Understanding
Information Transmission

Understanding Information Transmission

John B. Anderson

Rolf Johannesson

IEEE PRESS

A John Wiley & Sons, Inc., Publication

Library of Congress Cataloging-in-Publication Data:

Anderson, John B., 1945-
    Understanding information transmission/John B. Anderson and Rolf Johannesson.
       p. cm.
    Includes bibliographical references and index.
    ISBN 0-471-67910-0 (pbk.)
       1. Signal theory (Telecommunication) I. Johannesson, Rolf, 1946- II. Title.

TK5102.5.A535 2005
621.382′2—dc22   2004057151

Printed in the United States of America

10 9 8 7 6 5 4 3 2 1

Contents

About the Authors

Preface

Understanding Information Transmission is an introduction to the whole field of information engineering. Its seven chapters span the nature, storage, transmission, networking and protection of information. The book has two intentions: First, it is a second-year course book for new university programs in Information Technology (IT); secondly, it appears within the IEEE "Understanding Series" which was designed for those who wish to learn a new field on their own. In our case the field is the rapidly evolving field of IT. A special feature of the book is its treatment of the spectacular history of the subject, its people and inventions, and its social effects on all of us.

As a text, the book has been used in the required introductory course on Information in the first year of the Information and Communication Technology engineering degree program at Lund University in Sweden. The present version has been used for three years in that course. One of us (JBA) also worked within the IT program at Rensselaer Polytechnic Institute. Baccalaureate IT programs like these are starting up all over the world. Because they are so new it is worthwhile to look at their curriculum requirements.

These four-year IT programs combine courses from a variety of information disciplines. A typical curriculum might consist of courses in communication engineering, signal processing, software engineering, programing, computer science, mathematics (discrete mathematics, probability, linear algebra/complex variables), man–machine issues, psychology, and linguistics. To this may be added in some countries a proportion of liberal arts, economics, and management electives. Certain traditional engineering courses, for example, thermodynamics, mechanics, and materials, are often squeezed out. The prerequisites for our book are those for a course early in this structure. We assume a modest first-year university (U.S.) or gymnasium (Europe) preparation in mathematics (specifically, calculus, complex variables, and elementary probability) and physics (electromagnetic waves and DC electrical circuits). Review appendices are offered to help a reader who is missing parts of the prerequisites. Information engineering is a subject that is full of mathematics, and Chapter 2 is devoted to the core mathematical techniques of the discipline. The chapter develops Fourier transforms and bandwidth, linear systems and convolution, and some circuit ideas.

An IT degree program can be administered by an electrical engineering (EE), computer engineering, or computer science department, or possibly by a school of information technology. A program offered by one of the first three is necessarily a compromise compared to a traditional electrical engineering or computer science program. A degree recipient lacks circuit, fields and waves, and physics/ device courses compared to an electrical engineer; he or she lacks advanced programing, computer science and architecture courses compared to a computer science major. The combining of parts of the EE and computer science curricula, as well as courses from the softer sciences, places a special strain on IT programs. These compromises are present in the pages of *Understanding Information Transmission*. It is necessary to skip over many details. Furthermore, an understanding of the information processing discipline must be achieved in one book rather than several, and in an IT program this must occur at an early point in the curriculum.

The pedagogy behind this book and its choice of contents evolved over many years. A book like this can only arise from thousands of encounters with students, and we would like to acknowledge first the students and colleagues who made it possible, and especially the students in the first three years of the Infocom Program at Lund University. Next we wish to thank the Information Technology Department at Lund, which set aside significant resources for the preparation of the book. Particularly, we are grateful to Lena Månsson and Doris Holmqvist, whose enthusiasm and outstanding skill at Latex made it possible to complete this manuscript. Within IEEE and Wiley, thanks go to the production staff at Wiley and to our editors Tony VenGraitis and John Griffin, whose warm support we enjoyed from the first day. Thanks also are due to our colleague James Massey and to Oliver, the world's leading canine information theorist, for debating many issues with us. Finally, we are indebted to Jennifer Bissett for transforming her views of information transmission into a striking cover.

JOHN B. ANDERSON
ROLF JOHANNESSON

Lund, Sweden
December 2004

Chapter 1

Introduction: First Ideas and Some History

This book is about the transmission of information through space and time. We call the first *communication*. We call the second *storage*. How are these done, and what resources do they take?

These days, most information transmission is digital, meaning that information is represented by a set of *symbols*, such as 1 and 0. How many symbols are needed? Why has this conversion to digital form occurred? How is it related to another great change in our culture, the computer?

Information transmission today is a major human activity, attracting investment and infrastructure on a par with health care and transport, and exceeding investment in food production. How did this come about? Why are people so interested in communicating?

Our aim in this book is to answer these questions, as much as time and space permit. In this chapter we will start by introducing some first ideas about information, how it occurs, and how to think about it. We will also look at the history of communication. Here lie examples of the kinds of information we live with, and some ideas about why communication is so important. The later chapters will then go into detail about communication systems and the tools we use in working with them. Some of these chapters are about engineering and invention. Some are about scientific ideas and mathematics. Others are about social events and large-scale systems. All of these play important roles in information technology.

Understanding Information Transmission. By John B. Anderson and Rolf Johannesson
ISBN 0-471-67910-0 © 2005 the Institute of Electrical and Electronics Engineers, Inc.

1.1   WHAT IS COMMUNICATION?

Communication is the transfer of information.

Information occurs in many ways. It can take the form of postal letters, email, bank statements, parking tickets, voice, music, pictures, moving video. It is easy to name many more. The *medium* that carries information can be electromagnetic waves, electricity through wires, writing on paper, or smoke signals in the air. The *delay* of transfer can vary. A short letter can be delivered in tenths of a second in an online chat room, seconds or minutes by email, a day or two by postal priority mail, and perhaps months by low-priority mail. The *quality* of transfer can also vary. Voice and music can be compact disk quality, ordinary radio quality, telephone quality, or something worse, like a military or taxi radio. The form of information, and the medium, delay, and quality of its transmission, are all things with which engineers must deal, and quantify.

Sometimes information appears in forms that are hard to quantify. A letter is just words, but a voice speaking the same words can be happy, sad, threatening, and so on, and carry more information. Information of this sort can be abstract and almost impossible to describe in words; examples are the feelings and impressions that are present in music or art. Philosophers and mathematicians alike have posed the question, "What is information?" We can give at least three answers. Information can be *data*, in the sense of a bank statement, a computer file, or a telephone number. Data in the narrowest sense can be just a string of binary symbols. Information can also be *meaning*. The meaning of the bank statement might be that your account is overdrawn and will now be closed, and the meaning of the symbols in the computer file may be that you have won the lottery and should quit your job. Another idea was proposed by the mathematicians Hartley and Shannon in the middle of the last century. They said that information was the degree that uncertainty was reduced by knowing symbols, and they gave a formula to measure it. Shannon's ideas lie at the heart of the modern engineering idea of information, and we will look at them in detail in Chapter 5. Until then, we will measure information of the symbolic kind by simply counting the symbols.

Many forms of information, such as text and data, are inherently symbolic. Others, such as voice and video, are originally analog waveforms, and can be transmitted or stored in this form or converted to a symbolic form. There are many engineering reasons to do this, and in theory there is no loss in doing so. We will call this process source *conversion*. It is often called by more technical names, such as source coding, data compression, change of format, or analog-to-digital (A to D) conversion; what these are is only a change in form. There are laws that govern it, and state, for example, how many symbols are needed for voice or video. We will look at that in Chapters 2 and 5. Sometimes information is converted from one symbolic form to another. Emails, for example, are converted from the text symbols $A,B,C,\ldots$ to the binary symbols 1 and 0. When information is converted to a simple, standard form such as these binary symbols, both the public and engineers alike say that it is in *digital form*.

A conversion to a form intended for transmission or storage is called *modulation*. In this process, analog or digital forms are converted to electromagnetic waves as in radio, magnetized regions as in a hard disk, or pits in a film as in a compact disk (CD), to name a few. Within radio and wire modulation many ways exist. These include modulating the amplitude, frequency or phase of a radio or electrical waveform. As an example of the proper use of language, we might say that "voice was converted to digital form and the resulting bits are phase modulated for transmission." Waveform information such as voice and video may be modulated directly in its analog form or converted to digital form. We will take a close look at modulation in Chapter 4.

The need for modulation seems obvious, but it is a good idea to review why it is needed. A good modulation method is one that fits the medium. For example, an efficient means of modulating magnetic domains on a disk may not be the best one on a CD or over a radio link. Radio channels are especially interesting because the physics of antennas and transmission depend very much on frequency. For all sorts of subtle reasons, microwaves are required in space; 20 MHz is suitable for transcontinental transmission during the daytime, 6 MHz is suitable at night, and 20 kHz is needed for submarines at any time. Another reason for modulation is to keep signals from interfering; if two signals are modulated to different radio frequencies, they will not disturb each other.

An interesting philosophical point about all of this is that modulation is inherently an analog process. The last circuit in radio transmitters and disk drives is always an analog one. Symbols do not have length or weight or field intensity, but magnetic domains and electromagnetic waves do. We need to measure this physical reality, and buy and sell and control it.

1.1.1 Noise

A proverb says "Death and taxes are always with us." The equivalent of these in communication is noise. Except at absolute zero—not a very interesting temperature—noise is always with us.

Noise takes many forms. For two people having a conversation, traffic noise may be the problem. For people sending smoke signals, it might be fog. A definition of noise might be any unrelated signal in the same time or place or frequency band. Because most communication is one way or another electrical, it is electrical noise that is most interesting for us, and within this, thermal, or "white" noise. This noise stems from the motions of molecules, something that is present in all materials and at all temperatures above absolute zero. It is true that there is a cosmic background noise in the universe, but most often the dominant source of white noise is the receiver itself, in the front part where the signal is first applied. Sometimes it is this unavoidable noise level that limits communication. Other times a nonthermal source dominates. Everyday examples are interference from switched currents in neighboring wires, electrical activity in the radio medium, for example, the ionosphere, and other signals in the same channel. It is also possible that a signal can interfere with itself in such a way that versions of the signal are hard to separate and act like noise to each other. In video transmission, the interfering version is called a ghost, in audio, it is an echo. If there are several interferers, and they lie close in time, the result is a smear in video, a garble in audio.

There are several general rules about noise. First, signals decay as they propagate, so that sooner or later a fixed noise level, however small, becomes significant. Secondly, only the ratio of signal energy E to noise energy N matters, not the absolute value of either. The important ratio is called the signal-to-noise ratio, abbreviated SNR. In communication, this ratio E/N is expressed in decibels[1] (abbreviated dB), which by definition is computed as $10 \log_{10}(E/N)$. We can observe this rule in everyday life. If two people are talking in a room and a party starts up, they must now talk louder; the ratio of their speech to the background noise must stay the same. Almost always, the same rule applies to electrical communication. The implications are that if signals are weak, as they are from outer space, the receiver must be very good, with a low noise; conversely, if noise is high, it may be overcome, but only by large signal power.

1.1.2 Measuring Communication

With symbols, we can simply count them. The situation is actually more subtle, because some symbols can contribute more to the message than others. But more on this must await Chapter 5. Here we want to gain an overall impression of how to measure analog signals, both analog sources of information and the analog signals that transmit digital information.

Important measures of a communication system are its *energy, bandwidth, processor requirement, distortion*, and *delay*. In the real world, these all cost money. In general, they all trade off against each other; that is, reducing the cost of one increases the cost of the others. Distortion, for example, can be reduced by consuming more energy or bandwidth, or by more expensive processing or longer transmission delay. There are many other tradeoffs and some are less intuitive; for example, choosing a transmission method with wider bandwidth can lead to a lower signal energy requirement or a lower distortion.

We can look at energy and bandwidth in a little more detail now, saving the full treatment for Chapters 2 and 4. For the moment, think of processing, distortion, and delay as fixed at some convenient level. Energy is a familiar quantity. With digital transmission, it is convenient to think of energy per bit, denoted E_b (in joules). If T seconds are devoted to the transmission of each bit, then the power is E_b/T watts. With analog waveforms, the power of the waveform is easy to think about. Bandwidth is more difficult. To start, we should point out that there are two meanings of the word. Often in engineering and almost always in the general public, bandwidth refers to the bit rate of a service in bits/second. For example, one might say a video system has higher bandwidth than a voice system, meaning that it

---

[1] With a slight misspelling, this unit is named after the great communication pioneer Alexander Graham Bell; a bel is a power ratio whose log base 10 is 1. Bell is discussed in Section 1.3.

requires more bits/s. To communication engineers this is an abuse of notation; bandwidth is the width of frequencies that is required to send the signal. The two meanings are related, but in a complicated way that varies strongly with the modulation method and the quality desired. The simplest digital modulation methods take, very roughly, 1 Hz of bandwidth for each bit per second transmitted. As an example, standard low-tech digitized telephone speech runs at 64 kbits/s, and this therefore would need roughly 64 kHz of bandwidth. As a second example, a short email might convert to 1000 bits, and to send it in 20 s (certainly competitive with the post office!) would imply 50 bits/s for 20 s, and a bandwidth consumption of 50 Hz. The bandwidth of a brief letter is thus very much smaller than sending the same spoken words. As the saying goes, a picture is worth a thousand words. In fact, the engineering reality is that a picture costs the bandwidth of a thousand *spoken* words, but more like 100,000 written words.

Communication engineers compute bandwidth by the Fourier transform, which is described in Chapter 2. A view that gives some simple intuition is the following water pipe analogy. Transmitting information is like transmitting water. Signal energy E corresponds roughly to the initial pressure of the water. Signal bandwidth W is the size of the pipe. Signal noise N is the friction of the pipe. The total water carried per second is the product of pipe size and pressure, reduced by the effect of friction. Actually, information transfer obeys a relation more like (bandwidth) $\times$ log (signal-to-noise ratio), but the water analogy gives the right feel.

It can be seen from the email example above that there are tremendous variations in the parameters of different information sources. Before going further, it would be useful to give rough measures for some of them. These will serve temporarily before we study sources in more detail in Chapter 3.

Messages

These include short emails, paging calls, and orders for a taxi service, for example. Length is perhaps 1000–10,000 bits (200–2000 ASCII characters). Delay of several seconds to several minutes is acceptable. Error rate should be very low, less than 10^{-9}. Transmission speed can be as low as 100s of bits/s.

Telephone Speech

As an analog signal, speech has a bandwidth of about 3500 Hz and requires an SNR of 30–40 dB (this is the ratio of signal power to noise power; 30 dB is a factor of 1000). Transmission must be nearly real-time. As a digital signal converted from analog, speech has a bit rate of 64 kbits/s if converted in a simple way, and perhaps 5 kbits/s if converted in a complex way. Bit error rate needs to be in the range 10^{-2} to 10^{-5}.

CD-Quality Music

As a high-quality analog signal, music has a bandwidth of about 22 kHz and needs an SNR of about 90 dB. Delays of up to several seconds can be tolerated in reproduction. As a digital signal converted from analog, standard stereo CD music requires 1.41 Mbits/s. Error rate must be low, less than 10^{-9}.

Television

As an analog signal, ordinary television has a bandwidth of about 4 MHz and requires an SNR of 20–30 dB. As a digital signal converted from analog, video requires about 40 Mbits/s if converted in a simple way, and perhaps 0.5–2 Mbits/s if converted in a complex way. Delays of up to several seconds can be tolerated in broadcasting and much more in tape playback. An error rate of 10^{-5} is tolerable. High-definition television (HDTV) requires 5–10 times the bandwidth and bit rate.

1.2   WHY DIGITAL COMMUNICATION?

The last 30 years has seen a conversion of the entire communication business from analog to digital transmission, that is, from waveforms to symbols. This revolution has been so complete that most of our study in this book is devoted to digital transmission. Why is this?

There are many compelling reasons. We will list them in approximate order of importance.

1. *Cheap hardware*. Beyond all else, the collapse in the price of electronics has propelled the digital revolution. An oft quoted empirical rule is Moore's Law, which states that the price of signal processing drops by half every 18 months. It is hard to grasp how momentous this price fall really is. As a small example, take the diode. In the 1950s, a diode was a vacuum tube that cost more than US$5 in today's money; today its cost has dropped at least 10 million fold. What would happen if the price of fuel or housing dropped that much?

2. *New services*. A great many new services are inherently symbolic, and are therefore digital. These include electronic banking, airline reservations, the web, email, to name just a few. We choose to live and work in a widely distributed way, which makes these services all the more necessary. Voice, music, and video can be transmitted in either analog or digital form, but these new services are only digital.

3. *Control of quality*. Even if all signals were voice, music, and video, digital transmission would still offer special advantages. These are subtle to understand, but they are nonetheless important. Digital transmission works in a way that tends to set a desired distortion level initially and then keeps it nearly fixed at that value. This will be discussed in Chapter 3. Analog transmission tends to start at a high quality and get worse at each conversion or retransmission step. Digital systems thus have the advantage when there are many such steps. We can stop momentarily and look at two classic examples, a recording/playback chain and a transmission system with repeaters.

It is often thought that a high-quality music recording medium must be digital, but this is not necessarily so. High-quality music is a matter of finding a medium with the bandwidth, SNR, and dynamic range required and this is possible with analog media.[2] The problem in recording is more that recording/playback is actually a chain of many processors. These include microphones, their lines, mixing, recording, remixing and re-recording several more times, storage in some medium, replay from the medium, playback processing, amplification, speaker reproduction. Quality is lost at every step. A digital system maintains its bits essentially unchanged from end to end. Once a quality level is agreed upon, it never changes.

The second example is a long-distance transmission system that is based on a chain of many short links with amplifiers (called repeaters) that boost the signal after each link. The system could be a chain of 50 km line-of-sight microwave links; a more modern example is an under-ocean light fiber system, which would need a reforming of the bit-carrying light waveform every 100 km. As an analog signal is passed from link to link, it picks up a certain quantity of noise each time, which cannot be removed. After, say, 100 links, the noise has grown 100-fold. A way of looking at this is that each link needs to have 100 times the quality that the whole system will have. This may only be achieved by a 100-fold increase in the signal-to-noise ratio in the links. A digital system that carries bits encounters quite a different set of rules. The bits have a certain probability of error. After 100 links the laws of probability say that the probability overall will be about 100 times larger. To achieve a desired probability overall, then, about 100 times lower probability is needed in each link. We will see in Chapter 4 that this can be done with only a 60% increase in signal-to-noise ratio in the links.

4. *Flexibility of transport and switching.* If all signals have a common format as bits, the same system can carry them. Switching the bits and combining them into streams of different speeds and sizes are much easier. The same line can carry bits that control, for example, a telephone system as carries the voice itself. In reality, the bits from different services can require very different error rates, and so combining of services is not straightforward, but digital transmission is nonetheless vastly simpler when many services must be carried. Networking is the subject of Chapter 7.

5. *Interference rejection.* It is a fact that mobile systems, which tend to be limited by interference from other users, can fight interference better if messages are carried in digital form. This raises the number of users that the system can carry, and therefore lowers cost per user.

6. *Security.* Message security is inherently difficult with analog systems, since another user need only listen in. Analog encryption methods exist, but they

---

[2] For example, a 33 rpm vinyl disk is much inferior to a compact disk, but when the same physical disk is sped up to 45 rpm, its playback quality is almost that of a CD.

are inherently weak. Digital encryption is performed by adding unknown bits and can be made virtually impossible to decipher. New services, such as electronic banking, tend to need more security than voice or video, and this multiplies the digital advantage. Security will be studied in Chapter 6.

1.3 SOME HISTORY

AT&T stock is the greatest investment in the world. When times are good, all stocks go up; when times are bad, people pick up the phone and complain to each other. . .

Source: Heard in the halls of American Telephone Telegraph Company, the giant company that ran tele-communications in the United States from the 1880s to the 1980s.

This section recounts events in the long and fascinating history of telecommunication. Thinking about history as a list of dates and inventors can be misleading, since trends and individual inventions most often arise in confusion and in many different places at once. Fields can have unquestioned leaders, to be sure, but most of history happens in a rather muddy way. Information transmission evolved in a series of dramatic subrevolutions, which will form the structure of this section, and with most of them, the innovation arose in many places. Sometimes, as with the telegraph, the advent was rather sudden; other times, as with computer software, it was confused and drawn out. It is also important to realize that every major innovation in technology is accompanied by major social and political change. It can hardly be otherwise: a major shift in something as important as communication cannot occur in isolation. And someone has to finance the revolution. Like the people who gave their last dollar to AT&T in order to tell their friends how bad things were, someone has to think communication is worth paying for. The act of financing something as huge as information transmission is itself a major social and political event.

We can gain insight into these changes in our culture by studying history. However, the process of social change is subtle and not that easy to track. Historians say that the effects of a major change, such as the invention of radio, do not make themselves fully felt for as much as 50 years. This means, for example, that whatever we feel the effect of the Internet has been on us, the *real* effect on our civilization will not be known for something like 40 more years. In the meantime, we are the experimental guinea pigs.

Present-day telecommunication arose over the last two centuries because of four great trends. These were the invention of electric signaling technology (telegraph, telephone, radio, and so on), scientific and mathematical understanding of these (otherwise how could we work with them?), the advent of microcircuits—chips (which made the equipment small, fast, reliable, and very cheap), and the software concept (which makes possible complex algorithms). It is interesting to observe that telecommunication from the telegraph up to television was based on science known in the 1800s. We will see the details of this presently. Only with data networking and the Internet did communication make use of the technology of the mid 1900s, namely computer software and microcircuitry.

We will now take a look at the revolutions of information transmission in the order they occurred. They are the telegraph, telephone, radio, television, cable TV, mobility, and the Internet. Some of the important events are given in Table 1.1. We want particularly to find out the following:

- What technology supported each innovation?
- What caused the social and political sectors to take an interest in the innovation? Why did they invest in it?
- In turn, what were the social and political effects of the innovation?

1.3.1 The Telegraph

The first demonstration of an electric telegraph was between Washington, D.C., and Baltimore in 1844; the inventor and promoter were both Samuel F. B. Morse (1791–1872) (Box 1-1). Morse was actually a portrait artist, but he had an active intellect, and some 15 years before, had been struck by the thought that electricity might propagate down a wire and carry a message for some distance. Morse was aware of and capitalized on the discoveries of Henry, Faraday, and Ampère, who were American, British, and French scientists, respectively, who worked during the period 1800–1840. Joseph Henry in particular had discovered electromagnetic induction: He strung a loop of wire around his school classroom and discovered that passing a current through it would create a current in a similar but disconnected loop in the room. A moment's thought shows that Henry had in a sense demonstrated a telegraph and in fact even radio. But it is difficult today for us to imagine how little was known in the 1800s about electricity. Both the telephone and the telegraph were devised without any concept of atoms or moving charges. Morse worked from the simple fact that connecting a battery at one end of his wire caused a magnetic response at the other end. For their part, the public identified electricity only with lightning; they called the telegraph the *lightning line*.

It was not enough for Morse to recognize that electricity—whatever that was— would cause magnetism at a distance. How could this electricity carry text information? He invented the Morse code for that purpose, and for that matter, he invented the key with which to send it. Here we see an important factor in producing a real innovation. One must capitalize not only on a scientific discovery, but devise an entire *system* that puts it to convenient and economic use. With minor changes, the Morse code is still in use today, and it is shown in Table 1.2. Morse devised a code based on sequences of long and short pulses called dots and dashes that represented different text letters.[3] He also conceived the idea of using short words to represent common letters such as "e" and "i" and long words to represent uncommon letters such as "z." These principles are still used today in coding information.

---

[3] There is also a certain rhythm between dots and dashes and between letters that serves to distinguish letters and words. The modern name for signaling by pulses of different lengths is pulse-width modulation.

Table 1.1   Major events in telecommunication history. Note that many of these did not occur at a specific time, or have a single person associated with them.

Year	Event
ca. 1820	Oersted shows electric currents create magnetic fields
1830–1840	Henry discovers induction; Faraday shows magnetic fields produce electric fields
1834–1842	Various telegraphs demonstrated
1844	Morse commercial telegraph, Baltimore to Washington
1864	Maxwell publishes his theory of electromagnetism
1866	First permanent transatlantic telegraph
1860–1876	Various telephone demonstrations by Bell and others
1878	First telephone exchange installed by Bell, at Hamilton, Canada
1887	Experiments by Hertz verify Maxwell
1895–1898	Marconi and others demonstrate radio over significant distances
1901	First transatlantic radio message by Marconi, UK to Canada
1904; 1906	Fleming announces diode; DeForest announces triode
1906	Fessenden transmits speech 320 km
ca. 1918	Armstrong devises superheterodyne receiver
1920	First modern radio broadcast by KDKA, Pittsburgh
ca. 1925	Mechanical TV system demonstrations by Baird, London
1924	Pulse and noise theories of Nyquist
1928	Gaussian thermal noise papers of Johnson and Nyquist
1929	Zworykin demonstrates electronic TV system
ca. 1933	Armstrong devises FM
1936	TV broadcasting begins, by BBC London
ca. 1940	First use of radar
1945–1950	Early computers constructed
1947	Transistor demonstrated by Brattain, Bardeen, and Shockley, Bell Labs.
1949	First error-correcting code, by Hamming
1948–1949	Shannon publishes his theory of information
1947–1949	Shannon and others devise signal space and sampling theory
1950–1955	Beginnings of computer software and microwave transmission
1953	First transatlantic telephone cable
ca. 1958	First chips demonstrated by Kilby and others
ca. 1960	Error-correcting codes begin rapid development
1960	Laser announced by Schawlow and Townes, Bell Labs.
ca. 1965	Communication satellites using active transponders Long-distance communication to space probes begins
ca. 1970	Low-loss optical fibers demonstrated Large-scale integrated circuits appear
1971	First microprocessor chip, Intel 4004
ca. 1977	Digital telephone trunks first installed
1979	Images received from Jupiter
ca. 1980	Digital optical fiber telephone trunks begin
1985–1990	Cellular mobile telephones become widespread in Europe
1992	First digital mobile telephone system, GSM, begins in Europe
ca. 1996	Use of the Internet accelerates

BOX 1-1

Samuel Morse financed his first demonstration through a grant from the U.S. Congress. This first example of government support in communication was no more trouble free

Samuel Morse (1791–1872)
(Photo Courtesy of Noel Collection, www.noelcollection.org)

than it is today. It required five years for approval, and many congressmen thought the idea was dishonest or mystical. Opponents equated the telegraph with hypnotism and a sect that predicted the Second Coming of Christ for that year (see ref. [1], p. 10). Before we judge the congressmen too harshly, we should remember that in the public mind, electricity was lightning and nothing else. Despite these problems, Morse's demonstration on May 24, 1844 was a great success. Three days later, Morse played an important role in a political party convention by relaying critical information from a meeting in Baltimore to a candidate in Washington. This settled his difficulties with disbelieving politicians. By 1846, Morse had constructed a telegraph between New York and Washington, and the telegraph had been used to report on a war that had broken out that year. By 1861, a telegraph line had crossed the North American continent.

The idea of signaling by some symbolic means over distances was not new in 1844. For some 50 years, and especially in Britain, entrepreneurs and governments had experimented with lights, semaphore (a system with two flags), and even smoke signals over short distances. The systems were not successful because they took too much time, they needed relays to go even moderate distances, and they were too subject to error. The telegraph solved all these problems in an economic way.

Table 1.2   The Morse code, in its present-day international version, with some punctuation and non-English symbols

A ·—	K —·—	T —	0 —————
B —···	L ·—··	U ··—	1 ·————
C —·—·	M ——	Ü ··——	2 ··———
D —··	N —·	V ···—	3 ···——
E ·	O ———	W ·——	4 ····—
F ··—·	Ö ———·	X —··—	5 ·····
G ——·	P ·——·	Y —·——	6 —····
H ····	Q ——·—	Z ——··	7 ——···
I ··	R ·—·	Ä ·—·—	8 ———··
J ·———	S ···	Å ·——·—	9 ————·
	. ·—·—·—	? ··——··	
	, ——··——	— —····—	
	: ———···	' ·————·	

Morse was successful with politicians at first, but this was not to continue. He himself felt that the telegraph should be operated by the government for the public good, but the Congress took no further interest, feeling that government should not control such things, and the exploitation of the invention in the United States passed to private industry. The telegraph grew like wildfire, much as the Internet has done in our time, and within 20 years was dominated in the United States by the giant Western Union Company. By 1880, Western Union was the largest company in the United States, the first of the giant media companies that we know so well today. The telegraph also grew rapidly in Europe and everywhere else, but in all these cases it was financed and run by the governments, who felt just as strongly that governments *should* control the telegraph. The system came to be called the PTT (Posts-Telegraph-Telephone) method. Only recently have both the American and the European models been overturned. More about this will follow.

Why did the telegraph catch on so rapidly? It is said that the greatest single cause was the advent of cheap, daily newspapers, the so-called "penny papers" of the era. The public liked them, the papers needed news with immediacy, and the public therefore liked the telegraph. More slowly, the public came to see that the telegraph was relatively cheap and that they could use it themselves. The telegraph required huge investment that stretched over a wide geography, but it had a high *bandwidth* for its day; that is, it could divide its cost by many, many messages. A secondary cause of the telegraph's success was the rapid industrial expansion at the time, which needed a method to manage finance and production data. Governments were interested because countries and empires were growing in size, and the managing of these and of various military adventures needed better communication.

We have seen now the scientific basis of the telegraph (electricity) and how the inventor made it practical (wires, a code, the telegraph key). We have seen how it was financed (government in Europe, privately in the United States) and why it grew rapidly. But what was the effect of the telegraph on the culture around it? Once created, what did the monster do to its creators?

Historians say that the telegraph fostered a wider idea of nationality; that is, the idea that people have of their nation and culture now applied to much wider stretches of land and numbers of people. In the business world, markets in different locations became more tightly coupled. Transport became easier—transport and communication work in a symbiosis, in which each requires the other in order to be efficient. Morse himself foresaw some of this and spoke of the "one neighborhood" that he thought the telegraph would bring. But it was only a century later that McLuhan's concept of the "global village" [2] became a topic of everyday discussion.

We can take a closer look at the military use of the telegraph. After the telegraph, those who administered empires and wars no longer had the autonomy they once enjoyed. It used to be that a general or a governor of the outpost of an empire was sent far away, did the best he could, and either perished or reported back victory many months later. In the War of 1812 in the United States, for example, a significant part of the war occurred *after* the peace treaty. The Crimean War (1857), the American Civil War (1861–1865) and the Franco–Prussian War (1870) were the first to use the telegraph. The device was used for intelligence, to order troop movements—and most significantly—to direct the wars from the respective capitals. Now the political leaders, not the generals, were in charge. As for the generals, they no longer needed to be in the battle to know what was going on; they could sit in a bunker a distance away and learn from the telegraph. A severe modern example of leading from afar is given by Hitler's micromanaging from Berlin of the Eastern Front in World War II. What would have happened if Hitler had left war to the experts on the scene?

1.3.2 The Telephone

As with the telegraph, the scientific effect that underlay the telephone was simply the fact that electricity propagated down a wire. There was no theory of charged particle flow, and no-one had ideas about whether brute electricity could carry what today we call a waveform. Alexander Graham Bell (1847–1922), a Scot who had emigrated to Canada and later the United States, is the person identified today with the invention of the telephone. His first demonstration of the telephone, that is, a microphone, electricity carrying a waveform, and a reproducer, was in Boston in 1876. He was not trying to demonstrate voice transmission. Rather, he was trying to send several telegraph signals down the same wire line by interrupting different frequency tones, and he noticed that something resembling a voice could be transmitted.[4] This first demonstration was only between two rooms. Bell soon returned to Canada and demonstrated telephone calls over several kilometers at Brantford, Canada. The first telephone exchange was in Hamilton, Canada, in 1878. Like

---

[4]Today, this is called frequency division multiplex. It was an effective technique with telegraph and is used today in every kind of transmission.

Morse, Bell was not originally a scientist or engineer, and was by trade a teacher of the deaf. This, however, gave him a deep understanding of voice and hearing, which was surely an advantage in his work with the telephone.

As with the telegraph, the initial commercial development of the telephone took place within private finance and industry. In a pattern that would repeat with later communication innovations, there were major battles around 1880 among patent holders, which ended for whatever reason with Bell victorious, and this is in part why we today connect the telephone with Bell.[5] There were, however, many other contributors. One that should be mentioned, who narrowly lost out in the patent battles, is Elisha Gray. Also, one must mention those who made pioneering contribution to the business organization, especially A. Vail and G. G. Hubbard.

In North America, the telephone underwent a rapid development during the period 1880–1900, with the chief service being short, telegraph-like voice messages between businesses. It was relatively cheap and easy to install wires and an "apparatus" consisting of simply a coil for the earphone and a button filled with carbon for the microphone. Connections were made by boys who ran around a room connecting ends of wires. With these boys appeared for the first time the concept of *switching* in a network. As the telegraph had been before, the telephone was viewed initially as a point-to-point communication system, that is, one that permanently connected two users at opposite ends of a wire. Bell was the prophet of a new switching view (Box 1-2).

The concept of message-based charging was also devised, in which the user paid for each call and was not forced to pay all at once for the installation of expensive lines. Aside from the fact that it carried voice, the telephone was thus fundamentally different from telegraph in two more ways—it served almost everyone directly, and connections were set up and taken down in a switched way.

We see that the telephone in North America began as a private business whose service was aimed at the entire public. In Europe, the telegraph was already organized in the PTT mode, and telephone was absorbed into that structure. It was natural to see telephone as an adjunct to the telegraph, as a service that delivered short, nonreal-time messages, and perhaps mainly for this reason, the development of telephone as a universal public service was delayed in Europe. Even radio initially was seen in Europe as a mobile form of the telegraph.

The telephone steadily evolved toward the universal medium that it is today. Switching became mechanized with the invention in 1892 of the dial switch by Almon Strowger.[6] Longer distance telephony depended on such new technology as the loading coil (M. Pupin and G. Campbell, 1899) and the vacuum tube (de Forest, 1906). Transcontinental long distance between San Francisco and New York was finally demonstrated in 1915, with the elderly Bell making the

---

[5]Bell's basic patent, U.S. Patent 174465, applied for in February 1876, is said to be the most valuable patent ever issued by the U.S. Patent Office.

[6]Strowger did not work for a telephone company. He was an undertaker in St. Louis who felt that the telephone operators were being paid off to direct calls to his competitors; he therefore proposed a machine that eliminated people from telephone switching. Some examples of his remarkably robust solution were still in service in the 1970s.

first call. About 40% of the public had a telephone by 1925 in countries such as the United States and Sweden, and by 1965–1970, almost 90%. By the 1910s in the United States and Canada, the telephone business grew into a private but heavily regulated monopoly. In the United States this was the American Telephone and Telegraph Company, more commonly called the Bell Telephone System. It was

---

BOX 1-2

As early as 1878 Alexander Graham Bell wrote that:

> ... it is conceivable that cables of telephonic wires could be laid underground or suspended overhead communicating by branch wires with private dwellings, Counting Houses, shops, Manufactuaries, etc., etc., uniting them through the main cables with a Central Office where the wires could be connected together as desired establishing direct communication between any two places in the city. Such a plan as this though impracticable at the present moment will, I firmly believe, be the outcome of the introduction of the telephone to the public...

Source: de Sola Pool [3]

Here in this quotation we even see the words "Central Office," which survives to the present day as the English phrase for the basic telephone switching node. One says, for example, that "Lund University telephones are organized as the 222 central office." This kind of switching, called generically circuit switching, survived until the Internet, which uses the packet switching method. We will discuss the distinction between these methods in Chapter 7. The quotation also contains the telling phrases "private dwelling" and "introduction of the telephone to the public." Bell and his partners, especially Vail, advocated that the telephone should serve ordinary people, and almost all of them at that. Fortunately, the telephone was not intrinsically an expensive technology. Eventually, universality was promoted in some countries by undercharging for local service and overcharging for long distance and for business service.

---

agreed that a significant part of the profits would support Bell Laboratories, which became the largest source of communication innovation in the world. It is astonishing to count the inventions that this institution brought to the world. The laser, fibers, information theory, and the transistor are some of them. One can argue that such a regulated organization, with a strong public service outlook, was a European PTT by another name. Be that as it may, the public-monopoly/PTT organizational form lasted until the 1980s. Today telephone service all over the world is evolving toward private profit-making forms—and we must do without Bell Laboratories.

To sum up, the scientific basis of the telephone was again electricity and the inventions that made it practical were simple: just an earphone, a microphone, and the switching concept. The financing evolved to a PTT/government-regulated-company form. Historians believe that the telephone evolved so rapidly because it was *instant*. The user completed the call, the conversation was real time, there were no intermediaries such as delivery boys, and the whole process could be "friendly" from beginning to end. All of this was aided by the business decision to make the service universal. Finally, telephones were cheap. We will see these aspects working in all later communication revolutions as well.

It is a little harder to see the effect of the telephone on the culture around it. (For one thing, it is hard to imagine life without it.) Social historians feel that the telephone allowed the activities of most people—not just generals and politicians—to take place at a distance, to become geographically spread. Families, businesses, and jobs could function even though they were not in direct contact. One first thinks of continental distances here, but any activity more spread out than a few rooms was profoundly affected by the telephone. It is said that the modern skyscraper is impossible without the telephone.

The telegraph is hardly present today and its chief significance is in how it led to other technologies and ways of social organization. The telephone, however, looks to the eye much as it did in the late 1800s and has lasted 120 years. However, this is because the service it provides has evolved with the times. First it replaced telegraphic business messaging, then it carried messages for the general public. By the 1960s on a per-minute basis it as often carried relationships between people, 40 minute personal encounters—an advertising slogan then was "Reach Out and Touch Someone." Today telephone traffic is more than half *data*. The old voice network has morphed into a new entity. More about this will come when we take up the Internet.

1.3.3 Radio

In its first 25 years, radio was based entirely on technology of the 1800s. As we have seen, it can even be said that Henry sent the first radio message in the early 1800s. The conscious idea of radio came only after the publication of Maxwell's theory of electromagnetic waves in 1873. His theory gathered together many earlier discoveries; it predicted that radio waves should exist, that they should radiate, and that all such waves should move at the speed of light. It remained only to demonstrate waves at radio frequencies, and this was done during the period 1885–1889 by the German Heinrich Hertz, over just a few meters, and again in 1892 by the Briton Oliver Lodge over a hundred meters.

The most successful demonstration of radio waves was by, of course, Guglielmo Marconi (1874–1937) near Bologna in 1895. He not only extended the range to kilometers, but much more importantly, he conceived of radio as a communication medium and he had the business acumen and the flair for publicity to promote it. In rapid succession, he transmitted the outcome of the Americas Cup race from offshore New York to the downtown newspapers (1899), crossed the Atlantic (12 December 1901; see Fig. 1.1), and even installed a radio link (1899) between British Queen Victoria's summer house and her yacht.[7]

---

[7]As related by Lebow [1], p. 68, Marconi intruded upon Victoria's privacy at one point as she sat in her garden. Her majesty was not amused, and not knowing what else to call history's first radio installer, said "Get another electrician!". He is said to have replied, "England *has* no Marconi."

Figure 1.1   Marconi, with transmitter–receiver equipment from the 1900–1920 era (photo courtesy of IEEE History Center)

Marconi performed many other demonstrations. However exciting these were, Marconi was also at work acquiring patents and setting up a business, which after 1899 was called the Marconi Wireless Telegraph Company. As evident in the name, Marconi saw radio as a means of telegraphy, in fact telegraphy between ships, where wires were impossible. Here is the origin of our present-day term wireless, although we apply it today to telephones. (For 50 years after Marconi, the British word for any kind of radio was "wireless".) Marconi's company was a great success. His product was effective and well priced and it revolutionized shipping; for 25 years this wireless telegraphy was the main commercial application of radio.

As we have mentioned, Marconi worked with established technology for which the theory was known. Early radio transmitters were spark transmitters, which worked by keying a spark to jump across a gap; waves were produced just as they are produced during ignition interference from a car engine. The principle here was soon improved by Nikola Tesla, a Croatian living in New York, who devised a coil that greatly increased the spark; various coupling systems could be added that served to localize somewhat the emissions to a frequency band. Power levels were routinely 1–5 kW.[8] The early receiver was a so-called coherer, a tube

---

[8] The full 5 kW passed through the key; operation of a large spark transmitter was not for the fainthearted. The nickname for a ship's radio operator was "sparks."

full of iron filings that would stick together somewhat and be more conductive when a radio wave passed through them; the filings had to be jarred apart again once a Morse symbol was detected. Marconi discovered by trial and error that low frequencies would follow the curvature of the Earth and make long distance communication possible. This occurs for good reasons, but was counter-intuitive according to the physics of the time, which predicted straight line propagation. Radio in general was much more counter-intuitive than the telephone and telegraph. Even though Marconi could not work out all the physics of radio, he, like Morse and Bell, had a solid instinct for what was possible, and to this he added a strong talent for entrepreneurship and publicity.

Radio in the period 1895–1920 thus used the technology of the 1800s and this limited it to entirely different applications than it has today. It was a medium in need of new technology. This radio soon found and the result was a second revolution that we today call broadcasting. Some of the technology is easy to describe and some is much more subtle.

Certainly the spark transmitter was a weak point and one line of development attacked this. The transmitter was limited in power; it splattered emissions all over the frequency band, and it could not send voice. V. Poulsen, a Danish engineer, devised around 1902 a method to modulate the sparks, and in 1906 the Canadian Reginald Fessenden adapted the method and transmitted the first speech broadcast (Box 1-3).

BOX 1-3

The first speech broadcast was Christmas Eve December 24, 1906 from Brant Rock, MA, United States. Reginald Fessenden transmitted among other things Christmas songs with himself as singer and some violin playing. The quality was said to be awful, but perhaps because of the familiar tunes, ships at sea that heard the transmission found it impossible to deny what they were hearing, and Fessenden went down in history as the first radio broadcaster. Fessenden had proposed an entirely different way to generate radio waves. Just as a rotating machine can produce AC current at 50 or 60 Hz, a special purpose alternator can produce much higher frequencies, and if these are attached to the proper antenna, the result will be high-power radio transmission at one pure frequency. Voice can be transmitted by modulating the field of the alternator. Fessenden contracted with General Electric Company around 1905 to produce such a machine, but it was primarily General Electric's brilliant engineer Ernst Alexanderson who perfected the method. The Alexanderson alternator was a magnificent machine; later versions could transmit hundreds of kilowatts at high efficiency and at frequencies exceeding 100 kHz. They dominated long-distance radiotelegraph transmission for several decades after 1915. Alexanderson's father was professor at Lund University in Sweden. Ernst emigrated in 1901, ending up in Schenectady, New York State, the research headquarters of General Electric. Ernst Alexanderson died in his 90s after an epic research career at General Electric that included some 400 patents; the alternator was only a small chapter in this output. The last Alexanderson alternator, located in Grimeton, Sweden, was shut down in 1986. An account of Alexanderson is given in ref. [4]. In a peculiar historical reversal, one of the authors of this book (JBA) worked many years in Schenectady at the very same laboratory and emigrated to become professor at Lund.

A second line of research and development, with many more consequences, was the vacuum tube. In 1883 the inventor Edison observed the fact that current will flow in a vacuum through the space between two electrodes. Edison could think of no interesting application, and his only further contribution was its name: the Edison effect. It was the Briton James Fleming who observed in the period 1896–1906 that an AC current would pass in only one direction. He devised the name *diode* for such a two-element vacuum tube (today we borrow the word to mean a two-element semiconductor). Although we must skip the scientific details, a one-way circuit element is the key to converting radio frequencies into a waveform we can see or hear. Fleming thus replaced the troublesome coherer receiver with a noise-free device having in theory perfect sensitivity. Soon after, in 1907, the American Lee de Forest suggested the *triode* tube, a device that contained a third element that could interrupt and control the charge flow through the tube. Avoiding again the electronic reasons, we simply give the significance of his invention: it was the key to amplification.[9] With amplifiers, sensitive receivers were possible and more versatile transmitters, as well as long-distance telephony and much else. From the triode came electronics, which has had an incalculable effect on us all.

A third crucial development stream was electronic circuitry. This is more subtle, and a place to start is a famous disaster, the sinking of RMS *Titanic* in April 1912. After hitting an iceberg, the ship used its powerful radio transmitter to call for help. Unfortunately, all radio operators in the area covered the same whole frequency band—neither transmitters nor receivers worked in the narrow "channels" that we use today. Because *Titanic*'s transmitter was so powerful, and because it constantly transmitted greetings from wealthy passengers, other ships had given up radio operations. As a consequence, distress calls were not heard until too late. However, once the ship did sink, the news spread to shore instantly via the other ships' radio sets. The drama of the sinking, reported in real time, caught the public imagination and had many consequences. Radio became an important medium overnight; the U.S. government took it seriously for the first time and organized its own Marconi-like service (it was placed within the Navy). More amateurs and research scientists alike became interested, and the technology began to evolve rapidly. A prime need was better circuitry.

The vacuum tube and the Alexanderson transmitter made possible amplification and signals that occupied a narrow, channelized bandwidth. A new rank of inventors combined tubes and other elements into better circuits. The foremost of these was the American Edwin Armstrong (1890–1954). His first major invention was the regenerative receiver, a means of using a triode tube to provide much higher sensitivity. However, his greatest invention, U.S. Patent 1,342,885, granted June 8, 1920, is still the basis of virtually all radio receivers today. Its operation was subtle and its

---

[9]de Forest, however, had no idea why the device worked. Despite a technical education at Yale University, he resolutely explained his device in mystical terms and called it an Audion. de Forest had many other peculiarities, which are well described in Lewis [5]. A lesson we can take is that inventions can occur even when the inventor has little idea what he or she is doing. A warning, however: a patent office may rule against you if you resolutely give a false explanation for your invention.

title inscrutable—the *superheterodyne receiver*. His idea is described in Chapter 4. The significance of it was that it allowed receivers to be built with extreme sensitivity and selectivity. The last means that the receiver detects only the desired signal and not those right next to it in the frequency band, in the way that we are accustomed to today. However obvious this strategy may seem, it in fact takes a deep knowledge of electronics to make it work. The result of Armstrong's invention was *channelized communication*, in which each user occupies one frequency and seldom interferes with others.

Before leaving Armstrong, we mention his other great invention, frequency modulation (around 1933). Frequency modulation (FM) caused Armstrong much political and scientific pain. Not the least cause of this was the subtlety of a principle contained within it, which Armstrong was the first to advocate in a concrete way: a signaling method that occupies a wider range of frequency, such as FM, can transmit with less power, for the same received quality. In communication theory, this is called the principle of power–bandwidth tradeoff.

However, with FM we get ahead of ourselves. At the end of World War I, the radio revolution had in fact hardly begun. What was to come was radio broadcasting, transmitting from one to many.[10] Broadcasting had its origins in amateur radio (ham radio). In an environment lacking regulations, amateurs sent out whatever they wished, and many, hams in the other sense, perhaps, talked and played music at some length. Their audience was other amateurs, and as 1920 approached, a variety of people constructed receivers, sometimes out of bits of junk.[11] A well-known such amateur was Frank Conrad of Pittsburgh, Pennsylvania, and he was hired by the Westinghouse Company to send out interesting programs, as a means to increase the sales of Westinghouse radio receivers. The date was November 2, 1920 and Westinghouse asked Conrad to broadcast the results of that night's 1920 national election. Radio broadcasting quickly became a sensation. By 1925, radio commercials had been devised, as well as news, religious broadcasting, and music transmission. Soon after, stations were formed into networks. By 1930, radio broadcasting had taken its modern form, or to be more precise, the modern form of television, which would replace its function in 20 more years.

In Europe, radio came soon after, with the formation of the British Broadcasting Corporation (BBC) in 1922. However, the decision was made by most countries that radio was to be used strictly for the public good, run by an accountable public corporation and paid for by license fees. This system carried over to television, and dominates many European countries to the present day, alongside a weaker commercial sector. A public broadcasting system was eventually set up in the United States in the 1960s, but it accounts for only perhaps a tenth of broadcasting there.

---

[10] Before 1920 the word broadcasting in English meant only the spreading of seed in a field. Pioneering broadcasters thought they were spreading ideas around like seeds. Similarly, the French adopted the word *diffusion*. The Swedish, however, simply adopted *sända*.

[11] Not all amateurs behaved in socially acceptable ways. There was a definite amount of what today would be called hacker activity. After 1912, there was a partial effort to discipline amateurs, another consequence of the *Titanic*.

To sum up, radio began as a straightforward use of discoveries in the 1800s about electromagnetic waves. Until 1920, it was in reality a wireless telegraph service. Its major growth was in the new broadcasting form, and this grew technologically out of the vacuum tube and early electronics. Broadcasting survives today as television, which had to await some further new technology. Early radio never required major finance, and it quickly found its early role as wireless telegraphy. The technology soon settled into a pattern of expensive transmitters/cheap receivers, which made it easy to gain rapid public acceptance for broadcasting.

Radio thus had an easy birth. Its effect on our culture is a major topic among historians, and indeed, the public. Before 1920, musical entertainment and plays were for the well off, and all others had to entertain themselves. Radio entertainment completely changed this. The sale of pianos after 1920, for example, dropped in inverse proportion to the sale of radios. Pop culture and top-40 radio became concepts, and huge profits were to be made. Entertainment and discourse changed from multiway to one-way, from the transmitter down to the listener. More seriously, it became easier to control large numbers of people by propaganda, both political and commercial. The powerful in society pay careful attention to what comes out of the broadcasting media. Is radio/television good or bad for us? Do we yet understand what this powerful medium has done to us?

1.3.4 Television

About television there is less to say, because television, historically, is an evolution from radio, not a revolution. By 1930 the pattern of networks, entertainment and news, paid for by advertising in some countries and license fees in others, was set for radio, and television followed the same pattern. Of course, television adds pictures. It is thus more immediate and arresting, more "friendly." Entertainment, especially sports and theatre, and bloody war reports are all more effective with pictures. Television is not expensive.[12] But all this is a completion of a revolution begun by radio.

In its technology television was based on the evolution of the electronics that began with the invention of the vacuum tube. For a brief period, a mechanical system was attempted, based on a photoelectric cell and a hole pattern in a rotating disk. The chief proponent was J. L. Baird in England. He demonstrated systems in the mid-1920s and there were BBC broadcasts with one in 1936. However, an all-electronic system soon proved to be much more practical. It was based on a string of electronic inventions: the cathode ray tube (demonstrated long before), electronic camera tubes (1923–1927, by P. Farnsworth and the Russian V. Zworykin, both living in the United States), and high-frequency radio technology (1930–1950). Zworykin demonstrated a complete electronic system in the late 1920s, and the

---

[12]It is interesting to observe that the cost of a television receiver in 2001, roughly US$200, is that of a single vacuum tube in 1927 in deflated money.

BBC began broadcasts with a similar system in 1936.[13] Later important technology advances included microwave radio (early 1950s), which made possible national live networks, color television (mid-1950s), and communication satellites (early 1960s), which made possible international live television. Today, most nonlocal television distribution is by satellite.

The effect of television on the human race is incalculable, as anyone knows. Many books have been written on how television changes society. Television changed and continues to change how people view the world and themselves. For many years, television has been the chief source of news in the Western world. Yet television is poor at local news, subtle stories, technical matters, and stories that are not primarily visual; in some countries television news is presented as entertainment or viewed as a money-making activity. Because television news is relatively expensive and demands visual content, disasters, wars, and the like are reported, which can be easily reached; viewers tend to think that these exist and others do not. Entertainment television, especially the commercial kind, is severely affected by the lowest-common-denominator problem: to optimize profit, programs must be directed toward the social center of the audience and to no particular locality. In reality, none of us are average; we are all unusual in a variety of ways and we relate to some home base. How to regulate the content of this powerful medium is an unsolved problem that will be with us for many years.

A case in point is how television has affected politics. A major early event was the 1952 broadcast of an American political convention in which General Eisenhower was nominated for the U.S. Presidency. People everywhere became aware of such conventions in a new way, and the conventions shifted from meetings to decide issues to opportunities to influence the public. Today, 50 years later, few people watch political conventions, but television is a major tool of political information and control. Television news is easily corrupted—given a spin—by politicians and other leaders. Political speeches in some countries are written and produced by staff, not by the leaders themselves. Historians say that politics has now evolved so that it has a strong tendency to choose leaders who are effective on television, and only secondarily those with deep political knowledge and expertise. What will be the effect of this on us? Here is a good example of a serious unintended consequence, that came only many years after an innovation.

1.3.5 Cable Systems

Another smaller innovation in communication was the construction of cable networks. While cable had less effect than radio and its offspring television, it was an important step in the *networking* of society. That trend has led to the Internet. It also led to yet another generation of the radio/television monster.

---

[13] An early broadcast was the coronation of King George VI in 1937. At the coronation of the next sovereign, Elizabeth II, the BBC and the Canadian Broadcasting Corporation again made history with the first transatlantic broadcast. However, film had to be *carried* across the Atlantic by relays of jet fighter aircraft. Since they almost kept up with the sun, the broadcast seemed nearly real time.

Cable television originated quite early, as a means to bring television from a tall, expensive community antenna to towns that were, for example, remote or located in valleys. The technology was coaxial cable (a center conductor inside a polyethylene tube, surrounded by a metallic shield), with repeater amplifiers every 300–800 m. This was sufficient to carry ten or so channels, and it proved affordable in densely settled areas. In the United States, cable was limited by law to difficult signal areas, but by the early 1970s, and especially in Canada, it began to saturate other builtup areas, and it soon became a sort of medium on its own.

Cable is only a local distribution method and it requires in its modern form a complementary widescale distribution of its channels by satellite. The first commercial international satellite system was set up by the INTELSAT Consortium in 1965. The first domestic system was the Canadian Anik system, launched in 1974. By the 1980s many providers competed to sell satellite relay channels. Today, cable-delivered TV competes with direct distribution by satellite to homes. This service first appeared in Europe, after 1990.

A subtle effect of cable was that it linked together all the dwellings in a town. Although cable is seldom used as a two-way medium, it *can* be if the user wishes, and hugely more information can be exchanged than over the older telephone system. Thoughtful observers saw this. Cable was the inspiration for and the startup of what today we call broadband networking. That, probably, is the next phase of the Internet.

It is also interesting to note that cable in its early stages was said to be a savior of humanity in that it would make available unlimited education and culture, free, somehow, of commercial exploitation and sundry corruptions. It is remarkable that the same was said about most other communication innovations. *Plus ça change, plus c'est la même chose.*

The main significance of cable was that it brought many more channels to the home viewer. This extended and completed the radio/television news and information phenomenon that we have discussed. What is more, cable ended the dominance of broadcasting by a few large networks. Both profit-making networks and license-supported public broadcasters now had to compete with superstations, single production facilities that could be far away in an alien country and free of the usual laws affecting air broadcasting. These superstations vary from cooking and sports channels to movie outlets to central news channels such as CNN and Skynews. We have not felt the full effect of this new kind of television. A system that provides 100 unregulated channels to watch can only be described as chaotic. It is interesting that in countries with strong publicly owned television, such as Germany and Sweden, the public stations manage to retain a strong influence.[14]

---

[14] Is one central news outlet, like CNN, a contradiction in terms? Perhaps all news is perceived locally, from the viewer's cultural point of view. Can a central broadcaster in a country at war really report a neutral point of view? These are questions for us to think about. Information transmission has consequences!

1.3.6 Mobility

There is nothing new about mobile radio. As we have seen, radio at its beginning was a wireless message service. By 1922, there were experiments with fire and police mobile radio. By the mid 1930s, mobile radio broadcast receivers were appearing in cars.[15] Mobile telephony for the general public slowly grew, and became less expensive and clumsy to use. Eventually a service emerged that would be recognizable today, except that the handheld telephone was considerably larger. These services used analog frequency modulation, worked at either 400 or 800 MHz, and were cellular, meaning that many transmitters covered small patches of land and the user was handed off from one to the other as he moved around. In the United States, the system was called AMPS (Advanced Mobile Phone System), and it was one of the last contributions of the old Bell System. Various similar systems, the so-called First Generation systems, appeared in the rest of the world at the same time. In Scandinavia it was the NMT (Nordic Mobile Telephone) system, which entered operation in 1981 as the world's first cellular system. Although these systems were analog, they played an important role in acquainting the public with the virtues of a simple mobile telephone system. The area in the world with the fastest growth was Scandinavia.

The explosion of public interest in mobile telephony came with the digital Second Generation. The cutting edge was in Europe and the system was the GSM one[16] that we still use today. First tests were carried out in 1986 and GSM began to be installed in the mid-1990s. Public use of mobile telephony grew dramatically with GSM for several reasons. In part, digital telephony was inherently more efficient and it adapted easily to other services such as email. High-frequency radio and digital circuitry were dropping rapidly in price and size in any case. And GSM offered for the first time a more subtle advantage: *roaming*. Because it was unified over many countries—and now over much of the world—and because its software procedures made identification of visiting telephones easy, people could roam over much of the Earth and use the same telephone. All these factors combined to make a very attractive product, and public use of mobile telephones doubled in the first years of the Second Generation. In some countries now there are more mobile users than fixed users. In a sense that has not previously existed, public telecommunication has achieved *mobility*.

The Second Generation had a more difficult birth in North America because it fractured into three incompatible technologies. Roaming is thus harder. This has delayed the step upward to higher public use, but it should arrive in time. The success of GSM shows the critical role of *standardization* in the success of a new technology. More often, standardization is imposed by a monopoly company, as

---

[15] An early pioneer in radios for cars was the present mobile radio giant Motorola Inc. It took its name from this early product.

[16] GSM originally meant *Groupe Spéciale Mobile*, which was a working group within a larger entity of European PTTs; when the system became a big success, history was rewritten, and GSM was redefined to mean Global System for Mobile communication.

happened with the telegraph and telephone, but in the GSM case it stemmed from a Europe-wide agreement among companies and PTT authorities.

It seems clear that mobile communication will progress to a Third Generation, although it is hard to predict when. By this term is meant a system that has higher bandwidth (so that it can handle music and video) and a combining of mobility with Internet access. The Third Generation is thus a fusion of a database (the Internet) with communication to it.

1.3.7 The Internet

Certainly the major information revolution in our own time is the Internet. This innovation has only just begun, but it has taken already many twists and turns, and its development echoes past revolutions.

The Internet is a classic example of an innovation that originated in many difference places,[17] and in fact a *lack* of overall organization is a principle of the net, as we shall see. Out of Internet history, we can select some events as follows.

The reality of the Internet is software, and the Internet stems from the whole history of computer software, from 1950 to the present. Server technology, originally called "real time computing," came in the late 1950s with large military systems (sometimes unsuccessful) and SABRE, the first airline reservation system (a major success). In the early 1960s the technique of *packetizing* was devised by a number of researchers, including P. Baran at Rand Corporation (United States), R. Kahn at Advanced Research Projects Agency (ARPA) in Washington, a branch of the U.S. military, and D. Davies at the British National Physics Laboratory. In this method of transmission, data sources are reduced to packets of uniform size, and each can have its own address associated with it and take in principle its own path through the network. This was a shift from the older circuit switching paradigm, in which dedicated pathways are connected between two users. The Bell System in the United States, being wedded to the circuit switched telephone system, was slow to embrace packet switching, and a proto-Internet that used packets had to arise somewhere else.

The place was ARPA, and a project director named J. C. R. Licklider. One of ARPA's activities was to identify promising new research areas and start pilot research efforts at widely distributed universities. Licklider wanted a communication system that would join these workers together in a virtual research group and would not demand any particular computer system; because the researchers needed to exchange data and documents, a network with seconds or minutes of delay was acceptable. Packet switching was a natural solution. The network was known as ARPANET and initially had four nodes. Later promotion and growth of ARPANET was largely due to L. Roberts and R. Kahn.

[17] In an echo of telephone history, at least five individuals have claimed to be the inventor of the Internet, including most famously, a politician who ran for President of the United States. A proverb says, "Success has many fathers, but failure is an orphan."

The next phase in the evolution was the devising of TCP/IP (Transmission Control Protocol/Internet Protocol) in 1979 by Kahn and Vinton Cerf, again at ARPA. This TCP/IP was a set of uniform interconnection rules that could be used by dissimilar computers. It was imposed on top of existing networks and it passed around packets. It created a network that was open to anyone who adopted the rules. In the jargon of the trade, it was "interoperability after the fact." The most interesting and perhaps unsettling consequence of TCP/IP was that control of the network left ARPA, and in fact left any sort of control. Any node that wished could enter or leave the net without affecting the other nodes,[18] and no-one built or owns the Internet. At this point, the Internet was essentially complete. It remained for user terminals to become cheap enough so that the net would become universal, and this came with the personal computer. The shift happened at ordinary research desks and at businesses around 1990 and in the home in the late 1990s.

In and around these events, there are some interesting subtleties to explore. We have not mentioned the cost of the Internet. In fact, the additional network infrastructure was almost free. *The Internet was imposed on the existing telephone system.* It has often been predicted that the telephone system would disappear and be replaced by some kind of digital network; in reality, a sort of opposite event happened, the telephone system became the physical network for the Internet. While it is true that some users have high-speed lines, what makes the Internet universal and convenient today is that it works through telephone lines. This fact is crucial: no new network had to be financed and laid. What assembled the telephone system—plus some other links—into the Internet was some software and the one-by-one addition of servers. The result is a system that supports email, the mainstay of the early Internet. Today we are trying to move away from slow telephone lines and convert to a higher-capacity Internet. The hoped-for new network will be broadband and based on a heavy modification of the telephone system or on fibers. But this will require for the first time heavy investment. In 2002 it is not at all clear who will provide this capital.

Another subtlety of the Internet development is that it required user terminals with considerable computing power. We cannot use the Internet as we do the telephone, by putting a finger in a telephone dial. Working with servers and TCP/IP requires computer power, as do the many algorithms that support Internet services. The Internet is *software based.* Fortunately, the means to do this came along as the PC.

The PC and its associated software has come to be dominated by a giant company, Microsoft, in a replay of earlier events in communication history. This company does not control the Internet itself, as did AT&T the U.S. telephone system, but rather the means of using some of its services. The historical role of Microsoft is probably to impose standardization on these services, something that history shows is needed for a technology revolution to take hold. Domination by a near monopoly is one way standardization takes place.

---

[18] However, a node list is kept and passed around to all nodes, and a central administration registers node and subnet names and avoids conflicts in the names.

Another subtlety is that the Internet is data and text based, and if it is to be used in a two-way fashion, the user needs computer expertise, and more problematic, needs to be able to compose written text. Those who cannot are excluded. Probably, "information appliances" will be devised that work around these difficulties. In any case, a major use of the Internet is to access databases (surfing), and this is mostly a one-way process. It is interesting that services such as fax transmission, which stems from the 1930s, developed along with the Internet. In part, these were made cheaper by technology, but it may also be that they provided a way around the need to compute and compose text.

To conclude, the Internet depended on computers and software, and grew rapidly once the first was cheap, since no other investment was needed. The first wave of the Internet was email, which was an extension of earlier services, namely telephone and postal mail. The second wave seems to be database access and probably downloading of music, text, and video. These services extend still further the conversion of widely distributed families, businesses, and nations into virtual villages, or as Bell wrote long ago, one neighborhood. The Internet will evolve much further and have many implications, but they are not easy to see from here.

The Internet is the only communication revolution that originated in a government (let alone military) laboratory. It is perhaps ironic that today it has not only left the military, but in fact left the control of anyone at all. It is also unique among major innovations in that it featured no great patent battles and was not a giant corporation. Perhaps it is inevitable that regulation will be imposed, as happened with the telephone, the hackers will be purged, as they were with early radio, and the profit motive will take over, as it seems to have with broadcasting. We will have to wait and see. If the Fifty Year Dictum holds, we can check again in 2040.

1.4 A FEW REMARKS ON INTELLECTUAL HISTORY

The previous section was devoted to inventions and inventors, industrialists and the public. Often, but not always, an invention capitalizes on new scientific thought. Before stopping, we should review briefly mathematical and scientific advances that relate to information transmission. More will be found about these in the chapters to follow, and especially in Chapters 2, 4, and 5.

We have already mentioned the scientific discoveries of Henry and Faraday, and their culmination in Maxwell's 1864 theory of electromagnetic waves. These scientific ideas inspired radio. The phenomenon of electricity was much easier to understand in terms of the atomic theory of matter and the idea of charge carriers like the electron and proton. These ideas became well known around the beginning of the 1900s. This was long after electricity was applied to communication, but the ideas of course were most welcome. Modern physics in the form of relativity theory, quantum physics, semiconductors, and crystal structure began to appear after 1900 as well, but these had little effect on communication until after 1950. In 1947 Shockley, Brattain, and Bardeen developed the transistor at Bell Laboratories, a device that was based on semiconductor physics. Many other semiconductor devices followed, and our modern electronics is the result. Within 10 years the laser followed at the same laboratory, the invention of Schawlow and Townes.[19] All of these researchers were physicists, who developed inventions based outright on the physics of the first half of the 1900s.

An intellectual history of another sort underlies how we think mathematically about information transmission. Our everyday tools of Fourier transforms, probability theory, and linear algebra are all developments of the 1800s, which entered undergraduate university courses only after World War II. Fundamental 20th-century mathematical innovations include the theories of H. Nyquist (1924, 1928), born in Nilsby, Sweden, who worked at Bell Laboratories. From his work [7–9] come our ideas of thermal noise, pulse waveforms, and signal sampling. Perhaps the greatest of these theoreticians was Claude Shannon, who also worked at Bell Laboratories. His publications of 1948–1949 [11, 12] are the basis of our present view of information and of how to make communication reliable. Shannon's ideas about information are the subject of Chapter 5. In ref. [12] Shannon also created the modern theory of signal sampling and of "signal space," a theory that describes signals as points in the Euclidean geometry of the ordinary physical world. Signal space theory was proposed independently and a little earlier by Kotelnikov [10]. Modern system theory, and especially the analysis of linear systems, arose during the period 1950–1970. Finally, we must mention J. von Neumann, the Hungarian-American who conceived the stored-program computer. From this came software, and without software and programs, it is hard to imagine any part of modern information transmission.

1.5 CONCLUSIONS

In this chapter we have introduced the basic ideas of information, its transmission and storage, which will be explored in the rest of the book. We have done this by describing energy and bandwidth, modulation and conversion, and the basic information types, such as text, voice and video. An important event in recent times is the digitization of communication. This occurred above all because digital processing is cheap; the digital form also gives us a standard transmission form and allows much better control of quality.

The largest part of this introduction has been devoted to history. Here we find all the different forms of information transmission, along with the inventions that made them possible and the fundamental changes that they caused in our civilization.

Innovation and entrepreneurship lie at the heart of information transmission. It is interesting to list their characteristics as they have appeared in telecommunication history.

---

[19] See ref. [6] for an excellent description of the birth of the laser and similar devices.

- One does not need to know an underlying theory in order to invent. Rather, one needs to observe carefully, create, and suggest a complete and useful system.

- Some innovations must be financed, some can evolve in small increments, and some are built on existing systems and need no finance.

- Huge corporate monopolies often control innovations, but they generally pass to another form. To have a major effect, a telecommunication system must be standardized, and this often occurs through monopoly.

- Successful innovations tend to be those that answer a business or public need. That need may not be consciously felt.

- Every major innovation has consequences, usually unintended, and almost never understood in advance.

REFERENCES[20]

1. *Lebow, I. L. 1995. *Information highways and byways*. IEEE Press: New York.
2. McLuhan, M. and Powers, B. R. 1989. *The global village: Transformations in world life and media in the 21st century*. Oxford Univ. Press.
3. de Sola Pool, I. 1977. *The Telephone's first century—and beyond*. Crowell: New York.
4. Nilsson, B. V. 1987. *Ernst Alexanderson*, Teleböckerna Nr. 5, Televerket Sweden, Farsta, Sweden (in Swedish).
5. *Lewis, T. 1991. *Empire of the air*. HarperCollins: New York.
6. Chiao, R. Y. ed. 1996. *Amazing light*. IEEE Press: New York.
7. Nyquist, H. 1924. Certain factors affecting telegraph speed. *Bell System Tech. J.*, April, 324–346.
8. Nyquist, H. 1928. Certain topics on telegraph transmission theory. *Trans AIEE*, 47, 617–644.
9. Nyquist, H. 1928. Thermal agitation of electric changes in conductors. *Phys. Rev.*, 32, 110–113.
10. Kotelnikov, V. A. 1947. The theory of optimum noise immunity. Ph.D. Thesis, Molotov Energy Institute, Moscow, January 1947; available under the same name from Dover Books, New York, 1968 (R. A. Silverman, translator).
11. *Shannon, C. E. 1948. A mathematical theory of communication. *Bell System Tech. J.*, 27; reprinted in *Claude Elwood Shannon: Collected Papers*, Sloane, N. J. A. and Wyner, A. D., eds, IEEE Press: New York, 1993.
12. Shannon, C. E. 1949. Communication in the presence of noise. *Proc. IRE*, 37, 10–21; reprinted in *Claude Elwood Shannon: Collected Papers*, Sloane, N. J. A. and Wyner, A. D., eds, IEEE Press: New York, 1993.

[20]References marked with an asterisk are recommended as supplementary reading.

Chapter 2

Mathematical Methods of Information Transmission: Why Sinusoids?

The dramatic evolution of microelectronics has fueled an equally dramatic development in information transmission by making very complex implementations possible. Such systems require advanced theoretical methods for structural analysis—heuristic methods are not sufficient any longer. In this chapter we look at the core mathematical methods used in information transmission.

First we introduce linear, time-invariant systems. We show that such a system can be characterized by its impulse response, that its output signal can be obtained from the input signal and the impulse response by an operation called convolution. A sinusoidal input signal always yields a sinusoidal output signal. Furthermore, linear, time-invariant systems are of great practical importance and can, for example, be used to shape the frequency contents of signals. An important tool for design and analysis of linear, time-invariant systems is the *Fourier transform*, which we will treat carefully. Finally, we will discuss the concept of bandwidth.

2.1 LINEAR, TIME-INVARIANT (LTI) SYSTEMS

A *system* is something that transforms an input signal $x(t)$ into an output signal $y(t)$, where both signals are functions of time. If we do not impose any restrictions upon the system there is not much we can do in order to analyze it. Therefore we shall introduce two properties that lead to a great simplification of the mathematical analysis and, thus, to a better understanding of the system behavior.

Understanding Information Transmission. By John B. Anderson and Rolf Johannesson
ISBN 0-471-67910-0 © 2005 the Institute of Electrical and Electronics Engineers, Inc.

A system $\mathcal{L}$ is generally said to be *linear* if, whenever an input $x_1(t)$ yields an output $\mathcal{L}(x_1(t))$ and an input $x_2(t)$ yields an output $\mathcal{L}(x_2(t))$, we also have

$$\mathcal{L}(\alpha x_1(t) + \beta x_2(t)) = \alpha \mathcal{L}(x_1(t)) + \beta \mathcal{L}(x_2(t)) \tag{2.1}$$

where α, β are arbitrary real or complex constants.

The formulation of the *linearity condition* (2.1) is somewhat abstract, so we illustrate it in Figure 2.1, where the upper part corresponds to the left-hand side of (2.1) and the lower part to the right-hand side of (2.1). Notice that, according to the linearity condition (2.1), the outputs $y(t)$ from both parts must be the same for a linear system!

When we extend the linearity condition (2.1) to infinite sums (integrals) we must assume that the system $\mathcal{L}$ is "sufficiently smooth or continuous"—"small" changes in the input must give "small" changes in the output.

The linearity condition (2.1) can be replaced by the two more simple conditions

$$\mathcal{L}(x_1(t) + x_2(t)) = \mathcal{L}(x_1(t)) + \mathcal{L}(x_2(t)) \tag{2.2}$$
$$\mathcal{L}(\alpha x_1(t)) = \alpha \mathcal{L}(x_1(t)) \tag{2.3}$$

Notice that both conditions (2.2) and (2.3) must be true for (2.1) to be true.

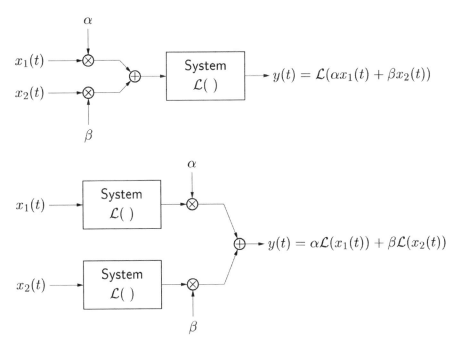

Figure 2.1 Illustration of the linearity condition (2.1)

Let us now take a closer look at condition (2.2). If we assume that both inputs $x_1(t)$ and $x_2(t)$ are zero, that is, $x_1(t) = x_2(t) = 0$, and insert this into condition (2.2), then we obtain

$$\mathcal{L}(0 + 0) = \mathcal{L}(0) + \mathcal{L}(0) \tag{2.4}$$

Hence, we conclude that $\mathcal{L}(0) = 0$. In other words, for a linear system the input zero must result in the output zero. This is an important observation.

In electrical engineering the linearity condition is often replaced by the equivalent requirement that the principle of *superposition* holds: a system is said to be linear if the output resulting from an input that is a weighted sum of signals (left-hand side of (2.1)) is the same as the weighted sum of the outputs obtained when the input signals are acting separately (right-hand side of (2.1)).

Many telecommunication systems are linear or can be regarded as approximately linear. Systems that are not linear are called *nonlinear systems*. In some cases nonlinear behaviors are needed. For example, in Chapter 5 we shall briefly discuss error correcting coding. Then the *encoding* procedure on the transmitting side is usually linear but the *decoding* procedure on the receiving side is always nonlinear.

From a practical point of view the second restriction that we impose on systems is much less severe. We say that a system $\mathcal{I}$ is *time-invariant* if a delay of the input by any amount of time causes only the same delay of the output. In other words, the system as such does not change its behavior with time. In mathematical writing: a system $\mathcal{I}$ is time-invariant if when $y(t) = \mathcal{I}(x(t))$ then

$$y(t - \tau) = \mathcal{I}(x(t - \tau)) \tag{2.5}$$

holds for all *delays* or *shifts* τ. If a system is time-invariant, then its reflexes do not "grow old."

In the remainder of this chapter we shall only consider systems that are both linear and time-invariant (LTI).

Let us consider the moment when a baseball is hit by a bat. Then a very large force acts on the ball during a very short time. Such a force is called an *impulsive force*. In electrical engineering impulsive forces are important tools when we study linear systems. We shall illustrate this by charging a capacitor instantaneously.

Consider the capacitor given in Figure 2.2a. We shall charge it using a rectangular current pulse with amplitude $1/\varepsilon$ and duration ε; hence, we charge the capacitor with $(1/\varepsilon) \cdot \varepsilon = 1$ C, (that is, one coulomb or ampere-second). The current pulse is shown in Figure 2.2b together with the charge on the capacitor. In Figure 2.2c we have reduced the pulse duration by a factor of 2 while keeping the charge at 1 C.

Clearly if we let the pulse duration approach 0, while keeping the charge (that is, the area of the pulse) at 1 C, the function $q(t)$ will approach the *unit step function*

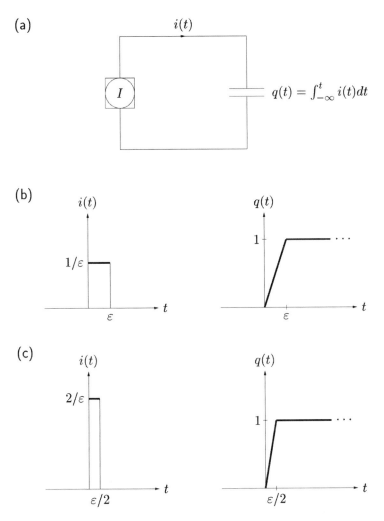

Figure 2.2 Charging a capacitor "instantaneously"

$u(t)$, which is defined as

$$u(t) \stackrel{\text{def}}{=} \begin{cases} 0, & t < 0 \\ \dfrac{1}{2}, & t = 0 \\ 1, & t > 0 \end{cases} \tag{2.6}$$

and shown in Figure 2.3.

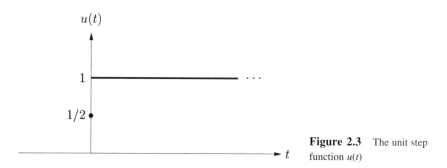

Figure 2.3   The unit step function $u(t)$

When the duration of our pulse approaches 0, the pulse approaches the *delta function* (sometimes called *Dirac's delta function*[1] or, by electrical engineers, the *unit impulse*) denoted $\delta(t)$ and characterized by

$$\delta(t) = 0, \qquad t \neq 0 \tag{2.7}$$

and

$$\int_{-\infty}^{\infty} \delta(t)\, dt = 1 \tag{2.8}$$

Using the delta function, the capacitor charge $q(t)$ can be written

$$q(t) = \int_{-\infty}^{t} \delta(t)\, dt = u(t) \tag{2.9}$$

(Heuristic argument for Eq. (2.9): for $t < 0$, the pulse has not started and hence the integral $= 0$, but for $t > \varepsilon/2$, the whole pulse is included in the integral, which then is 1.)

The delta function $\delta(t)$ is defined by the property

$$\int_{-\infty}^{\infty} \delta(t) g(t)\, dt = g(0) \tag{2.10}$$

[1] Paul Dirac (1902–1984) was an English physicist and Nobel Laureate (1933) who played an important role in the development of quantum mechanics.

where $g(t)$ is an arbitrary function, continuous at $t = 0$. From Eq. (2.10) it follows that

$$\int_{-\infty}^{\infty} \delta(t) g(t_0 - t) \, dt = \int_{-\infty}^{\infty} \delta(t_0 - t) g(t) \, dt = g(t_0) \qquad (2.11)$$

where $g(t)$ is an arbitrary function, continuous at t_0.

We should not regard the delta function as an ordinary function; it is a *generalized function* or *distribution*.

Two generalized functions $a(t)$ and $b(t)$ are said to be equal in *distributional sense* if

$$\int_{-\infty}^{\infty} a(t) \varphi(t) \, dt = \int_{-\infty}^{\infty} b(t) \varphi(t) \, dt \qquad (2.12)$$

for all *test functions* $\varphi(t)$. A test function $\varphi(t)$ is a function that has derivatives of any order and that has *compact support*, that is, $\varphi(t) \neq 0$ only for a finite interval of the time axis.

The derivative of a generalized function $g(t)$ is defined by

$$\int_{-\infty}^{\infty} g'(t) \varphi(t) \, dt \overset{\text{def}}{=} -\int_{-\infty}^{\infty} g(t) \varphi'(t) \, dt \qquad (2.13)$$

Notice that this definition is consistent with formal integration by parts:

$$\int_{-\infty}^{\infty} g'(t) \varphi(t) \, dt = [g(t) \varphi(t)]_{-\infty}^{\infty} - \int_{-\infty}^{\infty} g(t) \varphi'(t) \, dt$$

$$= 0 - \int_{-\infty}^{\infty} g(t) \varphi'(t) \, dt \qquad (2.14)$$

where the last equality follows from the fact that $\varphi(t) = 0$ for $t = \pm\infty$ [$\varphi(t)$ has compact support!].

Consider the unit step function $u(t)$ given by Eq. (2.6). To derive its derivative we use definition (2.13) and obtain

$$\int_{-\infty}^{\infty} u'(t) \varphi(t) \, dt = -\int_{-\infty}^{\infty} u(t) \varphi'(t) \, dt = -\int_{0}^{\infty} \varphi'(t) \, dt$$

$$= -[\varphi(t)]_{0}^{\infty} = -\varphi(\infty) + \varphi(0)$$

$$= \varphi(0) = \int_{-\infty}^{\infty} \delta(t) \varphi(t) \, dt \qquad (2.15)$$

From Eq. (2.15) we conclude that

$$u'(t) = \delta(t) \tag{2.16}$$

which is consistent with

$$\int_{-\infty}^{t} \delta(t) \, dt = u(t) \tag{2.17}$$

(cf. Eq. (2.9)).

EXAMPLE 2.1

That

$$t\delta'(t) = -\delta(t) \tag{2.18}$$

holds for all test functions $\varphi(t)$ can be shown as follows:

$$
\begin{aligned}
\int_{-\infty}^{\infty} t\delta'(t)\varphi(t) \, dt &= -\int_{-\infty}^{\infty} \delta(t)(t\varphi(t))' \, dt \\
&= -\int_{-\infty}^{\infty} \delta(t)(\varphi(t) + t\varphi'(t)) \, dt \\
&= \int_{-\infty}^{\infty} (-\delta(t))\varphi(t) \, dt - \int_{-\infty}^{\infty} \delta(t)t\varphi'(t) \, dt \\
&= \int_{-\infty}^{\infty} (-\delta(t))\varphi(t) \, dt - 0\varphi'(0) \\
&= \int_{-\infty}^{\infty} (-\delta(t))\varphi(t) \, dt
\end{aligned}
$$

where the first equality follows from definition (2.13).   ∎

2.1.1 Impulse Responses

We shall now show how the unit impulse $\delta(t)$ can be used to characterize a linear, time-invariant system. Let $\delta(t)$ be the input to an LTI system and let the *impulse response* $h(t)$ be the corresponding output (Fig. 2.4).

For an LTI system we can apply the inputs of Table 2.1 and get the corresponding outputs. It follows from Eq. (2.11) that the last left expression is the input $x(t)$, and hence we will call the corresponding right expression the output $y(t)$.

In Table 2.1, we have exploited the linearity (twice) and the time-invariance (once) in order to obtain the output $y(t)$ of an LTI system with input $x(t)$.

Figure 2.4   The impulse response of a linear, time-invariant system

By changing the integration variable we also have

$$y(t) = \int_{-\infty}^{\infty} x(\tau)h(t-\tau)\,d\tau = \int_{-\infty}^{\infty} x(t-\tau)h(\tau)\,d\tau \qquad (2.19)$$

The integral in Eq. (2.19) appears quite often in various mathematical and engineering problems. It is called a *convolution* and is usually denoted

$$y(t) = x(t) * h(t) = h(t) * x(t) \qquad (2.20)$$

It is the hitherto most important result in this chapter. In words, *the output y(t) of a linear, time-invariant system is the convolutional of its input x(t) and impulse response h(t)*. We have shown the miraculous result that interchanging the input $x(t)$ and the impulse response $h(t)$ does not change the output $y(t)$; a mathematician would say that the *commutative law* holds for the convolution.

The delta function $\delta(t)$ acts like an identity (like 0 in ordinary addition and 1 in ordinary multiplication) when we evaluate the convolution:

$$\delta(t) * g(t) = g(t) * \delta(t) = g(t) \qquad (2.21)$$

In particular, when the input $x(t) = \delta(t)$, we obtain the output

$$y(t) = \delta(t) * h(t) = h(t) * \delta(t) = h(t) \qquad (2.22)$$

which, as expected, is the impulse response.

Table 2.1   LTI inputs and corresponding outputs

Input		Output	
$\delta(t)$	$\mapsto$	$h(t)$	(definition of $h(t)$)
$\delta(t-\tau)$	$\mapsto$	$h(t-\tau)$	(time-invariance)
$x(\tau)\delta(t-\tau)$	$\mapsto$	$x(\tau)h(t-\tau)$	(linearity; cf. Eq. (2.3))
$\int_{-\infty}^{\infty} x(\tau)\delta(t-\tau)\,d\tau$	$\mapsto$	$\int_{-\infty}^{\infty} x(\tau)h(t-\tau)\,d\tau$	(linearity; extension of Eq. (2.2) to infinitely many terms)

We now give three examples to illustrate how the output of a linear, time-invariant system can be obtained by evaluating the convolution between the input and the impulse response.

EXAMPLE 2.2

Consider an LTI system with impulse response (Fig. 2.5)

$$h(t) = \begin{cases} 1, & -\frac{1}{2} \leq t \leq \frac{1}{2} \\ 0, & \text{otherwise} \end{cases} \tag{2.23}$$

and input

$$x(t) = \begin{cases} 2, & 0 \leq t \leq 1 \\ 0, & \text{otherwise} \end{cases} \tag{2.24}$$

The output can be written as the convolution

$$y(t) = x(t) * h(t) = \int_{-\infty}^{\infty} x(t - \tau)h(\tau)\, d\tau \tag{2.25}$$

Since $h(\tau)$ is 0 outside the interval $[-\frac{1}{2}, \frac{1}{2}]$ the integral in Eq. (2.25) can be simplified to

$$y(t) = \int_{-\frac{1}{2}}^{\frac{1}{2}} x(t - \tau)\, d\tau \tag{2.26}$$

In Figure 2.6 we show the input time-reversed and time-shifted, that is, $x(t - \tau)$ as a function of τ.

Since the integral (2.26) is evaluated over the interval $[-\frac{1}{2}, \frac{1}{2}]$ it follows from the illustration to the left in Figure 2.6 that the output $y(t)$ is 0 both for $t < -\frac{1}{2}$ and for $t \geq \frac{3}{2}$. When

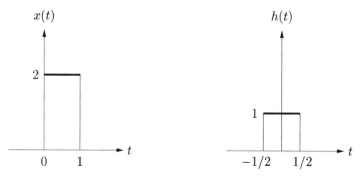

Figure 2.5   Input $x(t)$ and impulse response $h(t)$ for the LTI system in Example 2.2

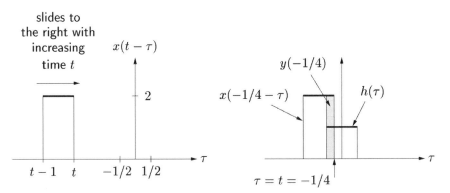

Figure 2.6   The time-reversed and time-shifted version of $x(t)$ (left), and the time-reversed input $x(-\tau)$ sliding across the impulse response $h(\tau)$ (right)

t is in the interval $[-\frac{1}{2}, \frac{1}{2}]$ we have

$$y(t) = \int_{-\frac{1}{2}}^{\frac{1}{2}} x(t - \tau)\, d\tau = \int_{-\frac{1}{2}}^{t} 2\, d\tau = 2[\tau]_{-\frac{1}{2}}^{t} = 2t + 1, \quad -\frac{1}{2} \leq t \leq \frac{1}{2}$$

This situation is illustrated on the right in Figure 2.6. The output is obtained as the area of the overlapping part (in time) of $x(t - \tau)$ and $h(\tau)$ as $x(t - \tau)$ slides along the τ-axis. In the figure we show the situation for $t = -\frac{1}{4}$. The shaded area corresponds to the output $y(-\frac{1}{4})$. Notice that the area of the overlapping part increases linearly with time t until $t = \frac{1}{2}$. Hence the output $y(t)$ increases linearly with time t in the interval $-\frac{1}{2} \leq t \leq \frac{1}{2}$.

When t is in the interval $[\frac{1}{2}, \frac{3}{2}]$ we have

$$y(t) = \int_{-\frac{1}{2}}^{\frac{1}{2}} x(t - \tau)\, d\tau = \int_{t-1}^{\frac{1}{2}} 2\, d\tau = 2[\tau]_{t-1}^{\frac{1}{2}}$$

$$= 1 - 2(t - 1) = -2t + 3, \quad \frac{1}{2} \leq t \leq \frac{3}{2}$$

as illustrated to the left in Figure 2.7.

We summarize this as

$$y(t) = \begin{cases} 0, & t < -\frac{1}{2} \\ 2t + 1, & -\frac{1}{2} \leq t < \frac{1}{2} \\ -2t + 3, & \frac{1}{2} \leq t < \frac{3}{2} \\ 0, & t \geq \frac{3}{2} \end{cases}$$

The output $y(t)$ is shown to the right in Figure 2.7.   ■

We notice that the maximum value of the output, that is, $y(\frac{1}{2})$, is obtained when the two signals are on top of each other. The width of the output $y(t)$ is the sum of the widths of the input $x(t)$ and the impulse response $h(t)$. These facts are true in general with convolutions.

The next example is a variant of the previous one.

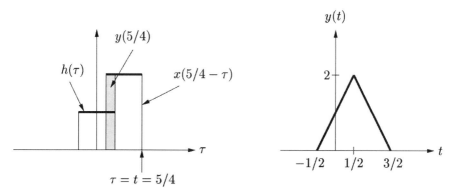

Figure 2.7   The time-reversed input $x(-\tau)$ sliding across the impulse response $h(\tau)$, and the output $y(t)$ for the LTI system in Example 2.2

EXAMPLE 2.3

Consider an LTI system with impulse response

$$h(t) = \begin{cases} 1, & -1 \leq t \leq 1 \\ 0, & \text{otherwise} \end{cases}$$

and the same input as in the previous example; that is, the input $x(t)$ is given by Eq. (2.24). The output is obtained as

$$y(t) = x(t) * h(t) = \int_{-\infty}^{\infty} x(t - \tau)h(\tau)\, d\tau$$

$$= \int_{-1}^{1} x(t - \tau)\, d\tau = \begin{cases} 0, & t < -1 \\ 2t + 2, & -1 \leq t < 0 \\ 2, & 0 \leq t < 1 \\ -2t + 4, & 1 \leq t < 2 \\ 0, & t \geq 2 \end{cases}$$

The signals are shown in Figure 2.8. Notice that during the sliding the area of the overlapping part of $x(t)$ and $h(t)$ is a constant in the interval $0 \leq t \leq 1$. Notice also that the width of the output $y(t)$ is the sum of the widths of the input $x(t)$ and the impulse response $h(t)$.

EXAMPLE 2.4

Consider an LTI system with impulse response

$$h(t) = e^{-t}u(t) \tag{2.27}$$

and input $x(t)$ given by Eq. (2.24); these signals are shown in Figure 2.9.

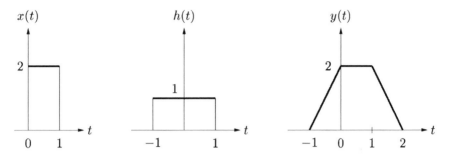

Figure 2.8 Input $x(t)$, impulse response $h(t)$, and output $y(t)$ for the LTI system given in Example 2.3

As in the previous examples we obtain the output as the convolution (cf. Fig. 2.10)

$$
y(t) = x(t) * h(t) = \int_{-\infty}^{\infty} x(\tau)h(t-\tau)\,d\tau
$$
$$
= 2\int_{0}^{1} h(t-\tau)\,d\tau = 2\int_{0}^{1} e^{-(t-\tau)}u(t-\tau)\,d\tau \tag{2.28}
$$
$$
= \begin{cases} 0, & t < 0 \\ 2\int_{0}^{t} e^{-(t-\tau)}\,d\tau, & 0 \le t < 1 \\ 2\int_{0}^{1} e^{-(t-\tau)}\,d\tau, & t \ge 1 \end{cases}
$$

The integrals are easily evaluated as

$$
2\int_{0}^{t} e^{-(t-\tau)}\,d\tau = 2e^{-t}\int_{0}^{t} e^{\tau}\,d\tau = 2e^{-t}[e^{\tau}]_{0}^{t}
$$
$$
= 2e^{-t}(e^{t} - 1) = 2(1 - e^{-t}) \tag{2.29}
$$

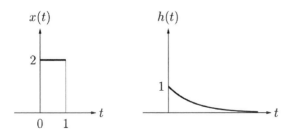

Figure 2.9 Input $x(t)$ and impulse response $h(t)$ for the LTI system given in Example 2.4

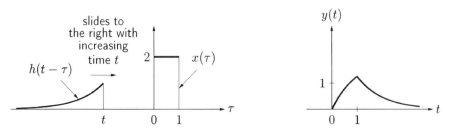

Figure 2.10   The time-reversed impulse response $h(-\tau)$ sliding across the input $x(\tau)$, and the output $y(t)$ for the LTI system in Example 2.4

and

$$2\int_0^1 e^{-(t-\tau)}\, d\tau = 2e^{-t}\int_0^1 e^{\tau}\, d\tau = 2e^{-t}[e^{\tau}]_0^1$$
$$= 2e^{-t}(e-1) = 2(e-1)e^{-t} \tag{2.30}$$

Hence, we have

$$y(t) = \begin{cases} 0, & t < 0 \\ 2(1-e^{-t}), & 0 \le t < 1 \\ 2(e-1)e^{-t}, & t \ge 1 \end{cases} \tag{2.31}$$

which is illustrated in Figure 2.10.   ∎

If we study the outputs $y(t)$ for the previous three examples we notice that the output $y(t)$ in Example 2.4 starts at time $t = 0$. This is in contrast to the outputs $y(t)$ in Examples 2.2 and 2.3 where the output starts at time $t = -\frac{1}{2}$ and $t = -1$, respectively. At a first glance this is somewhat odd since the corresponding input does not start until $t = 0$! These two outputs appear *before* the corresponding inputs! Such systems are called *noncausal*.

A system is said to be *causal* if the reaction always comes after the action—that is, if the output $y(t_0)$ at any given time t_0 is influenced only by inputs at times $t \le t_0$. Thus, for a causal system we have the output

$$y(t) = x(t) * h(t) = \int_{-\infty}^{\infty} x(\tau)h(t-\tau)\, d\tau = \int_{-\infty}^{t} x(\tau)h(t-\tau)\, d\tau \tag{2.32}$$

where the last equality follows from the causality condition. Since this equality must hold for all inputs $x(t)$ we conclude that the impulse response $h(t-\tau)$ must be zero for $\tau > t$, that is, $h(t)$ must be zero for $t < 0$. *The nonzero portion of the impulse response $h(t)$ for a causal system starts at time $t = 0$ or later.*

Clearly, the LTI system in Example 2.4 is causal. The output $y(t)$ from a causal system can be written as

$$y(t) = \int_{-\infty}^{t} x(\tau)h(t-\tau)\, d\tau \tag{2.33}$$

or, equivalently, as

$$y(t) = \int_{0}^{\infty} x(t-\tau)h(\tau)\, d\tau \tag{2.34}$$

Although we can only realize (build) systems, which operate on real time, that are causal it is sometimes useful to study noncausal systems; they might be simpler to analyze mathematically and could be good approximations of causal systems.

2.2   ON THE IMPORTANCE OF BEING SINUSOIDAL

From both theoretical and practical points of view the *sinusoid* must be regarded as the most important and most basic signal in communication engineering. Mathematically the sinusoid can be written either as a *sine signal* or a *cosine signal*. The general expression for a bi-infinite sine signal is

$$s_s(t) = A \sin(\omega_0 t + \phi), \qquad -\infty < t < \infty \tag{2.35}$$

where A is the *amplitude*, $\omega_0 = 2\pi f_0$ is the *radian frequency* (f_0 is the *frequency* in Hz), and ϕ is the *phase-shift* of the signal.[2] We assume that all signals in this section are bi-infinite. The sine signal $s_s(t)$ is shown in Figure 2.11.

The general expression for a bi-infinite cosine signal is

$$s_c(t) = A \cos(\omega_0 t + \phi) \tag{2.36}$$

The sine signal is simply equal to the cosine signal shifted to the right by $\pi/2$, that is,

$$s_s(t) = A \sin(\omega_0 t + \phi) = A \cos(\omega_0 t + \phi - \pi/2) \tag{2.37}$$

or, equivalently, the cosine signal is equal to the sine signal shifted to the left by $\pi/2$, that is,

$$s_c(t) = A \cos(\omega_0 t + \phi) = A \sin(\omega_0 t + \phi + \pi/2) \tag{2.38}$$

---

[2] Here and hereafter we have used the convention of writing ω or ω_0 instead of $2\pi f$ or $2\pi f_0$, etc.

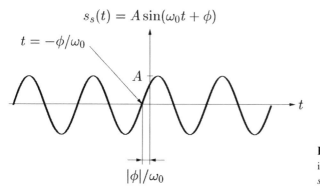

Figure 2.11   The bi-infinite sinusoidal signal $s_s(t) = A\sin(\omega_0 t + \phi)$

Furthermore, the sine and cosine signals are derivatives of each other:

$$\frac{ds_s(t)}{dt} = \frac{d(A\sin(\omega_0 t + \phi))}{dt} = A\omega_0 \cos(\omega_0 t + \phi) = \omega_0 s_c(t) \qquad (2.39)$$

and

$$\frac{ds_c(t)}{dt} = \frac{d(A\cos(\omega_0 t + \phi))}{dt} = -A\omega_0 \sin(\omega_0 t + \phi) = -\omega_0 s_s(t) \qquad (2.40)$$

In Table 2.2 we list some useful identities involving the sinusoids.

Let us return to the sinusoid in Figure 2.11. Clearly, it is periodic. We call the *period* T_0; then we have, for example,

$$A\cos(\omega_0(t + T_0) + \phi) = A\cos(\omega_0 t + \phi) \qquad (2.41)$$

Since the cosine has period 2π we conclude that

$$\omega_0 T_0 = 2\pi$$

or, equivalently,

$$T_0 = \frac{2\pi}{\omega_0} = \frac{1}{f_0} \qquad (2.42)$$

Since T_0 is the duration of a period in seconds (s), we have f_0 periods per second (s^{-1}), or f_0 hertz (Hz). Notice that $f_0 = 0$ corresponds to an infinite period, that is, to a constant signal, often called DC, which stands for *direct current*.

Table 2.2   Some trigonometric identities

1a	$\sin \alpha = -\sin(-\alpha) = \sin(\pi - \alpha)$
	$= \cos(\pi/2 - \alpha) = \mp \cos(\alpha \pm \pi/2)$
1b	$\cos \alpha = \cos(-\alpha) = -\cos(\pi - \alpha)$
	$= \sin(\pi/2 - \alpha) = \pm \sin(\alpha \pm \pi/2)$
2	$\sin^2 \alpha + \cos^2 \alpha = 1$
3a	$\sin(\alpha \pm \beta) = \sin \alpha \cos \beta \pm \cos \alpha \sin \beta$
3b	$\cos(\alpha \pm \beta) = \cos \alpha \cos \beta \mp \sin \alpha \sin \beta$
4a	$\sin \alpha \pm \sin \beta = 2 \sin \dfrac{\alpha \pm \beta}{2} \cos \dfrac{\alpha \mp \beta}{2}$
4b	$\cos \alpha + \cos \beta = 2 \cos \dfrac{\alpha + \beta}{2} \cos \dfrac{\alpha - \beta}{2}$
4c	$\cos \alpha - \cos \beta = -2 \sin \dfrac{\alpha - \beta}{2} \sin \dfrac{\alpha + \beta}{2}$
5a	$\sin \alpha \sin \beta = \dfrac{1}{2}(\cos(\alpha - \beta) - \cos(\alpha + \beta))$
5b	$\sin \alpha \cos \beta = \dfrac{1}{2}(\sin(\alpha - \beta) + \sin(\alpha + \beta))$
5c	$\cos \alpha \cos \beta = \dfrac{1}{2}(\cos(\alpha - \beta) + \cos(\alpha + \beta))$
6a	$\sin 2\alpha = 2 \sin \alpha \cos \alpha$
6b	$\cos 2\alpha = \cos^2 \alpha - \sin^2 \alpha$
7a	$\sin^2 \alpha = \dfrac{1 - \cos 2\alpha}{2}$
7b	$\cos^2 \alpha = \dfrac{1 + \cos 2\alpha}{2}$
8a	$\tan \alpha = \dfrac{\sin \alpha}{\cos \alpha}$
8b	$\cos \alpha = \dfrac{\cos \alpha}{\sin \alpha}$

In school (or from Appendix A) we all learned about complex numbers and in particular about Euler's remarkable formula for the *complex exponential*:[3]

$$e^{j\phi} = \cos \phi + j \sin \phi \qquad (2.43)$$

where $j = \sqrt{(-1)}$; $\cos\phi$ and $\sin\phi$ are the *real part*, $\Re\{e^{j\phi}\}$, and *imaginary part*, $\Im\{e^{j\phi}\}$, of $e^{j\phi}$, respectively.

Since it is in general easier to operate with exponentials instead of sinusoids we shall mostly use the bi-infinite *complex exponential signal*

$$
\begin{aligned}
s_e(t) &= A e^{j(\omega_0 t + \phi)} \\
&= A \cos(\omega_0 t + \phi) + jA \sin(\omega_0 t + \phi) \\
&= s_c(t) + js_s(t) \qquad (2.44)
\end{aligned}
$$

---

[3] Leonhard Euler (1707–1783) was a Swiss mathematician, who was Professor in mathematics in Berlin and St. Petersburg. He is considered to be one of the most productive mathematicians of all time.

as input when we study our linear, time-invariant systems. We will, as well, get a complex signal as output. If $h(t)$ is real (as we assume here and hereafter), then the output corresponding to just the cosine input $s_c(t)$ is simply the real part of the complex output. We illustrate the situation in Figure 2.12, where we consider the input $x(t) = e^{j\omega_0 t}$. Both the real and imaginary parts should be handled at the same time by considering the complex exponential since this will be much simpler than handling one of the parts!

We are now well prepared to study linear, time-invariant systems using the complex exponential signal $e^{j\omega_0 t}$ as their inputs. In the previous section we showed that the output from an LTI system is the convolution of its input and impulse response. Hence, if we let the input be $x(t) = e^{j\omega_0 t}$, then we have the output

$$y(t) = x(t) * h(t) = e^{j\omega_0 t} * h(t)$$

$$= \int_{-\infty}^{\infty} e^{j\omega_0(t-\tau)} h(\tau)\, d\tau = \int_{-\infty}^{\infty} e^{j\omega_0 t} e^{-j\omega_0 \tau} h(\tau)\, d\tau$$

$$= e^{j\omega_0 t} \int_{-\infty}^{\infty} h(\tau) e^{-j\omega_0}\, d\tau$$

$$= H(f_0) e^{j\omega_0 t} \tag{2.45}$$

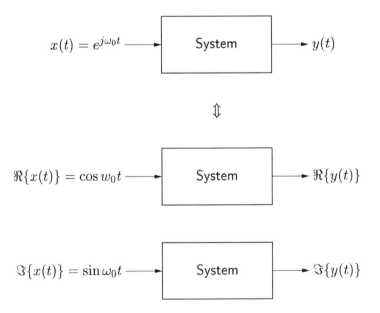

Figure 2.12   A complex input signal through a linear, time-invariant system can be split into its real and imaginary parts

Here

$$H(f_0) \stackrel{\text{def}}{=} \int_{-\infty}^{\infty} h(\tau)e^{-j\omega_0\tau}\,d\tau \tag{2.46}$$

is called the *frequency function* (or, sometimes, the *transfer function*) for the LTI system with impulse response $h(t)$.

The frequency function is in general a complex function of the frequency. It is sometimes convenient to write it as

$$H(f) = A(f)e^{j\phi(f)} \tag{2.47}$$

where

$$A(f) = |H(f)| \tag{2.48}$$

is called the *amplitude function* and

$$\phi(f) = \arctan \frac{\mathcal{I}\{H(f)\}}{\mathcal{R}\{H(f)\}} \tag{2.49}$$

is called the *phase function*. Notice that the frequency function $H(f)$ (and, thus, $A(f)$ and $\phi(f)$ as well) depends only on the LTI system, which is characterized by its impulse response $h(t)$, and does *not* depend on the input $x(t) = e^{j\omega_0 t}$. The output (2.45) can be written as

$$y(t) = H(f_0)e^{j\omega_0 t} = A(f_0)e^{j(\omega_0 t + \phi(f_0))} \tag{2.50}$$

where $A(f_0)$ and $\phi(f_0)$ describe the change in amplitude and phase, respectively, which is introduced by the LTI system. If we study Eq. (2.50) we notice immediately that when the input is the complex exponential signal $e^{j\omega_0 t}$, then the output of an LTI system is also a complex exponential signal; the LTI system does not change the shape of the signal, only its amplitude and phase.

> *For a linear, time-invariant system with a (bi-infinite) sinusoidal input, we obtain always a (bi-infinite) sinusoidal output!*

Furthermore, for general LTI systems it is only for sinusoidal input signals that the corresponding output signals have the same shape as the inputs. In the previous section we gave three different LTI examples, all with the same square pulse input signal; the three corresponding outputs looked quite different both from each other and from the input. We should also remark that the *sinusoidal in–sinusoidal out* property holds in general only for systems that are both linear and time-invariant. A mathematician would say that the complex exponential $e^{j\omega_0 t}$ is an *eigenfunction* of a *linear, time-invariant operator*.

Such LTI systems appear everywhere in information transmission. We can see then that sinusoids are well worth a deeper study. Appendix B is devoted to sinusoids and circuit theory.

2.3 THE FOURIER TRANSFORM

In Section 2.1, we introduced the impulse response $h(t)$ of a linear, time-invariant system and showed that the output $y(t)$ corresponding to the input $x(t)$ can be expressed as the convolution (2.20)

$$y(t) = x(t) * h(t) = h(t) * x(t)$$

In Section 2.2, we studied the important but very special case when the input was an exponential sinusoidal, that is, $x(t) = e^{j\omega_0 t}$. This input has only one frequency, namely f_0, and the corresponding output is obtained as (2.45)/(2.46), namely

$$y(t) = H(f_0)e^{j\omega_0 t}$$

and

$$H(f_0) = \int_{-\infty}^{\infty} h(\tau)e^{-j\omega_0 \tau}\, d\tau$$

is the frequency function for the LTI system with impulse response $h(t)$. This output has also only one frequency and the value $H(f_0)$ of the frequency function at this frequency specifies how the amplitude and phase of the sinusoidal input of frequency f_0 are changed by the LTI system.

Suppose now that the input is not sinusoidal but is a general function $x(t)$. Which frequencies does $x(t)$ contain? How is this input changed by the LTI system? The answer to the second question can be obtained by the convolution (2.20) but what about the first question? Let us be more specific: Which frequencies does, for example, the *rectangular pulse* in Figure 2.13

$$\text{rect}(t) = \begin{cases} 1, & |t| < \frac{1}{2} \\ 0, & |t| > \frac{1}{2} \end{cases} \tag{2.51}$$

contain?

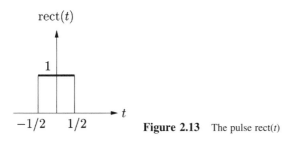

Figure 2.13   The pulse rect(t)

BOX 2-1

J. B. Joseph Fourier (1768–1830)

Jean Baptiste Joseph Fourier showed early talents for mathematics. At the age of 14 he had completed the study of the six volumes of Bézout's *Cours de mathematique*. When he was 19 he decided to become a priest, but he was unsure that he was making the right decision. Luckily for us he did not take holy orders. Fourier was taught by such famous mathematicians as Lagrange and Laplace. At the age of 29 he succeeded Lagrange as the chair of analysis and mechanics at École Polytechnique, Paris. At this time Fourier was renowned as an outstanding teacher. In 1807 he completed his important mathematical work on the theory of heat, *On the Propagation of Heat in Solid Bodies*. Both Lagrange and Laplace objected to Fourier's expansions of functions as trigonometrical series, what we now call Fourier series. Fourier's inability to convince them shows how new his views were. His life was not without problems since his theory of heat continued to provoke controversy.

Fourier's work inspired more than a century of later work on trigonometric series and the theory of functions of a real variable. His work has turned out to be the pillar on which modern telecommunication theory rests.

There is a mathematical way of solving this problem, namely using the *Fourier transform* (Box 2-1) of the signal $x(t)$ given by the formula

$$X(f) = \int_{-\infty}^{\infty} x(t)e^{-j\omega t}\, dt \tag{2.52}$$

where $\omega = 2\pi f$. This function is in general complex, with

$$X(f) = A(f)e^{j\phi(f)} \tag{2.53}$$

where $A(f) = |X(f)|$ is called the *spectrum* of $x(t)$ and $\phi(f)$ its *phase*. We can also represent $x(t)$ in terms of its Fourier transform via the *inversion formula*

$$x(t) = \int_{-\infty}^{\infty} X(f)e^{j\omega t} \, df \tag{2.54}$$

Equations (2.52) and (2.54) define a *Fourier transform pair* denoted

$$x(t) \leftrightarrow X(f) \tag{2.55}$$

To show the inversion formula we use the identity

$$\int_{-\infty}^{\infty} e^{j\omega t} \, df = \delta(t) \tag{2.56}$$

This distributional identity is both important and useful. We first sketch a proof[4] of an equivalent equality obtained by interchanging the variables f and t in identity (2.56).

Lemma 2.1

$$\int_{-\infty}^{\infty} e^{j\omega t} \, dt = \delta(f) \tag{2.57}$$

Proof.   Insert the limit

$$1 = \lim_{n \to \infty} e^{-|t|/n}, \quad \text{all } t \tag{2.58}$$

into

$$\int_{-\infty}^{\infty} \left(\int_{-\infty}^{\infty} e^{j\omega t} \cdot 1 \cdot dt \right) \varphi(f) \, df$$

where $\varphi(f)$ is a test function, and obtain

$$\int_{-\infty}^{\infty} \left(\lim_{n \to \infty} \int_{-\infty}^{\infty} e^{j\omega t - |t|/n} \, dt \right) \varphi(f) \, df$$

$$= \int_{-\infty}^{\infty} \lim_{n \to \infty} \left(\int_{-\infty}^{0} e^{(j\omega + n^{-1})t} \, dt + \int_{0}^{\infty} e^{(j\omega - n^{-1})t} \, dt \right) \varphi(f) \, df$$

$$= \int_{-\infty}^{\infty} \lim_{n \to \infty} \left(\frac{1}{j\omega + n^{-1}} - \frac{1}{j\omega - n^{-1}} \right) \varphi(f) \, df$$

$$= \int_{-\infty}^{\infty} \lim_{n \to \infty} \frac{2n}{1 + (\omega n)^2} \varphi(f) \, df \tag{2.59}$$

We notice that

$$\lim_{n \to \infty} \frac{2n}{1 + (\omega n)^2} \begin{cases} = 0, & \omega \neq 0 \\ \to \infty, & \omega = 0 \end{cases} \tag{2.60}$$

---

[4] We say "sketch a proof" since we do not justify the interchange of limit and integral in Eq. (2.59). The reader can find this detail in refs. [2, 3].

Furthermore, it is easily shown that

$$\int_{-\infty}^{\infty} \frac{2n}{1 + (\omega n)^2} \, df = 1 \tag{2.61}$$

Hence, from Eqs. (2.60) and (2.61) we conclude that

$$\lim_{n \to \infty} \frac{2n}{1 + (\omega n)^2} = \delta(f) \tag{2.62}$$

in distributional sense and we have shown that

$$\int_{-\infty}^{\infty} \left(\int_{-\infty}^{\infty} e^{j\omega t} \, dt \right) \varphi(f) df = \int_{-\infty}^{\infty} \delta(f) \varphi(f) \, df \tag{2.63}$$

This proves that Eqs. (2.57) and (2.56) hold in distributional sense.

Now to the inversion formula. Inserting expression (2.52) into the right-hand side of Eq. (2.54) yields

$$\begin{aligned}
\int_{-\infty}^{\infty} X(f) e^{j\omega t} \, df &= \int_{-\infty}^{\infty} \left(\int_{-\infty}^{\infty} x(\tau) e^{-j\omega \tau} \, d\tau \right) e^{j\omega t} \, df \\
&= \int_{-\infty}^{\infty} x(\tau) \left(\int_{-\infty}^{\infty} e^{j\omega(t-\tau)} \, df \right) d\tau \\
&= \int_{-\infty}^{\infty} x(\tau) \delta(t - \tau) \, d\tau = x(t) \tag{2.64}
\end{aligned}$$

where we have used Eq. (2.56) to obtain the third equality and Eq. (2.10) to obtain the last equality.

Consider now the sinusoidal signal $\cos \omega_0 t$. Which frequencies does it contain? In order to answer this fundamental question we invoke Euler's formula (2.43)

$$e^{j\omega_0 t} = \cos \omega_0 t + j \sin \omega_0 t$$

Insert $-t$ instead of t in Eq. (2.43) and exploit that the cosine is an even function, that is, $\cos(-\omega_0 t) = \cos \omega_0 t$, and that sine is an odd function, that is, $\sin(-\omega_0 t) = -\sin \omega_0 t$; then we obtain

$$e^{-j\omega_0 t} = \cos \omega_0 t - j \sin \omega_0 t$$

and adding the two yields that

$$\cos \omega_0 t = \frac{e^{j\omega_0 t} + e^{-j\omega_0 t}}{2} \tag{2.65}$$

Let us evaluate the Fourier transform of $\cos \omega_0 t$:

$$
\begin{aligned}
X(f) &= \int_{-\infty}^{\infty} \cos \omega_0 t e^{-j\omega t}\, dt \\
&= \int_{-\infty}^{\infty} \frac{e^{j\omega_0 t} + e^{-j\omega_0 t}}{2} e^{-j\omega t}\, dt \\
&= \frac{1}{2}\int_{-\infty}^{\infty} e^{j(\omega_0 - \omega)t}\, dt + \frac{1}{2}\int_{-\infty}^{\infty} e^{j(-\omega_0 - \omega)t}\, dt \\
&= \frac{1}{2}\delta(f_0 - f) + \frac{1}{2}\delta(-f_0 - f)
\end{aligned}
\tag{2.66}
$$

where the last equality follows from Eq. (2.57). Since $\delta(f)$ is even, that is, $\delta(-f) = \delta(f)$, we can rewrite Eq. (2.66) as

$$
\begin{aligned}
X(f) &= \int_{-\infty}^{\infty} \cos \omega_0 t e^{-j\omega_0 t}\, dt \\
&= \frac{1}{2}\delta(f - f_0) + \frac{1}{2}\delta(f + f_0)
\end{aligned}
\tag{2.67}
$$

Hence we have the Fourier transform pair

$$
\cos \omega_0 t \leftrightarrow \frac{1}{2}\delta(f - f_0) + \frac{1}{2}\delta(f + f_0)
\tag{2.68}
$$

which is illustrated in Figure 2.14. We get half of a unit impulse at frequency f_0 and, perhaps somewhat surprisingly, half of a unit impulse at frequency $-f_0$.

How shall we interpret a negative frequency? Clearly, we cannot have a negative number of periods per second. So a negative frequency is simply a mathematical construction; it is mathematically convenient to split the frequency content of a signal into two equal parts—half at positive frequencies and half at the corresponding negative frequencies. We will see later that the negative frequency concept is useful in analyzing signal modulation.

Taking this interpretation into account we conclude that, as expected, the sinusoid $\cos \omega_0 t$ contains only a single frequency, namely f_0.

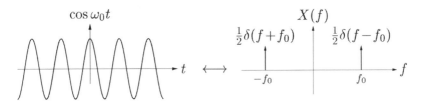

Figure 2.14   The sinusoid $\cos \omega_0 t$ and its Fourier transform

Let us now return to the rectangular pulse rect(t) given by Eq. (2.51) and shown in Figure 2.13. The frequency content of $x(t)$ is readily obtained as

$$
\begin{aligned}
X(f) &= \int_{-\infty}^{\infty} \text{rect}(t) e^{-j\omega t} \, dt \\
&= \int_{-\frac{1}{2}}^{\frac{1}{2}} 1 \cdot e^{-j\omega t} \, dt = \left[\frac{e^{-j\omega t}}{-j\omega} \right]_{-\frac{1}{2}}^{\frac{1}{2}} \\
&= \frac{1}{j\omega} (e^{j\pi f} - e^{-j\pi f}) \\
&= \frac{1}{j\omega} (\cos \pi f + j \sin \pi f - \cos \pi f + j \sin \pi f) \\
&= \frac{\sin \pi f}{\pi f} \overset{\text{def}}{=} \text{sinc}(f) \qquad \text{with } f = \omega / 2\pi
\end{aligned}
\tag{2.69}
$$

and we have the Fourier transform pair (Fig. 2.15):

$$
\text{rect}(t) \leftrightarrow \text{sinc}(f)
\tag{2.70}
$$

Clearly we have $|\text{sinc}(f)| > 0$ for all frequencies for which f is *not* an integer; that is, the signal rect(t) contains an infinite interval of frequencies! The extremely high frequencies are needed to build up the positive step at $t = -\frac{1}{2}$ and the negative step at $t = \frac{1}{2}$. We also notice that

$$
X(0) = \int_{-\infty}^{\infty} \text{rect}(t) \, dt = \int_{-\frac{1}{2}}^{\frac{1}{2}} 1 \cdot dt = 1
$$

or, alternatively,

$$
X(0) = \lim_{f \to 0} \text{sinc}(f) = \lim_{f \to 0} \frac{\sin \pi f}{\pi f} = 1
$$

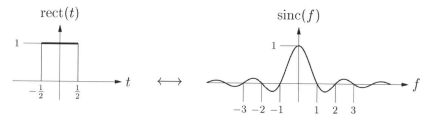

Figure 2.15   Function rect(t) and its Fourier transform sinc(f)

2.3.1 Properties of the Fourier Transform

We now give a list of properties of the Fourier transform that make it the important tool it is. The major ones are listed in Table 2.3, where the exponent $*$ denotes the complex conjugate. The behavior of many information systems is directly explained by one or more of these.

The linearity property follows immediately from the definition of the Fourier transform. The inversion formula was shown in Eq. (2.64). The translation property is easily shown as follows:

$$\int_{-\infty}^{\infty} x(t - t_0)e^{-j\omega t}\, dt = \int_{-\infty}^{\infty} x(\tau)e^{-j\omega(\tau + t_0)}\, d\tau$$

$$= e^{-j\omega t_0}\int_{-\infty}^{\infty} x(\tau)e^{-j\omega \tau}\, d\tau = X(f)e^{-j\omega t_0}$$

Properties 4–10 and 12 of Table 2.3 are shown in Problem 2.6 at the end of this chapter. We shall prove the convolution in the time-domain Property 11 since it

Table 2.3   Properties of the Fourier transform

1.	Linearity	$ax_1(t) + bx_2(t) \leftrightarrow aX_1(f) + bX_2(f)$
2.	Inverse	$x(t) = \int_{-\infty}^{\infty} X(f)\, e^{j\omega t}\, df$
3.	Translation (time shift)	$x(t - t_0) \leftrightarrow X(f)\, e^{-j\omega t_0}$
4.	Modulation (frequency shift)	$x(t)\, e^{j\omega_0 t} \leftrightarrow X(f - f_0)$
		$x(t)\cos \omega_0 t \leftrightarrow \dfrac{1}{2}X(f + f_0) + \dfrac{1}{2}X(f - f_0)$
5.	Time scaling	$x(at) \leftrightarrow \dfrac{1}{|a|}X(f/a)$
6.	Differentiation in time	$\dfrac{d}{dt}x(t) \leftrightarrow j\omega X(f)$
7.	Differentiation in frequency	$tx(t) \leftrightarrow -\dfrac{1}{j2\pi}\dfrac{d}{df}X(f)$
8.	Integration in time	$\int_{-\infty}^{t} x(\tau)\, d\tau \leftrightarrow \dfrac{1}{j\omega}X(f)$
9.	Duality	$X(t) \leftrightarrow x(-f)$
10.	Conjugate functions	$x^*(t) \leftrightarrow X^*(-f)$
11.	Convolution in time	$x_1(t) * x_2(t) \leftrightarrow X_1(f)X_2(f)$
12.	Multiplication in time	$x_1(t)x_2(t) \leftrightarrow X_1(f) * X_2(f)$
13.	Parseval's formulas	$\int_{-\infty}^{\infty} x_1(t)x_2^*(t)\, dt = \int_{-\infty}^{\infty} X_1(f)X_2^*(f)\, df$
		or, when $x_1(t) = x_2(t)$,
		$\int_{-\infty}^{\infty} |x(t)|^2\, dt = \int_{-\infty}^{\infty} |X(f)|^2\, df$

is an important link between convolution and the Fourier transform:

$$\int_{-\infty}^{\infty} x_1(t) * x_2(t) e^{-j\omega t} \, dt$$

$$= \int_{-\infty}^{\infty} \int_{-\infty}^{\infty} x_1(\tau) x_2(t - \tau) e^{-j\omega t} \, d\tau \, dt$$

$$= \int_{-\infty}^{\infty} \int_{-\infty}^{\infty} x_1(\tau) x_2(v) e^{-j\omega(v+\tau)} \, d\tau \, dv$$

$$= \int_{-\infty}^{\infty} x_1(\tau) e^{-j\omega\tau} \, d\tau \int_{-\infty}^{\infty} x_2(v) e^{-j\omega v} \, dv$$

$$= X_1(f) X_2(f)$$

Since the output $y(t)$ of an LTI system is the convolution of its input $x(t)$ and impulse response $h(t)$ it follows from this and Property 11 that the Fourier transform of its output $Y(f)$ is simply the product of the Fourier transform of its input $X(f)$ and its frequency function $H(f)$, that is,

$$Y(f) = X(f)H(f) \tag{2.71}$$

Equation (2.71) describes in a compact manner how the frequency contents of the input signal is shaped by an LTI system: it is multiplied by $H(f)$.

Electrical *power* is defined as the product of the voltage and the current, that is,

$$p(t) = v(t)i(t) \tag{2.72}$$

Power is measured in watts [W]. Electrical *energy* is defined as

$$e(t) = \int_{-\infty}^{t} p(\tau) \, d\tau \tag{2.73}$$

and measured in watt-seconds [W-s].

Let $x(t)$ be the voltage or current of a source. Often when we discuss energy we assume that such a source is connected to a 1 Ω resistor; then the quantity

$$\int_{-\infty}^{\infty} |x(t)|^2 \, dt$$

equals the energy delivered by the source to the resistor. This lends a special meaning to Parseval's formula, Property 13, which can be proved as follows:

$$
\int_{-\infty}^{\infty} x_1(t)x_2^*(t)\, dt
$$

$$
= \int_{-\infty}^{\infty} \left(\int_{-\infty}^{\infty} X_1(f)e^{j2\pi ft}\, df \right) \left(\int_{-\infty}^{\infty} X_2^*(v)e^{-j2\pi vt}\, dv \right) dt
$$

$$
= \int_{-\infty}^{\infty}\int_{-\infty}^{\infty} X_1(f)X_2^*(v)\left(\int_{-\infty}^{\infty} e^{j2\pi(f-v)t}\, dt \right) df\, dv
$$

$$
= \int_{-\infty}^{\infty}\int_{-\infty}^{\infty} X_1(f)X_2^*(v)\delta(f-v)\, df\, dv
$$

$$
= \int_{-\infty}^{\infty} X_1(f)X_2^*(f)\, df
$$

If we let $x_1(t) = x_2(t) = x(t)$, with $x(t)$ applied across a $1\ \Omega$ resistor, then Parseval's formula shows how the power is distributed over the frequencies.

In Table 2.4 we list some useful Fourier transform pairs. We establish the Fourier transform pair (c) by calculating the inverse Fourier transform of $2/j\omega$:

$$
x(t) = \int_{-\infty}^{\infty} \frac{2}{j\omega} e^{j\omega t}\, df = 2\int_{-\infty}^{\infty} \underbrace{\frac{\cos \omega t}{j\omega}}_{\text{odd}}\, df + 2j \int_{-\infty}^{\infty} \underbrace{\frac{\sin \omega t}{j\omega}}_{\text{even}}\, df
$$

$$
= \frac{2}{\pi} \int_{0}^{\infty} \frac{\sin \omega t}{f}\, df = \left\{ \begin{array}{ll} 1, & t > 0 \\ 0, & t = 0 \\ -1, & t < 0 \end{array} \right\} = \operatorname{sgn}(t)
$$

We have used that

$$
\int_{0}^{\infty} \frac{\sin x}{x}\, dx = \frac{\pi}{2} \tag{2.74}
$$

Since the unit step function $u(t)$ can be written as

$$
u(t) = \frac{1}{2}\operatorname{sgn}(t) + \frac{1}{2} \tag{2.75}
$$

we can simply add half of the Fourier transforms of $\operatorname{sgn}(t)$ and the constant 1, which yields $1/j\omega + \frac{1}{2}\delta(f)$ as the Fourier transform of $u(t)$.

The Fourier transform pairs (g)–(m) are established in Problem 2.7. The pair (n) is very useful in deriving various results; its validity is proved in refs [2, 3].

Table 2.4   Fourier transform pairs

(a)	Impulse in time	$\delta(t) \leftrightarrow 1$
(b)	Impulse in frequency	$1 \leftrightarrow \delta(f)$
(c)	Sign function	$\operatorname{sgn}(t) = \begin{cases} 1, & t > 0 \\ 0, & t = 0 \\ -1, & t < 0 \end{cases} \leftrightarrow \dfrac{2}{j\omega}$
(d)	Unit step function	$u(t) = \begin{cases} 1, & t > 0 \\ 1/2, & t = 0 \\ 0, & t < 0 \end{cases} \leftrightarrow \dfrac{1}{j\omega} + \dfrac{1}{2}\delta(f)$
(e)	Complex exponential	$e^{j\omega_0 t} \leftrightarrow \delta(f - f_0)$
(f)	Cosine function	$\cos \omega_0 t \leftrightarrow \dfrac{1}{2}\delta(f - f_0) + \dfrac{1}{2}\delta(f + f_0)$
(g)	Sine function	$\sin \omega_0 t \leftrightarrow \dfrac{1}{2j}\delta(f - f_0) + \dfrac{1}{2j}\delta(f + f_0)$
(h)	Rectangular pulse	$\operatorname{rect}(t) \leftrightarrow \operatorname{sinc}(f) = \dfrac{\sin \pi f}{\pi f}$
(i)	Sinc pulse	$\operatorname{sinc}(t) \leftrightarrow \operatorname{rect}(f) = \begin{cases} 1, & |f| < 1/2 \\ 0, & |f| > 1/2 \end{cases}$
(j)	Triangular pulse	$\begin{cases} 1 - |t|, & |t| < 1 \\ 0, & |t| > 1 \end{cases} \leftrightarrow \operatorname{sinc}^2(f)$
(k)	Gaussian pulse	$e^{-\pi t^2} \leftrightarrow e^{-\pi f^2}$
(l)	One-sided exp. $(\alpha > 0)$	$e^{-\alpha t} u(t) \leftrightarrow \dfrac{1}{\alpha + j\omega}$
(m)	Double-sided exp. $(\alpha > 0)$	$e^{-\alpha|t|} \leftrightarrow \dfrac{2\alpha}{\alpha^2 + \omega^2}$
(n)	Impulses spaced T sec apart	$\displaystyle\sum_{i=-\infty}^{\infty} \delta(t - iT) \leftrightarrow \dfrac{1}{T}\sum_{j=-\infty}^{\infty} \delta\left(f - \dfrac{j}{T}\right)$

EXAMPLE 2.5

The spectrum of the rect(t) signal is sinc(f); thus, the spectrum is concentrated around $f = 0$. Now multiply the rect(t) signal by $\cos \omega_0 t$. The Fourier transform of a product is the convolution of the spectra of its factors:

$$\operatorname{rect}(t) \cos \omega_0 t \leftrightarrow \operatorname{sinc}(f) * \left(\frac{1}{2}\delta(f - f_0) + \frac{1}{2}\delta(f + f_0)\right) \tag{2.76}$$

The convolutions with the impulses are easily evaluated:

$$\operatorname{sinc}(f) * \left(\frac{1}{2}\delta(f - f_0) + \frac{1}{2}\delta(f + f_0)\right)$$

$$= \frac{1}{2}\int_{-\infty}^{\infty} \operatorname{sinc}(f - v)\delta(v - f_0)\,dv + \frac{1}{2}\int_{-\infty}^{\infty} \operatorname{sinc}(f - v)\delta(v + f_0)\,dv$$

$$= \frac{1}{2}\operatorname{sinc}(f - f_0) + \frac{1}{2}\operatorname{sinc}(f + f_0) \tag{2.77}$$

that is, half of the spectrum is shifted so that it is concentrated around the frequency f_0 and the other half so that it is concentrated around the frequency $-f_0$. We say that the signal rect(t) is *modulated* by the carrier $\cos \omega_0 t$ in the sense that after the modulation its spectrum is centered around $\pm$ the *carrier frequency f_0*. Modulation will be discussed in detail in Chapter 4.

EXAMPLE 2.6

Consider the nonperiodic signal $x(t)$. If we sum copies of $x(t)$ taken T seconds apart we obtain the *periodic* signal

$$\sum_{i=-\infty}^{\infty} x(t - iT) = x(t) * \left(\sum_{i=-\infty}^{\infty} \delta(t - iT) \right) \tag{2.78}$$

Then, using Property 10 and Fourier transform pair (n), we obtain the pair

$$\sum_{i=-\infty}^{\infty} x(t - iT) \leftrightarrow \frac{1}{T} X(f) \left(\sum_{j=-\infty}^{\infty} \delta\left(f - \frac{j}{T} \right) \right)$$

$$= \frac{1}{T} \sum_{j=-\infty}^{\infty} X\left(\frac{j}{T} \right) \delta\left(f - \frac{j}{T} \right) \tag{2.79}$$

■

In the next section we will use the Fourier transform to discuss the fundamental concept of bandwidth.

2.4   WHAT IS BANDWIDTH?

The *bandwidth* of a signal is a fundamental concept whose meaning requires some elaboration. In this section we introduce two kinds of bandwidth; the first one is inspired by the Fourier transform and the second by the sampling theorem. We then consider the relationship between these two notions of bandwidth.

As an introductory example we use the signal

$$x(t) = \text{sinc}(2t/T) \tag{2.80}$$

shown in Figure 2.16. Its "main lobe" has width T. Combining Fourier transform pair (i), that is, $\text{sinc}(t) \leftrightarrow \text{rect}(f)$, with the time-scaling property, $x(at) \leftrightarrow |a|^{-1} X(f/a)$, yields

$$\text{sinc}(2t/T) \leftrightarrow \frac{T}{2} \text{rect}(fT/2) = \begin{cases} \dfrac{T}{2}, & |f| < \dfrac{1}{T} \\[2mm] 0, & |f| > \dfrac{1}{T} \end{cases} \tag{2.81}$$

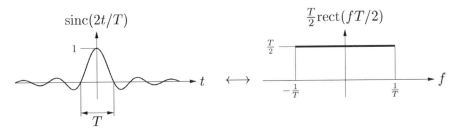

Figure 2.16 The Fourier transform pair sinc($2t/T$) $\leftrightarrow \frac{T}{2}$ rect($fT/2$)

The nonzero frequency content of the signal sinc(t/T) is confined to the *frequency band* (or *interval*) $[-\frac{1}{T}, \frac{1}{T}]$ as we see from Eq. (2.81) or the corresponding Figure 2.16. It is quite obvious that we must say that the signal sinc($2t/T$) has a bandwidth of $W = 1/T$ Hz and to call this its "Fourier bandwidth" since it is closely related to the Fourier transform.

It is not always so easy to quantify the Fourier bandwidth of a signal as it was in the above simple example. The signal $x(t) = $ rect(t/T) has the Fourier transform Tsinc(fT), which is nonzero outside any finite frequency band that we might consider (Fig. 2.17). This is true for the Fourier transform of every signal whose nonzero values are limited to a finite time interval. What then should we say is the Fourier bandwidth of such a signal?

In practice, we usually have to restrict our signals to frequencies inside a certain agreed finite band, $[-W, W]$ say. But such a hard restriction on the frequency content of a signal cannot be combined with the assumption of finite time-duration! To be able to speak of the Fourier bandwidth of a general signal, we need to use a softer restriction on its frequency content. A useful way to do this is to consider what fraction η of the energy of the signal $x(t)$ lies inside the frequency band $[-W, W]$, that is, to find the solution W of

$$\frac{\int_{-W}^{W} |X(f)|^2 \, df}{\int_{-\infty}^{\infty} |X(f)|^2 \, df} = \eta \tag{2.82}$$

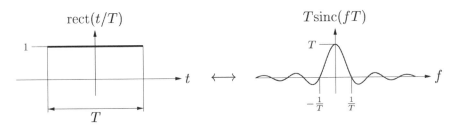

Figure 2.17 The Fourier transform pair rect(t/T) $\leftrightarrow T$ sinc(fT)

Letting $W = 1/T$ for our second example $x(t) = \text{rect}(t/T)$, we find by a straight-forward calculation that

$$\frac{\int_{-W}^{W} |X(f)|^2 \, df}{\int_{-\infty}^{\infty} |X(f)|^2 \, df} = \frac{\int_{-1/T}^{1/T} T^2 \text{sinc}^2(fT) \, df}{\int_{-\infty}^{\infty} T^2 \text{sinc}^2(fT) \, df} = 0.903 \tag{2.83}$$

About 90% of the energy of $\text{rect}(t/T)$ is contained within the frequency band $[-W, W] = [-1/T, 1/T]$.

With the above examples in mind, it seems reasonable to define the *Fourier bandwidth* of a signal to be the smallest value of W such that essentially all of its energy is confined to the frequency band $[-W, W]$. There is a certain arbitrariness to this definition, which reflects the fact that except for strictly band-limited signals there is no compelling absolute measure of Fourier bandwith. However, it certainly seems reasonable to say, for instance, that the signal $\text{rect}(t/T)$ has a Fourier bandwidth of $W = 1/T$ Hz as our definition implies. To be more precise, we could say that the "90%-energy Fourier bandwidth" of the signal $\text{rect}(t/T)$ is $W = 1/T$ Hz, but we will usually not have need for such precision.

Next we introduce the much celebrated sampling theorem [4, 5], which is an important tool in the study of information transmission and in many other areas.

Consider the function

$$\phi(t) = \sqrt{2W} \, \frac{\sin 2\pi Wt}{2\pi Wt} = \sqrt{2W} \, \text{sinc}(2Wt) \tag{2.84}$$

with Fourier transform (show this as an exercise; hint: use time scaling)

$$\Phi(f) = \frac{1}{\sqrt{2W}} \, \text{rect}\left(\frac{f}{2W}\right) = \begin{cases} \dfrac{1}{\sqrt{2W}}, & |f| < W \\ 0, & |f| > W \end{cases} \tag{2.85}$$

Thus, the function $\phi(t)$ is confined to the frequency band $[-W, W]$. Versions of $\phi(t)$ delayed by $\frac{k}{2W}$ form the set of *orthonormal functions*

$$\phi_k(t) = \phi\left(t - \frac{k}{2W}\right) = \sqrt{2W} \, \text{sinc}\left(2W\left(t - \frac{k}{2W}\right)\right) \tag{2.86}$$

where k is an integer. Orthogonality is an important notion in signal analysis. It means that

$$\int_{-\infty}^{\infty} \phi_k(t) \phi_l^*(t) \, dt = \begin{cases} e_k, & l = k \\ 0, & l \neq k \end{cases} \tag{2.87}$$

where e_k is the energy of $\phi_k(t)$. It holds here because

$$
\begin{aligned}
\int_{-\infty}^{\infty} \phi_k(t)\phi_l^*(t)\, dt &= \int_{-\infty}^{\infty} \Phi_k(f)\Phi_l^*(f)\, df \\
&= \frac{1}{2W} \int_{-W}^{W} e^{j\omega(l-k)/2W}\, df \\
&= \frac{2}{2W} \int_{0}^{W} \cos\left(\frac{\omega(l-k)}{2W}\right) df = \begin{cases} 1, & l = k \\ 0, & l \neq k \end{cases}
\end{aligned}
$$

The second equality follows from the fact that the Fourier transform of $\phi_k(t) = \phi(t - \frac{k}{2W})$ is (by time-shifting)

$$
\Phi_k(f) = \Phi(f)e^{-j\omega k/2W} \tag{2.88}
$$

Furthermore, since

$$
\int_{-\infty}^{\infty} |\phi_k(t)|^2\, dt = \int_{-\infty}^{\infty} |\phi(t)|^2\, dt = 1 \tag{2.89}
$$

for every integer k, these functions are *normalized* (energy $e_k = 1$, all k). A set of orthogonal and normalized functions is called an *orthonormal set of functions.*
 We are now prepared to formulate the *sampling theorem.*

Theorem 2.1 (Sampling Theorem) *If $x(t)$ is a signal whose Fourier transform is identically zero for $|f| \geq W$, then $x(t)$ is completely determined by its samples taken every $\frac{1}{2W}$ seconds in the manner*

$$
x(t) = \sum_{k=-\infty}^{\infty} x\left(\frac{k}{2W}\right) \mathrm{sinc}\left(2W\left(t - \frac{k}{2W}\right)\right) \tag{2.90}
$$

Proof. We can view the process of sampling as taking the product of the signal $x(t)$ with a train of impulses spaced $\frac{1}{2W}$ seconds apart. Then, sampling gives the following train of impulses $x^\dagger(t)$ whose coefficients are the samples of $x(t)$:

$$
x^\dagger(t) = x(t) \sum_{k=-\infty}^{\infty} \delta\left(t - \frac{k}{2W}\right) = \sum_{k=-\infty}^{\infty} x\left(\frac{k}{2W}\right) \delta\left(t - \frac{k}{2W}\right)
$$

We use Property 11 and Fourier transform pair (n) to compute the transform of $x^\dagger(t)$:

$$\sum_{k=-\infty}^{\infty} x\left(\frac{k}{2W}\right)\delta\left(t - \frac{k}{2W}\right) \leftrightarrow 2WX(f) * \sum_{l=-\infty}^{\infty} \delta(f - l2W)$$

$$= 2W \sum_{l=-\infty}^{\infty} X(f - l2W) \tag{2.91}$$

The *sampled* version of the signal $x(t)$ has a spectrum that can be written as copies of $X(f)$, that is, the spectrum of $x(t)$, spaced $2W$ Hz apart! If we multiply this periodic spectrum by $\frac{1}{2W}\text{rect}(\frac{f}{2W})$ we obtain $X(f)$. Hence, we conclude that

$$x(t) \leftrightarrow \left(2W \sum_{l=-\infty}^{\infty} X(f - l2W)\right)\left(\frac{1}{2W}\text{rect}\left(\frac{f}{2W}\right)\right)$$

By using Property 10, Eqs. (2.84), (2.85), and (2.91), we obtain

$$x(t) = \left(\sum_{k=-\infty}^{\infty} x\left(\frac{k}{2W}\right)\delta\left(t - \frac{k}{2W}\right)\right) * \text{sinc }(2Wt)$$

$$= \sum_{k=-\infty}^{\infty} x\left(\frac{k}{2W}\right)\text{sinc}\left(2W\left(t - \frac{k}{2W}\right)\right)$$

and the proof is complete.   □

The *sample points* $\{x(\frac{k}{2W})\}$ are taken at the rate $2W$ samples per second. If W is the smallest frequency such that the Fourier transform of $x(t)$ is identically zero for $|f| \geq W$, then the sampling rate $2W$ is called the *Nyquist rate*. The Nyquist rate is the minimum sampling rate for which $x(t)$ can be recovered from the resultant samples in the manner indicated by Eq. (2.90) in the sampling theorem.

It is well worth noting that if $x_1(t)$ and $x_2(t)$ are both time functions whose Fourier transform is identically zero for $|f| \geq W$, then their linear combination $a_1x_1(t) + a_2x_2(t)$ is also a time function whose Fourier transform is identically zero for $|f| \geq W$ for all real a_1 and a_2. This shows that *the set of all time functions whose Fourier transforms are identically zero for $|f| \geq W$ is a real vector space.*

Suppose now that W is specified and that $x(t)$ is any signal whose Nyquist rate for sampling is $2W$. By sampling $x(t)$ at its Nyquist rate, we obtain $n = 2WT$ samples in the interval of T seconds starting at time $-\frac{1}{2}\frac{1}{2W} = -\frac{1}{4W}$. We now assume that the length T of this time interval is very large so that $n \gg 1$. Because the functions $\text{sinc}\left(2W\left(t - \frac{k}{2W}\right)\right)$ are essentially 0 outside an interval of length $\frac{1}{W}$ seconds centered at their peaks, it follows from Eq. (2.90) that we can write

$$x(t) \approx \sum_{k=0}^{n-1} x\left(\frac{k}{2W}\right) \text{sinc}\left(2W\left(t - \frac{k}{2W}\right)\right), \qquad -\frac{1}{4W} < t < T - \frac{1}{4W} \qquad (2.92)$$

This equation expresses $x(t)$ as a linear combination of the n orthonormal functions $\phi_k(t) = \text{sinc}\left(2W\left(t - \frac{k}{2W}\right)\right)$ for $k = 0, 1, \ldots, n-1$. Another way to say this is that, over the considered interval of length T seconds, $x(t)$ lies in the n-dimensional subspace having the n orthonormal functions $\text{sinc}\left(2W\left(t - \frac{k}{2W}\right)\right)$ for $k = 0, 1, \ldots, n-1$ as a basis. But $x(t)$ is an arbitrary function such that its Fourier transform is identically zero for $|f| \geq W$. Recalling that the dimension of a vector space is the number of elements in a basis for the space, we can summarize as:

Theorem 2.2 (Dimensionality Theorem) *The set of time functions whose Fourier transforms are identically zero for $|f| \geq W$, when restricted to a time interval of length T where $2WT \gg 1$, forms a real vector space of dimension $n = 2WT$.*

The reason for demanding that $n = 2WT \gg 1$ is to get around the "edge effects" of the time interval. The basis function $\phi_k(t) = \text{sinc}\left(2W\left(t - \frac{k}{2W}\right)\right)$, whose values are "essentially 0" outside the interval of length $\frac{1}{W}$ seconds centered at its peak, does not in fact have its nonzero values confined to any finite time interval. More precisely, we should say that the values of $\phi_k(t)$ in magnitude go to zero as the reciprocal of their distance from the peak. What this means is that the n-term approximation of Eq. (2.92) is truly only an approximation to the restriction of the band-limited function $x(t)$ to the chosen interval of length T seconds. The error results from neglecting the small contribution from those basis functions outside, but close to the edge, of the time interval. When $n = 2WT \gg 1$, we can ignore these small contributions and treat Eq. (2.92) as if it were indeed an equality over substantially all of the considered interval of length T.

We now consider what makes the sinc functions so special. Let $\psi(t)$ be a normalized signal of Fourier bandwidth W Hz, which means that W is the smallest frequency such that essentially all of the energy of $\psi(t)$ lies in the band $[-W, W]$. Let T_N denote the smallest τ such that $\psi(t)$ is orthogonal to every time-shift of itself $\psi(t - k\tau)$ by a nonzero multiple of τ. We call T_N the *Nyquist-shift* of the basis signal $\psi(t)$. Note that the signals $\psi_k(t) = \psi(t - kT_N)$, all integer k, form an orthonormal set of signals with Fourier bandwidth W Hz. We leave it as an exercise to show that the Nyquist-shift of the signal $\phi_k(t) = \text{sinc}\left(2W\left(t - \frac{k}{2W}\right)\right)$ is $T_N = \frac{1}{2W}$ as the reader has already undoubtedly guessed. For $m \gg 1$, the signal

$$x(t) = \sum_{k=0}^{m-1} x\left(\frac{k}{2W}\right) \psi(2W(t - kT_N)) \qquad (2.93)$$

lies in the subspace of signals whose Fourier transform is essentially zero for $|f| \geq W$ consisting of that subset of signals that can be represented in terms of the basis functions $\psi_k(t) = \psi(t - kT_N)$, for $k = 0, 1, \ldots, m - 1$, and that are essentially time-limited to an interval of length $T = mT_N$. The number per second of these basis functions is $m/T = 1/T_N$; this leads us to define the *Shannon bandwidth B* of the basis signal $\psi(t)$ by $B = 1/2T_N$, or equivalently,

$$2B = 1/T_N \quad \text{basis functions per second} \tag{2.94}$$

(We have called this measure of bandwidth the "Shannon bandwidth" because Claude Shannon was the first to appreciate its great importance [7].) However, the full space of signals whose Fourier transform is essentially zero for $|f| \geq W$ and that are essentially time-limited to an interval of length $T = mT_N$ seconds has, according to the dimensionality theorem, dimension $n = 2WT$ while the dimension of the subspace of these signals that can be represented with $\psi(t)$ and its shifts is $2BT$. Thus we must have $2BT \leq 2WT$, or equivalently $B \leq W$. We have arrived at the following theorem [6]:

Theorem 2.3 (Fundamental Theorem of Bandwidth)   *The Shannon bandwidth B of a basis signal is at most equal to its Fourier bandwidth W; equality holds when the signal is a sinc function.*

The significance of $B < W$ is that the considered signal and its shifts can then represent only a proper subspace of the space of band-limited signals. The Shannon bandwidth can be thought of as the amount of bandwidth a signal *needs* and the Fourier bandwidth as the amount of bandwidth a signal *uses*. Because the usage of the Fourier spectrum is regulated (and sometimes sold) by authorities, a reasonable goal when designing communication systems is to make the Fourier bandwidth close to the Shannon bandwidth. When designing multi-user systems such as spread-spectrum systems for mobile telephony, the signals have a Fourier bandwidth that is much greater than their Shannon bandwidth. A spread-spectrum signal uses much more bandwidth than it needs!

EXAMPLE 2.7

Suppose that we would like to transmit binary data using the basis signal

$$\psi(t) = \frac{1}{\sqrt{3}} \left(\text{sinc}\left(\frac{3}{T}\left(t + \frac{T}{3}\right)\right) + \text{sinc}\left(\frac{3t}{T}\right) + \text{sinc}\left(\frac{3}{T}\left(t - \frac{T}{3}\right)\right) \right) \tag{2.95}$$

which consists of three sinc-pulses as illustrated in Figure 2.18. By combining the properties Linearity, Translation, and Time scaling in Table 2.3 with the transform pair (i) in Table 2.4

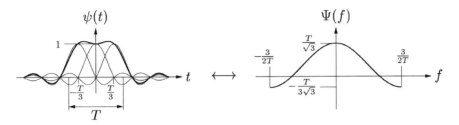

Figure 2.18   The triple-sinc signal and its Fourier transform

we obtain the Fourier transform of $\psi(t)$, that is,

$$\Psi(f) = \frac{T}{3\sqrt{3}}(\text{rect}(fT/3))(e^{j\omega T/3} + 1 + e^{-j\omega T/3})$$

$$= \frac{T}{3\sqrt{3}}(\text{rect}(fT/3))(1 + 2\cos(\omega T/3)) \tag{2.96}$$

which is shown to the right in Figure 2.18. The Fourier bandwidth of the signal $\psi(t)$ is seen to be $W = \frac{3}{2T}$. It is easy to check that the Nyquist-shift of this signal is $T_N = T$ and hence its Shannon bandwidth is $B = \frac{1}{2T}$. We see that

$$W = 3B \tag{2.97}$$

that is, this basis signal has a Fourier bandwidth that is three times its Shannon bandwidth.

EXAMPLE 2.8

Consider the basis signal

$$\psi(t) = \sum_{i=0}^{7} a_i \, \text{rect}\left(\frac{8}{T}\left(t - \frac{iT}{8}\right)\right) \tag{2.98}$$

where the 8-tuple

$$a = (a_0, a_1, a_2, a_3, a_4, a_5, a_6, a_7) = (1, 1, -1, -1, 1, -1, 1, -1)$$

It consists of 8 rect-pulses and by combining the properties Linearity, Translation, and Time scaling in Table 2.3 with the transform pair (h) in Table 2.4 we obtain its Fourier transform

$$\Psi(f) = \frac{T}{8} \, \text{sinc}(fT/8)\left(\sum_{i=0}^{7} a_i \, e^{-j\omega i T/8}\right) \tag{2.99}$$

If we let the Fourier bandwidth be determined by the main lobe of the sinc function we have $W = 8/T$.

The smallest τ such that $\psi(t)$ is orthogonal to every time-shift of itself $\psi(t - k\tau)$ by every nonzero multiple of τ is $T_N = \frac{T}{4}$ (verify this as an exercise) and hence the Shannon bandwidth for the basis signal $\psi(t)$ is $B = \frac{4}{2T} = \frac{2}{T}$ and we obtain

$$W = 4B \tag{2.100}$$

that is, this basis signal has a Fourier bandwidth that is four times its Shannon bandwidth.

■

The rate at which we can modulate a basis signal is $2B$ where B is its Shannon bandwidth. Thus we will be interested in Shannon bandwidth when we study digital modulation. The Shannon bandwidth will also be exploited in Chapter 5 when we discuss the channel capacity of the band-limited Gaussian channel.

2.5   DISCRETE-TIME SYSTEMS

In the previous section we introduced sampling and saw how a continuous-time signal $x(t)$ could be converted to a train of impulses T seconds apart,

$$s(t) = x(t) \sum_{n=-\infty}^{\infty} \delta(t - nT) = \sum_{n=-\infty}^{\infty} x(nT)\delta(t - nT)$$

We regard the sequence $\ldots, x(-T), x(0), x(T), \ldots$ as the *discrete-time* version of $x(t)$. In the sequel we use square brackets to denote discrete-time signals. For example,

$$y[n] = \frac{1}{2}(x[n] + x[n - 1]) \tag{2.101}$$

denotes the output of a discrete-time system that computes the running average of the present input $x[n]$ and the previous input $x[n - 1]$.

A discrete-time system $\mathcal{L}$ is said to be linear and time-invariant (LTI) if the discrete-time counterparts to the linearity condition (2.1) and the time-invariance condition (2.5) both hold; that is, if

$$\mathcal{L}(\alpha x_1[n] + \beta x_2[n]) = \alpha\mathcal{L}(x_1[n]) + \beta\mathcal{L}(x_2[n]) \tag{2.102}$$

where α, β are arbitrary real or complex constants, and if

$$y[n - k] = \mathcal{L}(x[n - k]) \tag{2.103}$$

holds for all shifts k.

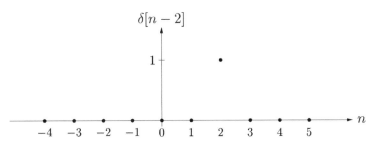

Figure 2.19   Shifted Kronecker's delta function

The discrete-time counterpart to Dirac's delta function $\delta(t)$ is called *Kronecker's delta function* $\delta[n]$, where

$$\delta[n] = \begin{cases} 1, & n = 0 \\ 0, & n \neq 0 \end{cases} \tag{2.104}$$

which is an ordinary function. In Figure 2.19 we show a shifted version of Kronecker's delta function. If the input to a discrete-time LTI system is Kronecker's delta function, then we obtain as output the discrete-time impulse response $h[n]$. An LTI system with a *finite impulse response*[5] $h[n]$ is called an *FIR system*, or an *FIR filter*, and can be realized with adders, multipliers, and unit delays as shown in Figure 2.20. Because the FIR filter in Figure 2.20 has m delays we say that it has *order m*.

The output of the FIR filter is simply

$$y[n] = h[0]x[n] + h[1]x[n-1] + \cdots + h[m]x[n-m]$$
$$= \sum_{k=0}^{m} h[k]x[n-k] \tag{2.105}$$

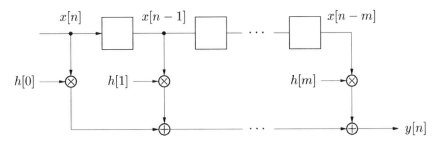

Figure 2.20   An *m*th order FIR filter

[5] This is a misnomer as $h[n]$ is the response to Kronecker's delta function $\delta[n]$, not to Dirac's impulse function $\delta(t)$. This abuse of terminology is so widespread that it cannot be avoided.

The sum in Eq. (2.105) is called a discrete-time *convolution* and is the counterpart of Eq. (2.19). Exploiting that $h[n] = 0$ for $n < 0$ and $n > m$ we can write Eq. (2.105) as

$$y[n] = \sum_{k=-\infty}^{\infty} h[k]x[n-k] = \sum_{k=-\infty}^{\infty} h[n-k]x[k] \qquad (2.106)$$

or, with the notation introduced in Eq. (2.20),

$$y[n] = h[n] * x[n] = x[n] * h[n] \qquad (2.107)$$

Sampled sinusoids play the same important role for discrete-time LTI systems as sinusoids do for continuous-time LTI systems. Let the continuous-time signal be

$$x(t) = e^{j\omega_0 t}, \qquad \omega_0 = 2\pi f_0$$

By taking samples T seconds apart we obtain the discrete-time signal

$$x[n] = x(nT) = e^{j\hat{\omega}_0 n} \qquad (2.108)$$

where $\hat{\omega}_0 = \omega_0 T$. The corresponding output from the discrete-time LTI system with impulse response $h[n]$ of order m is

$$
\begin{aligned}
y[n] &= h[n] * e^{j\hat{\omega}_0 n} \\
&= \sum_{k=0}^{m} h[k]e^{j\hat{\omega}_0 (n-k)} = \left(\sum_{k=0}^{m} h[k]e^{-j\hat{\omega}_0 k} \right) e^{j\hat{\omega}_0 n} \\
&= H(\hat{f}_0)e^{j\hat{\omega}_0 n} \qquad (2.109)
\end{aligned}
$$

where

$$H(\hat{f}_0) = \sum_{k=0}^{m} h[k]e^{-j\hat{\omega}_0 k}, \qquad \hat{\omega}_0 = 2\pi \hat{f}_0; \quad \hat{f}_0 = f_0 T \qquad (2.110)$$

is the *frequency function* of the discrete-time LTI system; it is the counterpart of the continuous-time frequency function $H(f)$ given by Eq. (2.46). We notice that for discrete-time LTI systems the important *sinusoidal in—sinusoidal out* property holds.

EXAMPLE 2.9

In Figure 2.21 we show the FIR filter for the running average given by Eq. (2.101).

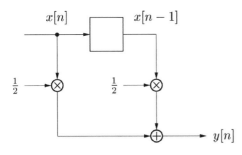

Figure 2.21   FIR filter of order 1 for the running average

The frequency function is

$$H(\hat{f}_0) = \tfrac{1}{2} + \tfrac{1}{2}e^{-j\hat{\omega}_0}$$

Suppose that we are sampling a sinusoid six times per period, then we get the input

$$x[n] = e^{j2\pi m/6}$$

which yields $\hat{f}_0 = 1/6$. Thus, we have

$$H(1/6) = \frac{1}{2} + \frac{1}{2}e^{-j2\pi/6} = \frac{1}{2} + \frac{1}{2}\cos\frac{\pi}{3} - j\frac{1}{2}\sin\frac{\pi}{3}$$

$$= \frac{3}{4} - j\frac{\sqrt{3}}{4} = \frac{\sqrt{3}}{2}e^{-j\arctan\,(1/\sqrt{3})}$$

Finally we have the output

$$y[n] = H(1/6)e^{j2\pi m/6}$$

$$= \frac{\sqrt{3}}{2}e^{j(\pi m/3 - \arctan(1/\sqrt{3}))}$$

2.6 CONCLUSIONS

In this chapter we introduced the mathematical methods that are of greatest importance when we study information transmission. These theoretical concepts have been
developed more rigorously than in most elementary texts, but it has also been our
intention to avoid the painstaking mathematical detail that is of limited interest in
engineering applications.

- A linear, time-invariant system is characterized by its impulse response and
  its output is the convolution of the input and the impulse response.
- The Fourier transform is the single most important tool. It relates the time and
  frequency properties of signals and provides us with an alternative method to

evaluate convolutions in the time domain by replacing them with multiplications of the corresponding functions in the frequency domain, then inverse transforming the result.

- The Fourier transform also provides us with the important insight that a signal that is strictly restricted to a finite time interval can not have a frequency content confined to a finite frequency interval and vice versa. This mathematical phenomenon leads to difficulties when we search for a practically meaningful definition of bandwidth.

REFERENCES

1. KAILATH, T. 1980. *Linear Systems*. Prentice-Hall: Englewood Cliffs, NJ.
2. BRACEWELL, R. N. 1986. *The Fourier transform and its applications*, 2nd edition, revised. McGraw-Hill: New York.
3. SCHWARTZ, L. 1966. *Mathematics for the physical sciences*. Addison-Wesley: Reading, MA.
4. SHANNON, C. E. 1949. Communication in the presence of noise. *Proc. IRE*, 37, 10–21; reprinted in *Claude Elwood Shannon: Collected Papers*, N. J. A. Sloane and A. D. Wyner, eds. IEEE Press: New York, 1993.
5. WOZENCRAFT, J. M. and JACOBS, I. M. 1965. *Principles of communication engineering*. Wiley: New York.
6. MASSEY, J. L. 1995. Towards an information theory of spread-spectrum systems, in *Code division multiple access communications*, edited by S. G. Glisic and P. A. Leppänen, 29–46. Kluwer Academic.
7. SHANNON, C. E. 1948. A mathematical theory of communications. *Bell System Tech. J.*, 27; reprinted in *Claude Elwood Shannon: Collected Papers*, N. J. A. Sloane and A. D. Wyner, eds. IEEE Press: New York, 1993.

PROBLEMS

1. (a) Show that

$$
x(t) = \begin{cases}
0, & t < 0 \\
\dfrac{4}{\epsilon^2}t, & 0 \le t < \dfrac{\epsilon}{2} \\
\dfrac{4}{\epsilon} - \dfrac{4}{\epsilon^2}t, & \dfrac{\epsilon}{2} \le t < \epsilon \\
0, & t \ge \epsilon
\end{cases}
$$

tends to $\delta(t)$ when $\epsilon \to 0$.

(b) Show that

$$
x(t) = \alpha e^{-\alpha t} u(t)
$$

tends to $\delta(t)$ when $\alpha \to \infty$

2. Consider an LTI system with impulse response

$$
h(t) = e^{-|t|}
$$

and input

$$x(t) = \begin{cases} 1, & 0 \le t \le 1 \\ 0, & \text{otherwise} \end{cases}$$

(a) Find its output.
(b) Is the system causal?
(c) Find its frequency function.
(d) Assume that the input is

$$x(t) = e^{j\omega_0 t}$$

Find the output.

3. Consider an LTI system with impulse response

$$h(t) = e^{-t}u(t)$$

(a) Find its frequency function.
(b) Assume that the input is

$$x(t) = e^{j\omega_0 t}$$

Find the output.
(c) Assume that the input is

$$x(t) = \cos \omega_0 t$$

Find the output.

4. Consider the circuit in Figure 2.22:
(a) Find the frequency function $H(f)$.
(b) Let $x(t) = \cos\omega_0 t$, where $\omega_0 = 10^3$ radian per second. Find $y(t)$.
(c) Let $x(t) = u(t)$.
Find $y(t)$.
Hint: Find first the impulse response $h(t)$.

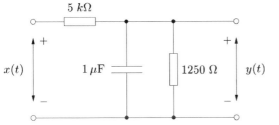

Figure 2.22

5. Consider the circuit in Figure 2.23:

   (a) Find the frequency function $H(f)$.

   (b) Let $x(t) = \cos\omega_0 t$, where $\omega_0 = 1$ radians per second. Find $y(t)$.

   (c) Let $x(t) = u(t)$. Find $y(t)$.

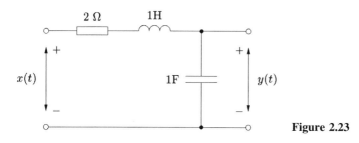

Figure 2.23

6. Consider the Fourier transform.

   (a) Prove the modulation property.

   (b) Prove the time scaling property.

   (c) Prove the differentiation in the time domain property.

   (d) Prove the integration in the time domain property.

   (e) Prove the duality property.

   (f) Prove the conjugate functions property.

   (g) Prove the multiplication in the time domain property.

7. Verify the Fourier transform pairs for the following time functions.

   (a) Sinc function

   (b) Rectangular pulse

   (c) Sinc pulse

   (d) Triangular pulse

   (e) Gaussian pulse

   (f) One-sided exponential function

   (g) Double-sided exponential function

8. (a) Find the Fourier transform of

$$x(t) = e^{at}u(-t), \qquad a > 0$$

   (b) Find the inverse Fourier transform of

$$X(f) = \frac{2a}{a^2 + \omega^2}, \qquad a > 0$$

   Hint: Use partial fraction expansion.

9. Consider the circuit in Figure 2.24:

(a) Find the frequency function $H(f)$.

(b) Find the impulse response $h(t)$.

(c) Let $x(t) = u(t)$ and evaluate $y(t) = x(t) * h(t)$ directly.

(d) Let $x(t) = u(t)$ and evaluate $y(t) = x(t) * h(t)$ via the Fourier transform.

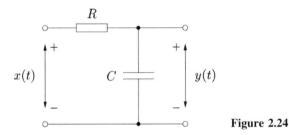

Figure 2.24

10. Find the spectrum of

$$x(t) = \begin{cases} (1 - |t|)\cos \omega_0 t, & |t| < 1 \\ 0, & |t| > 1 \end{cases}$$

11. Consider the circuit in Figure 2.25:

(a) Find the frequency function $H(f)$.

(b) Find the impulse response $h(t)$.

(c) Find the output $y(t)$ for the input $x(t) = \cos \omega_0 t$.

(d) Find the output $y(t)$ for the input $x(t) = u(t)$.

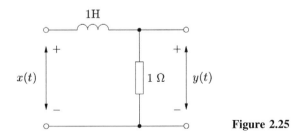

Figure 2.25

12. Consider the circuit in Figure 2.26:

(a) Find the frequency function $H(f)$.

(b) Let $x(t) = \frac{1}{2}\sin \omega_0 t$, where $\omega_0 = 1$ radian per second.
Find $y(t)$.

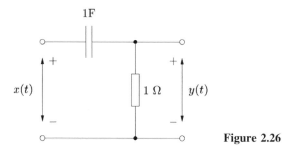

Figure 2.26

(c) Let $x(t) = u(t)$.
    Find $y(t)$.

13. Consider the circuit in Figure 2.27:

    (a) Find the impulse response $h(t)$.

    (b) Let $x(t) = u(t)$.
        Find $y(t)$.

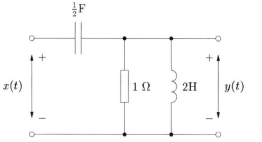

Figure 2.27

14. Consider the circuit in Figure 2.28
    Show that the output $y(t)$ for the input $x(t) = tu(t)$ is

    $$y(t) = (t - 1 + e^{-t})u(t)$$

15. Consider the circuit in Figure 2.29:

    (a) Find the frequency function $H(f)$.

    (b) Show that the impulse response is

    $$h(t) = \delta(t) + 2(t - 1)e^{-t}u(t)$$

    (c) Show that the output $y(t)$ for the input $x(t) = u(t)$ is

    $$y(t) = (1 - 2te^{-t})u(t)$$

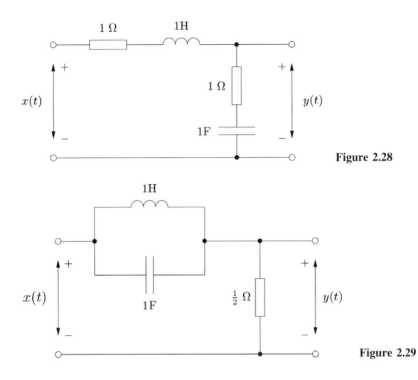

Figure 2.28

Figure 2.29

16. Consider an LTI system with impulse response

$$h(t) = \begin{cases} 1, & 0 \le t \le 1 \\ 0, & \text{otherwise} \end{cases}$$

and input

$$x(t) = \begin{cases} t, & 0 \le t \le 1 \\ 0, & \text{otherwise} \end{cases}$$

Find the output.

17. Consider the following basis signal

$$\psi(t) = \text{rect}(t/T)$$

(a) Find the Fourier bandwidth.
(b) Find the Nyquist-shift.
(c) Find the Shannon bandwidth.

18. Consider the triangular basis signal

$$\psi(t) = \begin{cases} 1 - \dfrac{2}{T}|t|, & |t| < T/2 \\ 0, & |t| > T/2 \end{cases}$$

    (a) Find the Fourier bandwidth.

    (b) Find the Nyquist-shift.

    (c) Find the Shannon bandwidth.

19. Consider the raised cosine basis signal

$$\psi(t) = \begin{cases} \frac{1}{2}(1 + \cos{(2\pi t/T)}), & |t| < T/2 \\ 0, & |t| > T/2 \end{cases}$$

    (a) Find the Fourier bandwidth.

        Hint: Rewrite $\psi(t)$ as $\frac{1}{2}\,\mathrm{rect}(t/T)(1 + \cos(2\pi t/T))$.

    (b) Find the Nyquist-shift.

    (c) Find the Shannon bandwidth.

Chapter 3

Information Sources: What is Out There to be Sent?

After a chapter of mathematics, we take a more descriptive turn. In this chapter we look at the main sources of information that need transmission or storage. In order of the number of bits they require, these are text, speech, music, still images, and moving video. All but the first can exist in either analog or digital form. We are interested in their bandwidth, in the quality needed for their reproduction, and in the number of bits they require in digital form. Another important element is how humans *perceive* sound and images. We do not perceive all that is there, and there is no sense transmitting information that no-one sees or hears. An illustration of this was an advertisement a few years ago for a television receiver, which showed a hungry cat looking at a yellow canary on the screen. The caption claimed that the colors were so realistic that even the cat was fooled. The fact is that cats are colorblind; furthermore, they catch mice and canaries primarily by their sense of hearing, which is concentrated in an audio range above that of humans. This TV is of little interest to the cat, since it mismatches both its sight and hearing. A cat needs quite a different receiver. What TV does a human need? What kind of telephone? What are the engineering parameters of such signals? We answer these kinds of questions now.

The tools in this chapter are bits, Hz, and decibels. The idea of breaking information into small, discrete pieces was introduced in Chapter 1. Here these pieces are *bits*, which are, roughly speaking, the amount of information in a variable that takes two values, 0 and 1. We will measure information sources throughout this chapter as the number of such variables it takes to represent them. A more careful investigation of the bit concept will come in Chapter 5. Another parameter of information is its

Understanding Information Transmission. By John B. Anderson and Rolf Johannesson
ISBN 0-471-67910-0 © 2005 the Institute of Electrical and Electronics Engineers, Inc.

bandwidth, the frequency band occupied by its analog form. Our understanding of the frequency concept comes from Fourier analysis and Chapter 2.

The last tool, decibels, is a new one and it needs a brief explanation. It is used to measure power and energy ratios that occur with signals. Communication engineers often talk about power ratios, and they measure these in decibels, abbreviated dB. A *bel* is a power ratio expressed as a base-10 log, and a decibel is $\frac{1}{10}$ of this log. Thus, if A and B are two powers with ratio A/B, their ratio expressed as decibels is

$$10 \log_{10}(A/B) \text{ dB} \tag{3.1}$$

If $A/B = 2$, the ratio in dB is $10 \log_{10}2 = 3.01$ dB; if $A/B = 10$, the ratio is $10 \log_{10}10 = 10$ dB; if $A/B = 100$, it is 20 dB. There is one tricky part about the decibel system. Sometimes A and B measure the absolute values of two quantities such as voltage or current, and the power ratio is now the square of A/B. Measured in dB, A/B must still be taken as a *power ratio*. The measure in this case is therefore

$$10 \log_{10}(A/B)^2 = 20 \log_{10}(A/B) \text{ dB} \tag{3.2}$$

For example, two signal voltages A and B such that $A/B = 2$ have ratio $20 \log_{10}2 = 6.02$ in dB.

3.1   WHAT IS TEXT?

By text we mean a collection of letters and other symbols that form words like this paragraph, or numbers on a bank statement, or a computer program, or an encrypted text, which might appear to be nonsensical numbers and letters.

Take a look at the following text. Read it quickly but carefully, and count the number of times the letter F appears.

> *FINISHED FILES ARE THE*
> *RESULT OF YEARS OF SCIENTIFIC*
> *STUDY COMBINED WITH THE*
> *EXPERIENCE OF YEARS.*

The answer may surprise you. It appears in the footnote below, and it illustrates how human perception affects text processing.[1]

To begin, however, we will look at how information transmission machines view text. There is a set of possible symbols called the symbol *alphabet*. In this English paragraph, it is the large and small letters AB...Z and ab...z, plus punctuation marks ?/:;() and so on, and one final important symbol, the space. Other languages add a few more characters such as åäö. Actually, these characters only make up a simplified alphabet sometimes called "typewriter text." A word

---

[1] There are six Fs. Did you guess three? Almost everyone does. The brain pays little attention to the preposition "of," especially when it sits in the middle of lines. Do we need to transmit "of"?

processing program[2] such as Latex works with many more. A few examples include italic letters *abc*..., Greek letters $\alpha\beta\gamma$..., calligraphic letters $\mathcal{ABC}$..., and instead of the simple space, a whole variety of spaces, such as the shim ‖, the quad | |, and the doublequad | | (the size of the space is between the verticals).

In digital transmission, all these characters are converted to words made of binary symbols; that is, the symbol alphabet is {0,1}. We can design a Simple Text Code as follows to make the simplest possible conversion of text: list the 26 letters of English, plus the space, plus the period '.' (to indicate the end of a sentence), plus Swedish å,ä,ö (just to be on the safe side); make a correspondence between these and the 5-bit binary words; the result is a 5-bit/letter text conversion code. Another simple conversion is the BCD (Binary Coded Decimal) one, which converts the numbers {0,1,...,9} to the 4-bit groups 0000,0001,0010,...,1000,1001. The groups simply count up in binary, with the least significant bit (LSB) on the right. A final everyday conversion in computer engineering is the hexadecimal one that equates the symbols {0,1,...,9,*A*,*B*,...,*F*} to the full list of 4-bit groups 0000,1000,0100,...,1111; the precise equivalence shows on the left in Figure 3.1.

BOX 3-1

ASCII stands for American Standard Code for Information Interchange. There have been several ASCII codes. The original one, adopted 1963, had 128 7-bit words. These converted typewriter text only, and some code words were reserved for instructions to the machinery, such as carriage return or end of message. A parity-check bit was added to make 8-bit words. The ASCII code shown in Figure 3.1 is a modern one used in Microsoft Windows and other places. Bits 1–4 are given by the hexadecimal symbols across the top of the block; bits 5–8 are the hex symbol down the side; the hex to bit equivalence is shown in the hex table. For example, the symbol "[" is hex B5, which becomes the left-to-right bits 1101 1010. The rectangular blocks in the table are positions reserved for use as instructions to the computing machinery. Some variant of ASCII is almost always used to convert standard text to bits.

A more complicated conversion is the ASCII one (Box 3-1). The code maps some 200 letters and symbols from a variety of languages into 8-bit words. The right side of Figure 3.1 shows the code. The term "ASCII file" has come to mean a text file that has been converted in this way. Many other conversions exist, of course; other symbols than those in Figure 3.1 can be transmitted and information need not be sent in 8-bit groups. Generically, we call these other information files simply binary files. Sometimes ASCII is used to transmit general binary files by means of a double conversion: The general symbols are converted to standard ASCII symbols, which are then converted to 8-bit groups. An example is given by email transmission of a text page that has been realized in Latex. All the font

---

[2] A word processing program adds relatively few new characters; a text *compositor* such as Latex adds many more and allows complete flexibility in setting up pages.

Binary to Hexadecimal

Binary	Hex
0000	0
1000	1
0100	2
1100	3
0010	4
1010	5
0110	6
1110	7
0001	8
1001	9
0101	A
1101	B
0011	C
1011	D
0111	E
1111	F

	0	1	2	3	4	5	6	7	8	9	A	B	C	D	E	F
0	■	■	■	■	■	■						■	■		■	■
1	■	■	■	■	■	■	■	■	■		■	■	■	■	■	■
2		!	"	#	$	%	&	'	(	)	*	+	,	-	.	/
3	0	1	2	3	4	5	6	7	8	9	:	;	<	=	>	?
4	@	A	B	C	D	E	F	G	H	I	J	K	L	M	N	O
5	P	Q	R	S	T	U	V	W	X	Y	Z	[	\	]	^	_
6	`	a	b	c	d	e	f	g	h	i	j	k	l	m	n	o
7	p	q	r	s	t	u	v	w	x	y	z	{	|	}	~	■
8	■	■	■	■	■	■	■	■	■	■	■	■	■	■	■	■
9	■	'	'	■	■	■	■	■	■	■	■	■	■	■	■	■
A		¡	¢	£	¤	¥	¦	§	¨	©	ª	«	¬	-	®	¯
B	°	±	²	³	´	µ	¶	·	¸	¹	º	»	¼	½	¾	¿
C	À	Á	Â	Ã	Ä	Å	Æ	Ç	È	É	Ê	Ë	Ì	Í	Î	Ï
D	Ð	Ñ	Ò	Ó	Ô	Õ	Ö	×	Ø	Ù	Ú	Û	Ü	Ý	Þ	ß
E	à	á	â	ã	ä	å	æ	ç	è	é	ê	ë	ì	í	î	ï
F	ð	ñ	ò	ó	ô	õ	ö	÷	ø	ù	ú	û	ü	ý	þ	

Figure 3.1   (Left) Hexadecimal conversion between 16-symbol and binary alphabets (LSB on left, the reverse of BCD). (Right) The ASCII character conversion code as used in Microsoft Windows. The two 4-bit ASCII bytes are shown in hexadecimal form: Bits 1–4 are the top hex symbol, bits 5–8 are the side symbol

size, text arrangement, italics, strange math symbols, and so on, of a text page are converted to Latex code, which is itself restricted to ASCII characters; these characters are then converted to bits by Figure 3.1.

As an example of ASCII file sizes, take the Latex file that created Chapter 1 of this book. This file contains about 45,000 characters, all of the ASCII type, and since each requires 8 bits, the total bit count of the file is about $8(45,000) = 360,000$. This works out to about 10,000 bits per page of text. This could probably be reduced by a third, using simple file compression. Most pages have areas of white space in the text, but a fully packed page might have (35 lines)(80 characters/line) = 2800 characters. At 8 bits/character, this is about 20,000 bits per page.

Sophisticated file compression can reduce text files much further. The theoretical basis for this is discussed under source coding in Chapter 5. In brief, one can use the probabilities of the characters in standard text, both the probability that a character occurs and the probability that one is followed by another. The most common letter in English is e, with probability about 0.12; this could be given a short binary codeword, and an unlikely letter like z can have a long one. q is always followed by u in English. Thus the u after q need not be transmitted at all; the equipment can simply add u to q automatically at reconstruction.[3] All of these strategies reduce the bit count of a text conversion. It has been estimated that a theoretically perfect compression would reduce English text to about 1.1–1.3 binaries per letter, ignoring the effect of capital letters and punctuation. This is four times

---

[3] But what would happen with the sentence, "James Bond talked to Q."? Rare exceptions are what make conversion algorithms difficult!

better than the 5 bit/letter Simple Text Code that was given above, and perhaps six times shorter than ASCII.

We measure the quality of text transmission by the *error probability* of the symbols. With ordinary text such as a novel, an error rate of a few percent is tolerable, although it is unpleasant. A ratio of 1 character per 10,000 (1 in 10 pages) is more typical of a well-produced book. Even this error rate is intolerable in a bank statement or a computer program, and rates of 10^{-8} to 10^{-10} or lower are required here. The acceptable error rate in fact depends very much on the customer and the type of text.

3.1.1 Nonalphabetic Languages

At least a quarter of the world's population uses a written language that is not based on a small alphabet of symbols. Chinese languages, as well as Japanese and Korean, are based on a system of pictograms. Writing well in Chinese or Japanese requires knowledge of several thousand of these. Converting them back and forth from digital form is an important subject in their respective countries.

One way to do this is to convert the pictograms to words in a roman alphabet and then encode the words. For example, Mao Tse-tung is a romanized transcription of several characters of a man's name.

3.2   WHAT IS SPEECH?

3.2.1   The Acoustic Nature of Speech

Human speech, or voice as we will often call it, is a succession of pieces of sound. These are produced by a part of the anatomy called the human vocal tract, which is shown in Figure 3.2. It includes the mouth, teeth, nose, and the tube leading down to the lungs that includes the larynx, or voice box. This last contains two vibrating flaps, the vocal cords, which produce a musical tone in the same way as the reed in an oboe or the vibrating lips applied to a trumpet. The rest of the vocal tract modifies this tone to form the different sound units of speech. We can break these sounds into three major groups, *voiced* sounds, *unvoiced* sounds, and silences. In the first, the vocal cords are operating and the rest of the tract forms a sound like the body of a wind instrument shapes sound. All the vowels are voiced sounds. With unvoiced sounds, the vocal cords are inactive, and only air is blown through the vocal tract. Some consonant sounds are unvoiced, including the "s" and the "k" in "sink" or the "s" and the "f" in "fish," but many are voiced, such as the "z" in English "zinc" or the "V" in "Volvo." You can demonstrate this for yourself by pronouncing the words while touching the voice box. The third sound type, silence, is of course the absence of sound, but it is nonetheless important. A tiny piece of silence between "to" and "order" helps us differentiate the spoken English phrases "to order" and "toward her." Speech is a rapid succession of these sounds, 5–10 per second,

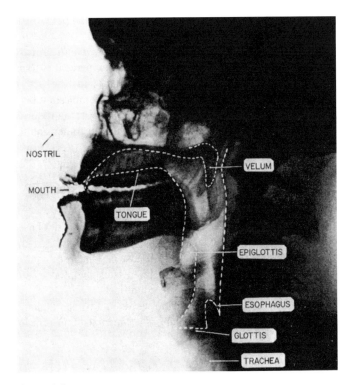

Figure 3.2   The human vocal tract.
Source: Flanagan et al. [7], © IEEE, used with permission.

much like words are a succession of letters. These sounds are what we must deal with when transmitting and storing speech.

Speech sound units are called *phonemes*. Altogether there exist some 75 distinct phonemes.[4] A given language does not include all of them. Swedish is the only language that uses the "sj" in "sju." The "th" in "there" is characteristic of English, and the vowel "ö" in German "Köln" or Swedish "kö" does not occur in English. Figure 3.3 shows examples of the waveforms of voiced and unvoiced sounds. The two types of waveforms are very different. Voiced sounds tend to be high-energy, repetitive waveforms, with an overall period of repetition called the *pitch period* that stems from the vocal cord vibration. There is a fine structure in the repetition that comes mainly from the vocal tract sound shaping. Unvoiced sounds are much lower in energy and look like random noise. These waveforms and the variations among them are what must be carried in analog speech transmission.

---

[4] This total does not include small variations that occur in the pronunciation of the same phoneme by different people or in different dialects of a language.

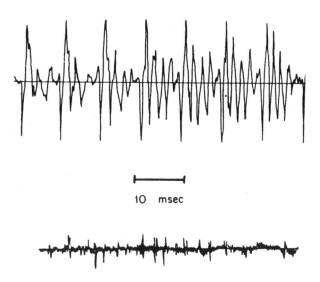

10   msec

Figure 3.3   Voiced and unvoiced speech waveforms, showing the phoneme |a| as in English "hot" and |sh| as in English "fish"

By taking the Fourier transform of speech sound waveforms, we see another, quite different set of characteristics. Some transforms are shown in Figure 3.4 as vertical plots of intensity (black is most intense) versus frequency, taken every 10 ms. The sentence spoken is "Why do I owe you a letter?" It is easy to see the different vocal resonances and how they migrate with time; the plot below shows the center positions of these precisely. The sentence here is mostly voiced, and the only clearly visible unvoiced region centers at time 1.45 s.

Although it is not visible in the figure, voiced sounds tend to have a substructure of lines in their spectrum. This is because the excitation for the sound is a tone; the spacing of the lines, more or less, is the fundamental of the tone, and the higher lines are its harmonics. The overall height of a plot of the lines versus frequency (their "envelope") does not trend uniformly down to zero but passes through several bumps. They occur because the tract is roughly a tube and any tube has such resonances. (You can demonstrate this fact by speaking through a paper tube.) Vocal tract resonances are called *formants*. They change as the tract is changed. The spectral position of the formant and its width are different for every phoneme, and tracking these parameters is one way to recognize or compress speech. Unvoiced sounds have a smooth spectrum without lines, because their excitation is random. Some formant structure can be present, because the vocal tract still modifies the sound.

There is also an overall average spectral shape to speech, which plays an important role in its transmission and digitizing. On the average, the energy in speech concentrates in the frequencies 100–800 Hz, above which it declines by a factor of about 16 for every doubling of frequency. Only 1% of the energy in speech lies above 4000 Hz. Speech has this characteristic because the vocal tract cannot easily produce other sounds; it is also true that we cannot hear outside

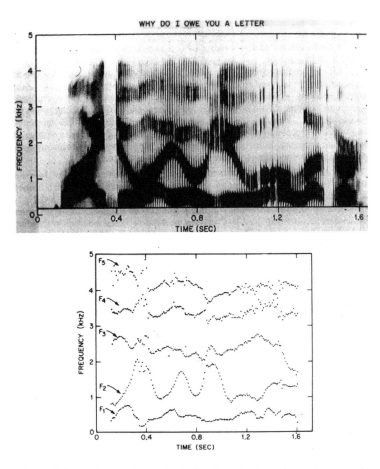

Figure 3.4   Fourier transforms of voiced and unvoiced speech sounds, arranged as successive transforms (top) versus time for the sentence "Why do I owe you a letter?" Bottom figure shows more precisely the five formant locations. *Source:* Atal and Hanauer [8], © American Institute of Physics, used with permission.

100–4000 Hz with enough precision to make the extra range useful for communication. We can break the 100–4000 Hz range into two important regions. The 100–800 Hz range carries most of the energy, and it is primarily this range that allows speaker *recognition*. The 800–4000 Hz range is where we distinguish the various phonemes; this is the *intelligibility* range. People who cannot hear enough of this range can recognize speakers, but not what the speakers are saying.

What all these facts mean is that telephone speech may be limited to the range 100–4000 Hz or less. A standard *toll* line[5] is limited to approximately

---

[5] Toll is a Bell System term; alternate terms are trunk or long distance. The terms mean that amplifiers or other processors are limiting the channel to 200–3400 Hz. Note that short telephone links consisting of just a pair of wires can have a much wider bandwidth.

200–3400 Hz, and this is what gives telephonic speech its peculiar quality. The lower frequencies add little to recognizability and they are hard to reproduce in the small handset earphone. Frequencies above do add intelligibility, but as a cost compromise they are ignored. There is a small price to pay: the difference between English "sit" and "fit" cannot be distinguished over a true toll line, because the formant that distinguishes the "s" and "f" lies above 3400 Hz. There are standard speech quality levels below telephone speech (more phonemes are lost; often the speaker is difficult to recognize), as well as above it (radio broadcast quality, CD quality). High-quality speech processing becomes the music problem, and we will come to that in the next section.

More about phonemes

We cannot discuss all the sounds of speech in detail, but it is worthwhile sketching them briefly, if only to show how complex the subject of speech synthesis and recognition really are. *Vowel* sounds are always voiced, and they can be thought of as produced by a box (the mouth) with a constriction (produced by the tongue). The constriction can be high or low in the mouth and located in different places front to back. An opening to the nose can be open or shut. *Consonants* are more diverse and are not all voiced. A *fricative* consonant has an incoherent excitation, a garble if voiced or air noise if not. Examples are (Swedish examples are given in parentheses): "th" in "then" or "thin" (no "th" in Swedish!), "v" in "vote" ("vecka"), "f" in "for" ("fyra"). *Plosive* consonants, also called stops, are built on the pattern closure/pressure buildup/sudden release. Examples are "b" in "bee" ("bok"), "p" in "pea" ("pil"), "g" in "go" ("gå"). However complicated vowels and consonants may be, there are even more layers to the phoneme problem. Phonemes tend to change, depending on sounds that come before or after. Some are dynamic, meaning that they are a motion from one basic sound to another. Affricates are slides between consonants. Diphthongs are slides between vowels; examples are "oy" in "boy" and "ay" in "May." "gå" in Stockholm and Skåne, a district in Southern Sweden, differ because the second has a diphthong.

As if this were not enough, pitch change, called *inflection*, carries meaning, too. In many languages we know that a question is being asked because the vocal cord pitch rises in a characteristic way during the sentence. Smaller-scale pitch changes can be important as well. Compare the spoken sentences "I live in the white house" and "I live in the White House" (meaning the one in Washington, D.C.); the difference in meaning is carried by a pitch pattern over the two-syllable phrase "white house." This kind of short range pattern is called a *tone*, and English and most languages actually use tones in rather noncritical ways. Swedish, however, is strongly based on a system of two tones that apply to multisyllable words (e.g., "anden" can mean the duck or the spirit, depending on tone). Chinese contains four or more, and they can modulate single-syllable words! For those unaccustomed to the language, these can be virtually impossible to hear. All of this complexity is not mere theory, because a speech recognition machine that does not recognize all the distinctions cannot possibly do a good job recognizing speech. The quickest way to develop sympathy for speech recognition software is to try to copy down phrases spoken in a language you do not know.

3.2.2 Speech as an Analog or Digital Signal

We have seen that telephone speech is a signal whose frequencies lie in the band 200–3400 Hz. Transmission systems introduce noise and the idea of "telephone" speech carries with it also a specification about how much noise is allowed. In an ordinary local telephone connection, it is a signal-to-noise power ratio (denoted SNR) of about 40 dB; that is, a power ratio of $10^{40/10} = 10,000$. When this ratio falls below about 27 dB (a ratio of 500), the speech will still be intelligible but most people will give up the call and try to get a clearer connection. Note here how the quality of analog telephone information is measured by an *SNR*, not by a probability of symbol error, as it would be with a text source.

To make speech a digital signal, it has to be converted from analog form. This requires a two-stage process. First, the signal has to be sampled at the *sampling frequency* to form the sequence $s(0), s(T), s(2T), \ldots$, and we learned in Chapter 2 that this must be done at a rate twice that of the highest signal frequency. In order to make some of the components easier to design, it is customary to sample a little faster. The standard sampling rate is thus taken as $2(4000) = 8000$ per second, which gives $T = 1/8000 = 0.125 \mu s$. The second stage is to convert each sample to bits. The straightforward way to do this is called pulse-code modulation, or PCM.[6] It will soon be clear that 8 bits/sample are required to meet the 40 dB SNR requirement for telephone speech. Under simple digital conversion, then, the bit rate is (8000 samples/s)(8 bits/sample) = 64,000 bits/s.

The converted signal is now in bit format, and it can be reproduced at the 40 dB quality level so long as the bits are unchanged. The measure of quality for the bits is error probability. As long as the error rate is 10^{-4} to 10^{-5} or less, it is difficult to hear errors in PCM telephone speech.

Because PCM is easily understood and often used, we will take time out to describe it. There are many more efficient methods that create fewer bits per sample by using, for example, the probabilities of the samples. The bits rates we calculate below may be reduced by 50–80%, depending on the complexity of the method. However, these are beyond the level of this book; further information on them appears in the general communication books in the References.

3.2.3 An Introduction to PCM

Figure 3.5 shows how a 3-bit PCM scheme works, and the picture may be extended to any number of bits. The picture shows amplitude versus time. The input to the scheme is an analog sample, and one sample arrives each T seconds, three altogether

---

[6]PCM need not use pulses and it is not a method of modulation as we use the term in this book. The name is a holdover from many years ago. PCM is simply a method of matching sample values to bits.

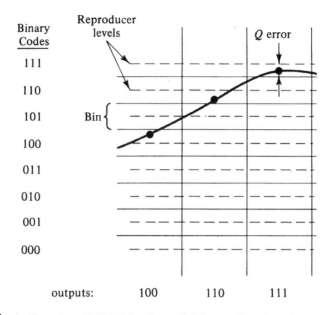

Figure 3.5 An illustration of 3-bit PCM analog-to-digital conversion. Three signal samples are converted to $3 \times 3 = 9$ bits

in the picture. The vertical scale is divided into 2^3 *bins*, each represented by a 3-bit code. The top bin extends actually to $+\infty$ and the bottom one to $-\infty$. A sample that lies in one of the eight bins will be forevermore given the *reproducer value* located at the dashed line, the middle of the bin in the six middle cases. The actual value of the sample is lost. The difference between the value and the reproducer level is the *quantizer noise*. Effectively, a PCM quantizer is defined by the set of bins and reproducer values.

It is not hard to show that the ratio of the signal energy to the quantizer noise energy must approximately follow the rule $\text{SNR}_{\text{dB}} = 6b - C_o$, where b is the number of bits per sample. This relation is called the "6 dB Rule." The value C_o depends on the overall scaling of the bins (fatter bins give a larger C_o). The rule is true because each addition of a bit cuts the bin size in half and the noise on the average is half as large; a factor of $\frac{1}{2}$ in noise amplitude is a noise energy reduction by 6 dB. A standard assumption in telephone PCM is that the difference between the top and bottom bins should be eight times the rms value of the signal; assuming this gives

$$\text{SNR}_{\text{dB}} = 6b - 7.3 \quad \text{(6 dB Rule for Telephone PCM)} \quad (3.3)$$

For any analog source and for most methods of converting to digital form, a 6 dB Rule with some constant will hold.

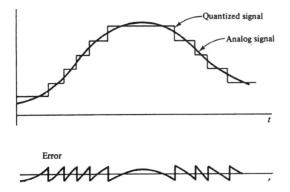

Error

Figure 3.6   Reconstruction error in PCM; error signal at bottom

Quantizer noise is not white noise, but it sounds like it to the ear. For standard 8 bit telephone PCM, the Rule predicts an SNR of about $6(8) - 7.3 \approx 41$ dB. Pulse-code modulation also produces a kind of noise called granular noise, which occurs when the sample lies outside the range of the bins. This sounds like a rough, scraping sound, riding above the speech sound.

At the receiving end of the transmission chain, the PCM bits must be converted back to speech. This is D-to-A conversion, also called reconstruction or down-conversion. An electronic circuit generates from the b PCM bits a voltage equal the bin reproducer value and holds it T seconds until the next b PCM bits arrive. The process is shown in Figure 3.6, which also shows the total waveform error caused by the reconstruction. A look at this shows that there are sudden jumps in the error, and a great deal of this distortion is out of band, meaning that the frequencies lie above those of the voice signal. It is thus important to remove them with a filter, since noise will be reduced without any damage to the original signal. If the voice system is based on the usual 200–3400 frequency range, then the filter should pass only frequencies below about 3400 Hz.

Many other details about PCM are given in the communication text references. For music and images, all the discussion here still applies, except the sampling frequency will be different.

3.3 WHAT IS MUSIC?

As a waveform, music is like speech. That is, most of its energy lies in a range 100–1000 Hz, above which there is a steady rolling off, and only 1%, more or less, lies above 4 kHz. It makes sense that we tend to like sounds that are like our speech. Sounds that do not have this balance, such as fire alarms and screeching train wheels, are not our favorite music. Nonetheless, high-fidelity music means a high level of realism, which means a frequency spectrum equal to the entire human range, roughly speaking, 20–20,000 Hz. It also means low background noise and a wide dynamic range, and the reproduction itself interacts strongly with the facts of human perception. Of course, the meaning and content of music goes far beyond engineering facts, but the last will be our focus now.

3.2.1 Music and Perception

First, some basics about music. We perceive both loudness and musical pitch more or less logarithmically. A power ratio of 1 dB between two sounds (a ratio of $1.26:1$) sounds quite small to us. Passages played by a full orchestra can vary by $30-40$ dB (a ratio of $1000-10,000$) in power. In the Western music system, the smallest pitch difference used to construct music is called a half-tone: two pitches are a half-tone apart if their frequencies are in the ratio $2^{1/12}:1$, which is $1.059:1$. A half-tone is the difference between two piano keys; if the note A is taken as 440 Hz, the half-tone above, $B^\flat$, has pitch $440(1.059) = 466$ Hz. Every 12 half-tones is an exact doubling of frequency, called an octave; on the piano this is the next A above and it comes at 880 Hz. The human ear hears all these half-tone intervals as more or less the same pitch change. A half-tone at low pitch thus varies only a little in pitch on an absolute scale, and a half-tone at high pitch varies a lot, even though we perceive them both as the same relative change in pitch. Reproducing music up to 20 kHz instead of 15 kHz thus adds only about 5 half-tones (5 keys on the piano) to what we think we hear, despite a difference of 5000 Hz; this is because $(2^{1/12})^5 \approx 20,000/15,000$.

As produced by instruments, musical tones consist of a fundamental rate of vibration plus components called overtones (or harmonics) that lie at integer multiples of the fundamental. These harmonics are part of what distinguish piano, trumpet, and guitar notes that have the same fundamental frequency. Typically, several harmonics are needed to establish the difference. For the A at 440 Hz above, at least the overtones at (2)(440) and (3)(440) Hz are needed. In terms of the fundamental frequency, the notes of a standard 88-key piano run from about 26 to 4190 Hz, and this approximately represents the range of musical instruments. A given struck note also has an "energy envelope," that is, a characteristic evolution of energy over time. Striking a large drum gives a strong initial sound followed by a longer ringing of the drum, all at a low pitch; striking a small metal object gives the same envelope, but at a high pitch.

Cats and bats hear at a higher range of frequencies than humans and it is fair to say that they hear something quite different from a musical performance. What parts do we perceive? While it is true that we perceive sound over $20-20,000$ Hz or more, we do not register it very accurately outside a range of, very roughly, $100-4000$ Hz. Our most acute hearing takes place over $800-3000$ Hz. It is here that we distinguish different music instruments and the information-bearing phonemes in speech. We also perceive here the *direction* of sound, and this is the critical range for stereo perception of music. Since we have two ears, we perceive a *stereo image*, a whole field of sound spread out in three-dimensional space. This image is generated in the brain by the audio cortex, which interprets the slightly different arrival times at the two ears. Outside of the $100-4000$ range, we have difficulty measuring both the direction and the loudness of sound, and for the most part we perceive simply its presence or absence. In perceiving a thunderstorm, we can locate the crack of the lightning but not the rumble of the thunder.

The space in which listening occurs adds to these problems. Low pitches, even if we could perceive their direction, do not tend to come from one place in a typical room or theatre, because their wavelength is too long (5–20 m) compared to the room dimensions. High frequencies present the opposite problem, and tend to focus only in certain spots; they do not disperse. For reproducing music, we can form some important conclusions. Accurate rendering is most critical in the middle range, since it establishes direction and distinguishes instruments. Low and high frequencies can be reproduced more approximately, with less attention paid to loudness relationships and directionality, except that high frequencies must be dispersed throughout the listening area.[7]

Two important elements in high-fidelity music are signal-to-noise ratio and dynamic range. Each places its own constraint on the reproduction process. When music at a continuous loudness is reproduced with a 40 dB SNR (music energy 10,000 times noise), most listeners are not aware of the noise if it is not concentrated in one frequency band. The dynamic range of music is perhaps 40–50 dB, taking the ratio of a full music ensemble to one instrument played very quietly.[8] But SNR and dynamic range interact with each other in a nasty way that makes the reproduction process much harder. We can explain this by taking a typical situation. Suppose the quietest sound to be recorded is a hushed single voice. We would like the recording noise level to lie 40 dB below this. Soon after in the recording comes a loud orchestra climax 45 dB louder; if the recording noise continues the same, the signal-to-noise during this passage will be *85 dB*, not 40. This is a real challenge for a recording or transmission medium. Compact disks are designed to achieve it, but the best that analog FM can do (see Section 4.2) is 60–70 dB, and this only in local broadcasting.

In reality, the chief source of noise in a CD-quality recording is probably the ventilation system in the recording hall or traffic outside. Many puzzles arise during recording. For example, all recording halls mould bass sounds and all have reverberation; since these effects cannot be removed, the art of recording becomes using them to best advantage. A deeper problem is what constitutes "fidelity" in a good recording. Fidelity to what? Often recordings are made by recording instrument groups in many separate channels and then mixing them together in a pleasing way. However, this destroys the original stereo image and the balance that the musicians had with each other, and replaces them with another reality. Fully electronic music has no stereo image except what the

---

[7]We see these rules in consumer equipment. A rule of thumb in expensive three-speaker systems says spend the most on the midrange. Sometimes in a cheaper system a single central woofer reproduces bass tones. Several manufacturers radiate very high frequencies from the back, so that they reflect off a wall and other objects and gain better dispersion than direct radiation out the front.

[8]Absolute loudness does not matter, only the ratio of loud to quiet. A rock concert is loud on an absolute scale, but has a smaller dynamic range, since the music tends to be continuously loud. A realistic rock loudness is achieved at playback, not in the recording medium.

mixing console creates. We will have to leave all these puzzles now to recording engineers and return to the actual signal processing.

3.3.2 Music as an Analog and Digital Signal

From the above discussion, music as a waveform signal is a 20 kHz bandwidth waveform. If it is CD quality, the SNR should be round 90 dB; a lower, more reasonable SNR for broadcasting might be in the range 50–65 dB. The bandwidth assumed for FM broadcasting in many parts of the world is 15 kHz, which, as we have seen, is perceptively only a slight loss.

As a digital signal, the music signals must first be sampled, then converted to digital form. From the sampling theorem in Chapter 2, the sampling rate should be twice the highest frequency, which would give 40 kHz; the standard sampling rate for CD music is a little higher, 44.1 kHz. Simple PCM conversion of these samples is governed by Eq. (3.3); it says that 16 bits should achieve an SNR of about $6 \times 16 - 7.3 \approx 89$ dB. The overall bit rate for stereo is thus $2 \times 44,100 \times 16 = 1.411$ Mbits/s. This is in fact the bit rate at the output of a standard CD player.

As a waveform, music is not much different from telephone speech. Yet the sampling rate 44.1 kHz is more than 5.5 times faster than the standard speech rate. Another way of looking at this is that to the music sampler, the music waveform seems to be moving very slowly. This says that previous samples of music rather strongly predict the present sample. Sophisticated digital conversion methods can take advantage of this predictability, and some of these reduce the 1.411 Mbits/s rate to 100 kbits/s or lower. Another way of simplifying recording, which works for both analog and digital music, is Dolby-type recording. Here the music is recorded at an easier SNR level, say 50 dB, which conserves the analog or digital medium. By some compensation method, loud passages are reduced and quiet passages are increased, so that the 50 dB SNR more or less applies to everywhere. At playback, the procedure is reversed. All these methods work well for playback in, for example, cars, but they produce odd effects that are noticeable with good equipment in a quiet listening room. The Dolby compensation, for example, can cause what small noise exists to move about in a "visible" way in the stereo image. For really demanding applications the CD with its simple 16-bit PCM has remained the method of choice.

The Compact Disk Recording System

Any method that reliably records 16 bits per sample at a 44.1 kb/s rate will have the same sound as a CD. But the CD recording system illustrates many important digital conversions and one important storage technology, and we therefore should pause to take a look at it.

The blocks in the recording process are shown in Figure 3.7a. Sampling and PCM A-to-D conversion produce a 1.411 Mb/s bit stream. This stream is

(a)

(b)

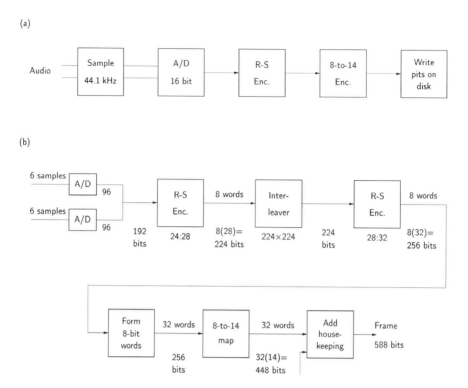

Figure 3.7   (a) Block diagram of the compact disk recording process; (b) More details about the center bit manipulations. For playback, reverse both diagrams

encoded by a Reed–Solomon error-correcting code. We will look at such error-correcting codes in Chapter 5; for now, we can say the R–S code adds some extra bits that will allow errors in the data bit stream to be corrected. After another special encoding, described later, the bits are written on the optical CD storage medium. The pattern of bits is carried by a long spiral of microscopic dents (called "pits") in a reflective film. At playback, the disk is rotated and the pattern read off by a finely focused beam of coherent light, generated by a laser, which tracks along the bit path. The beginning and end of a dent as it passes by signify data 1s. The remaining space signifies 0s, and the number of 0s is set by the amount of space that passes by, either at the bottom of a pit or in the film that surrounds the pit. The depth of the pits is a $\frac{1}{4}$ wavelength of the light, about $0.11\,\mu\text{m}$. The detection system works because at a pit boundary some light travels an extra $\frac{1}{2}$ wavelength and some does not, and this yields a partial cancellation in the reflected light, which can be detected. An electronic circuit watches for these dips, puts 1s at the dips and measures out some 0s in between. Other electronics automatically keep the laser beam pointed at the track and keep the disk running at the right speed. Circuits like these are typical of modern information storage systems, whether magnetic or optical. The reflecting film is enclosed by a 1 mm clear protective base. Dirt and imperfections in the base tend to be ignored by the detector because the laser beam is not focused there. Still, there can be small regions of defective pits in the film, and some method of correcting errors is needed.

We will next look in more detail at the bit processing that accompanies this laser detection. The major parts of this are shown in Figure 3.7b. The recording process runs from left to right; the playback process is the reverse. The basic recorded bit frame has 588 bits. It is obtained as follows.

- Six samples of each stereo channel are converted by 16-bit PCM to form 192 bits.
- Bits are added to these by a pair of Reed–Solomon error-correcting encoders; the outcome is 256 bits, which are formed into 32 8-bit words.
- Each of these words is mapped to a 14-bit word, a process called *8-to-14* encoding. The frame has now grown to 448 bits.
- 140 "housekeeping" bits are added; these aid in synchronization and in organizing the disk. The frame has now finally 588 bits.

The second and third items need further explanation. The R–S encoding occurs in two steps separated by an *interleaver*. Errors tend to occur in groups that reflect imperfections in the disk, and the interleaver is a device that scrambles the bit positions, so that what is a run of errors on the disk becomes scattered errors as seen by the R–S encoders. They have difficulty with long runs of errors but can easily correct the same overall rate if the errors are scattered. The first R–S encoder puts out 28 bits for each 24 that come in (there are 8 such groups in each 192-bit data frame), and the second puts out 32 for each 28; in between the interleaver scrambles 8 groups of 28. The end result is 256 bits.

The reason for the 8-to-14 encoding is more subtle. In actuality, the pits can be much smaller than the laser spot, and this markedly increases storage density on the disk. However, the pit edges cannot be too close, or the light cancellation effect will fail. A pit spacing limit is enforced by requiring at least two 0s between any two 1s in the final bit stream to be recorded. In order to make this happen, a special encoding is needed, the 8-to-14 encoding. It happens that out of all the 2^{14} 14-bit words, there are 256 that satisfy the at-least-2 0s constraint. This is enough to cover all the possible 8-bit word inputs. The 8-to-14 code is simply a one-to-one map from one set to the other. After the map the frame has grown to 448 bits. The housekeeping bits complete the frame.

All this bit processing nearly triples the frame size, but it leads to a much higher storage density and a very low error rate. The design of the overall disk system seeks to optimize the combination of these factors; that is, the processing cost, the storage available (here about 74 minutes), and the error rate (10^{-9} or less). For those wanting more detail, there is much written about the CD system. A few sources to start with are refs [1, 5, 6].

3.4 WHAT IS AN IMAGE?

An image is a two-dimensional array of light values. It must somehow be reduced to a one-dimensional waveform, at least for the kind of signal processing we have today. This is the scanning process, and the familiar kind of scan, consisting of successive lines across the image, is called a raster scan. Through this means, an image is reduced to a waveform source like speech and music. We want to look at the properties of the information in this waveform.

By *video* we mean a moving image. From a signal processing point of view, video is actually a succession of still images. Furthermore, each image usually closely predicts the next one, and this needs to be taken into account in an efficient storage and transmission system. These issues will be discussed in the next section.

Humans have been creating images since the Stone Ages, but it was not always so easy as today. Until the 1500s, drawing and painting were used in some languages, such as early Egyptian; they were used to commemorate events like battles, to interpret religious ideas in churches, and not much else. This began to change after 1550 with the invention of the camera obscura by Porta in Italy. This device used a pinhole, later a crude lens, to throw an image onto a small screen. Here for the first time was an image produced direct from nature. The discovery of chemicals affected by light came soon after, and their use to make temporary images came after 1750, but it was not until 1835 that H. F. Talbot discovered how to "fix" the image, that is, to stop the photochemical reaction and leave a permanent image. A number of such photographic processes were devised, all involving complex, wet chemical processes, but the real revolution occurred in 1884 when George Eastman (Box 3-2) in Rochester, New York, began selling a simple box camera that registered its images on dry chemicals adhered to a paper roll. With this, image processing became for the first time an activity of the general population.

Today, film coexists with electronic imaging, with its CCD cameras, magnetic storage, and laptop computer processing, but the information-handling ability of electronics will be inferior to film for some years to come.

How much information is in an image? To investigate this, we need to define a smallest image element of interest, the *pixel*,[9] and then count the number of pixels in the image. The number of distinct pixels per cm is called the resolution of an image. There is often a human observer somewhere, of course. In that case, we can imagine that the observer is standing at a distance such that the eye can just barely make out the pixels. A printing or other imaging process has a certain resolution, whether or not a human is looking; that is, it can resolve a certain number of pixels, or dots, per cm. The standard way to give the resolution of a fax, laser printer, or xerographic copier is in dots per inch (DPI), with 1 inch = 2.5 cm. This kind of machine prints either a black dot or no dot, which we can represent as a single bit of information, either 1 or 0. A lower quality copy machine resolves 300 DPI, a

---

[9]Pixel comes from the contraction of PICTure ELement. In some image processing, a pixel is simply called a dot.

BOX 3-2

George Eastman (1854–1932) was a brilliant industrialist and technologist who pioneered many aspects of the information industry that are familiar today. As we saw in Chapter 1, devising a revolution in technology usually requires that a whole *system* be invented. Eastman simplified the process of picture taking to the point where anyone could do it and almost anyone could afford it. His system, developed in the 1880s, included the dry-roll photographic paper, the simple Kodak box camera, plentiful advice, and a confidence-inspiring guarantee. (The word Kodak derived from the sound of the camera shutter.) Eastman finessed the parts of the process that could not be simplified by having the customer mail in the entire camera and exposed paper; by return mail came the pictures and the reloaded camera. The cost was US$10 for a *hundred* pictures. The public rapidly accepted this idea, and by 1900 the Eastman Company had a near monopoly on the world photographic business. As if this were not enough, Eastman, working with Edison and Dickson in 1889, invented the motion picture camera. This "system" required dry chemicals applied to a clear celluloid film, and thus was invented what we call "film." With these inventions, Eastman did far more than market a technology. He insisted that all processes and devices be mass-producible at low cost, and was one of the first technologists to think this way. He worked in a sort of partnership with the buying public. He was arguably the first to invest massively in basic research. Research for the Kodak color film process, which began in the early 1900s, is said to have required 25 years before it paid off, and it is still in progress. The idea of spending 25 years on a new product may be the one idea of Eastman's that we have forgotten today.

high-quality one 500–800, printing processes more than 2000, and standard 35 mm photography can resolve 3000 or more. Taking a standard page as 26×17 cm and the 300 dot resolution, we can compute the maximum number of bits in a picture as

$$17(26)(300/2.5)^2 = 6.36 \text{ Mbits} \qquad (3.4)$$

An old adage says that a picture is worth a thousand words. At the average rate of 40 bits/word that was used in Section 3.1, we can see that this is a gross underexaggeration. A picture is worth more like 150,000 words!

The picture in Eq. (3.4) might be unpleasant to look at, since it could be an entire sheet of salt-and-pepper random noise. More likely, it is mostly white space, with some words of text. Image processing systems such as a fax machine take advantage of this and send a special "white space" signal whenever possible; this greatly reduces the bit count in Eq. (3.4), almost to zero in the case of a page with just a few words.

Figure 3.8 shows magnified samples of three resolutions: On the left is a 300 DPI xerographic copy machine, the middle is a 600 DPI laser printer, and the right is book text at 800 + DPI. The 300 DPI works out to 12 dots per mm (see the mm scale). The dot size is obvious in the 300 DPI sample, and is almost invisible at 800 + DPI.

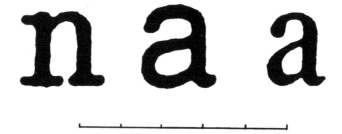

Figure 3.8   Magnified samples of three printers, showing differing resolutions. (Left) 300 DPI xerographic copy machine; (middle) 600 DPI laser printer; (right) book text at 800 + DPI. Millimeter scale as shown

This kind of image, consisting of black or white dots, is in a sense inherently digital. When the dots can take on shades of gray the image is said to be a *gray scale* image. A waveform of the intensity along a scan line is inherently an analog signal. The first practical fax machines appeared in the 1920s and transmitted news pictures by sending these analog scan lines by telephone or radio. (Less practical fax schemes had been proposed as early as 1891.) But the classic example of a scanned image is a single black and white television frame, and we will look at that now as an example of a gray scale image.

We will take the European PAL standard frame (world television systems are reviewed in Chapter 4). The PAL frame height is 625 lines; the width to height ratio is $4:3$. If we take the pixel as square with the height of a scan line, there are a total of

$$(625)(4/3)(625) \approx 520,000 \text{ pixels/frame} \tag{3.5}$$

The resolution is 833×625 per frame. For a 20 diagonal-inch (50 cm) screen, the pixels are about 0.5×0.5 mm. The pixel count in Eq. (3.5) is one-tenth the dots per page in Eq. (3.4). But now an analog waveform represents the intensity along a line. Suppose now that each pixel intensity is digitized by simple PCM at 6 bits per pixel. The distortion it causes will be nearly invisible. The total bits are now

$$(6)(520,000) = 3.1 \text{ Mbits/frame} \tag{3.6}$$

This value is not too different from the 300 DPI laser printer number in Eq. (3.4). In fact, printers of this type can create an image with an apparent gray scale and a resolution roughly that of TV. They do this by modulating the density of black dots against the white background, in combination with a resolution that is 10 times that of the TV screen.[10]

---

[10]More precisely, the resolution of our 20 inch screen is $12/0.5 = 24$ times worse, but the paper page must be doubled to be of the same physical size.

The PCM rate in the example here was taken as 6 bits/pixel because a human viewer has difficulty seeing an improvement from any more. However, the "True-color" computer image standard specifies 8 (see Problem 3.9). Actually, choosing the best combination of bits/pixel and resolution is a tricky problem. From Eqs. (3.5) and (3.6), these trade off against each other for a fixed number of bits per frame. Some photos of different PCM tradeoffs appear in Chapter 1 of ref. [9].

Digital image processing started in earnest with the space exploration of the 1960s, where PCM was found to be the best way to send pictures back from the Moon and nearby planets. With the planets, images were recorded onboard, and the PCM bits sent back very slowly, with error-correcting coding. (The slow speed boosted the transmission energy per bit; we will look at that in Chapter 4, and error correction in Section 5.3.) None of this would have been possible with analog transmission.

As with speech and music, a great deal of compression is possible in the PCM bit count of a gray scale image. If the image is a landscape or portrait for humans to look at, there will be a very strong correlation between the intensity of a pixel and those next to it. There will also tend to be a structure of edges and regions of constant tone. These can be used—perhaps at a considerable cost for computing—to compress the bit count to a few percent of Eq. (3.6). It is a step harder to compress images where the detail matters, such as aerial photographs. How humans perceive images and color plays a role (Box 3-3), but we will discuss that under the video heading, where it plays the major role.

BOX 3-3

The human eye contains around 10^8 light sensors, some 20–100 times those in an ordinary digital camera. About ten million of these lie in the fovea and the spacing here is 3 μm, about 28 times finer than a 300 DPI printer, and only a few times the wavelength of the light itself. Including the effect of the iris and the more light-sensitive peripheral vision, the dynamic range of the eye is about 10^7; simple PCM would need 17 bits per sensor output to capture this (we borrow the audio 6 dB Rule Eq. (3.3)). Color is sensed by the fovea cells and there appear to be three types. These have relatively wide responses centered in the blue, green, and red; the peak responses lie near 0.47, 0.54, and 0.61 μm, respectively. Taken together, these cells have peak sensitivity in the green at 0.56 μm, and a bandwidth of 0.40–0.70 μm. Their differentiation is enough to give us the color we perceive. Electronic sensors extend this range into the infrared, but overall, present-day electronics have difficulty equaling the performance of the eye.

Today, digital image transmission is widely used because of all the things that are easy to do with digital signal processing. Images with motion blurring, noise, poor focus or color can be enhanced or restored. Computer algorithms can recognize features such as tumors, fingerprints, and whole faces. Digital images, being bits, can be stored by general purpose media. Most compression algorithms are digital, so that fax and HDTV, which need compression to be practical, need to be digital image technologies. Everyday use of fax had to await the drop in the cost of signal processing that occurred in the 1980s. Image processing is a fascinating specialty, and further information about it can be found in the advanced references [9–11].

3.5 WHAT IS VIDEO?

Video is moving pictures, or to be precise, the presentation of a sequence of still images to give that impression. The major example of video is broadcast television. Starting with the very idea of sequencing images, television depends on the properties of human vision at every turn. We start with that.

3.5.1 Human Visual Perception

In human vision, images are registered on the retina of the eye. It contains a small central region, the fovea, that registers a detailed image, and a large surrounding area that registers a peripheral image. With training, we can become consciously aware of some details in the peripheral image, but we see poorly there and use it mostly to sense low light levels and motion coming from the side. In watching a scene, the eye darts rapidly about in a pattern that allows the fovea to scan an area of interest in the image. Our vision ignores the great majority of the image that is set before it at any one instant. This is a frustrating fact for image reproduction: At any one time, almost all the very large bit rate discussed in Section 3.4 is not perceived. Yet we cannot know where the viewer will focus, and so all the image must ordinarily be reproduced in detail.

In the brain, human perception tends to organize an image into edges and regions of nearly constant tone. These objects make up a face or landscape, and we have a highly developed capacity to recognize the overall organization of a scene, even if many small details have changed. If noise causes patterning in a tonal area or jaggedness in an edge, we perceive it easily. Image compression techniques need to take account of all these facts. Motion itself has its own perception facts. One that has many consequences is persistence of vision: an image flashed before us seems to persist for a brief time, about 60 ms, and if the next image comes soon enough, we perceive a continuing image; if the next one has moved, we think we see motion. Another consequence is that we tend to perceive the average of the recent images in the video sequence. This means that noise in successive frames is averaged by the eye; the signal-to-noise ratio in an isolated frame is low compared to what we perceive the video to have.

The physics of light and color largely began with Isaac Newton and his treatise *Opticks* (1704). Newton showed that white light was composed of colors and he said that seven primary colors were needed to form all the others. In 1861, Maxwell demonstrated that in fact only three were needed, what we call the additive primary colors: red, green, and blue (abbreviated henceforth RGB).[11] Human

---

[11] These form colors through addition, as in, for example, color TV displays or projection through film. Paint and print work via reflected light, and use the subtractive primaries yellow, magenta, and cyan. In printing, it is easier to render colors if a fourth ink, black, is added.

color perception is not perfectly understood—for example, it is not necessarily based on three primary colors. However, constructing a color image from red, green, and blue works well, and seems to have some basis in the physiology of the eye. It is the method used in all television systems.

While television camera and display systems are based on RGB, transmission of TV is not. This is because the eye is not too sensitive to errors in the RGB levels. The RGB levels are converted to three special variables y, i, and q, which are defined from facts about human perception. This works as follows. We do not perceive white when all three RGB intensities are equal; rather, a pixel appears white when

$$y = 30\%r + 59\%g + 11\%b \tag{3.7}$$

where r, g, and b are the intensities. The y, called the *luminance* value, is the total brightness of the pixel, measured as intensity of human "white." Humans also perceive color values with considerably less resolution than brightness. A thought experiment illustrates this. Imagine a pixel size such that alternating light and dark pixels are just barely resolved as such. If the alternating tones are changed to red-orange and blue-green, both with similar brightness, the image will appear to be simply gray. Before the pixels will appear as alternating color, they must be 3–6 times larger in area, depending on the colors. In color television, there is much less perceptual information in the colors as opposed to the brightness. The transformation (3.7) isolates a variable y, which contains most of the picture information (to a human) and can be sent with greater care. We will see in Section 4.4 that 80% of the transmission power is devoted to y.

The variables i and q carry what is left of the image, and by elimination this must be the color information. Together, these are the *chromaticity* of the pixel. If one is too big at the expense of the other (the most common transmission error), the result will be a change in the hue of the color; the eye is less sensitive to this than to a brightness error. If both i and q are too big or too small, the result is an error in the saturation (the degree of pastel) of the color. Again, this is a relatively harmless error. Much further detail on color perception and TV and image processing is available in ref. [9].

3.5.2 Video as an Analog and Digital Signal

We can form a simple estimate of the bandwidth of a video signal by analyzing a worst-case image that consists of alternating light and dark patches, whose intensity varies according to a sine wave; the estimate does not differ much from a sophisticated analysis based on optics and sampling theory. Let alternation occur at the television pixel rate in Eq. (3.5). The frequency of the sinewave will be $520,000/2 = 260,000$ cycles/frame. In the PAL system, 25 complete frames are sent per second; the frequency of the sinewave is thus

$$(\text{frame rate})(4/3) \times (\text{line count/frame})^2 = (25)(260,000) = 6.5 \text{ MHz} \tag{3.8}$$

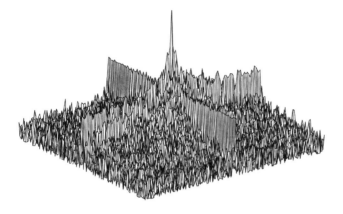

Figure 3.9 Three-dimensional Fourier transform plot for a portrait of Albert Einstein. The transform magnitude (vertical axis) is logarithmic; two-dimensional frequency origin is in the middle, at sharp peak. *Source:* Tomas Eriksson, Lund University, reproduced with permission

In actuality, the PAL standard bandwidth for the luminance signal y is taken as 4.4 MHz, because such a busy picture is not of much interest. The corresponding color signals need only another 0.5 MHz.

Video signals do not always need such a wide bandwidth. In fact, 1–2 MHz provides a satisfactory picture if the screen size is small. Figure 3.9 shows a plot of the spectrum of a single frame of video. The frequencies here are "spatial," meaning that they are measured in cycles per unit distance; the plot is also two-dimensional, since the video has width and height. The origin of the width and height frequency coordinate system is in the center. We can see that the video spectrum strongly concentrates at low frequencies. The spectrum amplitude is logarithmically plotted because the variation is so large.

Narrow video bandwidth causes a moderate smearing if it is extreme, and a "ringing" at vertical edges in the picture; this means that there are one or more faint traces of the edge next to the true edge. With a little effort, the bandwidth can be computed from the number and spacing of these traces. The bandwidth can be reduced still further by reducing the frame rate. *Slow scan* TV refers to systems with both reduced frame rate and image bandwidth. The result can be video with a bandwidth of only 100s of kHz. A familiar kind of video with reduced resolution is the standard VHS analog video recorder. Its resolution is 200–300 lines, corresponding to an analog bandwidth of about 1.5 MHz. Resolution trades off against how much video can be recorded on a given tape, and the public preferred this trade.[12] As for signal-to-noise ratio, video has a lower requirement than speech because of the visual averaging of frames; 20 dB is sufficient.

---

[12]At the time VHS was introduced, there was in fact a competing analog system called Betamax, which had higher quality. Nonetheless, the marketplace rejected it.

As a digital signal, video waveforms with simple PCM conversion have a very high bit rate. By repeating the estimate in Eq. (3.6) at 25 frames per second, we obtain close to 80 Mbits/s. We can get another estimate by applying the sampling theorem of Chapter 2 to the PAL video signal. We need to include in the signal both the brightness and color signals, plus various system signals, and the standard total signal bandwidth is 5 MHz. The theorem states that we must sample at twice this rate, and 6-bit PCM will give

$$2(5 \text{ MHz})(6 \text{ bits}) = 60 \text{ Mbit/s}. \tag{3.9}$$

This is a very large bit rate. Various video compression techniques can reduce it to the $2-5$ Mbit/s range, but at considerable processing cost.

3.5.3 High-Definition Television

The opposite of slow scan is high-definition TV, or HDTV. By increasing the number of scan lines and increasing the analog bandwidth in keeping with Eq. (3.8), a higher resolution can be obtained, but it is evident that the bandwidth grows fast, as the square of the number of scan lines. A reasonable goal for HDTV is to approach the resolution in a good movie theatre, which is that of 35 mm film. Movies tend to be wide-screen, and HDTV has adopted therefore a width : height ratio of 16 : 9. A second goal is that quality should be good enough for large-screen viewing in the home; this means a screen of 1 m or larger diagonal measure, viewed from 2 m away. There are many different HDTV and near-HDTV standards in the world. At the top end of these is a 1080-line 16 : 9 system with 24 frames/s. For this, the analog bandwidth calculation in Eq. (3.8) works out to

$$(24)(16/9)(1080)^2 \approx 50 \text{ MHz} \tag{3.10}$$

counting only the brightness component.

Analog television with such a bandwidth was developed in Japan in the 1980s and saw limited use there, but in most broadcast and recording situations, it is too large to be practical. What had evolved instead is a technology that first digitizes the HDTV video and then heavily compresses it to a final bit rate in the $10-20$ Mbit/s range. The compression technology is far beyond our scope. But in brief: a Fourier transform is taken of the images and certain parameters of that are digitized; what is transmitted is not the present parameters, but their *difference* from the previous frame, a technique called interframe coding; furthermore, the system tries to predict motion in the scene, and it transmits only the error in the prediction; last, the number of bits per frame is not constant, but can grow temporarily if more bits are needed for a troublesome scene. Some further details of this are in Couch [4], and at a simpler level in Lebow [1]. The final bit stream has a rate near 20 Mbit/s, and it can be transmitted in the channel used by ordinary analog television, which has a $6-7$ MHz bandwidth. Observe here how HDTV is forced to be digital, for the reason that only a digital format allows the bandwidth compression processing that makes it practical.

A set of international standards called MPEG[13] has evolved around HDTV, and includes digital standards for slow scan, standard, and high-definition TV. MPEG-1 is equivalent to 240-line standard television, about the resolution of a VHS recorder. The same strong compression techniques as above are used to produce a data rate in the range 1–3 Mbit/s. The standard MPEG-2 covers both standard and HDTV and has a bit rate of 3–20 Mbit/s, depending on the quality desired. Note that variable rates in these MPEG methods present no problem with CD recording, because the CD system can read out the bits at different rates as they are needed.

At this writing, it is impossible to say how prevalent HDTV will become. Some parts of it, for example the 16 : 9 picture size (but not the high resolution), have gained acceptance in Europe. But the cost, both for program production, transmission, and reception, is much higher. Do people want HDTV at the breakfast time? History shows that public acceptance is notoriously hard to predict.

3.6 CONCLUSION

In this chapter we have sketched the most common information sources. We have characterized them in terms of their analog bandwidth, the signal-to-noise ratio and resolution that they require, and the bit rate they demand once converted to digital form. Perhaps the chief lesson is that this bit rate varies tremendously, from a few thousand bits for a text message, to tens of thousands per second for speech, to a few megabits for an image, to as much as 80 Mbit/s for video. A picture is not worth a thousand words, but is in fact worth hundreds of thousands, and a moving picture is worth many millions.

The very different nature of information sources is the first thing to take into account in designing a transmission system. A text messaging system, for example, cannot be adapted to send images in any practical way. We must also account for different quality requirements and for human perception.

REFERENCES[14]

1. *LEBOW, I. L. 1998. *Understanding digital transmission and recording*. IEEE Press: New York.
2. *RABINER, L. R. and SCHAFER, R. W. 1978. *Digital processing of speech signals*. Prentice-Hall, Englewood Cliffs, N.J.
3. *STARK, H., TUTEUR, F. B. and ANDERSON, J. B. 1988. Modern electrical communications, 2nd ed. Prentice-Hall, Englewood Cliffs, N.J.
4. *COUCH, L. W. 2001. *Digital and analog communication systems*, 6th ed. Prentice-Hall, Upper Saddle River, N.J.
5. Special Issue on Digital Audio. 1985. *IEEE ASSP Mag.*, 2 (4).

[13] MPEG = Motion Picture Experts Group, a subdivision of the International Standards Organization (ISO).

[14] References marked with an asterisk are recommended as supplementary reading.

6. CHEN, P. 1986. The compact disk ROM: How it works. *IEEE Spectrum*, 23 (4), 44–49.

7. FLANAGAN, J. L. et al. 1970. Synthetic voices for computers. *IEEE Spectrum*, 7 (10), 22–45.

8. ATAL, B. S. and HANAUER, S. L. 1971. Speech analysis and synthesis by linear prediction of the speech wave. *J. Acoust. Soc. Am.*, 50, 637–655.

9. *WEEKS, A. R. Jr. 1996. *Fundamentals of electronic image processing*. SPIE Optical Engineering Press: BELLINGHAM, WA; copublished with IEEE Press: New York.

10. RUSS, J. C. 1992. *The image processing handbook*. CRC Press: Boca Raton, FL.

11. GONZALEZ, R. C. and WOODS, R. E. 1992. *Digital image processing*. Addison-Wesley: Reading, MA.

PROBLEMS

1. (a) Two signals have powers 1 W and 20 W. Find their ratio in decibels.

   (b) At the input to a receiver, a signal power of 100 μW is observed; when the signal is taken away, noise alone is observed to have power 1 μW. What is the SNR in dB?

2. (a) A current of 1 A flows through a 10 Ω resistor. Later, 15 A is measured there. What is the ratio of these currents, when expressed in decibels?

   (b) The measurements of the receiver in Problem 3.1(b) are repeated, but this time a voltmeter is used instead of a power meter and the typical signal and noise voltages are measured. Otherwise nothing has changed. What do you expect the voltage ratio to be?

3. This problem discusses the size in bits of various files that might store the text of Chapter 1 of this book. To start, estimate roughly the word count of Chapter 1.

   (a) Suppose that Chapter 1 is converted to bits using the Simple Text Code in Section 3.1 (capital letters only, plus the space, represented by 5 bits). Roughly how long is the file in bits?

   (b) Repeat, using ASCII to convert the file to bits.

   (c) The actual Latex file was about 90,000 bytes. Compare this to your answer in (b). What can you say about the efficiency of Latex at representing complicated text? Give reasons for your answer.

4. A digital music transmission system is to have bandwidth 5 kHz and signal-to-noise ratio 60 dB. Use the sampling theorem and the Six-dB Rule of PCM to estimate how many bits/ second are required in the system.

5. A spacecraft sends back to Earth five different telemetry signals from its instruments. These are analog signals, and after some observations on the actual signals it is concluded that three of them have bandwidth 20 Hz, one has bandwidth 50 Hz, and one has bandwidth 200 Hz.

   (a) At what rate in samples per second should each of these be sampled?

   (b) Each sample is converted to bits at the rate of 8 bits per sample. Estimate the total bit rate that the spacecraft must send back to Earth.

6. The good ship *Whisky on the Rocks* is monitoring an underwater area with its sonar system. It is desired to make a permanent surveillance recording of everything *Whisky* picks up. A sonar signal has highest frequency 300 Hz and needs to be recorded with 30 dB signal-to-noise ratio. The recording is done digitally. Estimate how many bits are required to store each hour's worth of sonar signal. Allow 20% extra sampling rate in order to make the electronics simpler.

7. Estimate the bit rate of an HDTV video system whose quality is the same as that of a good movie theatre.

   Here are some reasonable assumptions that you can make: (i) 35 mm film (35×25 mm field); (ii) 3000 DPI film resolution; (iii) 24 frames/s; (iv) 8 bits to digitize each pixel.

8. Picturephone was a telephone equipped with a small TV screen that was introduced in the 1960s. It was not a commercial success; among other things, customers did not want to put on their clothes to make a telephone call. Perhaps it is time for another attempt to sell this telephone. Propose a design for the video part that uses ordinary PCM and has an overall bit rate of 64 kbit/s. Assume that the screen is 8×8 cm and that a low picture quality and a low "slow scan" frame rate are acceptable. Recall that the bit rate is the product

$$(\text{bits/pixel}) \times (\text{lines//frame})^2 \times (\text{frames/s})$$

   Juggle these three factors to produce a system you think is acceptable.

9. The "True-color" computer image standard devotes 8 bits to each of the three RGB components for a pixel.

   (a) Compute the bits that are required to display a standard Super VGA color image composed of 1024×768 pixels.

   (b) A standard called RS170 converts a single standard NTSC television frame (i.e., two interlaced half-frames) to a computer image. Make a reasonable estimate of the bits produced from a black and white frame. Repeat for a color frame, assuming that the True-color standard is used. (You will have to consult Section 4.4 for the NTSC parameters.)

Chapter 4

Transmission Methods: How is Information Sent?

Communication is the transfer of information, through either space or time. In this chapter we look at the chief ways that the transfer is actually made. These can be broken into two wide classes, analog and digital communication. The work in this chapter is partly descriptive, partly mathematical. The methods in Chapter 2 play a major role. First, bandwidth is an important measure of communication efficiency, and this is calculated by Fourier methods. Secondly, radio communication circuitry works almost entirely with sinusoids. Thirdly, most circuits are linear.

Modulation converts the signals and bits from the sources in Chapter 3 into a new form, chosen to suit the channel. We begin by looking at the channel through which the signals must pass, since this plays a major role in choosing a way to send them. It is easy to overlook the storage channel. This is as much a channel as a radio or a pair of telephone wires. The storage medium, as well as a radio or wire medium, can cause errors, and modulation needs to be designed to counter this. After channels, we will go first to analog, then to digital modulation methods.

4.1 COMMUNICATION CHANNELS

A rough breakdown of electrical communication channels is as follows:

1. Wires, cables, and glass fibers, used when it is possible to connect together the transmitter and receiver;
2. Radio, when one or both is moving, or in a location not known in advance;
3. The storage channel.

We will take these now one at a time.

Understanding Information Transmission. By John B. Anderson and Rolf Johannesson
ISBN 0-471-67910-0 © 2005 the Institute of Electrical and Electronics Engineers, Inc.

4.1.1 Wire, Cables and Fibers

Wire Channels

The oldest and simplest channel is a pair of wires. The wire-pair channel goes back to the telegraph and the dawn of electrical communication. Today it is with us in the form of the telephone wires that enter our houses. In most towns, it is still a wire pair that runs from our telephones or computers out to the area's telephone switch. From there onward, calls probably travel by another means, most likely glass fiber. The weak link in this chain is the wire pair, and despite its antiquity, the wire pair is therefore still the object of much attention.

A pair of wires acts like a lowpass electrical filter; that is, it passes low frequencies more readily than high ones. The frequency at which a filter begins seriously to reduce a signal is called the filter's *cutoff* frequency. The tricky fact about the wire pair is that the cutoff depends on its length. A 100 m pair has cutoff in the megahertz range, but a 30 km pair has a kilohertz cutoff and will barely carry voice signals. This effect is at the heart of how a wire channel works, and so we need to discuss it.

A wire pair is a special kind of circuit called a distributed parameter circuit that has R, L, and C like the circuits in Appendix B, but distributed continuously along the wires.

A special analysis can be performed that shows that a complex voltage signal $v_0(t) = V_0 e^{j\omega t}$ at radian frequency ω, when placed at the input, propagates down the wire and declines exponentially. At time t its value is

$$v(t) = V_0 e^{j\omega t} e^{-y\gamma} \qquad \text{at distance } y \tag{4.1}$$

Here y is distance in meters, V_0 is a constant, and frequency f in Hz and radian frequency are related by $\omega = 2\pi f$. The parameter γ is called the propagation constant of the wire pair; it is a complex number given by the formula

$$\gamma(\omega) = \sqrt{(R(\omega) + j\omega L)(G + j\omega C)}, \qquad \omega = 2\pi f \tag{4.2}$$

Here R is the resistance down the wire pair in ohms (Ω) per meter; similarly, C and L are the capacitance and inductance measured per meter. Any two objects have capacitance and inductance between them, and in the case of two wires, some thought will show that it has to grow linearly with the wire length. G in Eq. (4.2) is the conductance in Ω^{-1} across the medium between the two wires, and in our case here we will set it to zero.

The resistance R actually depends on frequency, and in fact has the form $R(\omega) \approx K_o \sqrt{\omega}$ at high frequencies. This is because of the *skin effect*, a phenomenon that has a major effect on signaling through wires and cables. Alternating currents tend to travel near the surface of a conductor, the higher the frequency, the nearer the surface. At a high enough frequency, all the signal current is forcing its way through a skin some tens of microns thick.

The voltage $v(t)$ at y meters down the wire pair in Eq. (4.1) depends strongly on frequency. If $v_0(t)$ is $\Re\{V_0 e^{j\omega t}\} = V_0 \cos \omega t$, with $\omega = 2\pi 200$ rad/s ($f = 200$ Hz), then by the rules in Section 2.2, the voltage at y is the real part of Eq. (4.1), namely

$$\Re\left\{V_0 e^{j\omega t} e^{-y\gamma(\omega)}\right\} = \Re\left\{V_0 e^{j(2\pi 200)t} e^{-y\gamma(2\pi 200)}\right\} \tag{4.3}$$

The factor $e^{-y\gamma}$ is a complex number, as so $v(t)$ is a cosine, but with a phase shift and a reduced amplitude. A typical value for $\gamma(\omega)$ at $\omega = 2\pi 200$ might be $0.059 + i0.059$ per km (for more, see Example 4.1). Thus $e^{-y\gamma}$ at, say, $y = 10$ km, becomes

$$e^{-y\gamma} = 0.463 - 0.310i = 0.557\angle - 0.59 \text{ rads}$$

and $v(t)$ at 10 km down the wire pair becomes $0.557 V_0 \cos(2\pi 200t - 0.59)$. This is a reduction by 5.1 dB (i.e., $20 \log_{10} 0.557$), and it grows much worse at higher frequencies. The expression $e^{-y\gamma(\omega)}$, $\omega = 2\pi f$, is the transfer function $H(f)$ introduced in Section 2.2, for the circuit defined by the wire pair. That is, $V_0 e^{j2\pi ft}$ applied at the input yields $H(f)V_0 e^{j2\pi ft}$ after y meters. The length y wire pair is a linear circuit, like those in Chapter 2.

EXAMPLE 4.1

The classic example of the wire pair is the wires in the cables that connect our telephones to the local telephone switch. These range from a few hundred meters in length up to 30 km for connections in the countryside. For a look at this important channel, we can use Eqs. (4.1) and (4.2) together with the R, L, C parameters for ordinary 22 AWG copper wire, a common kind in local cables. The parameters per kilometer are approximately $L = 0.60$ mH, $C = 0.05$ μF and $R \approx 0.2\sqrt{\omega}$ Ω, $\omega > 2\pi 50k$, $R = 110$ Ω otherwise. We are interested now only in the attenuation that the wires make in the different frequency components, and this is the absolute value of the ratio $V_0 e^{j2\pi ft} e^{-y\gamma}/V_0 e^{j2\pi ft}$. At length y it is

$$|e^{-y\gamma}| = e^{-y\Re\{\gamma\}} \tag{4.4}$$

Figure 4.1 plots this attenuation in dB against log frequency for three wire lengths, 1, 10, and 20 km. From the plot, we can see that the wire pair is usable at least out to 1 MHz (the 20 dB loss is easily made up by an amplifier). However, the 10 km line has a loss of 60 dB (reduction in power by 10^6) at 100 kHz, and the 20 km is hopeless above a few thousand Hz.

The results in the example have major implications for building universal wide bandwidth data networks. They describe the so-called *last mile problem*: It is easy to interconnect whole towns and regions with very wide band single channels, such as glass fibers, which carry high speed data, but to run such a line to each home is too expensive. We must depend on the telephone lines that exist there already, and these have wide bandwidth only when they are short.

Advanced modulation methods do exist that can carry data rates in the 0.1– 1 Mbit/s range over wire pairs when they are short enough. These are called DSL

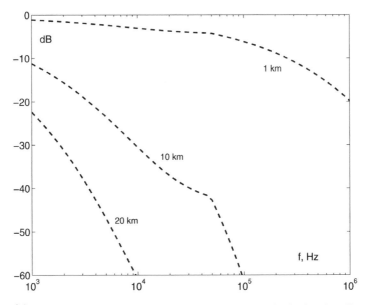

Figure 4.1   Attenuation in dB versus frequency for AWG 22 wire pair with length 1, 10, and 20 km. Note logarithmic frequency scale

(digital subscriber line) technologies. Sometimes a high data rate is needed only in one direction; these are ADSL (asymmetric DSL) methods. Such DSL methods measure the channel as it actually exists and then adapt the bit rate accordingly.

Coaxial Cable Channels

A coaxial cable consists of an inner wire conductor, surrounded by a dielectric tube made of plastic such as polyethylene, around which is placed a shielding metal tube. The mathematics of propagation for this wire within a tube system is similar to that of the wire pair, with one difference: The propagation works at much higher frequencies. For the same path length, cables carry a hundred times higher bandwidth, which means, one way or the other, a hundred times the information transfer. Since the return path is the outer shield, which is grounded, the inner conductor is protected from external electrical noise. Also, when the cable is used to carry power to a transmitting antenna, the shield helps prevent the power from radiating beforehand.

Coaxial cables are familiar as the TV distribution systems in houses and neighborhoods. With a receiver–transmitter *repeater* that regenerates the signal every few hundred meters, cables will carry 100 or more television channels. The cable material is relatively easy to work with. Fibers are cheaper, need few repeaters, and carry much more bandwidth, but as with telephone lines, the fact that cables are already installed and paid for almost everywhere gives them a major advantage over fibers. Here again is the last mile problem, and it says that cable will be with us for many years to come.

Fiber Optic Channels

The optical fiber is based on a universal principle of physics that states that light bends and is reflected when it passes through a change in refraction index. This is illustrated in Figure 4.2, which shows the core within a cladding construction of the simplest kind of fiber. Both core and cladding are designed to transmit light with very little loss, but the cladding has a lower refraction index, which causes internal reflection as shown. When the indices of the two materials are nearly the same, the reflection angle θ_o is small and most of the light is trapped and propagates as if down a pipe.

A laser diode generates a modulated signal at the fiber input and a photosensitive diode detects the light at the output. In a digital transmission, the light is simply switched on and off, but this can be done even at gigabit rates, so the fiber has a very high capacity. In addition, the whole structure is as thin as a human hair, so that many independent fibers can be bundled together. Propagation losses grow worse at shorter wavelengths but light containment works better; the best compromise between the two effects occurs at wavelengths $0.8-1.5$ μm, in the near-infrared region. Modern fiber materials have very small loss factors of 0.5 dB/km or less, and paths of $60-100$ km are possible. By a succession of such links with repeaters in between, oceans can be crossed and cities connected at very low cost on a per-bit basis. Compared to other costs in an information transmission system, fixed, long-distance fiber links are virtually free. They are our major means of communication over fixed links.

4.1.2 Radio Channels

In radio channels, electromagnetic waves propagate freely, without being confined to wires or fibers. Nonetheless, objects in the path affect the waves, as does the medium through which the waves pass. That medium can be space, the atmosphere, charged particle regions like the ionosphere, or even the sea. The best radio frequency depends strongly on these factors. Table 4.1 shows the breakdown of the

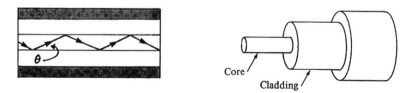

Figure 4.2 Construction of a light fiber, showing propagation down the fiber when the geometry and critical angle are in the right relationship

Table 4.1   Radio frequency bands, with some properties and uses for each band

Frequency band	Band name	Comments
10–100 kHz	Extra low frequency (ELF)	Underwater communication
100–500 kHz	Low frequency (LF)	Follows Earth surface
500–3000 kHz	Medium wave (MW)	Follows Earth with loss; some ionosphere reflection at night
530–1610 kHz		MW broadcast band
3–30 MHz	Shortwave (SW, or HF)	
3–10 MHz		Reflected by ionosphere, night
10–30 MHz		Reflected by ionosphere, day
30–300 MHz	Very high frequency (VHF)	FM, TV broadcasting; primarily line of site (LOS)
300–1000 MHz	Ultra high frequency (UHF)	Mobile radio; only LOS
1–10 GHz	Microwave	Wideband links, Earth and space; LOS
10–100 GHz	Millimeter wave	Space links; affected by rain; LOS
>200,000 GHz	Infrared	Optical fiber links

radio spectrum into bands, with a few notes on how each band is used. We look first at radio in space, because here nothing modifies the propagation; then we move on to more complicated radio channels.

The Space Channel

By a space channel we mean a radio channel that has white noise but otherwise has unimpeded propagation, without reflection, absorption, or any other damaging effects. Communication between spacecraft and planets is the classic example.

Unlike the case with the wire pair, empty space does not damage the transmission. Radio waves simply propagate according to the inverse-square law, which states that the density of radio power diminishes as $1/d^2$, where d is distance. Antennas collect the power, there is noise, and there are some losses at the transmitter and receiver, in the manner sketched in Figure 4.3. At the end of it all, there is a ratio of signal to noise at the receiver, which is what sets the quality level of the received information. Adding up all the gains and losses in order to arrive at a signal-to-noise ratio (SNR) is called forming a *link budget*. The budget starts with a transmitter power P_t, from which may be deducted some losses in the transmitter circuits. Next comes the transmit antenna. We can take both the transmitter and receiver antennas as parabolic dishes; this, or something similar, is what they usually are in radio communication at high frequencies and beyond short distances. The physics of a transmit antenna are such that it focuses power in a desired direction. The transmitted power P_t seems much bigger at the other end, in a ratio given in

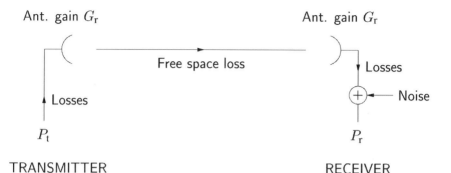

Figure 4.3   A picture of the major items in a space channel link budget, including transmitter and receiver circuit losses and antenna gains, and the free space loss. P_t is the transmitter power and P_r is the received power

theory by the formula

$$G = \frac{4\pi A}{\lambda^2} \qquad (4.5)$$

where G is called the antenna gain, A is the dish area, and λ is the radio wavelength. We can see that the gain is proportional to area and to the inverse *square* of wavelength.

At the receive end, the antenna works to collect power, much as a dish lying on the ground would collect rainwater. The gain from this collecting is proportional to the dish area. In sum, it can be shown that the power collected at the receiver is given by

$$P_r = P_t G_t G_r \left(\frac{\lambda}{4\pi d}\right)^2 \qquad (4.6)$$

Here G_t and G_r are the transmitter and receiver antenna gains, both computed from Eq. (4.5). What remains, the quantity $(\lambda/4\pi d)^2$, is called the *free space loss* (FSL). It measures the effect of distance and spreading as the radio wave propagates. We show the FSL in Figure 4.3 as a loss.

Gaussian Noise   This completes the budget except for noise. In a space channel, and in most channels, noise appears at the front of the receiver. We have therefore shown it adding there in the figure. It is tempting to think that noise is present in the medium itself, but this is usually not the dominant source. At the front of the receiver, the incoming power P_r terminates at some load resistor or amplifier called the "termination," and it is here that noise normally enters the picture. The termination has a temperature, and this creates white thermal noise whose power N obeys the formula (Box 4-1)

$$N = kT_K B_m \quad \text{(Watts)} \tag{4.7}$$

Here k is Boltzmann's constant (1.28×10^{-23}), T_K is absolute temperature in degrees Kelvin, and B_m is the bandwidth over which the measurement takes place in Hz, counting positive frequencies. A single sample of this noise will have a Gaussian probability distribution with zero mean and variance $N/2$. The outcome of such a sample takes the bell-shaped probability distribution given by

$$f(x) = \frac{1}{\sqrt{N\pi}} e^{-x^2/N}, \quad \text{all } x \tag{4.8}$$

The noise is called white because it has a uniform, flat energy density at all frequencies. A plot and some further discussion about this distribution is given in Appendix C.

Much further information on link budgets, antennas, and noise appears in the starred communication textbooks in the reference list. Now we give an example of a link budget.

BOX 4-1

The Gaussian noise formula (4.7) was worked out in theory and demonstrated in practice in 1928 in the papers of Nyquist [8] and Johnson [9] at Bell Laboratories in the United States. It stems from the molecular theory of heat. In rare cases, the noise entering the antenna from the outside environment is larger; an antenna on Earth pointed up always sees 20 K infrared radiation from the atmosphere, and an antenna in space pointed at space sees the 3 K background radiation in the universe. As the measurement bandwidth B_m grows, it is true that the power N grows without limit. But the white noise model only applies up to 100 GHz or so. This is enough to cover all of radio communication, and so to radio engineers, noise is truly "white." There are some interesting facts in Eq. (4.7) about receiver design. First, N depends on temperature, so we can reduce noise by reducing temperature. Secondly, N grows with bandwidth; thus the receiver bandwidth should be as small as possible without damaging the signal. A third way to reduce noise is to use quieter amplifying circuits. Unless there is noise out in the medium to work on, these three are the only ways to reduce noise at the receiver output.

EXAMPLE 4.2

In the last 30 years a number of spacecraft have visited the planets in the solar system and sent back images and data. We will take a look at the link budget for a Mars-to-Earth link. A careful look at Eqs. (4.5) and (4.6) shows that higher frequencies travel with less loss than lower ones; this is because the focusing effect in the antennas works better at short wavelengths. For this reason, a relatively high frequency is used, 8.4 GHz (wavelength 3.6 cm). The distance d is 4×10^8 km in the worst case. The most powerful transmitter that can be sent to Mars puts out 200 W. The transmit antenna at the spacecraft is a 5.4 m dish that is deployed after launch; its gain is measured to be 51 dB (i.e., $G_t = 10^{5.1} \approx 126,000$). The receive antenna is huge, a 70 m steerable dish[1] with measured gain 73 dB. The antenna terminates in a special amplifier that is actually inside the antenna feed; it is cooled with liquid gas and has an equivalent noise temperature in the neighborhood of 20 K. We can subtract altogether 5 dB for losses in various receiver and transmitter connections. From Eq. (4.6) we can compute the power that reaches the receiver. It is

$$
\begin{aligned}
P_r &= P_t G_t G_r \left(\frac{\lambda}{4\pi d}\right)^2 \times (5 \text{ dB loss factor}) \\
&= (200 \text{ W})(10^{5.1})(10^{7.3})(0.036 \text{ m}/4\pi 4 \times 10^{11} \text{ m})^2 (10^{0.5}) \\
&= 8.2 \times 10^{-15} \text{ W}
\end{aligned}
\tag{4.9}
$$

This is the received power. The noise that the receiver adds is given by Eq. (4.7), and it depends on the receiver bandwidth. That in turn depends on the bit rate in the link. Digital transmission methods are covered in Section 4.3, and for now we can just state that 5 Mbit/s will be transmitted and that it will occupy 5 MHz of RF spectrum. The noise power is then

$$
\begin{aligned}
N = kTB_m &= (1.38 \times 10^{-23} \text{ J/K})(20 \text{ K})(5 \times 10^6 \text{ Hz}) \\
&= 1.4 \times 10^{-15} \text{ W}
\end{aligned}
\tag{4.10}
$$

Note the crucial effect of the low receiver input temperature. The ratio P_r/N is thus about $8.2 \times 10^{-15}/1.4 \times 10^{-15} = 5.9$, which is enough to give a bit error rate of about 0.0003 (this is justified in Section 4.3). It will be enough perhaps for some data types, but for others a lower rate is needed. It can be obtained by a number of means: error-correcting codes, more power, bigger antennas, higher frequency, or a slower transmission rate.

Terrestrial Radio

When radio communication is brought down to Earth, radio waves no longer propagate in a simple manner. They are subject to reflection, *refraction* (bending because of changes in the refraction index), *diffraction* (re-radiation from small objects and openings), and absorption (due, e.g., to rain). Even when there is line-of-sight contact between transmitter and receiver, these effects can reduce or even completely cancel the radio signal. At microwave frequencies, a typical radio link is 50 km in length and needs 20–40 dB extra power, depending on the reliability that is required (30 dB will yield service 99.99% of the time over average terrain). Shortwave radio (3–30 MHz) actually depends on reflection from the ionosphere in order to work over international distances. The ionosphere in turn depends for its success

---

[1] It is located in Goldstone, CA, United States, and may be seen in a number of movies about space and alien visits. The antenna is a major part of the cost of the link.

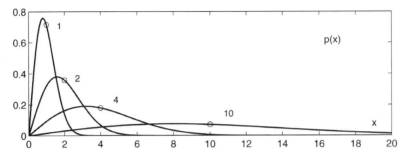

Figure 4.4   The Rayleigh amplitude distribution, when the mean amplitude is 1, 2, 4, 10. The position of the mean in the distribution is shown by a small circle

as a radio mirror on radiation from the Sun. Different frequencies must accordingly be used during night and day; even with several frequencies available, shortwave contact across continental distances cannot be guaranteed more than 90–95% of the time.

Mobile radio channels present special problems because line-of-sight contact is ordinarily not present. *Rayleigh fading* is the term used to describe the situation where radio waves come in more or less equally from all directions, with random delays. It can be shown (see the starred texts) that the received amplitude x of the radio wave is randomly changing in accordance with the Rayleigh distribution

$$p(x) = \begin{cases} \dfrac{x}{\rho} e^{-x^2/2\rho} & x > 0 \\ 0 & \text{otherwise} \end{cases} \tag{4.11}$$

The mean value of the amplitude is $\sqrt{\pi\rho}/2$. Usually, the front of the receiver is still the dominant noise source, a white noise that stays fixed while the signal amplitude moves up and down according to distribution (4.11). This distribution of power can be an unpleasant one to deal with. Figure 4.4 shows the distribution for several mean values, and it is clear that the distribution has a wide spread and x has considerable probability of taking a value well below the mean.

EXAMPLE 4.3

For example, suppose that a Rayleigh fading signal has average amplitude $\sqrt{10}$, and that with the noise present, this gives good performance. The mobile link is unacceptable when the received power drops by a factor of 4. This is an amplitude drop by 2, to $\sqrt{10}/2$. At any given time, what is the probability that this happens? The calculation method is taken from probability theory. It is done by integrating $p(x)$. The probability that the amplitude is less than u is $\int_0^u p(x)dx = 1 - e^{-u^2/2\rho}$. For average amplitude $\sqrt{\pi\rho/2} = \sqrt{10}$, ρ is 6.4. We take $u = \sqrt{10}/2$ and get that the probability integral is 0.18. The link thus fails 18% of the time. With the same average power but no Rayleigh fading, the link will almost always work well.

This amplitude fading is not all that affects a mobile radio signal. Since one or both ends are moving, the radio signal is Doppler shifted. The classical Doppler relation states that a speed v leads to a frequency shift

$$\delta f = v/\lambda \text{ Hz} \qquad (4.12)$$

where λ is the wavelength measured at rest. This relationship is in fact a method used by police to catch speeders. At 100 km/h and the 850 MHz frequency of GSM telephones, δf is

$$(100 \text{ km/h})/(3600 \text{ s/h})(0.353 \text{ m}) = 79 \text{ Hz}$$

(At police radar frequencies, which are higher, it is more like 1000 Hz.) In reality, the Doppler effect is more troublesome than this, because under Rayleigh conditions the radio waves come from all directions. For a direction at angle ϕ to the receiver, the apparent velocity is $v \cos \phi$ and therefore what arrives is a smear of frequencies in the range $f_0 - \delta f \leq f \leq f_0 + \delta f$, where f_0 is the rest frequency in the transmission.

Frequencies are smeared for another more subtle reason. In Chapter 2 we saw from the Fourier transform that a signal that varies in amplitude will have a transform with a range of frequencies. An amplitude-faded signal thus cannot avoid being at the same time a frequency-smeared signal, even when there is no motion. In addition to frequency smearing, there is also a smearing of the signal in time because the signal arrives by multiple paths that each have their own delay. This simultaneous confusion in frequency and time, called *dispersion*, when added to the fading in amplitude, is what is characteristic of fading.

As a mobile terminal moves about the countryside, it of course encounters small regions of better and worse propagation. This is yet another effect called *shadowing*, since the terminal is moving rapidly in and out of radio "shadows." These changes in signal strength tend to be large, and the Rayleigh effect rides on top of them. When all the effects are added up, mobile radio becomes quite a challenge to the engineer. It is important, for example, that signal changes in the modulation occur over longer times than the time dispersion and over greater frequencies than the frequency dispersion. At the same time, a lot of extra signal energy must be transmitted to guard against deep fades.

4.1.3 Storage Channels

A storage channel moves information from one time to another, but it is nonetheless a channel and it has error probability and possibly distortion, just like other channels. The most common storage methods are magnetic and optical ones. Optical storage channels record information in microscopic pits in a surface and recover the

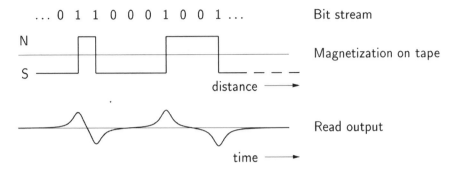

Figure 4.5 An illustration of binary magnetic recording and playback. The magnetization along a track shifts between N and S whenever a binary 1 appears

information by sensing the pits optically. The compact disk storage system is typical. It is described in Section 3.3 and we will not look further at optical methods here.

Magnetic storage works by magnetizing alternating regions along a narrow strip, or "track," in a magnetic film. This is done as the film passes by a write head, and in binary digital recording, the head induces short saturated regions of two kinds, either north (N) or south (S). The bits are read back by a read head, which is basically a loop of wire held close to the moving track. From physics, the current induced in this loop is proportional to the rate of change of the magnetic field that passes by. Therefore, the loop picks up not absolute magnetization but *changes* between N and S. As in optical storage, then, it is necessary to encode the information bits in the shifts from one region to the next.

A typical digital magnetic recording process is illustrated in Figure 4.5. A sequence of bits to be stored appears in the stream shown. The strip of magnetic film is magnetized by the write head either N or S as shown, with the direction reversing at the appearance of each binary 1. The magnetic regions down the strip are shown in the middle of the figure. A read head will produce the voltage versus time shown at the bottom, with a positive peak at each S–N transition and the opposite at a N–S transition. The peaks have a certain width that depends on the read loop geometry and on how fast the magnetization can change; this limits the storage density along the track. The storage circuitry knows the rate that bits appear along the track, and when it sees a peak of either polarity it puts out a 1; otherwise it puts out a 0.

A typical magnetic tape accepts 3000 or more bits per cm arranged in nine parallel tracks. Eight tracks carry data, with the ninth acting as a stream of parity checks on the other eight.[2] Special circuits keep the output synchronized properly with the framework that was written on the tape and break the output down into words of data. Dust along the surface can affect the readout, and more important,

---

[2] A simple parity check scheme would be to require that the sum of the bits across the nine tracks is an even number. More on parity check schemes appears in Chapter 5.

the magnetic film can have regions that will not accept magnetization properly. Recording systems try to spot such regions and either skip over them or correct the errors that they cause. Computer hard disks use a technology similar to this tape technology.

4.2 ANALOG MODULATION

Modulation changes the form of a signal and converts it to a different band of frequencies. Without modulation, we would all have to take turns communicating over the same frequency range, and placing each of us in a separate frequency range is one good reason to modulate. Another reason for frequency shifting is that a particular medium may work much better at one frequency than another. Shifts to another form, such as the digital form, may also make communication more efficient over a given medium or network. Once in a while, no modulation at all is best—whales have evolved to use the lower audio frequencies at very long distances under water, because these give the best propagation. Modulation is a matter of what works best, and of allowing more than one user in a medium.

Most modulation methods employ *carrier* transmission. A carrier modulation method shifts the information signal from its natural frequency range to a new, higher range. Soon, we will use Fourier analysis to see how the signal is "moved." The amount of the shift is called the carrier frequency f_0. Sometimes a sinusoid at frequency f_0 is clearly present in the modulated signal, and can be said to "carry" the signal. In other methods it is not, and here f_0 is simply the size of the shift; f_0 is sometimes called the center frequency in that case. Once the signal is shifted, it is a *bandpass* signal. Such a signal has frequencies in only a narrow range around some f_0; narrow means small in comparison to f_0. Before the shift, the original signal is called a *baseband*, or sometimes simply a lowpass, signal. This is because it has a frequency range that includes or is at least close to DC. One way to describe a bandpass signal mathematically[3] is to write

$$s(t) = A(t) \cos[\omega_0 t + \phi(t)], \qquad \omega_0 = 2\pi f_0 \qquad (4.13)$$

Here $A(t)$ is the amplitude and $\phi(t)$ is the phase of a sinusoid with radian frequency ω_0. Both $A(t)$ and $\phi(t)$ are baseband signals, with frequencies in a relatively narrow range around DC. Any bandpass signal at all can be expressed in terms of two signals $A(t)$ and $\phi(t)$ by using Eq. (4.13).

4.2.1 Amplitude Modulation

Signals that carry speech, images, and video are inherently analog, and so analog modulation is important for these. It is clear from Eq. (4.13) that there are two attributes of a bandpass signal that we could think of modulating, namely $A(t)$

---

[3] We will see a second way in Section 4.3.

and $\phi(t)$. In the first case we have amplitude modulation, and in the second, phase or frequency modulation. We will look now at the first of these.

The study of amplitude modulation starts with the Modulation Property of Fourier transforms, which is Property 4 in Table 2.3 and Example 2.5. It states that if $g(t)$ has transform $G(f)$, then the Fourier transform of $g(t) \cos 2\pi f_0 t$ is

$$g(t) \cos 2\pi f_0 t \leftrightarrow \frac{1}{2}[G(f + f_0) + G(f - f_0)] \tag{4.14}$$

The left-hand side is precisely the relationship in Eq. (4.13), if the phase $\phi(t)$ is set to zero. The Modulation Property states that the new spectrum will consist of two replicas of $G(f)$, one centered on $-f_0$ in the negative frequencies and the other on $+f_0$ in the positive frequencies. Taking the product $g(t) \cos 2\pi f_0 t$ thus carries out the most important modulator requirement: Move the baseband signal to a new frequency band.

We need to get a better feeling for what the new signals look like. Figure 4.6 at the top shows a piece, $g(t)$, of a randomly varying waveform that has frequencies spread uniformly through the range -5 to $+5$ kHz. Below it is the same signal, shifted up in frequency by 50 kHz. This is the signal $g(t) \cos 2\pi f_0 t$, and it has frequencies spread through the range 45–55 kHz (as with all real-valued time signals, there is also a mirror-image spectrum in the range -45 to -55 kHz). It is easy to see the influence of a 50 kHz sinusoid in the second picture, but here we must be careful. The signal energy *at* 50 kHz is infinitesimally small. The

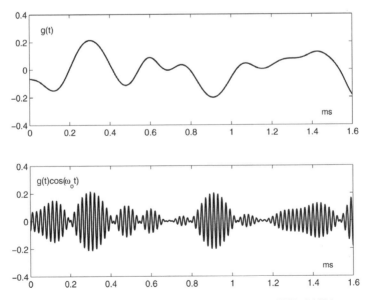

Figure 4.6   A random waveform $f(t)$ having spectrum in the range $[-5 \text{ kHz}, 5 \text{ kHz}]$ compared to the same waveform shifted in frequency to 45–55 kHz

energy in the shifted signal is spread continuously over the whole frequency range, and there are phase variations and other small shifts in what appears to be a 50 kHz sinusoid. Narrowband signals centered on an f_0 look like this. The "carrier" $\cos 2\pi f_0 t$ is not so much a physical component as it is a center frequency position in the bandpass signal.

With this insight, we can look at types of amplitude modulation. There are three main ones. They start with the general formulation

$$s(t) = A[1 + m_{AM}g(t)]\cos 2\pi f_0 t, \qquad g(t) \leq 1 \text{ (Ampl. Modulation)} \qquad (4.15)$$

Here, $g(t)$ is the audio or video signal and we have required that it be normalized so that its peak absolute value is 1. m_{AM} is a positive constant called the modulation index. We can define the three types as follows:

- When m_{AM} lies in the range $0 < m_{AM} < 1$, we have ordinary amplitude modulation, abbreviated henceforth as AM. The principle of AM is that the quantity $1 + m_{AM}g(t)$ must never be negative. Figure 4.7 at the top shows a time domain plot of a 500 Hz cosine $g(t)$ modulating a carrier with $f_0 = 5000$ Hz.[4] Here $A = 1.7$ and $m_{AM} = 0.59$, and it is said that the

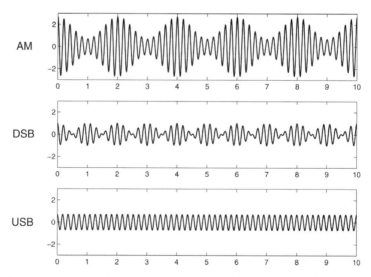

Figure 4.7 Illustration in the time domain of amplitude modulation. A 500 Hz sinusoid modulates a 5000 Hz carrier, using AM, AM-DSB, and AM-SSB. In all three, the power in the information-carrying sidebands is the same. (Time scale in ms)

---

[4] $f_0 = 5000$ Hz is of course not a practical carrier frequency, but the frequencies here are chosen to make the illustration clear. 500 Hz modulating a 1 MHz carrier cannot be printed clearly.

carrier is 59% modulated. Identity 5c in Table 2.2 shows that this signal is

$$s(t) = 1.7[1 + 0.59 \cos 2\pi500t] \cos 2\pi5000t$$
$$= 1.7 \cos 2\pi5000t + 0.5 \cos 2\pi4500t + 0.5 \cos 2\pi5500t \qquad (4.16)$$

Figure 4.8 is a frequency domain picture that shows what happens to the spectrum of a typical audio signal. In ordinary AM, the audio spectrum is shifted up (and down) by f_0. There are actually two components to the signal, a carrier component $A \cos 2\pi f_0 t$ and a modulation component

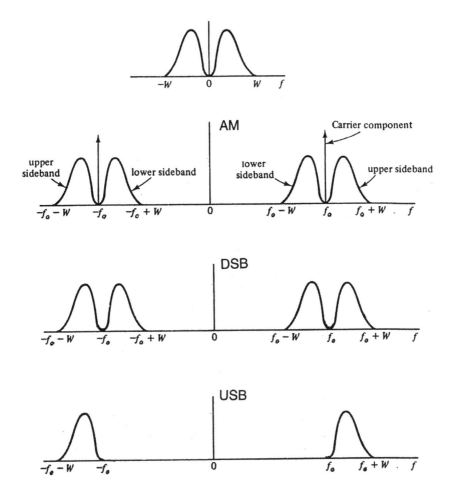

Figure 4.8   Illustration in the frequency domain of amplitude modulation. A typical speech signal (at top) modulates a carrier, using AM, AM-DSB, and AM-SSB. Both positive and negative frequencies are shown

$Am_{AM}g(t) \cos 2\pi f_0 t$. The first is an impulse function in frequency and is shown as an arrow with weight $A/2$.

- When $m_{AM} = 1$ and the "1" in Eq. (4.15) is replaced with 0, we get $s(t) = Ag(t) \cos 2\pi f_0 t$. This is *double-sideband* AM, abbreviated AM-DSB. The time signal in Figure 4.7 is quite different, and appears to have twice the rate of oscillation in its amplitude. This is actually an illusion: When the modulating $g(t) = \cos 2\pi 500t$ changes sign on its second half-cycle, it reverses the sign of the carrier (this is visible under careful examination), and there are in fact only five repeats of the full signal pattern. The signal is given by

$$s(t) = \cos 2\pi 500t \cos 2\pi 5000t = \tfrac{1}{2}\cos 2\pi 4500t + \tfrac{1}{2}\cos 2\pi 5500t \quad (4.17)$$

The audio frequency picture in Figure 4.8 is precisely that predicted by Eq. (4.14), since AM-DSB exactly carries out the Fourier Modulation Property. There is no carrier impulse. There are two replicas of the $g(t)$ spectrum; one, called the lower sideband, is reversed in frequency, and the other is the upper sideband. Both contain the same information, although one contains it frequency-reversed. All of this follows directly from the Modulation Property.

- Since the AM-DSB sidebands contain the same information, we can save spectrum by deleting one of them. What results is called *single-sideband AM*, abbreviated AM-SSB. If the upper one remains, we have upper sideband modulation (AM-USB), otherwise lower sideband (AM-LSB). A way to create SSB is to remove a sideband with an ideal bandpass filter that lets only the desired one through; Figure 4.8 shows the USB case. To obtain a general SSB expression in the time-signal form (4.15) is a good exercise in Fourier techniques but we will skip over it. For the case $g(t) = \cos 2\pi 500t$, the signal is shown in Figure 4.7; by removing the lower sideband in expression (4.17), we get that

$$s(t) = \tfrac{1}{2}\cos 2\pi 5500t \quad (4.18)$$

Some more details about amplitude modulation

It is clear in Figure 4.7 that the AM signal has much larger energy than the other two. This is because of the separate carrier component $1.7 \cos 2\pi 5000t$. The power in this component is not present in AM-DSB and is in fact completely wasted in AM. We can make a simple calculation the power in the AM carrier and sidebands by letting $g(t)$ in Eq. (4.15) be the sinusoid $\cos 2\pi \alpha t$, $\alpha \ll f_0$ and computing the power as

$$\lim_{T \to \infty} \frac{1}{T} \int_0^T s(t)^2 dt \quad (4.19)$$

After some trigonometry (some good exercise!), the result is the expression $\frac{1}{2}A^2 + \frac{1}{4}A^2 m_{AM}^2$. We can write the efficiency of AM, then, as the ratio

$$\mu = \frac{\frac{1}{4}A^2 m_{AM}^2}{\frac{1}{4}A^2 m_{AM}^2 + \frac{1}{2}A^2} = \frac{m_{AM}^2}{m_{AM}^2 + 2} \tag{4.20}$$

Since $m_{AM} \leq 1$, the power efficiency of AM with a sinusoid input cannot exceed $\frac{1}{3}$. Its efficiency in Figure 4.7 is only 14%, since $m_{AM} = 0.59$. The figure is drawn in fact so that all three modulations have the same energy in their information-carrying parts. With AM-DSB and AM-SSB, the efficiency is 100%. Although we will not prove it here, it can be shown[5] that the noise after demodulation is the same for all three methods in the figure, and that it depends only on the power in the sidebands.

With speech, the AM efficiency is even lower than Eq. (4.20) predicts. This is because speech is a less "friendly" waveform that has large isolated positive and negative peaks, and the waveform $m_{AM}g(t)$ must be small most of the time in order that the expression $1 + m_{AM}g(t)$ is never driven negative. Why then is AM commonly used for broadcasting? The answer lies in the simplicity of the receiver (Box 4-2). A circuit that extracts $g(t)$ from the modulated signal is called a *detector*. With ordinary AM, the crucial point is that in the modulated waveform *the amplitude follows $g(t)$*. This is because of the $1 + m_{AM}g(t) > 0$ condition, and it says that we need only make a circuit that somehow follows the size of the radio wave. Such a circuit is called an envelope detector and a simple example appears in Figure 4.9.

BOX 4-2

It is possible literally to build an AM receiver from junk. The natural mineral galena, sometimes found near coal piles, is a crude semiconductor. Capacitors can be made from chewing gum wrappers and inductors from old motor windings. Such "gum wrapper" radios were constructed by prisoners of war during the 1940s. The first radio receivers were hardly better. The only really essential element in a receiver based on Figure 4.9 is the diode, an element that conducts current in one direction only. The effect is to cut off the bottom of radio waveforms like those in Figure 4.7, leaving a waveform that basically follows $g(t)$.

Detectors for DSB and SSB are considerably more sophisticated. They work by shifting the sidebands back down to their original baseband position in the spectrum. An important advantage of SSB transmission is that it takes only half the radio bandwidth of AM or AM-DSB. Sometimes, however, this is a disadvantage. With AM-DSB in a crowded radio band, one sideband is often damaged by interference while the other is not, and an SSB receiver can be used on the one that remains clean. To

---

[5] See the starred references. The proof assumes white Gaussian noise at the front of the receiver and computes the SNR in the audio after detection. For AM, the carrier power is ignored.

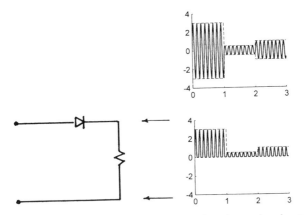

Figure 4.9   Input and output waveforms for a simple envelope detector based on a diode and resistor. The input is a sinusoid, amplitude-modulated by 3, then 0.5 then 1. The short-term average of the output follows this modulation. Note that a short-term average of the input is always zero!

sum up, the choice of an amplitude modulation method is a tradeoff among cost of equipment, power efficiency, and bandwidth. In fact, AM is by far the simplest method, AM-DSB and AM-SSB are much more power efficient, and AM-SSB is twice as bandwidth efficient.

4.2.2   Frequency Modulation

In frequency modulation (FM) we hold constant the amplitude factor $A(t)$ in Eq. (4.13). What is left to modulate is the phase component $\phi(t)$. This is a phase, not a frequency, but the frequency of a signal is *the derivative of its phase*; that is, if a signal passes through 2π radians of phase, we say that a cycle of frequency has elapsed. In a small space of time, we can say that a passage through angle $\Delta\phi$ in Δt seconds is a short-term frequency of $\Delta\phi/\Delta t$. Passing to the limit, we can define the *instantaneous frequency* of a signal to be the derivative of its phase, $d\phi/dt$. If we reverse the thoughts here we get that instantaneous phase is the integral of frequency. We define FM, then, by making the instantaneous frequency proportional to the modulating signal $g(t)$ and writing

$$s(t) = A \cos\left[2\pi f_0 t + m_{\mathrm{FM}} \int_{t_o}^{t} g(\tau)d\tau\right] \qquad \text{(FM Modulation)} \qquad (4.21)$$

where m_{FM} is a constant that scales the frequency swing that occurs, and t_o is when the modulation starts. By differentiating the entire phase of the cosine, we find that the instantaneous frequency of $s(t)$ is $f_0 + m_{\mathrm{FM}}g(t)/2\pi$ (in Hz). As with AM-DSB and AM-SSB, there is no separate carrier component in the signal, and f_0 merely

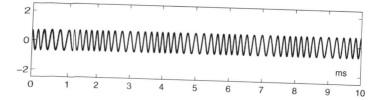

Figure 4.10   Illustration of FM in the time domain. A 500 Hz sinusoid modulates a 5000 Hz carrier, with modulation index $\beta = 2$. (Time scale in ms)

marks the center of the FM frequency swings. The quantity

$$\Delta f = \max_t \{m_{FM}g(t)/2\pi\} \qquad \text{(in Hz)} \tag{4.22}$$

is called the peak frequency deviation.

There are several ways to get a feel for this signal. The first is to set $g(t)$ equal a modulating sinusoid $\cos 2\pi f_m t$ and plot the time domain signal, as we did with AM. The peak frequency deviation is now $\Delta f = m_{FM}/2\pi$ Hz. Figure 4.10 is the plot when $f_m = 500$ Hz, $m_{FM} = 4\pi 500$ and the center frequency is $f_0 = 5000$ Hz.[6] The energy in this FM wave is the same as that in the AM-DSB and AM-SSB waves in Figure 4.7. The FM effect is subtle but clear: There are five rises and falls in the carrier frequency.

A second, more informative, way is to plot the spectrum of such a signal. The result is surprising and is shown in Figure 4.11. An important parameter in the plot is the ratio $\beta \triangleq \Delta f/f_m$, called the *FM modulation index*. It normalizes the frequency deviation to the frequency that causes it. In Figure 4.10, $\beta = 2$. The signal $s(t)$ in Eq. (4.21) now works out to be

$$A\cos[2\pi f_0 t + \beta \sin 2\pi f_m t] = A\cos[2\pi f_0 t + 2\sin 2\pi f_m t]$$

After some serious calculation, the Fourier transform works out to be

$$S(f) = A \sum_{n=-\infty}^{\infty} J_n(\beta)\cos[2\pi(f_0 + nf_m)t] \tag{4.23}$$

in which $J_n(\cdot)$ is a tabulated function called the Bessel function of the first kind of order n.[7] We do not have to worry about the fine details of this formula. The important point is that the single spectral impulse at f_m Hz in the modulating $g(t)$ has spread into an *infinite array* of impulses at $f_0 + nf_m$, $n = 0, \pm 1, \pm 2, \ldots$, in the spectrum of $s(t)$. They are spaced every f_m Hz. Bessel function properties are such that the

---

[6] Here again, f_0 is not a practical center frequency, but is chosen to make the FM effect visible. A practical f_0 would be 10 MHz or more.

[7] A good tabulation appears in the text by Stremler [5].

olds more or less for practical audio and video signals, if we choose
the strong part of the spectrum.

4.4

broadcasting, the peak frequency deviation is limited by law to 75 kHz either
er frequency (150 kHz total positive bandwidth). Normally, the highest audio
kHz. We can imagine that only this tone is transmitted and take this as a worst-
he second form of Carson's Rule states that $2(15 \text{ kHz})(\beta + 1) = 150 \text{ kHz}$,
that the modulation index β would be 4 in such a case. A lower audio frequency
ved to have a bigger β. β plays a crucial role in the signal-to-noise ratio, as we
and it is important to have it as large as possible. What about a more interesting
usic, which is a mixture of many sinusoids? As we saw in Section 3.3, the
es in music are ordinarily in the 500–1500 Hz range, with a rapid drop at
encies. An index for real music cannot be precisely defined, but we can say
usually be in a range 5–20. In broadcasting, typically, m_{FM} in Eq. (4.22) is
such a way that Δf is 75 kHz. This will give the largest possible effective

ave been working with the index β for one more reason: It sets the FM
noise ratio. As with spectrum, the SNR in FM has some surprises for us.
e SNR at the beginning of a receiver as $(S/N)_{\text{in}}$, where S is the signal
d N is the background noise.[9] Similarly, let $(S/N)_{\text{out}}$ be the SNR for the
nted $g(t)$, after the detector circuit. Although we did not go through the
he fact is that for AM-DSB and AM-SSB modulation, $(S/N)_{\text{out}} =$
here is no change in the SNR during the detection process. For FM, the situ-
completely different. The proof is advanced, but we can give the outcome,
r $\beta \geq 1$ is very simple:

$$(S/N)_{\text{out}} \approx \frac{3\beta^2}{2}(S/N)_{\text{in}} \qquad \text{(FM SNR)} \qquad (4.25)$$

his is a remarkable result, which was hardly believed by some when FM was proposed.[10] In Example 4.4, the 15 kHz sinewave test signal will be detected with SNR
that is improved $(3/2)4^2 = 24$ times. In the broadcasting of ordinary voice and
music, an index of more like $\beta = 10$ applies, which leads to an SNR improvement
of 150 times (22 dB).

[9] N is typically caused by thermal noise in the first receiver circuit. A technical but important detail is that N should be measured in the same bandwidth that the signal occupies.

[10] Edwin Armstrong, the main inventor of FM, gave demonstrations of AM and FM transmissions in the 1930s over the same distance, with the same power and carrier frequency. FM sounded much better, but some listeners refused to believe it and accused him of faking the results. Compared to broadcast AM, FM is even better than Eq. (4.25) predicts, since ordinary AM wastes most of its power sending a separate carrier.

impulse weights $J_n(\beta)$ are symmetric abo.
certain value of nf_m. The values of the we
they are shown for several indices in Figure

Fortunately, it is not necessary to involve c
overall behavior is summed up in a way called
mate estimate of bandwidth given by

sigls. But it
freencies in

EMPLE

$$W_{RF} \approx 2(\Delta f + f_m) \qquad \text{(Devia}$$
$$= 2f_m(1 + \beta) \qquad \text{(Index }$$

Inary FM
sine cen
fry is 1:
chal. T
plies
allo
xt,
r
ch
u

Here W_{RF} is the effective bandwidth of the modulate
frequencies; the true bandwidth is infinite in theor
width includes about 99% of the signal power. The Rul
about twice the peak frequency deviation Δf (for large ∠
twice $f_m\beta$ (when β is significant).

Unfortunately, FM is a nonlinear modulation, and this n
spectrum of $g(t)$ into sinusoids and using Fourier analysis do
spectrum of the modulated signal; that is, the superposition pr
does not hold.[8] Technically, Carson's Rule applies only to sir

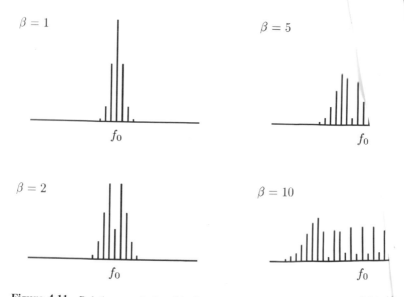

$\beta = 1$

$\beta = 5$

f_0

f_0

$\beta = 2$

$\beta = 10$

f_0

f_0

Figure 4.11   Relative magnitudes of the frequency impulses in an FM signal modulated I
when the modulation index is $\beta = 1, 2, 5, 10$

---

[8] Amplitude modulations are linear. This means that if $g_1(t)$ and $g_2(t)$ modulate to $s_1(t)$ and ,
respectively, then $ag_1(t) + bg_2(t)$ modulates to $as_1(t) + bs_2(t)$. When this property is combine
linearity of the Fourier transform, the spectrum of a complicated $g(t)$ after modulation can be f
by adding sinewave components. This is not true for FM.

As payment for this huge SNR improvement, we must "spend" more channel bandwidth, about a factor $\beta+1$ more, compared to AM or AM-DSB. What is happening here is an example of an important principle in communication theory called *power–bandwidth exchange*. The principle states that power and bandwidth may be exchanged for each other, given a fixed quality of the demodulated signal. As an example, we can compare sending a signal $g(t)$ with bandwidth 5 kHz by AM-DSB and FM. AM-DSB achieves a certain $(S/N)_{out}$ with a 10 kHz modulated signal bandwidth; alternately, FM with $\beta = 10$ consumes about 110 kHz bandwidth, but achieves $(S/N)_{out}$ with 150 times less power. An 11-fold bandwidth is exchanged for 150 times less power. The principle here applies not only to FM but to many other transmission methods. In the next section we look at digital transmission methods, and these too exemplify the principle. It appears also in Shannon's theory in Chapter 5.

In a real transmission or storage system, bandwidth and power each have a cost associated with them. Since bandwidth and power can be traded for each other, part of choosing a good modulation scheme is minimizing their total cost.

4.3 DIGITAL MODULATION

Analog modulation is easy to think about because voice and video analog waveforms occur naturally and in carrier modulation they simply drive the phase or amplitude of a sinusoid. Digital modulation is more subtle, because it transmits symbols. The information source needs first to be converted into these, and we cannot tell whether the source is voice or a bank statement just by looking at the signal. But an advantage is that all sources can now be carried in the same way.

In digital transmission, each symbol gets a T-second piece of time. The rate of transmission is $R_t = 1/T$ symbols/second. T is called the *symbol interval*. Each symbol also gets a piece of energy E_s (in joules), called the *symbol energy*. In most of this section we will take the symbols as binary. The usual symbol set, $\{0, 1\}$, is not very convenient when we study modulation, and it works better to take the set $\{+1, -1\}$ instead. By convention, the mapping between these two sets is taken as $0 \rightarrow +1$, $1 \rightarrow -1$. The symbols $\{0, 1\}$ are, after all, just mathematical abstractions, and could just as well take any other names, such as P and Q. The values $\{+1, -1\}$ will take on physical meaning in what follows; for example, they may represent voltages. The ideas in this section are easiest to explain in this binary case, but nonbinary transmission with 4, 8, 16,..., values is becoming increasingly important, and we will show at the end how the binary ideas extend to such cases.

Somehow, the symbol stream must be converted to a waveform, one whose bandwidth and power are in keeping with the medium through which the signal will go. The most common way is to let each symbol be carried by a pulse waveform $v(t)$. We will first consider the so-called baseband case, where the collection of pulses is actually what is sent; then, just as earlier in the chapter, we will look at how to create a carrier transmission, in which the signal spectrum is moved up to a new center frequency f_0.

To construct the baseband signal, let the nth symbol value be a_n. The pulse that carries it is centered at time nT and is multiplied by the symbol value a_n, so we write it as $a_n v(t - nT)$. The entire sequence of pulses can be written as

$$s(t) = \sqrt{E_s} \sum_n a_n v(t - nT) \tag{4.26}$$

where the index n runs over all the symbols. The factor $\sqrt{E_s}$ scales up the energy of the transmission to E_s per symbol. This kind of scheme is called *linear digital modulation*, after the fact that $s(t)$ is just a linear sum of all the time-shifted pulses.

Many pulse shapes are possible, and Figure 4.12 shows a few basic ones. An obvious choice is the simple square pulse, defined as $(1/\sqrt{T})\,\mathrm{rect}(t/T)$, which is function (h) in the Fourier transform pair list in Section 2.3 time-scaled by $1/T$. This pulse will serve us well to illustrate how digital transmission works, but it has a serious disadvantage in practical use: Its bandwidth is large. Any time-limited pulse has infinite bandwidth (see Section 2.4), but the square pulse is especially unpleasant. A substantial part of its energy lies outside the main spectral lobe.

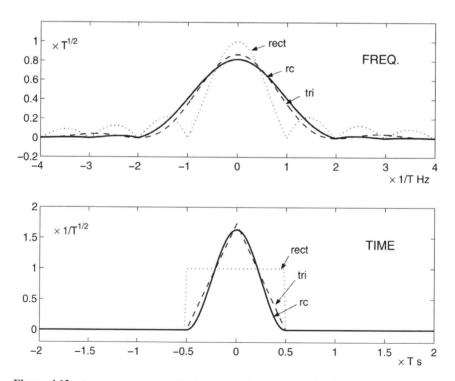

Figure 4.12   Some basic digital modulation pulses $v(t)$ (below) and their Fourier transforms $V(f)$ (above): The rectangular (rect), triangular (tri), and raised-cosine (rc) pulses

The other pulses in Figure 4.12 have a more compact spectrum. They are the triangle

$$v(t) = \begin{cases} \sqrt{3/T}(1 - 2|t|/T), & |t| < T/2 \\ 0, & |t| \geq T/2 \end{cases} \tag{4.27}$$

(compare to function (j) in the Section 2.3 list); and the raised-cosine (RC), which is a piece of cosine raised up to give

$$v(t) = \begin{cases} \sqrt{2/3T}(1 + \cos 2\pi t/T), & |t| < T/2 \\ 0, & |t| \geq T/2 \end{cases} \tag{4.28}$$

The coefficients $\sqrt{1/T}$, $\sqrt{3/T}$, and $\sqrt{2/3T}$ in these pulses are required so that all three have unit energy. This will make the symbol energy in Eq. (4.26) equal to E_s, no matter which pulse is used. We can string together any number of pulses $a_0v(t)$, $a_1v(t - T)$, $a_2v(t - 2T)$, ... to form a *pulse train*.

EXAMPLE 4.5

The pulse train generated by data $+1, +1, -1, +1$ is shown in Figure 4.13 for the rect and RC cases. Here $T = 1$ and the train has unit energy per symbol. Multiplying the train by $\sqrt{E_s}$ raises the energy to E_s per symbol. The Fourier transform of the whole train in the figure has precisely four times the energy of a single rect and RC pulse energy. Can you prove this?

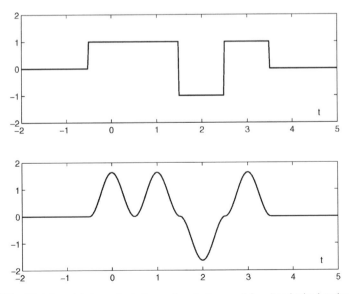

Figure 4.13   Digital modulation pulse trains made out of square (above) and raised-cosine pulses (below), when the symbol interval is $T = 1$. Both trains carry the data $+1, +1, -1, +1$

The power in the signal $s(t)$ is $(E_s \text{ joules/symbol})/(T \text{ s/symbol}) = E_s/T = E_sR$ watts. Power thus grows with the rate of symbol transmission. What is the bandwidth of $s(t)$? This is important because all transmission media have a bandwidth, and the signal should not exceed this. The standard telephone channel has a bandwidth of about 3.4 kHz, for example, and $s(t)$ should not be wider. Conversely, if $s(t)$ turns out to have a narrower bandwidth, we can think about sending faster. A different example is the coaxial cable that delivers television signals. A 1 km length of it might tolerate a signal with bandwidth as wide as 300 MHz. Now we can shorten T and send much faster. How much faster?

We use the Fourier transform as a tool to answer this question. Roughly speaking, the bandwidth of our signal is $1/T$ Hz; that is, it is the reciprocal of the time duration. This is the rough measure that was given in Section 2.4. It states that a digital transmission at a 1 megasymbol/s rate, for which $T = 10^{-6}$, will have a bandwidth of 1 MHz, more or less. Similarly, a transmission at a gigasymbol rate will have bandwidth around 1 GHz. This relationship is inescapable, but the transform will allow us to refine it.

We first need a result from Fourier theory about signals $s(t)$ that are a superposition of time-shifted $v(t)$ pulses. The result says that the transform of $s(t)$ has the same magnitude spectrum as $v(t)$ does; that is, $S(f) = V(f)$, to within a constant. We will not prove it here, but the proof is not difficult. Thus, we can concentrate on only $V(f)$.

The magnitude transforms of the three $v(t)$ pulses are also shown in Figure 4.12. It is worth taking a careful look at these transforms, because some important properties can be observed. The main part of all three spectra lies in the frequency range $[-1/T, 1/T]$ Hz. This happens because all three pulses last roughly T seconds; it is a statement of the "$1/T$" rule just given. A closer look, however, shows some differences in the compactness of the spectrum. The triangular pulse spectrum dies down faster at the edges of the spectrum than the rect spectrum, and the RC spectrum faster still. This happens because the triangle pulse is "smoother" than the rect, and the RC pulse is smoother still; the rect pulse has large jumps in it, the triangle has none but it has sharp corners, and the raised-cosine has neither jumps nor corners. Increasing the smoothness reduces the outer spectrum.

These outer parts of a spectrum are called its *sidelobes*. The triangle sidelobes are much smaller than the rect ones, and the RC spectrum seems to have none at all (a few are visible if the plot is magnified). During a radio transmission of our digital waveform, there may be other transmissions to the left and right of our main spectrum, and these will suffer interference unless the sidelobes are small. Although the sidelobes seem small in the figure, our transmission will devastate another nearby user who tries to communicate in the next channel with a partner who is far away.

Because of its relationship to bandwidth conservation and interference, the design of pulse shapes is an important part of digital communication. For a simple transmitter and receiver, it is also important that separate pulses act in a sense independently of each other, each in their own symbol interval, as they do in Figure 4.13. There is a theorem in communication theory, related to the sampling theorem of Section 2.4, that states as follows:

The narrowest bandwidth of any pulses that act independently is [−1/2T, 1/2T] Hz, where T is the symbol interval.

The proof of this and a full discussion about what is meant by "independent" pulses[11] is beyond our scope, but it can be found in the starred references. The modern theory of pulses began with two papers by Nyquist [10, 11] in the 1920s.

4.3.1 Detecting Pulse Waveforms

The signal $s(t)$ from Eq. (4.26) arrives at the receiver and passes through the first parts of it to a detector circuit, whose job it is to extract the data symbols a_n from the pulse waveform. By the time $s(t)$ reaches the detector, it may be warped, scaled up or down, full of echoes and noisy. Dealing with all these distortions is a challenging engineering problem. We can look at the most basic signal distortion, which is white noise added to the signal. As introduced in Section 4.1, white thermal noise is always present in received signals and it sets a basic limit on communication. A major theory exists about this. It derives detectors that minimize the probability of error in deciding a data symbol, when white noise has been added to the signal. The theory is quite complicated, and it derives several equivalent optimal detectors. The simplest of these to think about is based on *correlation*.

We will now describe the detector based on the correlation idea. To keep matters as simple as possible, take the binary data case and the pulse at time 0 that carries data symbol $a_0 = \pm 1$. Then what is sent is $s(t) = \sqrt{E_s}a_0 v(t)$ and what is received, $r(t)$, is either $+\sqrt{E_s}v(t)$ plus noise or $-\sqrt{E_s}v(t)$ plus noise; we do not know which. Note here that it is always possible to amplify the received signal so that $v(t)$ is again scaled by $\sqrt{E_s}$, or for that matter, simply 1. The noise will also be amplified; what matters is the ratio of the desired signal to the noise, not their actual values. Taking the correlation between $s(t)$ and $r(t)$ means finding out how much alike they are; mathematically, it means evaluating the integral $\int s(t)r(t)dt$. A large positive outcome means that $s(t)$ and $r(t)$ are positively correlated and that $r(t)$ probably came from $s(t)$, a value near zero means that they have little relation to each other, and a strong negative value means they are much alike, but one is the negative of the other. Actually, we do not need to measure precisely how alike signals are, but only compute which possibility, $+\sqrt{E_s}v(t)$ or $-\sqrt{E_s}v(t)$, is *more* like $r(t)$. This means comparing the two integrals

$$I_+ = +\int r(t)\sqrt{E_s}v(t)\,dt$$

$$I_- = -\int r(t)\sqrt{E_s}v(t)\,dt \tag{4.29}$$

---

[11] Independently acting pulses are not *required* in digital transmission; they only make the signal processing easier. For transmission in bandwidth narrower than $[−1/2T, 1/2T]$ Hz, the theorem says that dependent pulses are necessary, and such pulses are used in advanced narrowband schemes.

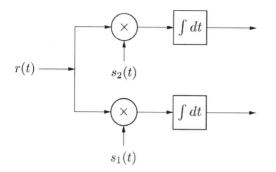

Figure 4.14 Implementation of the binary correlation receiver as two multipliers and two integrators. $r(t)$ is received; $s_1(t)$ and $s_2(t)$ are the two possible transmissions. The receiver asks which output is bigger.

If $I_+ > I_-$, then we decide a_0 is $+1$, because this is the more likely value; otherwise, we decide a_0 is -1.

Figure 4.14 shows a circuit that computes Eq. (4.29). There are many ways to implement the multiplier and integration blocks; for example, the integrator is a capacitor in an analog circuit and a summation in a microprocessor implementation. Signals $s_1(t)$ and $s_2(t)$ are $+\sqrt{E_s}v(t)$ and $-\sqrt{E_s}v(t)$. The receiver observes which of the right-hand outputs is larger.

A particular example of correlation detection is shown in Figure 4.15. The left picture is a transmitted triangle pulse (here $\sqrt{E_s}$ is set to 1 and the pulse is the one centered at time 0). White noise adds to the pulse, and it arrives as $r(t)$ on the right. The triangle is hardly visible to us, but the correlation detector can see it clearly. It performs the operation (T is 1)

$$\int_{-\frac{1}{2}}^{\frac{1}{2}} r(t)v(t)\, dt$$

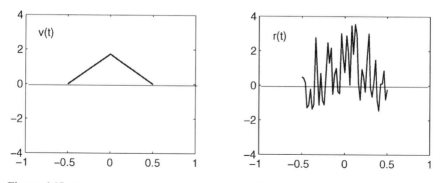

Figure 4.15 Illustration of correlation detection of a positive triangle pulse $v(t)$. White noise is added to produce the received signal $r(t)$. The correlation is $0.84 > 0$, indicating that the sent pulse was most likely positive.

and finds that $I_+ = 0.84$ and $I_- = -0.84$. This means that the transmitted pulse was most likely a positive triangle. When the next pulse arrives, the operation repeats, but this time the integration is over the interval $[T/2, 3T/2]$. Each decision is independent. For independent pulses and white noise, no receiver has a lower probability of error than this one.

By using probability theory, it is possible to derive an expression for the correlation detector error probability under white noise conditions. The details are too complicated for us now, but the mathematical outcome is simple. It is in terms of E_s and the *noise spectral density*, N_0, in watts per positive Hz. N_0 is simply the power in the noise spectrum measured per Hz of bandwidth. Since the noise is white thermal noise, N_0 does not vary over the band and is a constant. N_0 can be computed from Nyquist's theory or simply measured with an instrument.

According to noise theory, the total noise power in watts is $N = kT_K B_m$, as given by Eq. (4.7). B_m is the bandwidth over which the measurement is made, counting positive frequencies only. N_0 is therefore $N/B_m = kT_K$.[12] The probability depends only on the *ratio* E_s/N_0 and is given by the integral

$$P_e = \frac{1}{\sqrt{2\pi}} \int_{\sqrt{2E_s/N_0}}^{\infty} e^{-x^2/2} \, dx \triangleq Q(\sqrt{2E_s/N_0}) \tag{4.30}$$

The integral here appears often in physics and is tabulated as the so-called error function. A convenient approximation to Q is given by

$$Q(y) \leq \tfrac{1}{2} e^{-y^2/2}, \qquad y \geq 0 \tag{4.31}$$

Thus $P_e \leq \tfrac{1}{2} e^{-E_s/N_0}$.

Since so many digital modulations obey Eq. (4.30), it is useful to have a plot of it, and this is given in Figure 4.16. Note that both axes are logarithmic, the horizontal axis so because it is in dB. This is the usual way error plots are done in digital communication. As an example a ratio $E_s/N_0 = 5$, which is 7 dB, leads to $P_e \approx 7 \times 10^{-4}$.

Digital communication theory derives detectors for other kinds of noise, for pulses that overlap each other in complicated ways, and for modulation methods that are not linear superpositions of pulses. They do not exactly perform correlation, but they perform similar operations. The correlation principle is a strong one: It is intuitively pleasing, and if it is not precisely optimal it is usually close to it. Most digital detectors use some variant of it.

---

[12] For example, in Eq. (4.10), where $T_K = 20$ K, N_0 is $(1.38 \times 10^{-23} \text{ J/K})(20 \text{ K}) = 2.8 \times 10^{-22}$ W/Hz. Note that N_0 assumes that all calculations are referenced to positive frequencies.

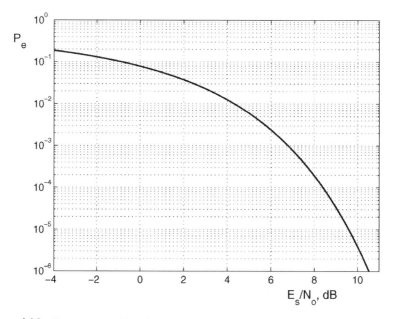

Figure 4.16   The error probability of binary signaling with independent pulses, as a function of E_s/N_0 (horizontal scale in decibels). For QPSK, use $E_s/2$ in place of E_s

4.3.2   Carrier Digital Modulation

Baseband digital transmission signals can be shifted up to a new center frequency. The resulting signal is a carrier digital modulation. Just as with amplitude modulation in Section 4.2, the Fourier Modulation Property (4.14) is the key, but now $g(t)$ is the baseband digital modulation signal. In a *linear* carrier digital modulation, $g(t)$ is the pulse train waveform in Eq. (4.26). The result is the new signal

$$s(t) = \sqrt{2E_s}\left(\sum a_n v(t - nT)\right)\cos 2\pi f_0 t \qquad (4.32)$$

When a_n is binary and $v(t)$ is a simple pulse like those in Figure 4.12, this kind of signaling is called binary phase-shift keying, or BPSK. The name comes from the fact that only two signals can be sent in a symbol interval, and they are sinusoids $180°$ apart in phase. If we ignore constants and look at the interval centered on 0, the signals are $+v(t)\cos 2\pi f_0 t$ and $-v(t)\cos 2\pi f_0 t$. The spectrum is the same as the ones in Figure 4.12, except that it is centered on f_0 Hz instead of 0 Hz. Note, however, that both the negative and positive frequencies in the baseband plot become positive frequencies in the BPSK spectrum; this means that the BPSK bandwidth is about $2/T$ Hz, instead of the $1/T$ that applied before. E_s is the symbol energy, as before. The error probability of BPSK is exactly the same as that of baseband binary transmission.

In carrier modulation, it is actually possible to send *two* such signals independently in the same bandwidth. The reason is the fact that

$$\int_{-T/2}^{T/2} g_1(t) \cos 2\pi f_0 t \; g_2(t) \sin 2\pi f_0 t \; dt = 0 \tag{4.33}$$

where $g_1(t)$ and $g_2(t)$ are baseband signals.[13] Actually, the result is strictly true only in the limit $f_0 \to \infty$, but the integral is approximately zero for practical f_0 and T. Communication engineers say that the two signals $g_1(t) \cos 2\pi f_0 t$ and $g_2(t) \sin 2\pi f_0 t$ are orthogonal,[14] or equivalently, that they are in quadrature; both words mean that they are at right angles to each other. The practical outcome is that each is invisible during the detection of the other.

We will demonstrate the last statement shortly, but first we will define a two-component signal that takes advantage it. A quadrature phase-shift keying (QPSK) signal is one with the form

$$s(t) = \sqrt{2E_s} \left(\sum a_n^I v(t - nT) \right) \cos 2\pi f_0 t$$

$$- \sqrt{2E_s} \left(\sum a_n^Q v(t - nT) \right) \sin 2\pi f_0 t \tag{4.34}$$

in which the data-bearing variables a_n^I and a_n^Q are binary. The two data streams are *independent* and the superscripts will help keep them apart.[15] If the a_n^I and a_n^Q are taken as the values $\pm 1/\sqrt{2}$, E_s is the energy per symbol; this can be demonstrated by showing that $\int s(t)^2 \, dt \to NE_s$ as $f_0 \to \infty$, where N is the number of symbols. Each of the a_n^I and a_n^Q in QPSK has the same error probability as the a_n in BPSK, if the energy per a is the same; that is, the QPSK case has the probability in Eqs. (4.30) and (4.31) if $E_s/2$ is substituted for the E_s there. The advantage of QPSK is that it carries twice as many data bits in the same bandwidth as BPSK. This is so important that BPSK is seldom used.

An example of a four-symbol QPSK signal based on square pulses is shown in Figure 4.17. Note how the two orthogonal carrier signals add to form the total QPSK signal. The square sinusoidal bursts make the QPSK operation easier to follow, but just as with baseband signaling, they are seldom used in practice because they produce large spectral sidelobes.

---

[13] What baseband really means here is that the bandwidth of both g functions is much less than f_0. The location of the T-interval in time makes no difference, so long as $T \gg 1/f_0$.

[14] More about orthogonality can be found in Section 2.4.

[15] The notation I and Q is traditional and refers to the names in-phase and quadrature, respectively, for the first and second terms in Eq. (4.34). The phase reference is taken as the cos phase, and the sin is in quadrature.

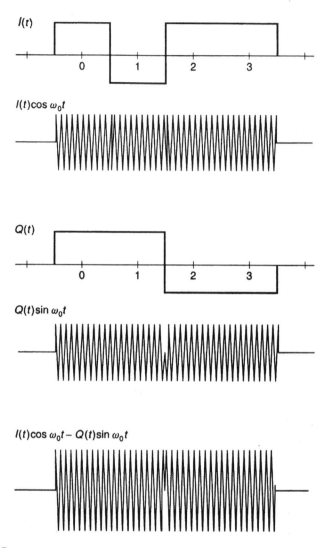

Figure 4.17   Four-symbol BPSK and QPSK signals, based on square pulses. The top signal alone is BPSK; add the top to the second to produce QPSK. Data values are $a_n^I = (1/\sqrt{2}) \times \{+1, -1, +1, +1\}$ and $a_n^Q = (1/\sqrt{2}) \times \{+1, +1, -1, -1\}$. $\omega_0 = 2\pi f_0$. *Source: Digital Transmission Engineering* [7], copyright 1998, IEEE Press, used with permission

Optimal detection of QPSK signals is done with the correlator detector or by several other methods that are equivalent. We can take a look at the same simple correlation procedure that we used before with baseband pulse trains. In QPSK transmission, there are several ways to apply the correlation idea, and we will choose one that illustrates the sine–cosine orthogonality. A symbol's worth of

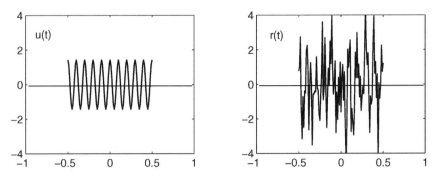

Figure 4.18 Illustration of correlation detection of a positive unit-energy square pulse $+ \text{rect}(t)$ $\cos 2\pi 10t$. White noise is added to produce the received signal $r(t)$. The cosine is completely invisible in the noise yet the correlation of the two yields $1.04 > 0$, indicating that the sent pulse is very likely the positive one.

received signal can take four forms, neglecting constants that are common to all:

$$+ v(t) \cos 2\pi f_0 t + v(t) \sin 2\pi f_0 t = [u(t)]$$
$$- v(t) \cos 2\pi f_0 t + v(t) \sin 2\pi f_0 t$$
$$- v(t) \cos 2\pi f_0 t - v(t) \sin 2\pi f_0 t$$
$$+ v(t) \cos 2\pi f_0 t - v(t) \sin 2\pi f_0 t$$

Let the transmitted signal $s(t)$ be the first of these, which we will denote $u(t)$; let $T = 1$ and take the pulse v as the one centered at 0, which occupies $[-T/2, T/2]$. Add severe white noise to $u(t)$. We can separately detect the data-bearing value a_n^I by correlating $r(t)$ against the two signals $+v(t) \cos 2\pi f_0 t$ and $-v(t) \cos 2\pi f_0 t$. No matter which $s(t)$ is sent, the correlation against the sine terms in $s(t)$ will be virtually zero because of orthogonality; the entire value of $\int r(t)s(t) \, dt$ will come from the remaining parts of $s(t)$, which are $\pm v(t) \cos 2\pi f_0 t$ plus noise. Figure 4.18 shows the cosine part of $u(t)$ on the left, scaled so that it has unit energy, and the cosine plus noise on the right. The baseband pulse $v(t)$ is $\text{rect}(t)$. The cosine is completely obscured in the received signal (the noise here has about twice the energy of the signal). Yet the correlation produces a perfectly clear outcome: The value of $\int r(t)u(t) \, dt$ is 1.04; when $u(t)$ is set to $-u(t)$, the correlation is -1.04. The highest correlation occurs when a_0^I takes its plus value, and so the detector decides this one. By correlating $r(t)$ instead against $+v(t) \sin 2\pi f_0 t$ and $-v(t) \sin 2\pi f_0 t$, we can decide the other data value, a_0^O.

EXAMPLE 4.6

For an example of QPSK in action, we can revisit the Mars communication of Example 4.2 and look more carefully at the bandwidth and error probability. The Mars link ran at 5 Mbit/s, which means that the QPSK symbol time is $T = (2 \text{ bit/symbol})/(5 \text{ Mbit/s}) = 4 \times 10^{-7} \text{ s/}$

symbol. The exact spectrum of the transmission depends on the transform of the baseband pulse $v(t)$, and some of these are given in Figure 4.12. Counting positive frequencies, the spectrum is very roughly twice $1/T$, or about 5 MHz. For a more precise picture, we scale the figure by 2.5×10^6 and change its center frequency to f_0, which was 8.2 GHz in Example 4.2. As an example of this, we can take $\text{rect}(t/T)$ transmission and define the bandwidth to include the main part of the spectrum plus the first sidelobes; from Figure 4.12, this means a bandwidth of $2(2/T) = 10$ MHz, centered on 8.2 GHz, which is the band [8.195, 8.205] GHz. Next, we estimate the probability of bit error. In order to use Figure 4.16, we need the energy per symbol E_s and the noise density N_0. The received power in Example 4.2 was 8.2×10^{-15} W. This is spread over 2.5 million QPSK symbols per second, and so $E_s = (8.2 \times 10^{-15})/(2.5 \times 10^6) = 3.3 \times 10^{-21}$ J/symbol. The noise density depends on the Kelvin temperature of the receiver in Example 4.2, and this was 20 K. As justified earlier in the section, $N_0 = kT_K$, where k is Boltzmann's constant and T_K is temperature. This formula gives $N_0 = (1.38 \times 10^{-23})(20) = 2.8 \times 10^{-22}$ W/Hz. The value to be used with Figure 4.16 to find the QPSK error probability is $(E_s/2)/N_0$, which is 5.9. This is 7.7 dB, which corresponds to a probability of somewhat above 10^{-4} in Figure 4.16. The precise value can be found from Eq. (4.30): It is 3.0×10^{-4}.

4.3.3 Nonbinary Digital Modulation

If a_n^I and a_n^Q take more than two values, more bits per symbol time can be sent with linear modulations of the type in Eq. (4.34). For example, if both take values in the set $\{-3, -1, +1, +3\}$, then there are $4 \times 4 = 16$ different transmissions of the type (a_n^I, a_n^Q), and the modulation carries $\log_2 16 = 4$ bits/symbol. The values (a_n^I, a_n^Q) scale the two baseband $v(t)$ pulses in Eq. (4.34). This kind of transmission, with equally spaced values in two dimensions, is called quadrature amplitude modulation (QAM). Such QAMs with 64 pairs (the set $\{\pm 5, \pm 3, \pm 1\}$), 256 pairs (set $\{\pm 7, \pm 5, \pm 3, \pm 1\}$), or even more are used in telephone line computer modems.

Figure 4.19 shows the case of PSK with 8 phases and an I-Q modulation called 16 QAM, which has 16 signals. The signals (a_n^I, a_n^Q) are represented by points in the plane. A picture like this is called a *signal constellation*.

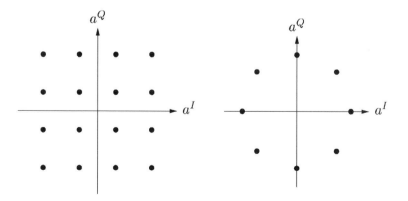

Figure 4.19   16-ary QAM and 8-PSK signal constellations

Quadrature amplitude modulation transmission is important because channel bandwidth is often much harder to get than signal power, and QAMs with 16, 64, and 256 points carry 2, 3, and 4 times as many data bits per Hz of bandwidth as QPSK. The detector for QAM is another variant of the correlator detector. Its probability of error is beyond our scope here, but the approach is similar to that for BPSK and QPSK. It is worth pointing out that QAM takes rapidly more energy per data bit as the number of points grows. At a fixed error rate, it can be shown that each increase by 4 in the number of points leads to a 4-fold increase in the energy per bit.[16] Here we see another example of the power–bandwidth exchange principle first introduced in Section 4.2. With analog FM, a wider bandwidth is exchanged for a much lower power requirement. With QAM, it is the opposite; bandwidth is saved, but much higher energy is needed.

What we have covered in this section accounts for many but not all digital modulation methods. Any carrier digital modulation can be expressed in the form

$$s(t) = \sqrt{2E_s}I(t)\cos 2\pi f_0 t - \sqrt{2E_s}Q(t)\sin 2\pi f_0 t; \qquad (4.35)$$

that is, as two baseband low frequency signals $I(t)$ and $Q(t)$ multiplying sin and cos, respectively. This form can in fact express any bandpass signal, not just a digital modulation. $I(t)$ and $Q(t)$ may be recovered from Eq. (4.35) through multiplication by $\cos 2\pi f_0 t$ and $\sin 2\pi f_0 t$, respectively. We will use this fact in the next section. For example, $s(t)\cos 2\pi f_0 t$ yields

$$\sqrt{E_s/2}I(t) + \sqrt{E_s/2}I(t)\cos 4\pi f_0 t - \sqrt{E_s/2}Q(t)\sin 4\pi f_0 t$$

(use Table 2.2). The first term is the scaled lowpass signal $I(t)$; the last two terms are high in the spectrum centered around frequency $2f_0$ and can be easily filtered away.

Some linear modulations employ pulses that overlap each other and do not act independently. This is in fact a necessity in very narrowband transmission. Other schemes have $I(t)$ and $Q(t)$ but do not work by superposing pulses. In still others $I(t)$ and $Q(t)$ are not independent of each other.

4.4 FM STEREO, TELEVISION, AND A LITTLE ABOUT ELECTRONICS

To bring the modulation story to a close, we will look at two more complicated information transmission systems that most of us experience every day, namely television and FM stereo. Both of these carry more than one kind of information at once, and they do it by combining several of the methods in the previous sections. The section will end with a brief discussion of radio electronics.

---

[16] See the starred references, and especially ref. [7], Section 3.5.

4.4.1 FM Stereo

Ordinary FM stereo broadcasting must transmit two information streams, the left and right channels of stereo sound. It does this by combining AM-DSB modulation with frequency modulation. First, some audio signal processing is required. The left and right stereo channels (call them L and R) are added to form an L + R signal and subtracted to form an L − R signal, and all signals are limited to a 15 kHz bandwidth. Next, the L − R signal double-sideband modulates a 38 kHz carrier, a process that moves it up to the frequency range 23–53 kHz. The 38 kHz sinusoid is called a subcarrier. The signal spectrum is shown in its new position in Figure 4.20. To the DSB signal is added the L + R signal, and finally, a small 19 kHz sinusoid cos 2π19000t called the pilot. The figure shows all three of these. It is the *combination* signal that is FM-modulated and transmitted by radio. The center frequency of this modulation lies in the range 88 – 108 MHz in ordinary broadcasting.

At the receiver, the double modulation process is reversed. First, the Figure 4.20 signal is recreated by FM demodulation. By means of filters, the L + R and the DSB L − R signal are separated from each other: A filter that passes only 0–15 kHz creates the L + R signal and another that passes only 23–53 kHz puts out the DSB L − R signal. Then an AM-DSB demodulator moves the L − R signal back down so that it is centered at 0 Hz. Forming the sum and difference of the two baseband signals gives the audio L and R signals: Adding L + R to L − R gives twice the left signal 2L and subtracting L − R from L + R gives 2R.

We can look more closely at this system and see some of the subtleties in its design. The 19 kHz pilot signal is sent along in order to help the receiver with its DSB demodulation. After the FM demodulation, the receiver filters out the 19 kHz sinusoid, and using a special circuit, it precisely doubles the sinusoid frequency in order to reproduce the 38 kHz subcarrier. With that in hand, the DSB demodulator can move the L − R signal precisely back to center frequency zero. Another aspect of the design is its *compatibility* with monaural FM transmission. By filtering away all but the L + R signal, a receiver ignores the stereo nature of the transmission and reproduces monaural audio. A good reason to do this is that

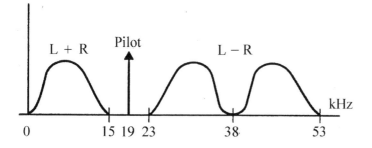

Figure 4.20   The FM stereo signal, prior to FM modulation, showing the sum and difference audio signals plus the DSB pilot. Only positive spectrum frequencies are shown

FM stereo does not work very well with weak radio signals. One cause is that the DSB L − R signal sits at high frequencies before the FM modulation, and it therefore has an effective modulation index β that is small; consequently, its SNR is poor. In any case, noise is more irritating to the ear during stereo reproduction than during monaural. What all this adds up to is that it is better to switch the receiver over to monaural reproduction during weak signal periods. If they are brief, the listener hardly notices, especially in a car or some other marginal environment.

The subchannel idea in FM stereo, whereby several information subchannels are stacked one above the other in the spectrum, can be used to stack up many signals. This is called *frequency division multiplexing*. It is common, for example, to stack as many as 24 analog telephone channels this way, so that all can travel on the same physical wire.

4.4.2 Television

Like FM stereo, television employs several modulation techniques in order to carry multiple signals. Now, however, there are at least six information streams to send, and every modulation method discussed in Sections 4.2 and 4.3 will be used in some way. There are actually many levels of complexity to color television and we can touch on only the main points. The next level of detail appears in the starred references, and particularly, in refs [3, 4].

We introduced video signals in Section 3.5. Video consists of a number of frames per second, either 25 or 30, with each frame broken down into either 525 or 625 scan lines. The intensity of red, green, and blue light along each line is given by three functions of time, $r(t)$, $g(t)$, and $b(t)$, and as given in Eq. (3.7), these are combined according to $y(t) = 0.30r(t) + 0.59g(t) + 0.11b(t)$ into the total brightness, or "luminance," signal $y(t)$. An ordinary video signal like this has a bandwidth of about 4 MHz. In addition to $y(t)$, color information must be transmitted, and this is carried by the same method as the L − R information in FM stereo. The television sound is a separate FM transmission placed just above the video transmission. This is the overall organization of the TV transmission. The details are carried out according to one of three world standards: NTSC (North and South America and Japan), SECAM (France and former USSR), and PAL (remainder of the world).[17] Some details about these systems appear in Table 4.2.

Now we can look at how several modulation methods are combined in order to carry the complete transmission. Figure 4.21a shows the location in the spectrum of the various component signals. The luminance $y(t)$ is the core signal. If it were transmitted by AM or AM-DSB, it would occupy too much bandwidth, as much as 12 MHz. Therefore, a variant of upper sideband modulation is employed. To an AM-USB signal is added a carrier (called the picture carrier, at f_P Hz) and a small part of the lower sideband, features that make the detection easier while keeping

---

[17] The abbreviations stand for National Television System Committee (the organization in the United States that developed the system in the 1940s and 1950s), *Sequential Couleur à Mémoire*, and Phase Alternating Line (a reference to the phase relationship between adjacent lines).

Table 4.2   Characteristics of the NTSC, PAL, and SECAM television standards

	NTSC	PAL	SECAM
Lines/frame	525	625	625
Frames/s	30	25	25
Lines/s	15,750	15,625	15,625
Video bandwidth (MHz)	4.2	5.0	6.0
Channel width (MHz)	6	7	8
Audio	FM	FM	FM[a]
Color subcarrier (MHz)	3.58	4.43	4.43
Compatible with B&W?	yes	no	no

[a] AM in France.

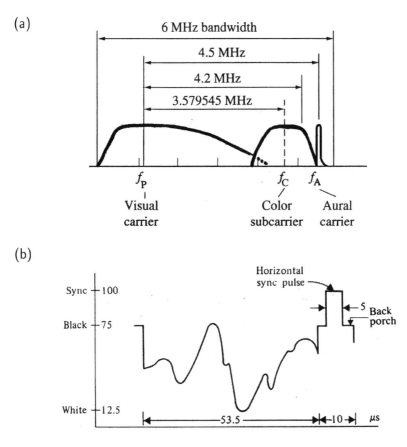

Figure 4.21   (a) 6 MHz standard NTSC television channel spectrum picture, showing luminance, color and audio signals, centered at f_P, f_C, and f_A MHz; (b) A luminance signal waveform during one scan line. The waveform has 53.5 μs of active picture information and 10 μs devoted to synchronization.

most of the bandwidth conservation. In order to transmit color, there must be altogether three independent signals, since the color components r, g, and b are independent. The signal $y(t)$ is one of these, and the other two are called $I(t)$ and $Q(t)$. These are modulated according to form Eq. (4.35), with subcarrier f_C equal either 3.58 MHz (NTSC) or 4.43 MHz (PAL and SECAM). Let us take a closer look at this. Equation (4.35) was set up as a general form for quadrature digital modulation, but as pointed out in Section 4.3, it is in fact a formulation for any bandpass signal. Furthermore, $I(t) \cos 2\pi f_C t$ and $Q(t) \sin 2\pi f_C t$ are orthogonal, meaning that $I(t)$ and $Q(t)$ can be demodulated separately (by multiplying the signal by $\cos 2\pi f_C t$ and $\sin 2\pi f_C t$, respectively). The subcarrier f_C is placed above the picture carrier f_P.

One more detail remains, how to compute I and Q. These are related to r, g, and b through

$$I(t) = 0.60r(t) - 0.28g(t) - 0.32b(t)$$
$$Q(t) = 0.21r(t) - 0.52g(t) + 0.31b(t) \tag{4.36}$$

This peculiar transformation was arrived at after much experiment and study of human perception. It renders colors in an apparently faithful way, and at the same time the bandwidth of I and Q is minimized.

The remaining television components are the sound and various synchronization signals. The sound is FM-modulated by an entirely separate transmitter. In the NTSC system, for example, the FM signal is placed 4.5 MHz above f_C and has a maximum deviation of $\Delta f = 25$ kHz.[18] Synchronization signals are critical to TV transmission, as well as to many other advanced information systems. In TV, the fundamental synchronization signal is the horizontal sync pulse, which tells the receiver when to begin a scan line. It is located at the beginning of each line in the luminance signal $y(t)$. Figure 4.21b shows a piece of an NTSC $y(t)$ signal, showing a line's worth of y with the next sync pulse; full white and black are certain levels as shown there, and the sync pulse rides on top.[19] Another synchronization signal, not shown in the figure, is placed on the so-called "back porch," just after the sync pulse. This is a short burst of the color subcarrier, $\cos 2\pi f_C t$. A circuit in the receiver extracts just this burst and synchronizes to it the oscillators used in the demodulation of I and Q. Without this feature, it is almost impossible to maintain color values.

There are several other synchronization signals in television and a great many fine details that we must skip over. The entire system is designed with exquisite attention to how humans perceive color and moving images.

---

[18] All the transmission standards also have a method of transmitting stereo sound.

[19] The sync pulse is thus the most powerful part of the video signal. Television transmitters range up to 2 MW or more. It has been said that if space aliens are tuned into Earth, the dominant signal they hear is our television sync pulses.

4.4.3   Some Radio Electronics

The electronic design of radio circuits is a fascinating special subject, as much an art as it is a science. Signals need to be generated, filtered, modulated, demodulated, shifted in frequency, and converted into and out of digital form. Appendix B gives some insight into how filters may be constructed that reject one signal while passing another. Myriad physical phenomena can be harnessed to generate and process radio signals. Choosing one and then overcoming its shortcomings to produce excellent performance are part of the radio art.

To give the flavor of radio engineering, we can look briefly at the *superheterodyne receiver* circuit (for more, see Box 4-3). It is described mathematically by the Fourier Modulation Property and some trigonometry. From Eq. (4.14), we have that the Fourier transform of the product $g(t) \cos 2\pi f_1 t$ is $(\frac{1}{2})[G(f+f_1) + G(f-f_1)]$. What happens if $g(t)$ itself is a radio signal $h(t) \cos 2\pi f_0 t$? From Table 2.2, we can write

$$
\begin{aligned}
h(t) &\cos 2\pi f_1 t \cos 2\pi f_0 t \\
&= h(t)[(\tfrac{1}{2}) \cos 2\pi (f_1 + f_0)t + (\tfrac{1}{2}) \cos 2\pi (f_1 - f_0)t] \\
&= (\tfrac{1}{2})h(t) \cos 2\pi (f_1 + f_0)t + (\tfrac{1}{2})h(t) \cos 2\pi (f_1 - f_0)t \\
&\leftrightarrow (\tfrac{1}{4})[H(f + f_0 + f_1) + H(f - f_0 - f_1)] \\
&\quad + (\tfrac{1}{4})[H(f + f_1 - f_0) + H(f - f_1 + f_0)]
\end{aligned}
\tag{4.37}
$$

BOX 4-3

The most important radio engineering system ever invented is probably the superheterodyne receiver, U.S. Patent 1,342,885, granted June 8, 1920. Invented around 1918 by Edwin H. Armstrong (1890–1954) in the United States, the idea is closely followed even today in virtually all radio receivers. A patent notice naming the patent assignee, Radio Corporation of America, appeared on the back of most radio and TV receivers at least through the 1950s. In 1918, the only components available were coils, capacitors, resistors, and crude vacuum tubes, plus a few very fuzzy circuit theory ideas, and no Fourier analysis. Armstrong's remarkable intuition was nonetheless able to pull together the superheterodyne receiver concept. Its unpronounceable name may be its only shortcoming. The word "superheterodyne" was formed from heterodyne, an old radio word that meant to multiply one radio signal by another so that the first is shifted in frequency, and super, meaning that the second signal lies at a higher frequency. This "superheterodyning" is the heart of Armstrong's receiver. Armstrong produced numerous other inventions, the most important of which was frequency modulation and some of its circuitry.

In other words, the radio signal that used to be centered at f_0 Hz has been moved through the multiplication by $\cos 2\pi f_1 t$ to two new spectral centers, $f_1 + f_0$ Hz and $f_1 - f_0$ Hz.

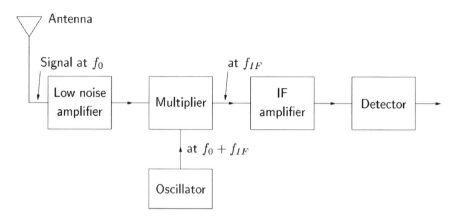

Figure 4.22   Block diagram of the superheterodyne receiver

Now imagine that $h(t) \cos 2\pi f_0 t$ is a desired radio signal. The signal $\cos 2\pi f_1 t$ will be generated internally in the receiver. The Armstrong concept was that no matter what f_0 is, f_1 should be chosen so that $f_1 - f_0$ is always the *same*. The nature of radio electronics is such that this provides a huge advantage. A block diagram of the full receiver is given in Figure 4.22.

The multiplication by $\cos 2\pi f_1 t$ sits in the middle of the diagram; $\cos 2\pi f_1 t$ comes from the radio frequency oscillator and $f_1 > f_0$. The multiplier produces one signal at $f_1 + f_0$, which is blocked by a filter and thrown away, and another signal at an $f_1 - f_0$ called the *intermediate frequency*, abbreviated IF. The stage that follows, called the IF amplifier, is carefully designed to amplify radio signals at this one special frequency; a huge gain is possible because of this restriction. In an ordinary AM receiver, the IF is 455 kHz, in FM reception it is 10.8 MHz, and in television it is about 45 MHz. After this comes a detector, whatever one the modulation method requires. Before the multiplication comes a special low noise amplifier. The first stage in any receiver almost entirely sets the white noise level in the receiver, and this amplifier is designed to keep the level as low as possible, while still providing a relatively small signal gain. The rules of electronics are such that large gain and low noise cannot be obtained from the same amplifier.

The overall goals of any receiver are to reject all signals in the spectrum except for one (this is called "selectivity"), to tune at will to different signals, to amplify a 10–100 microvolt signal to a level at which a detector can work (a volt or so), to detect the signal, and, finally, to introduce as little noise as possible. No one electronic circuit can do all of this. The parts of the superheterodyne receiver each take account of the electronic art in a different way, in such a way that all work together to accomplish these goals. Here are some of the electronic facts and how they are exploited.

- Certain electronic amplifier designs introduce very little noise, but these do a relatively poor job of rejecting nearby signals in the radio spectrum. They also have a relatively small amplification, $5-10$ or so. Therefore, this kind of amplifier is placed first; its relatively small gain is still enough to guarantee that almost all the SNR is established in the first stage.

- A nonlinear amplifier, a kind we ordinarily wish to avoid, makes a good multiplier circuit. An amplifier is thus designed to be mildly nonlinear, and this makes up the multiplier block. Multiplying is, however, a noisy process, and so the multiplier cannot come first. The radio is tuned by this oscillator, since the frequency $f_0 + f_1$ determines which input signal sits precisely at f_{IF}.

- Provided that it works at only *one* center frequency, a radio amplifier can be designed to provide high gain (10,000 or more) and strong rejection of nearby signals in the spectrum. But it has relatively high noise. Such an amplifier is thus placed in the middle of the receiver, and it becomes the IF amplifier. The selectivity of the amplifier also rejects any extra multiplier outputs.

- With a volt-range signal to work with, it is relatively easy to construct a detector. Each detector type takes advantage of different electronics. Amplitude modulation is detected with an envelope detector; FM can be detected by arrangements of RLC circuits (since these are frequency sensitive); DSB requires an oscillator and multiplier (to shift the signal down to baseband).

4.5   CONCLUSIONS

In this chapter we have described the basic analog and digital modulation methods. We have also looked at the major channel types and storage media. The properties of these are the first thing to consider when choosing a modulation method.

The amplitude modulation family contains several methods. Ordinary AM wastes power but is simple to use, and for this last reason it was important in the early days of radio. Double-sideband and single-sideband amplitude modulation conserve power or bandwidth or both. They are therefore favored when these are in short supply, and a little more money can be spent on the receiver. Frequency modulation has much wider bandwidth and here we began to see the power–bandwidth exchange principle in operation. Since FM has very high SNR and wide bandwidth, it is favored for high-quality broadcasting and its carriers are in the high megahertz range, where bandwidth is more available. Stereo FM and especially television illustrate how several modulation methods can be combined. They also illustrate how the nature of human perception can be exploited in a transmission system.

We also looked at digital modulation, with an emphasis on the basic linear (superposition of pulses) methods. These account for most applications. Digital demodulation is based on the principles of correlation and orthogonality. Digital techniques also exhibit the power–bandwidth exchange principle.

REFERENCES[20]

1. *LEBOW, I. L. 1995. *Understanding digital transmission and recording*. IEEE Press: New York.
2. NELLIST, J. G. 2001. *Understanding telecommunication and lightwave systems*, 3rd ed. IEEE Press: New York.
3. *STARK, H., TUTEUR, F. B. and ANDERSON, J. B. 1988. *Modern electrical communications*, 2nd ed. Prentice-Hall: Englewood Cliffs, N.J.
4. *COUCH, L. W. 2001. *Digital and analog communication systems*, 6th ed. Prentice-Hall: Upper Saddle River, N.J.
5. *STREMLER, F. G. 1990. *Communication systems*, 3rd ed. Addison-Wesley: Reading, MA.
6. *CARLSON, A. B. 1986. *Communication systems*, 3rd ed. McGraw-Hill: New York.
7. ANDERSON, J. B. 1998. *Digital transmission engineering*. IEEE Press: New York.
8. NYQUIST, H. 1928. Thermal agitation of electric changes in conductors. *Phys. Rev.*, 32, 110–113.
9. JOHNSON, J. B. 1928. Thermal agitation of electricity in conductors. *Phys. Rev.*, 32, 97–109.
10. NYQUIST, H. 1924. Certain factors affecting telegraph speed. *Bell System Tech. J.*, April, 324–346.
11. NYQUIST, H. 1928. Certain topics on telegraph transmission theory. *Trans. AIEE*, 47, 617–644.

PROBLEMS

1. A common way to specify the performance of a radio receiver is to give its *noise temperature*. The idea is to measure the actual noise power at the beginning of the receiver, and then assume that it comes from a resistor that is placed across the input. Often, in fact, there is just such a resistor in that position. The total white noise power obeys the law $N = kT_K B_m$ watts, which was given in Section 4.1. Suppose that the bandwidth B_m over which the power measurement takes place is 1 MHz. Find the power that will be observed if the resistor is at room temperature. (*Note*: By international agreement among radio engineers, this temperature is taken as 290 Kelvin; for the most accurate answer, you can take this value.)

2. A common microwave radio link is one that carries information over about 50 km at a frequency of 4 GHz. Suppose the antennas at both ends are 1 m diameter parabolic dishes, and suppose the transmitter power is 1 W. Use the dish formulas in Section 4.1 to estimate how much power arrives at the receiver. (Assume that the only power losses are the usual inverse square law propagation losses.)

3. Suppose the radio link in Problem 4.2 is used to carry 1 Mbit/s by QPSK modulation and the receiver is the one in Problem 4.1. The exact nature of the signal does not much matter here; what we really need is an estimate for the bandwidth of the signal that reaches the receiver. A good one is the "$1/T$ Rule" in Section 4.3, which in this case states that the signal will have bandwidth 1 MHz, the same as the bit rate.

   (a) Find the ratio of the signal power to the noise power at the beginning of the receiver, that is, the SNR. (Remember that the bandwidth at the receiver input should be limited to that of the signal itself.)

   (b) Suppose that an SNR of about 13 dB is enough to give a good error rate. Keep using the $1/T$ Rule to estimate bandwidth, and estimate the bit rate that this link can carry at an SNR of 13 dB.

[20] References marked with an asterisk are recommended as supplementary reading.

4. In general, it takes two lowpass signals to describe one bandpass signal. We saw that a bandpass signal may be represented in either of the following two equivalent forms:

$$A(t)\cos(2\pi f_0 t + \phi(t)), \qquad A(t) \geq 0$$
$$I(t)\cos 2\pi f_0 t - Q(t)\sin 2\pi f_0 t$$

Here all four of $A(t)$, $\phi(t)$, $I(t)$, $Q(t)$ are lowpass functions, with transforms closely grouped around 0 Hz. Write formulas for $I(t)$ and $Q(t)$ in terms of $A(t)$ and $\phi(t)$, and for $A(t)$ and $\phi(t)$ in terms of $I(t)$ and $Q(t)$. (Use the trigonometric identities in Table 2.2.)

5. The information signal $g(t)$ AM-modulates a carrier according to the standard formula $s(t) = A[1 + g(t)]\cos 2\pi f_0 t$. In AM, the power in the carrier is considered wasted. We can define AM efficiency as the power in the information-bearing sidebands divided by the total power in the transmission.

(a) Suppose $g(t) = (\frac{1}{2})\cos 2\pi 500 t$. f_0 is some very large value and $g(t)$ runs for a long time. What is the efficiency? (This problem can be done by finding the average energy of time signals, but it is easier to view the Fourier transforms.)

(b) Now let $g(t) = (\frac{1}{2})\cos 2\pi 500 t + (\frac{1}{2})\cos 2\pi 700 t$. What is the efficiency now?

6. (a) A single unit-height triangle pulse $v(t)$ (see transform pair (j) in Section 2.3) is AM-modulated at carrier frequency f_0 Hz, according to the modulation formula $s(t) = A[1 + v(t)]\cos 2\pi f_0 t$. The pulse has width T. Make a careful sketch of the transform $S(f)$ of $s(t)$. Plot both phase and amplitude of $S(f)$. Dimension the plot.

(b) Now let $v(t)$ be the decaying exponential $u(t)e^{-t}$ (as in transform pair (l) in Section 2.3). $v(t)$ is AM-DSB modulated, according to formula $s(t) = Av(t)\cos 2\pi f_0 t$. Make a careful sketch of the amplitude and phase of $S(f)$. Pay special attention to the symmetries of the phase above and below $\pm f_0$.

7. DSB-AM is described by the formula $s(t) = Av(t)\cos 2\pi f_0 t$. A basic way to perform detection is to multiply the received signal $s(t)$ by $\cos 2\pi f_0' t$. Here f_0' is a frequency close to f_0; since f_0 may not be precisely known at the receiver, it may be necessary to guess at it or find it by tuning.

(a) Give the spectrum of $s(t)\cos 2\pi f_0' t$. (Assume some typical shape for the $v(t)$ spectrum and show by a sketch where the various copies of it lie in your spectrum.)

(b) What further needs to be done to $s(t)\cos 2\pi f_0' t$ to complete the detector? Ideally, what should f_0' be?

(c) How would upper or lower sideband AM-SSB be detected using this method?

8. It is desired to send high-quality music by frequency modulation. The transmitter and radio path are such that the signal-to-noise power ratio that is actually present at the beginning of the receiver is 30 dB (a 1000 : 1 ratio). After FM detection, this should become 60 dB. The SNR in FM before and after detection obeys the relationship (4.25). We will use a 1 kHz test sinewave in order to work out a design for the FM modulation. The parameter β in Eq. (4.25) is the ratio $\Delta f/f_m$, where f_m is the 1 kHz and Δf is the maximum amount the carrier f_0 will deviate up and down.

(a) What must $\Delta f/f_m$ be in order to get the needed gain in the SNR?

(b) AM and AM-DSB would have a radio frequency bandwidth of $2(1\,\text{kHz}) = 2$ kHz this test signal. Roughly what is the bandwidth of our FM design?

9. Let the two sets of data symbols $\{+1, -1, +1, +1\}$ and $\{+1, +1, -1, -1\}$ be sent by QPSK digital modulation. The first group are $a_0^I, \ldots, a_3^I$ in the I signal $I(t) = \sqrt{2E_s} \sum a_n^I v(t - nT)$ in Eq. (4.34), and the second group are $a_0^Q, \ldots, a_3^Q$ in the Q signal $Q(t) = \sqrt{2E_s} \sum a_n^Q v(t - nT)$. The pulse $v(t)$ is the standard triangle pulse; $T = 1$. Figure 4.17 is based on the same data and may help you visualize the problem; note, however, that the figure is based on a *rect* pulse v.

   (a) Plot the two 4-symbol pulse trains $I(t)$ and $Q(t)$.

   (b) Find and plot the functions $A(t)$ and $\phi(t)$ in the first equivalent form in Problem 4.4. (The first of these is called the envelope of the signal and the second is its phase.)

10. In Section 4.3 were given three standard data pulses $v(t)$, the width-T rect, triangle and raised-cosine pulses. Show that all three, as given there, have unit energy.

Chapter 5

Information Theory and Coding: What did Shannon Promise?

When Claude E. Shannon (Box 5-1, 5-2) published his two-part monumental 1948 paper, "A Mathematical Theory of Communication" [1], he laid the foundation for the information age. He established an entirely new scientific field, *information theory*, which is the conceptual basis for communication. Shannon used the term *information* for what was being communicated and was able to quantify information for both sources and channels. According to Shannon, messages should be regarded as choices among alternatives. We can think of a message source as a random process—the messages are created at random. Shannon's information has nothing to do with the meaning of the message; it is a measure that quantifies the choices among alternatives.

In this chapter we shall first introduce Shannon's information theory; both his source coding theorem and his channel coding theorem will be discussed.

Shannon's source coding (data compression) theorem asserts that a communication source can be characterized by a parameter H_t, its output *uncertainty* (or *entropy*), such that the source can be represented by R_t binary digits per second if $R_t > H_t$, but not if $R_t < H_t$. The source is equivalent to one that generates H_t randomly chosen, equiprobable binary digits per second. This theorem was quickly accepted. It was not in conflict with older theories or experiences – source coding did not exist before 1948!

Shannon's most unexpected result is his channel coding theorem, which states that a communication channel can be characterized by a parameter C_t, the *channel capacity*, such that R_t randomly chosen binary digits per second can be transmitted over the channel virtually error-free if $R_t < C_t$, but significant distortion must occur if $R_t > C_t$. The quality of the channel is not important so long as it is high enough

Understanding Information Transmission. By John B. Anderson and Rolf Johannesson
ISBN 0-471-67910-0 © 2005 the Institute of Electrical and Electronics Engineers, Inc.

BOX 5-1

Part I: Claude Elwood Shannon grew up in Gaylord, Michigan. His childhood hero was Edison. Shannon obtained a master's degree in electrical engineering and a Ph.D. in mathematics from Massachusetts Institute of Technology, both in 1940. In his 1936 master's thesis, *A symbolic analysis of relay and switching circuits*, Shannon showed that Boolean algebra was the mathematical language to describe switching circuits. H. H. Goldstine, in his book *The Computer from Pascal to von Neumann*, called this work "one of the most important master's theses ever written...a landmark in that it changed circuit design from an art to a science." Before joining Bell Labs in 1941, Shannon spent a year at the Institute for Advanced Study, Princeton. During this time he began to develop the framework that led to the publication of "*A mathematical theory of communication*" in 1948, a paper that introduced the word "bit" for the first time, founded information theory, and remains as a monument in this field. Shannon understood the power that springs from encoding information in the language of 0s and 1s and from that a whole communications revolution has sprung. The idea that one could transmit words, sounds, pictures, and so on by sending 0s and 1s dates back (at least) to Sir Francis Bacon (1561–1626), but Shannon's recognition that randomly chosen binary digits could (and should) be used for measuring the generation, transmission, and reception of information was fundamentally new. (*To be continued.*)

to guarantee that $R_t < C_t$ holds. The key idea is that long information sequences should be encoded such that every information symbol has an influence on many of the binary digits that are transmitted over the channel. This was a radically new idea that laid the foundation for the field of error-correcting codes.

The scrambled adage that begins "Tu err 's humin. . ." hints at the need for something above the human in order to correct errors. But it is easy for man to

Part to II: Shannon's 1949 paper "*Communication theory of secrecy systems*" is considered to have transformed cryptology from an art to a science. These ideas were inspired by his work on encryption during World War II and led to a system that was used by Roosevelt and Churchill. Shannon did early work in artificial intelligence. He devised chess-playing programs, published in 1950. His electronic mouse, which he called Theseus, could solve maze problems. Also in the 1950s, Shannon built a computer just for fun, which did arithmetic with only Roman numerals. There are many stories about Shannon and his unicycle. In an obituary, in the New York Times, G. Johnson writes that Shannon: "...became known for keeping to himself by day and riding his unicycle down the halls [at Bell Labs] at night". Consistently, Shannon published the first (and only?) paper on a mathematical theory of juggling. In 1956 Shannon joined the faculty at M.I.T. He received numerous honorary degrees and awards. Shannon was very modest and the following quote is characteristic: "I've always pursued my interests without much regard to financial value or value to the world. I've spent lots of time on totally useless things."

correct errors as is illustrated by the form in which the above adage is given; in spite of a few typos the meaning of the text is easily understood. Information theory has contributed to a formalized and practical theory for error-correction.

Two practical algorithms for source coding (data compression) will be discussed and illustrated by examples. Then we introduce error-correcting codes and show how digital data can be protected against errors that occur during transmission over a communication channel or during storage in a memory.

5.1 INFORMATION THEORY: A PRIMER

Shannon's idea that information can be characterized by symbols to which probabilities are associated is at the heart of information theory. In order to formalize this approach we let X be a discrete random variable with finitely many outcomes denoted $x_1, x_2, \ldots, x_L$ and probability distribution $P_X(x)$. Shannon defined the *uncertainty* (or *entropy*) of a discrete random variable X to be the quantity[1]

$$H(x) \overset{\text{def}}{=} - \sum_{i=1}^{L} P_X(x_i) \log P_X(x_i) \tag{5.1}$$

We use the convention $0 \log 0 = \lim_{\epsilon \to 0} \epsilon \log \epsilon = 0$. Hence, $H(X)$ is well defined even if $P_X(x) = 0$ for some x.

The unit of the uncertainty is called the *bit*. One bit is the uncertainty of a binary random variable that is 0 or 1 with equal probability. If a binary random variable is 0 with probability 0.89 (and, hence, 1 with probability 0.11), then its uncertainty is

$$\begin{aligned} H(X) &= -0.89 \log 0.89 - 0.11 \log 0.11 \\ &= 0.50 \text{ bit} \end{aligned} \tag{5.2}$$

The uncertainty is a function only of the probability distribution of a random variable, not of the labels of the outcomes. The uncertainty of a randomly chosen binary digit that which assumes 0 or 1 with equal probability is the same as that for a fair coin flip.

EXAMPLE 5.1

The uncertainty of a fair coin flip with the two outcomes *Head* and *Tail* is

$$\begin{aligned} H(X) &= -P_X(\text{Head}) \log P_X(\text{Head}) - P_X(\text{Tail}) \log P_X(\text{Tail}) \\ &= -\tfrac{1}{2}\log\tfrac{1}{2} - \tfrac{1}{2}\log\tfrac{1}{2} = -\log\tfrac{1}{2} = \log 2 \\ &= 1 \text{ bit} \end{aligned} \tag{5.3}$$ ∎

Intuitively, the uncertainty of a random variable that assumes a certain outcome with certainty (probability 1) is zero, while the uncertainty is maximum if the random variable assumes all outcomes with the same probability. These important observations are formalized in the following.

Theorem 5.1   *The uncertainty $H(X)$ of the discrete random variable X with L outcomes is bounded as*

$$0 \le H(X) \le \log L \tag{5.4}$$

with equality on the left if and only if $P_X(x) = 1$ for some x, and with equality on the right if and only if $P_X(x) = 1/L$ for all x.

---

[1] Here and hereafter we write log for $\log_2$.

For a fair coin flip we have $L = 2$ and equality on the right in Eq. (5.4). Thus, as in Example 5.1 the uncertainty of a fair coin flip is $\log 2 = 1$ bit.

In the proof of these major inequalities we need the following simple inequality that is used so often in information theoretical derivations that it is commonly called the *Information Theory (IT) Inequality*.

IT Inequality   For any positive real number r

$$\log r \le (r - 1) \log e \tag{5.5}$$

with equality if and only if $r = 1$.

Proof.   Consider the graphs of $\ln r$ and $r - 1$ shown in Figure 5.1. They touch each other at $r = 1$ and since

$$\frac{d(\ln r)}{dr} = \frac{1}{r} \begin{cases} > 1, & r < 1 \\ < 1, & r > 1 \end{cases} \tag{5.6}$$

they never cross. Hence, we conclude that $\ln r \le r - 1$ with equality if and only if $r = 1$. Using the rule for changing the logarithmic base, viz., $\ln r = (\log r)/\log e$, completes the proof.   □

Proof of Theorem 5.1.   First we prove the left inequality. For the ith term in the sum of the uncertainty $H(X)$ we obtain

$$-P_X(x_i) \log P_X(x_i) \begin{cases} = 0, & P_X(x_i) = 0 \\ > 0, & 0 < P_X(x_i) < 1 \\ = 0, & P_X(x_i) = 1 \end{cases} \tag{5.7}$$

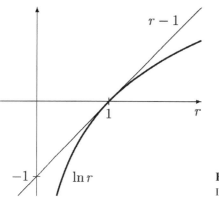

Figure 5.1   Geometric interpretation of the IT Inequality

We conclude that $H(X)$ is always nonnegative, and that $H(X) = 0$ if and only if $P_X(x_i)$ is either 0 or 1 for each i or, equivalently, if and only if $P_X(x_i) = 1$ for precisely one i.

To prove the right inequality we first notice that it is equivalent to show that

$$H(X) - \log L \le 0 \tag{5.8}$$

with equality if and only if $P_X(x_i) = 1/L$ for all L. Then we manipulate Eq. (5.8) such that we can apply the IT Inequality:

$$
\begin{aligned}
H(X) - \log L &= -\sum_{i=1}^{L} P_X(x_i) \log P_X(x_i) - \log L \\
&= -\sum_{i=1}^{L} P_X(x_i) \log P_X(x_i) - \sum_{i=1}^{L} P_X(x_i) \log L \\
&= -\sum_{i=1}^{L} P_X(x_i) \log(P_X(x_i)L) \\
&= \sum_{i=1}^{L} P_X(x_i) \log \frac{1}{P_X(x_i)L}
\end{aligned}
\tag{5.9}
$$

The second equality follows from the fact that $\sum_{i=1}^{L} P_X(x_i) = 1$. Now we apply the IT Inequality using $r = 1/(P_X(x_i)L)$ and obtain

$$
\begin{aligned}
H(X) - \log L &= \sum_{i=1}^{L} P_X(x_i) \log \frac{1}{P_X(x_i)L} \\
&\le \sum_{i=1}^{L} P_X(x_i) \left(\frac{1}{P_X(x_i)L} - 1 \right) \log e \\
&= \left(\sum_{i=1}^{L} \frac{1}{L} - \sum_{i=1}^{L} P_X(x_i) \right) \log e = (1 - 1) \log e = 0
\end{aligned}
\tag{5.10}
$$

with equality if and only if $1/(P_X(x_i)L) = 1$, or, equivalently, if and only if $P_X(x_i) = 1/L$, for all i. Notice that it was crucial to rewrite the sum $-\sum_{i=1}^{L} P_X(x_i) \times \log(P_X(x_i)L)$ as $\sum_{i=1}^{L} P_X(x_i) \log(1/P_X(x_i)L)$ in Eq. (5.9) before we applied the IT Inequality. Such a "trick" (often used in information theory) takes the act of proving theorems to the level of an art!

Let X be a binary random variable with outcomes x_1 and x_2. Then we have $P_X(x_1) = p$ and $P_X(x_2) = 1 - p$, which yields the uncertainty

$$H(X) = -p \log p - (1 - p) \log(1 - p) \tag{5.11}$$

Since we quite often encounter binary random variables we write

$$h(p) \stackrel{\text{def}}{=} -p \log p - (1-p) \log(1-p) \qquad (5.12)$$

and call $h(p)$ the *binary entropy function*. Its graph is shown in Figure 5.2 and in particular we notice that $h(0.50) = 1$ and $h(0.11) = h(0.89) = 0.50$.

Next we shall introduce *conditional uncertainty* and show the intuitively pleasing result that *conditioning can never increase uncertainty*. The conditional uncertainty (or conditional entropy) of the discrete random variable X with L outcomes given the discrete random variable Y with M outcomes is the quantity

$$H(X \mid Y) \stackrel{\text{def}}{=} -\sum_{i=1}^{L} \sum_{j=1}^{M} P_{XY}(x_i, y_j) \log P_{X|Y}(x_i \mid y_j) \qquad (5.13)$$

where $P_{XY}(x, y)$ is the joint probability distribution and $P_{X|Y}(x \mid y)$ is the conditional probability distribution.

As a counterpart (or, more precisely, a corollary) to Theorem 5.1 we have Theorem 5.2.

Theorem 5.2   *The conditional uncertainty $H(X \mid Y)$ of the discrete random variable X with L outcomes given the discrete random variable Y with M outcomes is bounded as*

$$0 \leq H(X \mid Y) \leq \log L \qquad (5.14)$$

with equality on the left if and only if for each y such that $P_Y(y) \neq 0$, $P_{X|Y}(x \mid y) = 1$ for some x, and with equality on the right if and only if for each y such that $P_Y(y) \neq 0$, $P_{X|Y}(x \mid y) = 1/L$ for all x.

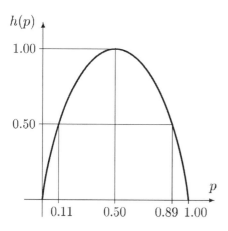

Figure 5.2   The binary entropy function

We shall now derive an important identity for uncertainties. Since a pair of random variables is also a random variable it follows from definition (5.1) that

$$H(XY) = -\sum_{i=1}^{L}\sum_{j=1}^{M} P_{XY}(x_i, y_j) \log P_{XY}(x_i, y_j) \tag{5.15}$$

From the definition of conditional probabilities it follows that

$$P_{XY}(x_i, y_j) = P_{X|Y}(x_i \mid y_j) P_Y(y_j) \tag{5.16}$$

Inserting Eq. (5.15) into Eq. (5.16) yields

$$H(XY) = -\sum_{i=1}^{L}\sum_{j=1}^{M} P_{XY}(x_i, y_j) \log(P_{X|Y}(x_i, y_j) P_Y(y_j))$$

$$= -\sum_{i=1}^{L}\sum_{j=1}^{M} P_{XY}(x_i, y_j) \log P_{X|Y}(x_i \mid y_j)$$

$$-\sum_{i=1}^{L}\sum_{j=1}^{M} P_{XY}(x_i, y_j) \log P_Y(y_j) \tag{5.17}$$

$$= H(X \mid Y) - \sum_{j=1}^{M} P_Y(y_j) \log P_Y(y_j)$$

$$= H(X \mid Y) + H(Y)$$

where we have used the marginal distribution

$$P_Y(y) = \sum_{i=1}^{L} P_{XY}(x_i, y) \tag{5.18}$$

Since the joint probability distribution $P_{XY}(x_i, y_j)$ in Eq. (5.16) can just as well be written

$$P_{XY}(x_i, y_j) = P_{Y|X}(y_j \mid x_i) P_X(x_i) \tag{5.19}$$

it follows that

$$\begin{aligned} H(XY) &= H(X) + H(Y \mid X) \\ &= H(Y) + H(X \mid Y) \end{aligned} \tag{5.20}$$

Identity (5.17) is easily generalized to a random vector with N component discrete random variables:

$$H(X_1 X_2 \ldots X_N) = H(X_1) + H(X_2 \mid X_1) + \cdots + H(X_N \mid X_1 X_2 \ldots X_{N-1}) \tag{5.21}$$

This identity is often called the *chain rule for uncertainty*.

EXAMPLE 5.2

Consider a fair die. Let the outcomes of the random variable X be the number of dots on the upper side of the die, and let the outcomes of the random variable Y be *Even* and *Odd* depending on whether the outcome of X is even or odd. Since we have six equiprobable outcomes of X and two equiprobable outcomes of Y, it follows that

$$H(X) = \log 6 = 2.58 \text{ bits}$$

and

$$H(Y) = \log 2 = 1 \text{ bit}$$

Suppose we know the outcome of Y, that is, whether we got an even or odd number of dots. Then we have only three possible outcomes for X; that is, the conditional uncertainty of X given Y is

$$H(X \mid Y) = \log 3 \text{ bits}$$

If we, however, know the outcome of X, for example, we get a "6" when we roll the die, then we know the outcome of Y with certainty! Hence, the conditional uncertainty of Y given X is

$$H(Y \mid X) = 0$$

Finally, if we combine the two random variables X and Y into the vector-valued random variable XY, we get in total 12 outcomes, but half of them cannot occur or, more precisely, the probability that they occur is 0; for example, the probability that the combination *6 dots* and *Odd* occurs is 0. Excluding the six impossible combinations leaves six equiprobable combinations and we have the uncertainty

$$H(XY) = \log 6 \text{ bits}$$

Alternatively, we can exploit the chain rule of uncertainty and write

$$H(XY) = H(X) + H(Y \mid X)$$
$$= \log 6 + 0 = \log 6 \text{ bits}$$

or

$$H(XY) = H(Y) + H(X \mid Y)$$
$$= 1 + \log 3 = \log 2 + \log 3$$
$$= \log 6 \text{ bits} \qquad \blacksquare$$

We have already mentioned that conditioning can never increase uncertainty, an important result that we formulate as Theorem 5.3.

Theorem 5.3   *For any two discrete random variables X and Y,*

$$H(X \mid Y) \leq H(X) \tag{5.22}$$

with equality if and only if X and Y are independent random variables.

Proof.   This proof is a slight variant of the proof of Theorem 5.1.

$$H(X \mid Y) - H(X) = -\sum_{i=1}^{L}\sum_{j=1}^{M} P_{XY}(x_i, y_j) \log P_{X\mid Y}(x_i \mid y_j)$$

$$+ \sum_{i=1}^{L} P_X(x_i) \log P_X(x_i)$$

$$= \sum_{i=1}^{L}\sum_{j=1}^{M} P_{XY}(x_i, y_j)\left(-\log \underbrace{P_{X\mid Y}(x_i \mid y_j)}_{\frac{P_{XY}(x_i,y_j)}{P_Y(y_j)}} + \log P_X(x_i) \right) \tag{5.23}$$

$$= \sum_{i=1}^{L}\sum_{j=1}^{M} P_{XY}(x_i, y_j) \log \frac{P_X(x_i)P_Y(y_j)}{P_{XY}(x_i, y_j)}$$

Next we let $r = P_X(x_i)P_Y(y_j)/P_{XY}(x_i, y_j)$ and apply the IT Inequality, then we obtain

$$H(X \mid Y) - H(X) \leq \sum_{i=1}^{L}\sum_{j=1}^{M} P_{XY}(x_i, y_j)\left(\frac{P_X(x_i)P_Y(y_j)}{P_{XY}(x_i, y_j)} - 1 \right) \log e$$

$$= \left(\sum_{i=1}^{L}\sum_{j=1}^{M} P_X(x_i)P_Y(y_j) - \sum_{i=1}^{L}\sum_{j=1}^{M} P_{XY}(x_i, y_j) \right) \log e \tag{5.24}$$

$$= (1 - 1)\log e = 0$$

with equality if and only if $r = P_X(x_i)P_Y(y_j)/P_{XY}(x_i, y_j) = 1$, that is, if and only if

$$P_{XY}(x_i, y_j) = P_X(x_i)P_Y(y_j) \tag{5.25}$$

for all i and j; Eq. (5.25) is simply the definition of independence of the discrete random variables X and Y.   □

Consider a discrete random variable X with uncertainty $H(X)$. Suppose we observe another discrete random variable Y. How much does this observation of Y reduce our uncertainty about X? Before the observation of Y we have simply the uncertainty $H(X)$, and after the observation of Y the uncertainty of X is reduced to $H(X \mid Y)$. The reduction of uncertainty of X due to the observation of Y is $H(X) - H(X \mid Y)$. Shannon regarded this difference in uncertainties as the *infor-*

mation the random variable Y gives about the random variable X. From Eq. (5.20) follows that

$$H(X) - H(X \mid Y) = H(Y) - H(Y \mid X) \qquad (5.26)$$

and we conclude that the reduction in the uncertainty of one random variable due to the observation of another random variable is symmetric in the two random variables. Each gives the same quantity of information about the other.

We introduce the notation

$$\begin{aligned} I(X; Y) &= H(X) - H(X \mid Y) \\ &= H(Y) - H(Y \mid X) \end{aligned} \qquad (5.27)$$

and since it is symmetric, that is, $I(X; Y) = I(Y; X)$, we follow Robert Fano and call it the *mutual information* between the random variables X and Y.

EXAMPLE 5.2   *(continued)*

Let us return to our die and calculate the mutual information between X and Y.

$$\begin{aligned} I(X; Y) &= H(Y) - H(Y \mid X) \\ &= 1 - 0 = 1 \text{ bit} \end{aligned} \qquad (5.28)$$

or, alternatively,

$$\begin{aligned} I(X; Y) &= H(X) - H(X \mid Y) \\ &= \log 6 - \log 3 = \log \tfrac{6}{3} = \log 2 = 1 \text{ bit} \end{aligned} \qquad (5.29)$$

The first alternative (5.28) can be interpreted as follows. By observing the number of dots, X, we remove all uncertainty about *Even/Odd*, that is, about Y. This uncertainty was 1 bit; thus, we obtain 1 bit of information about Y by observing X.

The second alternative (5.29) can be interpreted as follows. By observing *Even/Odd*, Y, we reduce the number of possible alternatives for X from six to three. Cutting the six equiprobable possibilities in two equiprobable halves corresponds to reducing the uncertainty by 1 bit; thus, we obtain 1 bit of information about X by observing Y. ∎

Consider the cascade of two processors shown in Figure 5.3. The random variable X can influence the random variable Z only via the random variable Y; this can

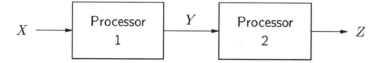

Figure 5.3   A cascade of processors used for the data processing inequality

be formally expressed as

$$P_{Z|XY}(z \mid x, y) = P_{Z|Y}(z \mid y) \tag{5.30}$$

for all x, y, z.

We can upper-bound the mutual information between X and Z as follows:

$$
\begin{aligned}
I(X; Z) &= H(X) - H(X \mid Z) \\
&\le H(X) - H(X \mid YZ) \\
&= H(X) - H(X \mid Y) \\
&= I(X; Y)
\end{aligned}
\tag{5.31}
$$

The inequality in Eq. (5.31) follows from the fact that further conditioning cannot increase the uncertainty, and the second equality follows from the fact that X and Z are independent given Y (see Eq. (5.30)). Similarly we have

$$
\begin{aligned}
I(X; Z) &= H(Z) - H(Z \mid X) \\
&\le H(Z) - H(Z \mid XY) \\
&= H(Z) - H(Z \mid Y) \\
&= I(Y; Z)
\end{aligned}
\tag{5.32}
$$

We summarize Eqs. (5.31) and (5.32) as the famous *data processing inequality*

$$I(X; Z) \le \begin{cases} I(X; Y) \\ I(Y; Z) \end{cases} \tag{5.33}$$

This inequality shows that no processing of data whatsoever, neither deterministic nor stochastic, can improve the inferences that can be made from the data. (By appropriate processing, the data can be made more easily accessible, but that is another story.)

5.1.1 Source Coding

We shall now discuss Shannon's source coding theorem, which relates the uncertainty of the source output to the probability of typical long sequences of source symbols.

Consider an unfair coin whose probability of *Head* is $p_H \ne 1/2$. Unless p_H is 0 or 1 there is not much we can say beforehand about the outcome of one coin toss. Let us therefore toss our coin n times. If n is chosen large enough, then we expect that the total number of *Heads* will be approximately np_H. By exploiting Chebyshev's inequality we can replace "large enough" and "approximately" by exact statements. Our intention is, however, only to give plausibility arguments for Shannon's source and channel coding theorems. Those who are interested in detailed proofs are referred, for example, to the textbook by Cover and Thomas [3].

Similarly, consider a source whose output is a sequence of independent and identically distributed binary digits 0 and 1 with probabilities p and $1 - p$, respectively. A sequence $x = x_1 x_2 \ldots x_n$ of n output symbols will consist of approximately np 0s and $n(1 - p)$ 1s when n is very large. The probability of the sequence is

$$Pr(x) \approx p^{np}(1 - p)^{n(1-p)} \tag{5.34}$$

We say that a sequence with roughly this probability is *typical*. Assuming that $p < 1/2$, the most probable output sequence is the sequence that consists of only ones; such a sequence is, however, not a typical sequence. Suppose we bet on horses. Then it is likely that we lose, but it would be very unlikely that we lose all the time; such a losing sequence is not typical!

Next we exploit the relation between logarithms and exponents and rewrite Eq. (5.34) as

$$
\begin{aligned}
Pr(x) \approx p^{np}(1 - p)^{n(1-p)} &= 2^{\log(p^{np}(1-p)^{n(1-p)})} \\
&= 2^{\log p^{np} + \log(1-p)^{n(1-p)}} = 2^{np \log p + n(1-p) \log(1-p)} \\
&= 2^{n(p \log p + (1-p) \log(1-p))} = 2^{-nh(p)}
\end{aligned}
\tag{5.35}
$$

where the binary entropy function $h(p)$ (see Eq. (5.12)) is the output uncertainty of the source.

All typical long sequences have approximately the same probability and from the law of large numbers it follows that the set of these typical sequences is overwhelmingly probable, that is, the probability that a long source output sequence is typical is close to one, and, hence, we conclude from Eq. (5.35) that there are approximately $2^{nh(p)}$ typical long sequences.

To obtain a formal definition of the typicality we introduce a positive number ϵ and let $T_\epsilon^{(n)}$ be the set of sequences $x = x_1 x_2 \ldots x_n$ such that

$$2^{-n(H(X)+\epsilon)} \leq P_X(x) \leq 2^{-n(H(X)-\epsilon)} \tag{5.36}$$

The set $T_\epsilon^{(n)}$ is called the *typical set* and it has the following properties:

1. If $x \in T_\epsilon^{(n)}$, then $P_X(x) \approx 2^{-nH(X)}$.
2. $Pr(T_\epsilon^{(n)}) > 1 - \epsilon$, for n sufficiently large.
3. $(1 - \epsilon)2^{n(H(X)-\epsilon)} \leq |T_\epsilon^{(n)}| \leq 2^{n(H(X)+\epsilon)}$.

A remark.   Property 1 is simply a reformulation of Eq. (5.36) and Property 2 follows from the law of large numbers. The right inequality of Property 3 can be shown as follows:

$$1 \geq \sum_{T_\epsilon^{(n)}} P_X(x) \geq \sum_{T_\epsilon^{(n)}} 2^{-n(H(X)+\epsilon)}$$

$$= 2^{-n(H(X)+\epsilon)} \sum_{T_\epsilon^{(n)}} 1 = 2^{-n(H(X)+\epsilon)} |T_\epsilon^{(n)}| \qquad (5.37)$$

where the second inequality follows from Eq. (5.36), and $|T_\epsilon^{(n)}|$ denotes the number of elements in the set $T_\epsilon^{(n)}$. The left inequality follows from Property 2 and Eq. (5.36) by a similar derivation.

To get a better feeling for typical sequences consider an urn with one black and two white balls. Suppose we take one ball from the urn, observe its color and put it back. This procedure is performed totally $n = 5$ times. The $2^5 = 32$ different combinations are shown together with their probabilities in Table 5.1.

Let X be a random variable that is BLACK and WHITE with probabilities $1/3$ and $2/3$, respectively. Then we have the uncertainty of X

$$H(X) = h(1/3) = 0.918$$

Let us arbitrarily choose $\epsilon = 0.138$ (15% of $h(1/3)$). Inserting these numbers into Eq. (5.36) implies that, for $\epsilon = 0.138$, a sequence is typical if its probability satisfies

$$0.027 \leq P_X(x) \leq 0.068 \qquad (5.38)$$

Those sequences that fulfill expression (5.38) are marked by $*$ in our table and we notice that we have 15 typical sequences. If we add their probabilities we get 0.6580. In other words, although the typical sequences constitute slightly less than half of the total number of sequences, they contribute almost $2/3$ of the total probability. Even if this result is not impressive it shows the tendency of typical sequences to be overwhelmingly probable. Let us now choose a smaller ϵ, namely $\epsilon = 0.046$ (5% of $h(1/3)$), and increase the length of the sequences. Then we obtain Table 5.2.

From the table we learn that for $\epsilon = 0.046$ we have $2^{953.4}$ typical sequences of length $n = 1000$. It is remarkable that for the length $n = 1000$, only a fraction $2^{953.4}/2^{1000} = 2^{-46.6} \approx 10^{-14}$ of all the sequences of this length is typical and this small fraction accounts for 99.8% of the total probability. To obtain a nontypical sequence of length $n = 1000$ from our urn experiment is highly unlikely. If we are not content with the probability 0.998 we simply extend the length of the sequences to $n = 2000$ and obtain typical sequences with virtual certainty.

So far we have discussed typical sequence only for sources that put out independent and identically distributed binary digits. The typicality arguments hold, however, for a very wide class of a source models; for example, Shannon generalized it to so-called *finite-state ergodic Markov sources* [1], which are rather useful models for languages.

Table 5.1 Five balls from an urn

Sequence	Probability	
● ● ● ● ●	1/3 1/3 1/3 1/3 1/3 $\Rightarrow$ 0.0041	
● ● ● ● ○	1/3 1/3 1/3 1/3 2/3 $\Rightarrow$ 0.0082	
● ● ● ○ ●	1/3 1/3 1/3 2/3 1/3 $\Rightarrow$ 0.0082	
● ● ● ○ ○	1/3 1/3 1/3 2/3 2/3 $\Rightarrow$ 0.0165	
● ● ○ ● ●	1/3 1/3 2/3 1/3 1/3 $\Rightarrow$ 0.0082	
● ● ○ ● ○	1/3 1/3 2/3 1/3 2/3 $\Rightarrow$ 0.0165	
● ● ○ ○ ●	1/3 1/3 2/3 2/3 1/3 $\Rightarrow$ 0.0165	
● ● ○ ○ ○	1/3 1/3 2/3 2/3 2/3 $\Rightarrow$ 0.0329	*
● ○ ● ● ●	1/3 2/3 1/3 1/3 1/3 $\Rightarrow$ 0.0082	
● ○ ● ● ○	1/3 2/3 1/3 1/3 2/3 $\Rightarrow$ 0.0165	
● ○ ● ○ ●	1/3 2/3 1/3 2/3 1/3 $\Rightarrow$ 0.0165	
● ○ ● ○ ○	1/3 2/3 1/3 2/3 2/3 $\Rightarrow$ 0.0329	*
● ○ ○ ● ●	1/3 2/3 2/3 1/3 1/3 $\Rightarrow$ 0.0165	
● ○ ○ ● ○	1/3 2/3 2/3 1/3 2/3 $\Rightarrow$ 0.0329	*
● ○ ○ ○ ●	1/3 2/3 2/3 2/3 1/3 $\Rightarrow$ 0.0329	*
● ○ ○ ○ ○	1/3 2/3 2/3 2/3 2/3 $\Rightarrow$ 0.0658	*
○ ● ● ● ●	2/3 1/3 1/3 1/3 1/3 $\Rightarrow$ 0.0082	
○ ● ● ● ○	2/3 1/3 1/3 1/3 2/3 $\Rightarrow$ 0.0165	
○ ● ● ○ ●	2/3 1/3 1/3 2/3 1/3 $\Rightarrow$ 0.0165	
○ ● ● ○ ○	2/3 1/3 1/3 2/3 2/3 $\Rightarrow$ 0.0329	*
○ ● ○ ● ●	2/3 1/3 2/3 1/3 1/3 $\Rightarrow$ 0.0165	
○ ● ○ ● ○	2/3 1/3 2/3 1/3 2/3 $\Rightarrow$ 0.0329	*
○ ● ○ ○ ●	2/3 1/3 2/3 2/3 1/3 $\Rightarrow$ 0.0329	*
○ ● ○ ○ ○	2/3 1/3 2/3 2/3 2/3 $\Rightarrow$ 0.0658	*
○ ○ ● ● ●	2/3 2/3 1/3 1/3 1/3 $\Rightarrow$ 0.0165	
○ ○ ● ● ○	2/3 2/3 1/3 1/3 2/3 $\Rightarrow$ 0.0329	*
○ ○ ● ○ ●	2/3 2/3 1/3 2/3 1/3 $\Rightarrow$ 0.0329	*
○ ○ ● ○ ○	2/3 2/3 1/3 2/3 2/3 $\Rightarrow$ 0.0658	*
○ ○ ○ ● ●	2/3 2/3 2/3 1/3 1/3 $\Rightarrow$ 0.0329	*
○ ○ ○ ● ○	2/3 2/3 2/3 1/3 2/3 $\Rightarrow$ 0.0658	*
○ ○ ○ ○ ●	2/3 2/3 2/3 2/3 1/3 $\Rightarrow$ 0.0658	*
○ ○ ○ ○ ○	2/3 2/3 2/3 2/3 2/3 $\Rightarrow$ 0.1317	
	0.9998	

Table 5.2 Typicality summary

n	$|\mathcal{T}_\epsilon^{(n)}|$	$Pr(\mathcal{T}_\epsilon^{(n)})$
100	$2^{92.6}$	0.660
500	$2^{474.9}$	0.971
1000	$2^{953.4}$	0.998
2000	$2^{1910.3}$	1.000

If we consider a source that outputs text, then the typical long sequences are the sequences of "meaningful" text while the nontypical sequences are simply garbled text. What is meant by "meaningful" is determined by the structure of the language; that is, by its grammar, spelling rules, and so on. If we have L letters in our alphabet, then we can compose L^n different sequences that are n letters long. Only approximately $2^{nH(X)}$, where $H(X)$ is the uncertainty of the language, of these are "meaningful." That is, only the fraction

$$\frac{2^{nH(X)}}{L^n} = \frac{2^{nH(X)}}{2^{n\log L}} = 2^{-n(\log L - H(X))} \tag{5.39}$$

which vanishes when n grows to infinity provided that $H(X) < \log L$, is "meaningful." For the ordinary written English $H(X)$ is about 1.5 bits/letter whereas $\log L = \log 26 \approx 4.7$ bits/letter.

Shannon illustrated by a simple example how increasing structure between letters will give better approximations to the English language. Assuming an alphabet with 27 symbols – 26 letters and 1 space – he started with an approximation of the first order, that is, the symbols are chosen *independently* of each other but with the actual probability distribution of English (12% E, 2% W, etc.):

```
OCRO HLI RGWR NMIELWIS EU LL NBNESEBYA
TH EEI ALHENHTTPA OOBTTVA NAH BRL
```

Then Shannon continued with the approximation of second order, where the symbols are chosen with the actual *bigram* statistics – when a symbol has been chosen, the next symbol is chosen according to the actual conditional probability distribution:

```
ON IE ANTSOUTINYS ARE T INCTORE ST BE S
DEAMY ACHIN D ILONASIVE TUCOOWE AT
TEASONARE FUSO TIZIN ANDY TOBE SEACE CTISBE
```

The approximation of the third order is based on the *trigram* statistics – when two successive symbols have been chosen, the next symbol is chosen according to the actual conditional probability distribution:

```
IN NO IST LAT WHEY CRATICT FROURE BIRS
GROCID PONDENOME OF DEMONSTRURES OF THE
REPTAGIN IS REGOACTIONA OF CRE
```

If we proceed in this manner we will obtain texts that look like English, that is, they are "meaningful" in the above sense, but they seem to carry no real meaning.

Consider the set of typical long output sequences of n symbols from a source with uncertainty $H(X)$ bits per source symbol. Since there are fewer than $2^{n(H(X)+\epsilon)}$ typical long sequences in this set, they can be represented by $n(H(X) + \epsilon)$ binary digits; that is, by $H(X) + \epsilon$ binary digits per source symbol. Suppose conversely that we have only $n(H(X) - 2\epsilon)$ binary digits available; then we can represent only the vanishing fraction $2^{n(H(X)-2\epsilon)}/((1-\epsilon)2^{n(H(X)-\epsilon)}) = (1-\epsilon)^{-1}2^{-n\epsilon}$ of the at least $(1-\epsilon)2^{n(H(X)-\epsilon)}$ typical long sequences.

We summarize our discussion in the following Theorem 5.4.

Theorem 5.4 (Source Coding)   *Let* $X = X_1 X_2 \ldots X_n$ *be the output sequence of a source with uncertainty* $H(X)$ *bits per source symbol. Then there exists a map between the set of output sequences* $x = x_1 x_2 \ldots x_n$ *and the set of typical long binary sequences of length* $n(H(X) + \epsilon)$ *such that the probability that the typical long sequence will not uniquely specify the source sequence is less than* ϵ.

Thus we can represent the source sequence $X = X_1 X_2 \ldots X_n$ essentially uniquely by using on the average $nH(X)$ binary digits.

Although it was only hinted at in our discussion of typical sequences, there exists a so-called *converse* to the Source Coding Theorem that states that we cannot represent the sequence $X = X_1 X_2 \ldots X_n$ essentially uniquely by using on the average fewer than $nH(X)$ binary digits.

5.1.2   Channel Coding

Since the typical long sequences are equiprobable and can always be represented by binary digits we can argue that it is sufficient to design a communication system to transmit sequences of equiprobable binary digits. Divide the entire sequence to be transmitted into *blocks* of K binary digits each. These blocks will be called *messages* and denoted $u = u_1 u_2 \ldots u_K$. A binary (N, K) *block code* B is a set of $M = 2^K$ binary N-tuples $v = v_1 v_2 \ldots v_N$ called *codewords*. N is called the *block length* and the quantity

$$R = \frac{\log M}{N} = K/N \tag{5.40}$$

is called the *code rate* and is measured in *bits per use* of the communication channel. The *transmission rate* R_t is measured in bits per second and is obtained by multiplying the code rate R by the number of transmitted channel symbols per second. If T seconds are used to send R bits, then we obtain the transmission rate as

$$R_t = R/T \text{ bits/s} \tag{5.41}$$

EXAMPLE 5.3

The $(3, 2)$ code $B = \{000, 011, 101, 110\}$ consists of $M = 2^K = 4$ codewords and has rate $R = 2/3$.   ∎

A *channel encoder* for an (N, K) block code $\mathcal{B}$ is a one-to-one mapping from the set of $M = 2^K = 2^{RN}$ binary messages of length K to the set of $M = 2^K = 2^{RN}$ codewords of length N.

EXAMPLE 5.4

$u_1 u_2$	$v_1 v_2 v_3$		$u_1 u_2$	$v_1 v_2 v_3$
00	000		00	110
01	011	and	01	101
10	101		10	011
11	110		11	000

are two different channel encoders for the rate $R = 2/3$ block code $\mathcal{B}$ given in Example 5.3. ∎

In Figure 5.4 we show a general digital communication system in which the signal processor on the transmitting side is split into a source encoder and a channel encoder, and the signal processor on the receiving side is split into a channel decoder and a source decoder. The outputs of the channel encoder, the codewords, are transmitted over the communication channel where it is likely that some of the symbols get corrupted by noise. The channel coding parts can be designed separately from the source coding parts, which simplifies the use of the same channel coding system for various sources.

The simplest models of digital channels, namely, the *binary symmetric channel* (BSC) and the *binary erasure channel* (BEC) are illustrated in Figure 5.5. For the binary symmetric channel both a 0 and a 1 are received correctly, that is, as a 0 and a 1, with probability $1 - \varepsilon$, and erroneously, that is, as a 1 and a 0, with

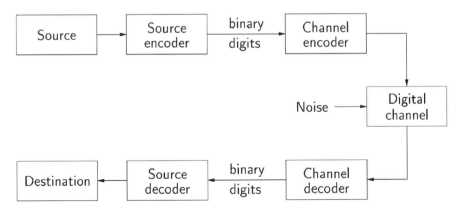

Figure 5.4   A digital communication system with separate source and channel coding

BSC

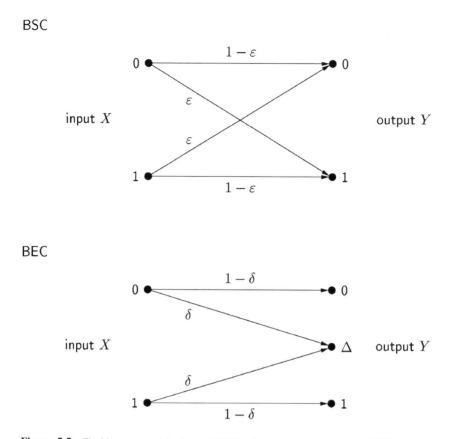

BEC

Figure 5.5   The binary symmetric channel (BSC) and the binary erasure channel (BEC)

probability ε. Similarly, for the binary erasure channel both a 0 and a 1 are received correctly with probability $1 - \delta$, but as an *erasure* Δ with probability δ.

Shannon modeled the *discrete memoryless communication channel* (DMC) as two alphabets, the input alphabet $\mathcal{X}$ and the output alphabet $\mathcal{Y}$, and a set of conditional probabilities $P_{Y|X}(y \mid x)$. If we transmit x then the received symbol y is randomly chosen according to the conditional distribution $P_{Y|X}(y \mid x)$. The number of output symbols does not have to be the same as the number of input symbols. The binary symmetric channel has two input symbols and two output symbols, while the binary erasure channel has two input symbols but three output symbols.

The channel is said to be *memoryless* if for all $i \geq 2$ the conditional probabilities

$$P_{Y_i|X_1X_2\ldots X_iY_1Y_2\ldots Y_{i-1}}(y_i \mid x_1x_2 \ldots x_iy_1y_2 \ldots y_{i-1}) = P_{Y|X}(y_i \mid x_i) \tag{5.42}$$

What happens to the sequence at time i is independent of what happened during the previous $i-1$ time instants.

For the binary symmetric channel and the binary erasure channel we have

$$\text{BSC:} \quad \begin{cases} P_{Y|X}(0 \mid 0) = P_{Y|X}(1 \mid 1) = 1 - \varepsilon \\ P_{Y|X}(1 \mid 0) = P_{Y|X}(0 \mid 1) = \varepsilon \end{cases} \tag{5.43}$$

$$\text{BEC:} \quad \begin{cases} P_{Y|X}(0 \mid 0) = P_{Y|X}(1 \mid 1) = 1 - \delta \\ P_{Y|X}(1 \mid 0) = P_{Y|X}(0 \mid 1) = 0 \\ P_{Y|X}(\Delta \mid 0) = P_{Y|X}(\Delta \mid 1) = \delta \end{cases} \tag{5.44}$$

In BPSK (see Section 4.3), the modulator generates, for example, the waveform

$$s_1(t) = \begin{cases} \sqrt{2E_s/T} \cos \omega t, & 0 \le t < T \\ 0, & \text{otherwise} \end{cases} \tag{5.45}$$

if the input is 1 and $s_0(t) = -s_1(t)$ if the input is 0. Assume that additive white Gaussian noise (AWGN) with zero mean and variance $N_0/2$ is added to the signal when it is transmitted over the channel. The optimum receiver is a matched filter whose output is sampled each T seconds (Fig. 5.6).

The output at sample time iT is a Gaussian random variable with mean $\mu = \pm \sqrt{E_s}$, where the sign is $+$ or $-$ according to the modulator input being 1 or 0, respectively, and the variance $\sigma^2 = N_0/2$. Suppose that we at the output of the sampler make a *hard decision*, that is, we take any matched filter output value above 0 as $+\sqrt{E_s}$, meaning symbol 1, and otherwise as $-\sqrt{E_s}$, meaning symbol 0. Then this BPSK modulation system can be modeled as the binary symmetric channel with crossover probability ε. The crossover probability is closely related to the signal-to-noise ratio E_s/N_0. Since the modulation system is symmetric in 0 and 1, we can without loss of generality assume that a 0 is sent. Then the crossover probability ε is simply the probability that a channel error occurs, that is, that the output from the sampler is positive (corresponding to a transmitted 1). It can be shown that this matched filter output is a Gaussian random variable with mean $\mu = -\sqrt{E_s}$, variance $\sigma^2 = N_0/2$, and

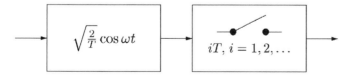

Figure 5.6 Matched filter receiver

probability density function $(\sqrt{2\pi\sigma^2})^{-1} \exp(-(x - \mu)^2/2\sigma^2)$. Thus, we obtain

$$
\begin{aligned}
\varepsilon &= \frac{1}{\sqrt{\pi N_0}} \int_0^\infty e^{-(x+\sqrt{E_s})^2/N_0} \, dx \\
&= \frac{1}{\sqrt{2\pi}} \int_{\sqrt{2E_s/N_0}}^\infty e^{-y^2/2} \, dy = Q(\sqrt{2E_s/N_0})
\end{aligned}
\tag{5.46}
$$

where the $Q(\ )$ function is given by Eq. (4.30).

If, for example, E_s/N_0 is 4 dB, then we obtain from Figure 4.16 that the cross-over probability ε for the corresponding BSC is approximately 10^{-2}. The BSC is often used as a model for the simple BPSK modulation system described above. The BEC model is applicable when we either are pretty sure whether a 0 or a 1 was sent, or we hardly get any guidance from the received signal about the transmitted signal in which case we simply declare an erasure Δ.

5.1.3 The Channel Coding Theorem

We shall now discuss the most sensational result in Shannon's 1948 paper, namely, his channel coding theorem, but as prerequisites we need a few more statements about typical long sequences.

As a straightforward extension of Eq. (5.36) we have

$$
2^{-n(H(XY)+\epsilon)} \leq P_{XY}(x, y) \leq 2^{-n(H(XY)-\epsilon)}
\tag{5.47}
$$

By combining the definition of conditional probabilities, $P_{X|Y}(x \mid y) = P_{XY}(x, y)/P_Y(y)$, (5.36), and Eq. (5.47) we obtain

$$
2^{-n(H(X|Y)+2\epsilon)} \leq P_{X|Y}(x \mid y) \leq 2^{-n(H(X|Y)-2\epsilon)}
\tag{5.48}
$$

which, as a counterpart to Property 3 of the typical set $T_\epsilon^{(n)}$, yields

$$
|T_\epsilon^{(n)}(X \mid y)| \leq 2^{n(H(X|Y)+2\epsilon)}
\tag{5.49}
$$

where $|T_\epsilon^{(n)}(X \mid y)|$ is the number of typical long sequences X that are *jointly typical* with the given typical long sequence y. Two sequences x and y are *jointly typical* if x and y are individually typical, that is, both satisfy Eq. (5.36), and the pair (x, y) is typical, that is, it satisfies Eq. (5.47).

Consider a channel with input X and output Y. Then we have approximately $2^{NH(X)}$ and $2^{NH(Y)}$ typical long input and output sequences of length N, respectively. Furthermore, for each typical long input sequence we have approximately $2^{NH(Y|X)}$ typical long output sequences that are jointly typical with the given input sequence (see Fig. 7); we call such an input sequence together with its jointly typical output sequences a *fan*. If the channel is very noisy, then the uncertainty about Y given X,

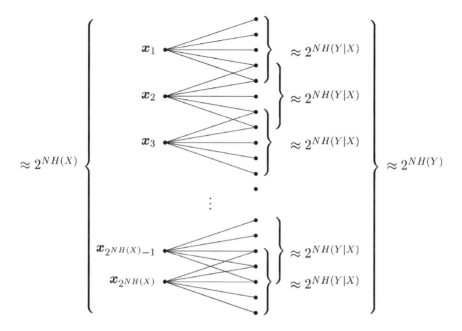

Figure 5.7   Illustration of our plausibility argument for Shannon's channel coding theorem

$H(Y \mid X)$, is large and hence the fans are large. On the other hand, if the channel is a straight wire, then the uncertainty about Y given X is zero, $H(Y \mid X) = 0$, and hence we have degenerate fans with only one output sequence per fan. (As an example we assume that we have a BSC with error probability $\varepsilon = 0.11$, then $H(Y \mid X) = 0.50$ (cf. Fig. 5.2) and, hence, each fan consists of approximately $2^{N \cdot 0.50}$ typical long output sequences.) Delete some of the fans in Figure 5.7 in such a manner that the remaining fans are nonoverlapping. Consider the remaining nonoverlapping fans. Clearly, we can have at most

$$\frac{2^{NH(Y)}}{2^{NH(Y|X)}} = 2^{N(H(Y)-H(Y|X))} = 2^{NI(X;Y)} \tag{5.50}$$

nonoverlapping fans. If we let the typical long input sequences corresponding to the nonoverlapping fans represent messages, then the number of distinguishable messages, $M = 2^K = 2^{RN}$, can be at most $2^{NI(X;Y)}$, that is,

$$2^{RN} = 2^{NI(X;Y)} \tag{5.51}$$

or, equivalently, the largest value of the rate R for nonoverlapping fans is

$$R = I(X;Y) \text{ bits/channel use} \tag{5.52}$$

Since we would like to communicate with as high code rate R as possible, we choose the input symbols according to the probability distribution $P_X(x)$ that maximizes the mutual information $I(X; Y)$; this maximum value is called the *capacity* of the channel,

$$C \stackrel{\text{def}}{=} \max_{P_X(x)} \{I(X; Y)\} \text{ bits/channel use} \tag{5.53}$$

In order to exploit the properties of our fans we let the encoder map the messages to the typical long input sequences that represent nonoverlapping fans, which requires that the code rate R is at most equal to the capacity of the channel, that is,

$$R \leq C$$

Then the received typical long output sequence is used to identify the corresponding fan and, hence, the corresponding typical long input sequence, or, equivalently, the message, and this can be done correctly with a probability arbitrarily close to 1.

If the fans overlap, which must occur if the code rate R exceeds the channel capacity C, that is, if $R > C$, some output sequences will appear in more than one fan and we would not be able to distinguish which was the sent message when these output sequences occur.

Having given these plausibility arguments based on typical long sequences we formulate Shannon's most dramatic and unexpected result:

Theorem 5.5 (Channel Coding) *Suppose we transmit information symbols at rate $R = K/N$ bits/channel use using a block code via a channel with capacity C. Provided that $R < C$ we can achieve arbitrary reliability, that is, we can transmit the symbols virtually error-free, by choosing N sufficiently large. Conversely, if $R > C$, then significant distortion must occur.*

In order to show that we can actually communicate arbitrarily reliable with a rate R as close to the channel capacity C as we wish, we consider the "reversed" fans in Figure 5.8 and use the following coding strategy:

- Choose the M codewords independently and randomly from the $2^{NH(X)}$ typical channel input sequences.

- To decode we look at the fan that corresponds to the typical output sequence that we receive. Only those typical input sequences in this fan that are codewords could have been sent; notice that there can be more than one such sequence. Choose any (!) one of these as the decision for the transmitted codeword.

To show that this strategy actually works we upper-bound the probability P_e that our decision is wrong. For each of the $M-1$ erroneous codewords we have the probability $2^{NH(X|Y)}/2^{NH(X)}$ of being chosen as one of the $2^{NH(X|Y)}$ typical input

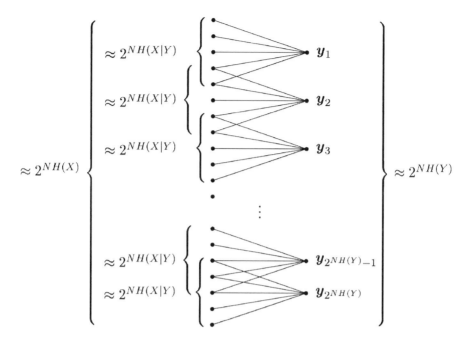

Figure 5.8   Illustration of the fans used in the proof of Shannon's channel coding theorem

sequences that could have caused the typical output sequence. Thus, we have

$$P_e \leq (M-1)(2^{NH(X|Y)}/2^{NH(X)})Pr(Y \text{ is typical})$$
$$+ Pr(Y \text{ is nontypical})$$
$$< (M-1)2^{-N(H(X)-H(X|Y))} + \epsilon$$
$$< M2^{-NI(X;Y)} + \epsilon$$

for N sufficiently large. Since the input symbols are chosen according to the capacity achieving probability distribution we obtain

$$P_e < M2^{-NC} + \epsilon$$
$$= 2^{-N(C-R)} + \epsilon \tag{5.54}$$

where we have used that $M = 2^{NR}$. We conclude from Eq. (5.54) that for rates R less than the capacity C our strategy yields an error probability as close to zero as we wish given that the sequences are sufficiently long. Shannon went one step further and showed that arbitrarily small error probability can even be achieved when $R = C$ (cf. [2]).

Before Shannon, the common belief was that an increase in reliability required an increase in the signal-to-noise ratio. Shannon showed that, provided the signal-to-noise ratio was high enough to cause the channel capacity to exceed the code rate, that is, $C > R$, then an increase in the reliability could be achieved without sacrificing the transmission rate. This was at the cost of increased block length N, that is, an increase in the complexity of the encoders and decoders. Some twenty-five years after Shannon's theoretical results, the micro-electronics revolution led to the development of very complex low-cost integrated circuits, paving the way for the use of codes in consumer products such as CD-players, mobile telephones, and high-speed modems.

EXAMPLE 5.5

Consider the BSC with crossover probability ε. From the symmetry of the channel it follows that the mutual information between the input X and the output Y, $I(X; Y)$ achieves its maximum when the input symbols 0 and 1 are used with equal probability; that is, when $P_X(x_i) = 1/2$, $x_1 = 0$, $x_2 = 1$. When the inputs are equiprobable, then, again, from the symmetry of the channel, it follows that the outputs are equiprobable and, hence, that the uncertainty of the output Y is $H(Y) = 1$. Thus we have the channel capacity

$$
\begin{aligned}
C_{\text{BSC}} &= \max\{I(X; Y)\} \\
&= \max\{(H(Y) - H(Y \mid X))\} \\
&= 1 - \left(-\sum_{i=1}^{2} \sum_{j=1}^{2} P_{XY}(x_i, y_j) \log P_{Y|X}(y_j \mid x_i) \right) \\
&= 1 + \sum_{i=1}^{2} \sum_{j=1}^{2} P_{Y|X}(y_j \mid x_i) P_X(x_i) \log P_{Y|X}(y_j \mid x_i) \qquad (5.55) \\
&= 1 + 2(1 - \varepsilon)\tfrac{1}{2}\log(1 - \varepsilon) + 2\varepsilon\tfrac{1}{2}\log \varepsilon \\
&= 1 + (1 - \varepsilon)\log(1 - \varepsilon) + \varepsilon \log \varepsilon \\
&= 1 - h(\varepsilon) \text{ bits/channel use}
\end{aligned}
$$

where $h(\varepsilon)$ is the binary entropy function (5.12). In Figure 5.9 we show the channel capacity for the binary symmetric channel as a function of the crossover probability ε. ∎

As expected the capacity is zero for $\varepsilon = 0.50$ since then the inputs and outputs of the channel are independent random variables. Notice that the channel is as good at ε as it is at $1 - \varepsilon$! Why?

5.1.4   The Gaussian Noise Channel

So far we have considered only channels with binary inputs. Now we introduce the time-discrete Gaussian channel whose output Y_i at time i is the sum of the input X_i and the noise Z_i,

$$
Y_i = X_i + Z_i \qquad (5.56)
$$

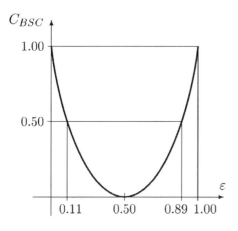

Figure 5.9 The channel capacity for the BSC

where X_i and Y_i are real numbers and Z_i is a Gaussian random variable with mean 0 and variance $N_0/2$. If we choose the inputs as an infinite subset of the reals with the numbers taken so far apart that they are distinguishable at the output after having been corrupted by the noise, then this scheme has infinite capacity; an infinite number of inputs can be received with an arbitrarily small error probability. What's the catch in our reasoning? The chosen set of inputs requires infinite energy! A natural limitation on the inputs is an average energy constraint; assuming a codeword of N symbols $x = x_1 x_2 \ldots x_N$ is transmitted, we require that

$$\frac{1}{N}\sum_{i=1}^{N} x_i^2 \leq E \tag{5.57}$$

where E is the signaling energy. It can be shown (see, for example, ref. [3]) that the capacity of a Gaussian channel with energy constraint E and noise variance $N_0/2$ is

$$C = \tfrac{1}{2}\log\left(1 + \frac{2E}{N_0}\right) \text{ bits/channel use} \tag{5.58}$$

Next we consider communication over a bandlimited channel with noise of power spectral density $N_0/2$. It is continuous in time and we assume that the frequency function is

$$H(f) = \text{rect}\left(\frac{f}{W}\right) = \begin{cases} 1, & |f| < W \\ 0, & |f| > W \end{cases} \tag{5.59}$$

that is, the channel cuts off all frequencies greater than W.

Suppose that we use basis functions $\psi(t)$ with Fourier bandwidth W and that they are transmitted at their Shannon rate $2B$ basis functions per second. Let P_s

be the power of any transmitted signal

$$s(t) = \sum_{k=1}^{N} s\left(\frac{k}{2B}\right) \psi\left(2B\left(t - \frac{k}{2B}\right)\right) \tag{5.60}$$

Suppose the channel is used over a time interval of T seconds. Then the energy per sample is

$$\frac{P_s T}{2BT} = \frac{P_s}{2B} \tag{5.61}$$

The noise has power $\frac{N_0}{2} 2W = N_0 W$ and its energy in the T seconds interval is $N_0 WT$ or

$$\frac{N_0 WT}{2BT} = \frac{N_0 W}{2B} \text{ Watt-seconds/sample} \tag{5.62}$$

Since the noise is white and Gaussian it can be shown that these noise samples are independent Gaussian variables with variance $N_0 W/2B$ and thus we can insert Eqs. (5.61) and (5.62) into Eq. (5.58) and obtain

$$\frac{1}{2}\log\left(1 + \frac{P_s/2B}{N_0 W/2B}\right) = \frac{1}{2}\log\left(1 + \frac{P_s}{N_0 W}\right) \text{ bits/sample} \tag{5.63}$$

Sampling with the Shannon rate $2B$ yields

$$2B \cdot \frac{1}{2}\log\left(1 + \frac{P_s}{N_0 W}\right) = B\log\left(1 + \frac{P_s}{N_0 W}\right) \text{ bits/s} \tag{5.64}$$

Finally, we maximize Eq. (5.64) by choosing the sinc-pulses as our basis functions, that is, we let the Shannon bandwidth be equal to its maximum value, $B = W$, which yields Shannon's famous formula for the channel capacity of the bandwidth limited Gaussian channel with two-sided noise spectral density $N_0/2$ [4]

$$C_t^W = W\log\left(1 + \frac{P_s}{N_0 W}\right) \text{ bits/s} \tag{5.65}$$

where W denotes the bandwidth in Hz and P_s is the signaling power in Watts.

Now we consider the Gaussian channel *without* bandwidth limitation. From Eq. (5.65) it follows that its capacity is

$$
\begin{aligned}
C_t^\infty &= \lim_{W\to\infty} W \log\left(1 + \frac{P_s}{N_0 W}\right) \\
&= \lim_{W\to\infty} W \frac{\ln\left(1 + \dfrac{P_s}{N_0 W}\right)}{\ln 2} \\
&= \lim_{W\to\infty} \frac{W}{\ln 2}\left(\frac{P_s}{N_0 W} - \frac{1}{2}\left(\frac{P_s}{N_0 W}\right)^2 + \cdots\right) \\
&= \lim_{W\to\infty}\left(\frac{P_s}{N_0 \ln 2} - \frac{W}{2\ln 2}\left(\frac{P_s}{N_0 W}\right)^2 + \cdots\right) \\
&= \frac{P_s}{N_0 \ln 2} \ \text{bits/s}
\end{aligned}
\tag{5.66}
$$

Let τ be a multiple of the pulse duration T and suppose that we transmit K information symbols during τ seconds. Then, since the signal energy during τ seconds is $P_s\tau$ we obtain the following energy per bit

$$
E_b = \frac{P_s\tau}{K}
\tag{5.67}
$$

The transmission rate $R_t = K/\tau$ bits/s, and, hence, we obtain

$$
E_b = \frac{P_s}{R_t}
\tag{5.68}
$$

Combining Eqs. (5.66) and (5.68) yields

$$
\frac{C_t^\infty}{R_t} = \frac{E_b}{N_0 \ln 2}
\tag{5.69}
$$

From Shannon's channel coding theorem it follows that for reliable communication we must have $R_t < C_t^\infty$. By combining this inequality with Eq. (5.69) we obtain that for reliable communication

$$
\frac{E_b}{N_0} > \ln 2 = 0.69 = -1.6 \ \text{dB}
\tag{5.70}
$$

which is the fundamental *Shannon limit* to signaling energy.

In any system that provides reliable communication over a Gaussian channel the signal-to-noise ratio E_b/N_0 must exceed the Shannon limit, -1.6 dB.

So long as $E_b/N_0 > -1.6$ dB, Shannon's channel coding theorem guarantees the existence of a system – although it might be very complex – for reliable communication over the channel.

Let us return to the bandwidth limited Gaussian channel with channel capacity given by Eq. (5.65). Assume that we use a rate $R = K/N$ bits/channel use block code to communicate at the *Nyquist rate*, that is, at a rate of $2W$ samples per second (cf. the sampling theorem in Section 2.4). As before we transmit K information symbols during τ seconds, which corresponds to

$$N = 2W\tau \quad \text{samples per codeword} \tag{5.71}$$

Since $R_t = K/\tau$ it follows from Eq. (5.71) that

$$R_t = 2WK/N = 2WR \text{ bits/s} \tag{5.72}$$

From Eq. (5.72) the important observation follows that assuming constant transmission rate R_t, the required bandwidth W is inversely proportional to the code rate R.

By combining Eqs. (5.68) and (5.72) we obtain

$$\frac{P_s}{WN_0} = \frac{E_b R_t}{(R_t/2R)N_0} = 2RE_b/N_0 \tag{5.73}$$

Inserting Eq. (5.73) into Eq. (5.65) and using the fact that for reliable communication we must have $R_t < C_t^W$, we obtain

$$R_t = 2WR < W \log\left(1 + \frac{2RE_b}{N_0}\right) \tag{5.74}$$

or, equivalently,

$$2^{2R} < 1 + \frac{2RE_b}{N_0} \tag{5.75}$$

Solving for E_b/N_0 yields

$$E_b/N_0 > \frac{2^{2R} - 1}{2R} \tag{5.76}$$

The limit of the right side of Eq. (5.76) when $R \to 0$ can be obtained as follows.

$$\frac{2^{2R} - 1}{2R} = \frac{e^{2R \ln 2} - 1}{2R} = \frac{2R \ln 2 + \dfrac{(2R \ln 2)^2 + \cdots}{2}}{2R} \qquad (5.77)$$

$$\to \ln 2 = 0.69 = -1.6 \text{ dB}$$

Thus, by letting $R \to 0$ in Eq. (5.76) we obtain, as expected, Eq. (5.70), that is, E_b/N_0 must exceed the Shannon limit, -1.6 dB.

In order to communicate close to the Shannon limit, -1.6 dB, we have to use both a code rate R and a transmission rate R_t close to zero! If we use a code of rate $R = \frac{1}{2}$, then it follows from Eq. (5.76) that in order to achieve reliable communication the required signal-to-noise ratio E_b/N_0 must exceed 0 dB,

$$E_b/N_0 > 1 = 0 \text{ dB} \qquad (5.78)$$

In Section 5.3 we shall study how encoding and decoding can be done in practice.

5.2 METHODS OF SOURCE CODING

In this section we shall discuss two different algorithms for source coding but first we introduce fixed-to-variable length coding (Fig. 5.10).

The source output U is a random variable taking on values in the K-ary alphabet $\mathcal{U} = \{u_1, u_2, \ldots, u_K\}$. The length of the codeword $X = X_1 X_2 \ldots X_W$ is a random variable W and for simplicity we assume that X_i, $i = 1, 2, \ldots, W$, are binary random variables.

Our goal is to find a mapping between the source output U and the codeword $X = X_1 X_2 \ldots X_W$ such that the *average codeword length*, that is, $\overline{W}$, is as small as possible; the average codeword length is

$$\overline{W} = \sum_{i=1}^{K} P_U(u_i) w_i \qquad (5.79)$$

Before we formulate the mapping we introduce a restriction that is somewhat subtle. We say that a sequence of length l is a *prefix* of a sequence if the first l symbols of the latter sequence are identical to those of the first sequence; in particular, a sequence is

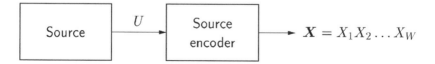

Figure 5.10   A fixed-to-variable length source coding scheme

a prefix of itself. Then we require that *no codeword is the prefix of another codeword* and call such a code a *prefix-free (instantaneous) source code*. Such a source code is instantaneously decodable; as soon as we have received a codeword the source decoder can output the corresponding source symbol. The mapping between source symbols and codewords for a prefix-free source code is clearly one-to-one, and, hence, we conclude that the uncertainty of the codeword is equal to the uncertainty of the source output, that is,

$$H(X) = H(U) \tag{5.80}$$

EXAMPLE 5.6

The sequence 10011 has the prefixes: 1, 10, 100, 1001, and 10011.

The source code with codewords {00, 01, 1} is prefix-free, but {00, 10, 1} is not, since 1 is prefix of 10. ∎

In the sequel we shall only consider prefix-free source codes.

EXAMPLE 5.7

The source code specified by the table

u	$P_U(u)$	x
u_1	0.45	0
u_2	0.30	10
u_3	0.15	110
u_4	0.10	111

can be illustrated by a (rooted) binary tree as shown in Figure 5.11. The average codeword length is

$$\overline{W} = \sum_{i=1}^{4} P_U(u_i) w_i$$

$$= 0.45 \cdot 1 + 0.30 \cdot 2 + 0.15 \cdot 3 + 0.10 \cdot 3 \tag{5.81}$$

$$= 1.80 \qquad \blacksquare$$

The codewords in the previous example correspond to vertices that are *leaves*, that is, vertices without outgoing branches. We call the remaining vertices, that is, the vertices with outgoing branches, *nodes*. The leftmost node is called the *root*. The probability of a node is the probability to go through that node on the trip from the root to a leaf. We have a neat little lemma about the depth of the leaves (cf. Massey [5]).

Lemma 5.6 (Path Length Lemma) *In a rooted tree with probabilities, the average depth of the leaves is equal to the sum of the probabilities of the nodes (including the root).*

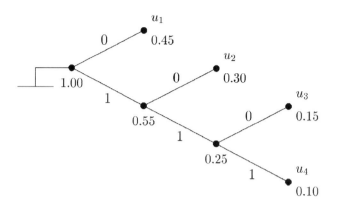

Figure 5.11   A binary tree representing the source code in Example 5.7

The proof of the Path Length Lemma is simple and left as an exercise.

EXAMPLE 5.6   *(continued)*

Since the average codeword length is the same as the average depth of the leaves we can use the Path Length Lemma and obtain

$$\overline{W} = 1.00 + 0.55 + 0.25 = 1.80 \tag{5.82}$$

in agreement with Eq. (5.81).   ■

Next we shall give a constructive procedure for designing an optimal, in the sense of shortest average codeword length, source code for a source output U. This algorithm is due to David Huffman [6] who discovered it when he in 1951 as a student chose to write a term paper instead of taking the final exam! "Huffman code is one of the fundamental ideas that people in computer science and data communication are using all the time," says Donald Knuth of Stanford University. We introduce the Huffman algorithm with an example.

Consider a random variable U taking on the six values in the set of outputs $\{u_1, u_2, u_3, u_4, u_5, u_6\}$ with probabilities

u	$P_U(u)$
u_1	0.30
u_2	0.20
u_3	0.20
u_4	0.20
u_5	0.05
u_6	0.05

Huffman's insight was that the longest codewords should be assigned to the least likely source symbols. Moreover, there exists a source code such that the two longest codewords differ only in the last code symbol. Hence, we build a rooted code tree "backwards" by assigning leaves to the source symbols and combining the two least likely leaves into a node whose probability is the sum of the probabilities of its leaves (Fig. 5.12a).

We have now reduced the problem to one with five values. Next we combine the two least probable vertices among the five, that is, the node in Figure 5.12a with one of the leaves u_2, u_3, and u_4. By arbitrarily choosing u_4 we obtain the structure shown in Figure 5.12b. Now we have reduced our problem to one with only four values. Proceeding in this way we finally obtain a Huffman tree shown in Figure 5.13. (Find the other two Huffman trees as an exercise.)

In Figure 5.14 we show a "straightened-out" version of the Huffman tree that has run wild in Figure 5.13. For this Huffman tree we obtain the Huffman code

u	$P_U(u)$	x
u_1	0.30	00
u_2	0.20	10
u_3	0.20	11
u_4	0.20	010
u_5	0.05	0110
u_6	0.05	0111

A straightforward calculation of the average codeword length yields

$$\overline{W} = \sum_{i=1}^{6} P_U(u_i)w_i$$

$$= 0.30 \cdot 2 + 0.20 \cdot 2 + 0.20 \cdot 2 + 0.20 \cdot 3 + 0.05 \cdot 4 + 0.05 \cdot 4 \qquad (5.83)$$

$$= 2.40$$

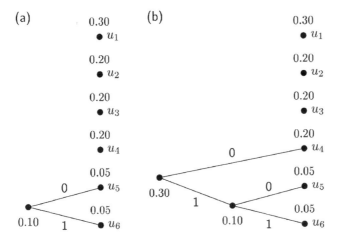

Figure 5.12   Growing a Huffman tree backwards

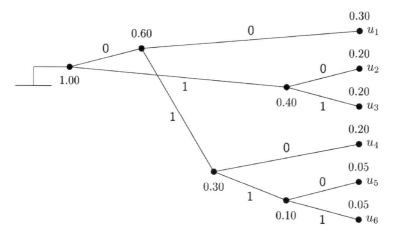

Figure 5.13   Complete Huffman tree grown backwards

Using the Path Length Lemma yields

$$\overline{W} = \sum_{\text{nodes}} Pr(\text{node})$$
$$= 1.00 + 0.60 + 0.40 + 0.30 + 0.10 \qquad (5.84)$$
$$= 2.40$$

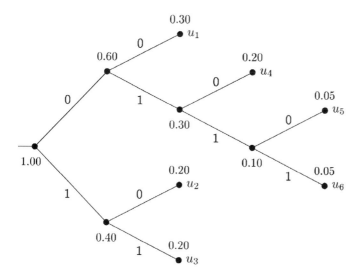

Figure 5.14   A "straightened-out" Huffman tree

We know from Shannon's source coding theorem that we cannot do better than the uncertainty of the source, which works out to

$$H(U) = -\sum_{i=1}^{6} P_U(u_i) \log P_U(u_i)$$

$$= -0.30 \log 0.30 - 0.20 \log 0.20 - 0.20 \log 0.20$$
$$- 0.20 \log 0.20 - 0.05 \log 0.05 - 0.05 \log 0.05$$
$$= 2.34$$

The Huffman code can be shown to be optimal, so we cannot do better than $\overline{W} = 2.40$ when coding the source in the previous example. We are 2.6% above the ultimate limit $H(U) = 2.34$, which cannot be reached if we encode consecutively the source symbols separately. If we jointly encode two consecutive and assumed independent source symbols, that is, use the Huffman code for the source

$u_i u_j$	$P_{U_1 U_2}(u_i u_j)$
$u_1 u_1$	0.0900
$u_1 u_2$	0.0600
$u_1 u_3$	0.0600
$\vdots$	$\vdots$
$u_6 u_6$	0.0025

we will obtain an average codeword length *per single source symbol* that is closer to the uncertainty of the source, $H(U) = 2.34$. As Shannon promised, encoding longer and longer strings will eventually get us arbitrarily close to the uncertainty of the source.

EXAMPLE 5.8

Consider a random variable U taking on the four values in the set of outputs $\{u_1, u_2, u_3, u_4\}$ with probabilities

u	$P_U(u)$
u_1	$\frac{1}{2}$
u_2	$\frac{1}{4}$
u_3	$\frac{1}{8}$
u_4	$\frac{1}{8}$

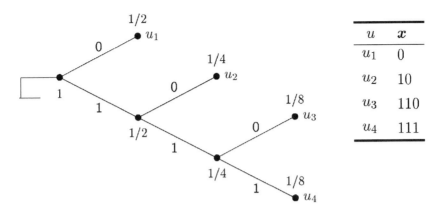

Figure 5.15   A Huffman tree and its corresponding Huffman code

The Huffman tree is shown in Figure 5.15 together with the Huffman code. The average code-word length is

$$\overline{W} = 1 + \tfrac{1}{2} + \tfrac{1}{4} = 1\tfrac{3}{4} \tag{5.86}$$

which happens to coincide with the uncertainty of the source output

$$
\begin{aligned}
H(U) &= -\sum_{i=1}^{4} P_U(u_i) \log P_U(u_i) \\
&= -\tfrac{1}{2}\log\tfrac{1}{2} - \tfrac{1}{4}\log\tfrac{1}{4} - \tfrac{1}{8}\log\tfrac{1}{8} - \tfrac{1}{8}\log\tfrac{1}{8} \\
&= 1\tfrac{3}{4}
\end{aligned}
\tag{5.87}
$$

$\blacksquare$

In our description of Huffman coding we treated the source output symbols as if they were independent of each other but this is far from the truth for real sources. Next we shall describe an entirely different method based on the dictionary technique. Both the transmitter and the receiver build up a dictionary incrementally, adding to it as each symbol (or group of symbols) is transmitted. The current version of the dictionary is used to encode the next portion of the source output.

5.2.1   The Lempel–Ziv–Welch Algorithm

The LZW algorithm is due to Lempel and Ziv [7] and Welch [8]. It is a so-called *universal source-coding algorithm*, which means that we do not need to know the source statistics to apply it. The algorithm is easy to implement and for long sequences it approaches the uncertainty of the source; it is asymptotically optimum.

BOX 5-3

In the old game "20 questions" the goal is to determine an object that belongs to a known set of objects by asking questions that will only be answered by "Yes" or "No". Assuming that we know the probability distribution on the objects we can identify the object by a series of questions that corresponds to the Huffman code for the objects. For example, suppose we have six objects with the probability distribution given after the continuation of Example 5.6. From the Huffman tree in Figure 5.14 we conclude that the first question should be "Is the object in $\{u_2, u_3\}$?" (Or, equivalently, "Is the object in $\{u_1, u_4, u_5, u_6\}$?") The answer determines the first binary digit in the codeword of the object. Suppose that the answer is "No", then we proceed in the tree and ask "Is the object u_1?" and so on, until we reach a leaf and, thus, have identified the object. The minimum average number of questions asked is the average codeword length of the Huffman code.

The source output sequence is sequentially parsed and divided into strings that have not appeared before. These strings are entered into a dictionary. When we start, the dictionary contains only the "empty" string *escape*, denoted by *, and the first letter u_1 at address 0 and address 1, respectively. During each step the encoder adds one *new* string to the dictionary and each new string is the concatenation of an old string and a new letter. Suppose that $u_1 u_2 \ldots u_t$ has already been encoded. In the next step the encoder finds the largest l such that the string $u_{t+1} u_{t+2} \ldots u_{t+l}$ is in the dictionary and is not the string that was most recently added to the dictionary, then the string $u_{t+1} u_{t+2} \ldots u_{t+l} u_{t+l+1}$ is added to the dictionary. The reason for this strange treatment for this most recent string is that it cannot be used immediately since, as we shall see later, the decoder at the receiver side will know the last letter u_{t+l+1} only after the following step!

Suppose we would like to compress the sentence

```
DO_NOT_TROUBLE_TROUBLE_UNTIL_TROUBLE_TROUBLES_YOU!
```

At step 1 we have only the empty string * and the letter D in the dictionary. Assuming that we use the ASCII code to represent our letters and symbols we need 8 binary digits to represent D. Next we come to O_N... in the sentence. We have $l = 0$ and, hence, $u_2 = $ O. But we need to encode also the address. Since $u_2 = $ O and this string is not in the dictionary yet, we encode the address 0 to the empty string. In general, to encode the address to one of the n strings in the dictionary we need[2] $\lceil \log n \rceil$ binary digits; for example, the decimal address 18, which is equal to $1 \cdot 2^4 + 0 \cdot 2^3 + 0 \cdot 2^2 + 1 \cdot 2^1 + 0 \cdot 2^0$, can be written in binary form using $\lceil \log 18 \rceil = 5$ binary digits as 10010. Thus, we need $\lceil \log(1) \rceil + 8$ binary digits to represent $u_2 = $ O. We proceed like this until we reach OT_T..., then $l = 1$ since at step 2 we had the string O. We add $u_5 u_6 = $ OT to the dictionary and use the

---

[2] The ceiling function $\lceil x \rceil$ denotes the smallest integer greater than or equal to x; for example $\lceil 3.4 \rceil = 4$ and $\lceil 7 \rceil = 7$.

address 2, which is one of four addresses, namely, 0, 1, 2, 3; hence, we need $\lceil \log 4 \rceil = 2$ binary digits to represent $u_5 = $ o.

In Table 5.3 we show how the dictionary develops when we parse the given sentence that consists of 50 letters and symbols. Without compression we would need as many as $50 \cdot 8 = 400$ binary digits to represent the sentence as a string of 50 ASCII symbols. If we sum the number of binary digits needed for the 38 steps shown in the table we get only 271 binary digits. If we use the ASCII character conversion shown in Figure 3.1 our sentence is compressed to the binary string shown in Table 5.4.

How do we recover the text from a compressed binary string? Clearly the first 8 bits form the ASCII character for the first source digit u_1. From Table 5.4 we obtain 00100010 which according to our conversion (Fig. 3.1) correspond to the character D. Since $\lceil \log 1 \rceil = 0$, we conclude that the following 8 bits, 11110010, also form a character, namely, o. The following bit is always an address; in this case, it is 0 and, hence, it is the address to Entry *, which implies that the following 8 bits, 11111010, form a character, which according to our conversion is the character _. The first 17 bits form always two characters and one address bit but the bits following this first address bit could be either characters or addresses. We have now built the first part of our dictionary:

Table 5.3 Dictionary for the sentence "Do not trouble Trouble until Trouble troubles you"

Step	Entry	# binary digits	Step	Entry	# binary digits
0	*	—	20	E_	$\lceil \log 19 \rceil$
1	D	8	21	_U	$\lceil \log 20 \rceil$
2	O	$\lceil \log 1 \rceil + 8$	22	UN	$\lceil \log 21 \rceil$
3	_	$\lceil \log 2 \rceil + 8$	23	NT	$\lceil \log 22 \rceil$
4	N	$\lceil \log 3 \rceil + 8$	24	TI	$\lceil \log 23 \rceil$
5	OT	$\lceil \log 4 \rceil$	25	I	$\lceil \log 24 \rceil + 8$
6	T	$\lceil \log 5 \rceil + 8$	26	L_	$\lceil \log 25 \rceil$
7	_T	$\lceil \log 6 \rceil$	27	_TRO	$\lceil \log 26 \rceil$
8	TR	$\lceil \log 7 \rceil$	28	OUBL	$\lceil \log 27 \rceil$
9	R	$\lceil \log 8 \rceil + 8$	29	LE_	$\lceil \log 28 \rceil$
10	OU	$\lceil \log 9 \rceil$	30	_TROU	$\lceil \log 29 \rceil$
11	U	$\lceil \log 10 \rceil + 8$	31	UB	$\lceil \log 30 \rceil$
12	B	$\lceil \log 11 \rceil + 8$	32	BLE	$\lceil \log 31 \rceil$
13	L	$\lceil \log 12 \rceil + 8$	33	ES	$\lceil \log 32 \rceil$
14	E	$\lceil \log 13 \rceil + 8$	34	S	$\lceil \log 33 \rceil + 8$
15	_TR	$\lceil \log 14 \rceil$	35	_Y	$\lceil \log 34 \rceil$
16	RO	$\lceil \log 15 \rceil$	36	Y	$\lceil \log 35 \rceil + 8$
17	OUB	$\lceil \log 16 \rceil$	37	OU!	$\lceil \log 36 \rceil$
18	BL	$\lceil \log 17 \rceil$	38	!	$\lceil \log 37 \rceil + 8$
19	LE	$\lceil \log 18 \rceil$			

Table 5.4 The compressed version of "DO_NOT_TROUBLE...". Individual characters and addresses are separated by "|", which are introduced during the recovery procedure

```
00100010|11110010|0|11111010|00|01110
010|10|000|00101010|011|110|000|0100101
0|0010|0000|10101010|0000|01000010|000
0|00110010|0000|10100010|0111|1001|101
0|01100|01101|01110|00011|01011|00100|0
0110|00000|10010010|01101|01111|10001
10011|11011|01011|10010|01110|000000|1
1001010|000011|000000|10011010|00101
0|000000|10000100|
```

Step	Entry
0	*
1	D
2	O
3	_

After a character follows always an address. Now we should be able to point out one of first three entries. Hence, the address must consist of $\lceil \log 3 \rceil = 2$ bits; in our example, the two bits following character _, that is, 00. Since this is the address to Entry * we know that the following 8 bits, 01110010, form a character, N. Then we have a 2-bit address, 10, which is the binary form of the decimal number 2 and thus the address to Entry O and we have obtained the following partial dictionary:

Step	Entry
0	*
1	D
2	O
3	_
4	N
5	O

Since the entry at Step 5 is the same as an earlier one (Step 2), we have to add another character at Step 5. To determine which character should be added we have to investigate Step 6. At this step the address consists of $\lceil \log 5 \rceil = 3$ bits. The next three bits are 000, that is, the binary form of the decimal number 0 which is the address to Entry *, telling us that the following 8 bits, 00101010, form a character, namely, T. We should have this character at both Step 5 and Step 6 since the character O was repeated; this yields

Step	Entry
0	*
1	D
2	O
3	—
4	N
5	OT
6	T

If we proceed in this manner we obtain the entries in Table 5.3 from which `"DO_NOT_TROUBLE_...''` immediately follows. (Notice that we cannot complete the entry at Step 5 until we have recovered the first character at Step 6.)

A highly optimized version of the LZW algorithm we have described is used widely in practice to compress computer files under both the UNIX© and Microsoft operating system, and in a CCITT standard for data compression for modems.

5.3 METHODS OF CHANNEL CODING

For channel coding (error correction) we have two main classes of codes, namely, *block codes*, which we first encountered when we discussed Shannon's channel coding theorem, and *convolutional codes*. We shall briefly discuss both classes.

5.3.1 Block Codes

The history of block codes goes back to 1947 when Richard Hamming (Box 5-4) had access to a computer only on weekends. He became very frustrated over its behavior: "Damn it, if the machine can detect an error, why can't it locate the position of the error and correct it?" [9]. This rather innocent outburst led to the remarkable development of error-correcting codes!

First we need some simple mathematical tools. A *field* is an algebraic system in which we can perform addition, subtraction, multiplication, and division (by nonzero numbers) according to the same associative, commutative, and distributive laws we use for real numbers. Here we need only the simplest field, namely, the *binary field*, $\mathbb{F}_2$, for which the rules of addition and multiplication are those of *modulo-two* arithmetic:

+	0	1
0	0	1
1	1	0

·	0	1
0	0	0
1	0	1

BOX 5-4

Richard W. Hamming (1915–1998)

Richard W. Hamming received his Ph.D. in mathematics in 1942 from the University of Illinois at Urbana-Champaign. He joined the Manhattan Project in Los Alamos, New Mexico, in 1945. There he maintained the computer systems used in developing the first atomic bomb. In 1946, Hamming left for Bell Labs, joining a group of applied mathematicians that included Claude E. Shannon, Donald P. Ling, and Brockway McMillan. In a 1993 interview Hamming told *IEEE Spectrum* that the four "were first-class trouble makers" who "did unconventional things in unconventional ways."

Hamming said that he believed that mathematicians do their best work early in their careers and retired from Bell Labs at the age of 61. But he then joined the Naval Postgraduate School at Monterey, California, where he worked for 21 years until his retirement in 1997.

Notice that since $1 + 1 = 0$, in $\mathbb{F}_2$, subtraction is the same as addition, which is very convenient. The addition of two n-tuples $x = (x_1 x_2 \ldots x_n)$ and $y = (y_1 y_2 \ldots y_n)$ is defined to be component-by-component addition in $\mathbb{F}_2$, that is,

$$x + y = (x_1 + y_1 \ x_2 + y_2 \ldots x_n + y_n) \tag{5.88}$$

Consider the (3, 2) block code $\mathcal{B} = \{000, 011, 101, 110\}$ introduced in Example 5.3. Then we have, for example,

$$(011) + (110) = (101) \qquad (5.89)$$

If the sum of any two codewords is a codeword, as it is here, then the code is said to be *linear*.

Suppose that the codeword $v = (v_1 v_2 \ldots v_N)$ is transmitted over the binary symmetric channel and that $r = (r_1 r_2 \ldots r_N)$ is the possibly erroneously received version of it, then the *error pattern* $e = (e_1 e_2 \ldots e_N)$ is defined to be the N-tuple that satisfies

$$r = v + e \qquad (5.90)$$

If we have one error, that is, e consists of one 1 and $N-1$ 0s, then one component in v is altered. Two errors cause two altered components in v. This observation motivated Hamming to introduce a distance, now known as the *Hamming distance* $d_H(x, y)$, between two n-tuples x and y as the number of components in which they differ; for example,

$$d_H(011, 110) = 2 \qquad (5.91)$$

The *minimum distance*, d_{min}, of a block code $\mathcal{B}$ is the minimum of all the Hamming distances between two nonidentical codewords of the code. For a linear block code the minimum distance is simply equal to the least number of 1s in a nonzero codeword. In general, a block code with minimum distance d_{min} will correct up to[3] $\lfloor (d_{min} - 1)/2 \rfloor$ errors. Alternatively, it can be used to *detect* up to $d_{min}-1$ errors.

Hamming constructed a class of *single-error-correcting* linear block codes with minimum distance $d_{min} = 3$. In Table 5.5 we specify an encoder mapping for the (7,4) *Hamming code* with $M = 2^4 = 16$ codewords.

The mapping in Table 5.5 is chosen to make the decoder simple. Consider the following array:

$$001$$
$$010$$
$$011$$
$$100$$
$$101$$
$$110$$
$$111$$

---

[3] The floor function $\lfloor x \rfloor$ is the largest integer less than or equal to x; for example $\lfloor 3.4 \rfloor = 3$ and $\lfloor 7 \rfloor = 7$.

Table 5.5   An encoder
mapping for the (7,4)
Hamming code

u	x
0000	0000000
0001	1101001
0010	0101010
0011	1000011
0100	1001100
0101	0100101
0110	1100110
0111	0001111
1000	1110000
1001	0011001
1010	1011010
1011	0110011
1100	0111100
1101	1010101
1110	0010110
1111	1111111

We notice that row i is simply i written as a binary number; for example, row 5 is $5 = 1 \cdot 2^2 + 0 \cdot 2^1 + 1 \cdot 2^0 = (101)$. Suppose we add component-wise modulo-two those rows in this array that correspond to the positions of the 1s in a codeword. For example, the codeword $v = (1101001)$ has 1s in positions 1, 2, 4, and 7. Hence, we add rows 1, 2, 4, and 7 in the array and obtain

$$
\begin{array}{c}
001 \\
010 \\
100 \\
\underline{111} \\
000
\end{array}
$$

For all codewords we obtain 000!

Assume that we would like to transmit the information 4-tuple $u = (1011)$ over a binary symmetric channel. Then we encode it, by using the mapping in Table 5.5, and obtain the codeword $v = (0110011)$. Let, for example, the sixth position be altered by the channel. Thus, we receive $r = (0110001)$. We return to our array, add position-wise modulo-two rows 2, 3, and 7 (the positions corresponding to the 1s in r) and obtain

$$
\begin{array}{l}
010 \\
011 \\
\underline{111} \\
110
\end{array}
$$

that is, the binary representation of 6; we flip the sixth position in $r = (0110001)$ and obtain the decision $\hat{v} = (0110011)$ for the codeword, which according to Table 5.5 corresponds to the decision $\hat{u} = (1011)$ for the information 4-tuple. This scheme yields the correct decision provided that at most one error occurs during the transmission over the binary symmetric channel.

Why does our scheme work? We can write the received 7-tuple as the sum of the codeword and the error pattern, that is, $r = v + e$. Remember that $1 + 1 = 0$! Because of this simple equality we can obtain the sum of the rows corresponding to the 1s in r by adding component-wise the sums of the rows corresponding to the 1s in v and e. Now we exploit the fact that the mapping in Table 5.5 is constructed such that the sum of the rows corresponding to the 1s in any codeword is 000, and, hence, we conclude that the sum of the rows corresponding to the 1s in r (this is the sum that the decoder computes) is equal to the sum of the rows corresponding to the 1s in e. But assuming at most one error during the transmission we obtain in case of no errors the sum of zero rows, which we interpret as 000 and then we accept r as our decision $\hat{v}$; in case of one error the sum contains one row, namely, precisely the row that is the binary representation of the position of the 1 in e. Hence, when we flip that position in r, we obtain the decision $\hat{v}$ for the codeword. If two or more errors occur, then they cannot be corrected by the Hamming code; we need a more powerful code if we would like to correct multiple errors.

How do we obtain the remarkable encoder mapping in Table 5.5? Since the Hamming code is linear the codewords corresponding to the information 4 tuples 1000, 0100, 0010, 0001 are of particular interest; these codewords form a so-called *generator matrix* for the (7,4) Hamming code:

$$
G = \begin{pmatrix} 1110000 \\ 1001100 \\ 0101010 \\ 1101001 \end{pmatrix} \tag{5.92}
$$

All codewords can be obtained as the product of the corresponding information 4-tuples and the generator matrix:

$$
v = uG \tag{5.93}
$$

For example, the codeword corresponding to $u = (1011)$ is according to Eq. (5.93) obtained as the position-wise modulo-two sum of the first, third, and fourth rows in G, that is,

$$
\begin{array}{ccccccc}
1 & 1 & 1 & 0 & 0 & 0 & 0 \\
0 & 1 & 0 & 1 & 0 & 1 & 0 \\
1 & 1 & 0 & 1 & 0 & 0 & 1 \\
\hline
0 & 1 & 1 & 0 & 0 & 1 & 1
\end{array}
$$

in agreement with the mapping in Table 5.5. Assume that we have a $K \times N$ generator G, then by the theory of matrices there exists an $(N - K) \times N$ matrix H with linearly independent rows such that[4]

$$GH^T = \mathbf{0} \tag{5.94}$$

From Eq. (5.94) follows immediately that

$$uGH^T = \mathbf{0} \tag{5.95}$$

that is, we have the fundamental result

$$vH^T = \mathbf{0} \tag{5.96}$$

which holds when v is a codeword and, in fact, only then.

In words, let v be a codeword, then if we add (position-wise modulo-two) the rows of H^T corresponding to the 1s in v we obtain the allzero $(N - K)$-tuple. This computation is a parity-checking procedure and thus we call the matrix H a *parity-check matrix* of our code. From the discussion of the Hamming code it should not come as a surprise to the reader that

$$
H^T = \begin{pmatrix}
0 & 0 & 1 \\
0 & 1 & 0 \\
0 & 1 & 1 \\
1 & 0 & 0 \\
1 & 0 & 1 \\
1 & 1 & 0 \\
1 & 1 & 1
\end{pmatrix}
$$

---

[4] T denotes the transpose of the matrix; that is, H^T is an $N \times (N - K)$ matrix, which is obtained from H by mirroring in its main diagonal.

The matrix H^T is simply the array we used when we introduced the Hamming code. It is easily verified that

$$GH^T = \begin{pmatrix} 1 & 1 & 1 & 0 & 0 & 0 & 0 \\ 1 & 0 & 0 & 1 & 1 & 0 & 0 \\ 0 & 1 & 0 & 1 & 0 & 1 & 0 \\ 1 & 1 & 0 & 1 & 0 & 0 & 1 \end{pmatrix} \begin{pmatrix} 0 & 0 & 1 \\ 0 & 1 & 0 \\ 0 & 1 & 1 \\ 1 & 0 & 0 \\ 1 & 0 & 1 \\ 1 & 1 & 0 \\ 1 & 1 & 1 \end{pmatrix} = \begin{pmatrix} 0 & 0 & 0 \\ 0 & 0 & 0 \\ 0 & 0 & 0 \\ 0 & 0 & 0 \end{pmatrix} = \mathbf{0}$$

in agreement with Eq. (5.94). Using linear algebra we can (easily) obtain the generator matrix G for a given parity-check matrix H and vice versa.

5.3.2 Convolutional Codes

When we study convolutional codes we regard the *information sequence* $\mathbf{u} = u_0 u_1 \ldots$ and the *code sequence* $\mathbf{v} = v_0^{(1)} v_0^{(2)} v_1^{(1)} v_1^{(2)} \ldots$ as semi-infinite; they start at time $t = 0$ and go on forever. Let us as an example consider the convolutional encoder shown in Figure 5.16. The information symbols are shifted into a register that in our example is of length two; it consists of two memory elements that each store one binary digit during one time interval and we say that the encoder has *memory* $m = 2$. Since we have one input sequence and two output sequences, the code rate is $R = 1/2$ binary digits/channel use; two output symbols per input symbol.

The two sequences $v_0^{(1)} v_1^{(1)} \ldots$ and $v_0^{(2)} v_1^{(2)} \ldots$ are serialized and interleaved before they are transmitted over the channel. The connections via the adders between the two memory elements and the two inputs of the serializer determine the error-correcting capability of the code. These connections represent two linear, time-invariant functions and, hence, the outputs of these functions are simply the convolutions between the corresponding inputs and the (time-discrete) impulse

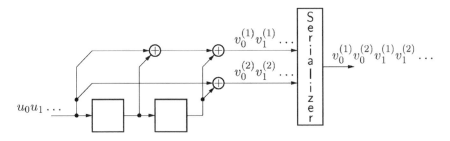

Figure 5.16   An encoder for a binary rate $R = 1/2$ convolution code

responses (cf. Chapter 2); hence, these codes are called *convolutional*. In general, convolutional codes are more powerful than block codes of comparable complexity.

The *state* of a system is a compact description of its past history which together with the present input suffices to determine the present output and the next state. For our convolutional encoder we can simply choose the state to be the contents of its memory; that is, at time t the state is

$$\sigma_t = u_{t-1}u_{t-2} \tag{5.97}$$

How many different states does our encoder have? Since the inputs are binary we have four different combinations of $u_{t-1}u_{t-2}$, namely, 00, 01, 10, 11; hence, we have four states.

If we are in state 00 at time t and $u_t = 0$, we output 00 and stay in state 00; if $u_t = 1$, then we output 11 and go to state 10; that is, at time $t+1$ we have $\sigma_{t+1} = u_t u_{t-1} = 10$.

If we are in state 01 at time t and $u_t = 0$, we output 11 and go to state 00; if $u_t = 1$, then we output 00 and go to 10.

If we are in state 10 at time t and $u_t = 0$, we output 10 and go to state 01; if $u_t = 1$, then we output 01 and go to state 11.

If we are in state 11 at time t and $u_t = 0$, we output 01 and go to state 01; if $u_t = 1$, then we output 10 and stay at state 11.

We can illustrate this behavior by using a *state-transition diagram* as shown in Figure 5.17. The branches are labeled $u_t/v_t^{(1)}v_t^{(2)}$. The state transition diagram is a compact description of the behavior of the convolutional encoder. As time progresses we jump from state to state according to the information sequence. By introducing a time axis G. David Forney [11] obtained the *trellis*, which is a less compact but remarkably powerful description of the same behavior. The trellis for our

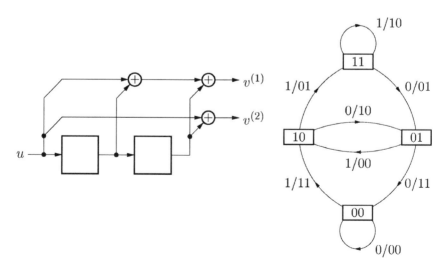

Figure 5.17   A rate $R = 1/2$ convolutional encoder and its state-transition diagram

encoder is shown in Figure 5.18. When we leave state σ_t it is understood that the upper and lower branches correspond to information symbols 0 and 1, respectively. Hence, in the trellis we label the branches only by the outputs $v_t^{(1)} v_t^{(2)}$.

As an example, the information sequence 0110... is encoded as the code sequence 00110101.... This code sequence corresponds to the bold trellis path shown in Figure 5.18.

We shall now by an example show how the optimum decoder for convolutional code sequences works. It was invented by Andrew Viterbi [10] and its optimality became obvious to Forney as soon as he had introduced the trellis [11]. These form two great contributions to the field.

Often, in practice, very long sequences of information symbols are encoded—typically, a few thousand binary digits. Then the sequence is *terminated* by encoding $m = 2$ dummy zeros that forces the encoder back to the 00 state; without this termination the decision for the last code symbols in a finite trellis would be very unreliable.

Assume for simplicity that only four information symbols should be transmitted. Together with the two dummy zeros we have six symbols that are encoded into a codeword of 12 code symbols. Suppose that we receive $r = 00\ 01\ 01\ 10\ 01\ 10$. The *Viterbi-algorithm* works as follows. For each time step starting from the first, at each state we compare subpaths leading to it and discard the one that is *not* closest (measured in Hamming distance) to the received sequence. The discarded path cannot possibly be the initial part of the path $\hat{v}$ that minimizes the Hamming distance between the r sequence and the codeword v. This is the *principle of nonoptimality*. What shall we do if both subpaths have the same distance to the received sequence? Clearly, in case of such a tie it does not matter—choose either one! If we are true to the principle of nonoptimality at each state in the trellis when we discard subpaths, then we must obtain (one of) the optimal (closest) path(s) when we reach the end of our trellis.

In Figure 5.19 we show the terminated trellis (for four arbitrary information symbols followed by two dummy zeros to force it to the 00 state) for our encoder and received sequence. We move through the trellis from left to right. The discarded poorer subpaths are marked with the symbol $\times$ on the branch that enters the

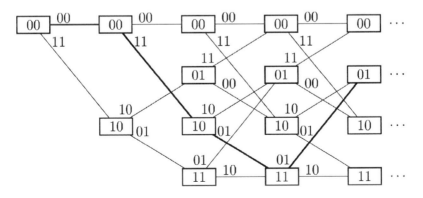

Figure 5.18 A trellis description of the encoder given in Figure 5.17

$r =$ 00   01   01   10   01   10

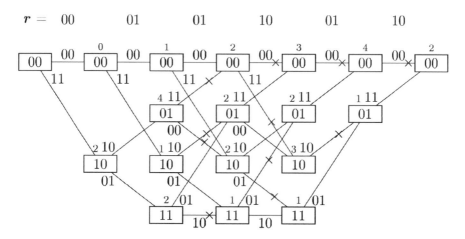

Figure 5.19   An example of Viterbi decoding

state where it is discarded. Above each state we write the number of errors (disagreements) between the surviving subpath leading to the state and the corresponding part of the received sequence.

Finally, when we have reached the end, that is, the rightmost 00 state, we can easily trace back (dodging the discarded paths) and obtain the unique survivor that is our decision $\hat{v} = 00$ 11 01 10 01 11 for the codeword, which corresponds to the information sequence $\hat{u} = 0111(00)$, where the last two binary digits are nothing but the known dummy zeros that were used to terminate the code sequence. If $\hat{v}$ was the transmitted codeword, then 2 errors occurred during the transmission.

After $m = 2$ steps we have reached four surviving subpaths and we will continue to have $2^m = 4$ surviving subpaths until we reach the terminating phase; then this number will be reduced by a factor of 2 until we reach the end of the trellis with only one survivor. This process is illustrated in Figure 5.20.

We saw above that we could correct a certain pattern of two errors, namely,

$$\hat{e} = r + \hat{v} = (00\ 01\ 01\ 10\ 01\ 10) + (00\ 11\ 01\ 10\ 01\ 11)$$
$$= 00\ 10\ 00\ 00\ 00\ 01 \tag{5.98}$$

where $\hat{e}$ is the decision for the error pattern. How many errors can we correct in general? The answer is related to the minimum Hamming distance between any two codewords in the trellis. Since a convolutional code is linear this value is equal to the least number of 1s in any nonzero codeword. By tracing the paths in the trellis shown in Figure 5.19 it is readily seen that this least number is 5 and that it is achieved, for example, by the codeword $v = 11\ 10\ 11\ 00\ 00\ 00$. For a convolutional code this least number is called the *free distance* and denoted d_{free}. In our example we have $d_{\text{free}} = 5$. As we argued when we introduced the minimum distance, we can correct all error patterns with $\lfloor (d_{\text{free}} - 1)/2 \rfloor$ or fewer errors. What about error patterns with more errors? The answer is that it depends;

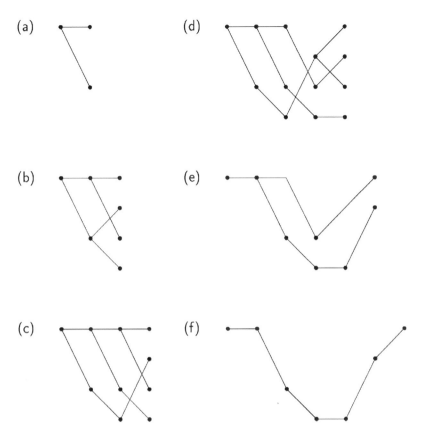

Figure 5.20   Evolution of subpaths through the trellis

if the errors are sparse enough we can correct many more! That is one reason why convolutional codes are so powerful.

The Viterbi decoding algorithm is as simple as it is ingenious. It is easy to implement and used in practice in a variety of products; for example, every mobile phone contains at least one implementation of the Viterbi algorithm. In practice, we often use convolutional encoders with as many as six memory elements that correspond to trellises with $2^6 = 64$ states; then for rate $R = 1/2$ the free distance is as large as 10.

Convolutional coding is treated in depth in ref. [12].

5.4 TRELLIS CODED MODULATION

Let us return to digital modulation discussed in Section 4.3. A common form of a digital modulated signal is

$$s(t) = \sqrt{E_s} \sum_{n=-\infty}^{\infty} (\sqrt{2}a_n^I \cos \omega_0 t - \sqrt{2}a_n^Q \sin \omega_0 t)v(t - nT) \qquad (5.99)$$

where a_n^I and a_n^Q are the in-phase and quadrature-phase data-bearing variables. The set of different pairs (a^I, a^Q) forms a *signal constellation* as discussed in Section 4.3. In Figure 4.19 we show the signal constellations for 16-ary QAM and 8PSK.

Suppose we transmit R_t bits/s over the Gaussian channel with bandwidth W, measured in positive frequencies. Then we have the *bandwidth efficiency* or *spectral bit rate* R_t/W (bits/s)/Hz. If we transmit at capacity, then it follows from Eq. (5.72) and Eq. (5.74) that

$$R_t/W = \log\left(1 + \frac{R_t}{W}\frac{E_b}{N_0}\right) \tag{5.100}$$

In Figure 5.21 we sketch R_t/W as a function of the signal-to-noise ratio E_b/N_0 according to Eq. (5.100). Shannon's coding theorem says that arbitrarily reliable communication is possible to the right of this curve but not to the left of it. For comparison we also show the bandwidth efficiency for four different modulations at the bit error probability $P_b = 10^{-5}$. For bandwidth, we have used the theoretical minimum for pulse modulations, which is the sinc-pulse bandwidth. Letting the consecutive sinc-pulses be T seconds apart, we use $\text{sinc}(t/T)$ with a $2T$ wide main lobe, then according to Fourier transform pair (i) in Table 2.4 combined with property 5 in Table 2.3, the Fourier bandwidth is $W = 1/2T$ Hz in agreement with our rule-of-thumb. The potential for improving these schemes by coding is large, for example, for 16-QAM this potential is 7.8 dB.

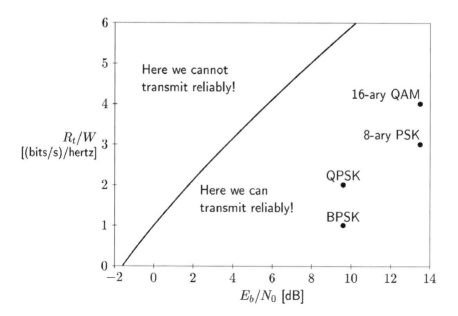

Figure 5.21   Bandwidth efficiency R_t/W versus signal-to-noise ratio E_b/N_0

Clearly we can improve the error performance by increasing the signaling energy. Alternatively we can delete some signal points from the constellation and increase the distance between the remaining signal points, but this reduces the data rate. A more clever approach is, surprisingly enough, to insert new signal points and create a *denser* constellation but at the same time introduce interdependencies between consecutive signal points by coding. Due to these interdependencies all *sequences* of signal points are not allowed and hence we obtain an increased distance between different sequences of signal points. We can pick up a larger gain in distance between sequences than what is offset by the decreased distance between individual signal points.

In Figure 5.22 we show one widely used structure for this kind of *modulation code*. The *minimum Euclidean distance* between two different *sequences* of signal points is denoted $d_{\mathrm{E}}^{(c)}$. We compare the performance of a modulation coding scheme with an uncoded scheme by computing the *asymptotic* (meaning for high signal-to-noise ratios) *coding gain*, defined as

$$\gamma = 10\log_{10}\left(\frac{d_{\mathrm{E}}^{2(c)}/E_b^{(c)}}{d_{\mathrm{E}}^{2(u)}/E_b^{(u)}}\right) \text{ dB} \tag{5.101}$$

where $d_{\mathrm{E}}^{(u)}$ is the minimum Euclidean distance between two different signal points in the constellation of the uncoded scheme, and $E_b^{(c)}$ and $E_b^{(u)}$ are the average bit energies per channel use of the coded and uncoded schemes, respectively.

We can illustrate the advantages of modulation codes by comparing the performance of a coded 8PSK scheme with an uncoded QPSK scheme. The method is a clever one suggested by G. Ungerboeck [13], which is based on forming subsets of the 8PSK constellation. Both schemes are two-dimensional and for a given pulse shape the bandwidth depends only on the number of modulation

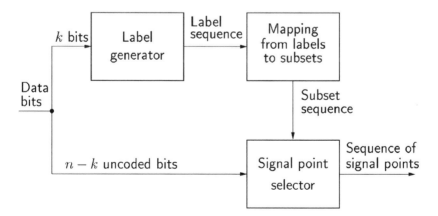

Figure 5.22   Encoder for a modulation code

pulses per second, which is the same in both cases. Furthermore, both schemes have the same rate $R = 2$ data bits per channel use.

In Figure 5.23 we show the various distances between the signal points in our two constellations. For simplicity we assume unit signal energy, that is, $E_s^{(c)} = E_s^{(u)} = 1$ or, in other words, the signal points are at distance 1 from the origin of coordinates. We see immediately for the uncoded QPSK scheme that the minimum squared distance

$$d_E^{2(u)}(\text{QPSK}) = d_1^2 = 2 \tag{5.102}$$

To find the distance for the 8PSK modulation code is more involved. First we have to specify the label generator and the mapping. Let us assume that we use the rate $R = 1/2$ convolutional encoder, which is shown together with three subsections of its trellis in Figure 5.24. This generates a set of subset labels.

We use Ungerboeck's selection method of *set partitioning* to successively obtain four subsets of the 8PSK constellation as illustrated in Figure 5.25. The mapping between the labels and the subsets is chosen in such a manner that the minimum Euclidean distance between different sequences of subsets is maximized. Trying all different mappings yields the one in Figure 5.25. A way to view this modulation code is that one data bit is carried in the 2-point subset and another data bit is used to select the signal point from the chosen subset $\mathcal{A}$, $\mathcal{B}$, $\mathcal{C}$ or $\mathcal{D}$.

The minimum Euclidean distance between sequences of subsets is obtained by comparing the label sequences for the state sequences $00 \to 00 \to 00 \to 00$ and $00 \to 10 \to 01 \to 00$ in the trellis. These state sequences correspond to the label sequences $00, 00, 00$ and $01, 10, 01$, or, equivalently, $\mathcal{A}, \mathcal{A}, \mathcal{A}$ and $\mathcal{B}, \mathcal{C}, \mathcal{B}$. Hence, the minimum squared Euclidean distance between sequences of subsets is (note that squared distances add)

$$\begin{aligned} d_E^{2(\text{seq})} &= d_E^2(\mathcal{A}, \mathcal{B}) + d_E^2(\mathcal{A}, \mathcal{C}) + d_E^2(\mathcal{A}, \mathcal{B}) \\ &= d_1^2 + d_0^2 + d_1^2 \\ &= 2 + (2 - \sqrt{2}) + 2 = 4.59 \end{aligned} \tag{5.103}$$

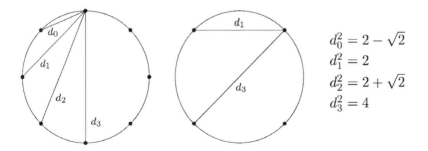

$$d_0^2 = 2 - \sqrt{2}$$
$$d_1^2 = 2$$
$$d_2^2 = 2 + \sqrt{2}$$
$$d_3^2 = 4$$

Figure 5.23   Distances between signal points in the 8PSK and QPSK constellations

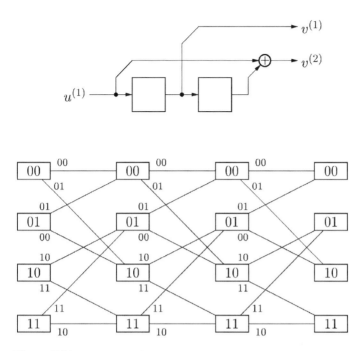

Figure 5.24   A rate $R = 1/2$ convolutional label generator and its trellis

where $d_{\mathrm{E}}^2(\mathcal{S}_i, \mathcal{S}_j)$ denotes the minimum squared Euclidean distance between subsets $\mathcal{S}_i$ and $\mathcal{S}_j$. Since the Euclidean distance between the two signal points within all these subsets is 2, the minimum squared Euclidean distance between two signal points within a subset is

$$d_{\mathrm{E}}^{2(\mathrm{sub})} = 4 \qquad (5.104)$$

Overall, the minimum squared Euclidean distance for the modulation code, $d_{\mathrm{E}}^{2(c)}$, is the minimum of the squared Euclidean distance for the set of sequences of subsets $d_{\mathrm{E}}^{2(\mathrm{seq})}$ and the squared Euclidean distance within the subsets $d_{\mathrm{E}}^{2(\mathrm{sub})}$, that is,

$$d_{\mathrm{E}}^{2(c)}(8\mathrm{PSK}) = \min\{4.59, 4\} = 4 \qquad (5.105)$$

The asymptotic coding gain for our 8PSK scheme over the uncoded QPSK scheme is

$$\gamma = 10 \log_{10} \frac{d_{\mathrm{E}}^{2(c)}(8\mathrm{PSK})}{d_{\mathrm{E}}^{2(u)}(\mathrm{QPSK})} = 10 \log_{10} \tfrac{4}{2} = 3 \text{ dB} \qquad (5.106)$$

The error correcting capability is in this example determined by the distances between the signal points within the subsets and (asymptotically) we will not gain

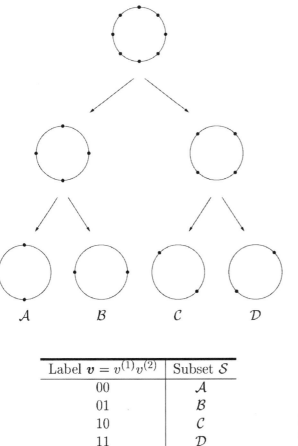

Label $\boldsymbol{v} = v^{(1)}v^{(2)}$	Subset $\mathcal{S}$
00	$\mathcal{A}$
01	$\mathcal{B}$
10	$\mathcal{C}$
11	$\mathcal{D}$

Figure 5.25   Set partitioning an 8PSK constellation, with the best label map

anything by using a more powerful rate $R = 1/2$ convolutional encoder as label generator! However, by carrying out the set partitioning until the subsets contain only one signal point each, we get $d_E^{(\mathrm{sub})} = \infty$ and remove the upper limit; hence $d_E^{(c)} = d_E^{(\mathrm{seq})}$. Then we can gain 6 dB or more. An example that gains 3.6 dB is shown in Figure 5.26.

A rate $R = 2/3$ convolutional encoder maps data bits directly to 8PSK phases and there is no concept of subsets. An 8-state version appears in Figure 5.26. Both the convolutional encoder and the 3-bit-to-8-phase map must be carefully designed. Many more details of these codes are given in ref. [14].

The Viterbi algorithm described in Section 5.3 is easily extended to decoding for this kind of modulation code. Above each state in the trellis we simply write the cumulative squared Euclidean distance between the surviving subpath leading

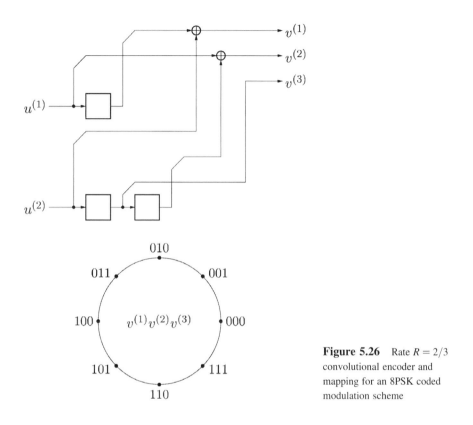

Figure 5.26   Rate $R = 2/3$ convolutional encoder and mapping for an 8PSK coded modulation scheme

to the state and the corresponding part of the received sequence. Poorer subpaths are discarded in the same way as before.

The introduction of trellis modulation codes led to much improved performance for voice-band modems.

5.5 CONCLUSIONS

In this chapter we first gave a brief introduction to Claude E. Shannon's information theory, which is the basis for modern communication technology. It provides guidelines for the design of digital communication systems. We then looked at some practical methods of source and channel coding.

- Source coding: Shannon modeled sources as discrete stochastic processes and showed that a source is characterized by the uncertainty of its output, $H(U)$, in the sense that the source output sequence can be compressed arbitrarily close to $H(U)$ binary digits per source symbol but not further.

- Shannon's most remarkable result concerns transmission over a noisy channel. He proved that it is possible to encode the source at the sender side and decode the possibly corrupted signal at the receiver side such that, if the source uncertainty is less than the channel capacity, that is, if $H(U) < C$, the source sequence can be reconstructed with arbitrary reliability. This is impossible if the source uncertainty exceeds the channel capacity.

- Huffman coding is a fixed-to-variable length optimal source coding procedure that uses the probability of the source symbols to obtain an encoding for single (or blocks of) source symbols into codewords that consist of variable length strings of binary digits such that the average codeword length is minimum.

  The LZW algorithm is a procedure that does not need to know the source statistics beforehand. It parses the source output sequence, recognizes fragments that have appeared before, and refers to the addresses of these fragments in an evolving dictionary. This algorithm is asymptotically optimum, easy to implement, and widely used in practice.

- Hamming codes constitute a much celebrated class of block codes. Their minimum distance is $d_{min} = 3$ and, thus, they correct all error patterns of single errors.

  Viterbi decoding is both an optimum and a practical method for decoding convolutional codes. It is widely used in mobile telephony and high-speed modems.

REFERENCES

1. SHANNON, C. E. 1948. A mathematical theory of communication. *Bell System Tech. J.*, 27, 379–423; 623–656.
2. GALLAGER, R. G. 2001. Claude E. SHANNON: A retrospective on his life, work, and impact (invited paper). *IEEE Trans Information Theory*, IT-47, 2681–2695.
3. COVER, T. M. and THOMAS, J. A. 1991. *Elements of information theory*. John Wiley: New York.
4. SHANNON, C. E. 1949. Communication in the presence of noise. *Proc. IRE*, 37, 10–21.
5. MASSEY, J. L. 1985. An information-theoretic approach to algorithms. In J. K. SKWIRZYNSKI, ed. *The impact of processing techniques on communications*, Series E, No. 91. NATO Advanced Study Institutes: Martinus Nijhoff, Dordrecht.
6. HUFFMAN, D. A. 1952. A method for the construction of minimum redundancy codes. *Proc. IRE*, 40, 1098–1101.
7. ZIV, J. and LEMPEL, A. 1978. Compression of individual sequences via variable-rate coding. *IEEE Trans Information Theory*, IT-24, 530–536.
8. WELCH, T. A. 1984. A technique for high-performance data compression. *IEEE Comput.*, 17, 8–19.
9. THOMPSON, T. M. 1983. *From error-correcting codes through sphere packings to simple groups*. Carus Mathematical Monographs No. 21, Mathematical Assoc. America.
10. VITERBI, A. J. 1967. Error bounds for convolutional codes and an asymptotically optimum decoding algorithm. *IEEE Trans Information Theory*, IT-13, 260–269.
11. FORNEY, G. D. Jr. 1967. Review of random tree codes. NASA Ames Res. Ctr. Contract NAS2-3637, Final Rep. App. A.
12. JOHANNESSON, R. and ZIGANGIROV, K. Sh. 1999. *Fundamentals of convolutional coding*. IEEE Press: Piscataway, N.J.

13. UNGERBOECK, G. 1987. Trellis-coded modulation with redundant signal sets, Parts I–II. *IEEE Communications Mag.*, 25, 5–21.

14. ANDERSON, J. B. and SVENSSON, A. 2003. *Coded Modulation Systems.* Plenum: New York.

PROBLEMS

1. Suppose that the random variable $X = X_1 X_2 X_3$ takes on the values in the set $\{000, 011, 101, 110\}$ with equal probability. Find:

   (a) $H(X_1)$

   (b) $H(X_1 X_2)$

   (c) $H(X_2 \mid X_1)$

   (d) $H(X_1 X_2 X_3)$

   (e) $H(X_3 \mid X_1 X_2)$

   (f) $I(X_1; X_3)$

   (g) $I(X_1 X_2; X_3)$

2. Consider the following experiment. We have one fair coin and one counterfeit coin that has *Head* on both sides. Choose randomly with equal probability one of the coins and flip it twice. How much information about the identity of the coin do we obtain from the total number of observed *Heads*?

3. Find the channel capacity for the binary erasure channel (BEC).

4. Find a Huffman code for the random variable U that takes on the six values in the set of outputs $\{u_1, u_2, u_3, u_4, u_5, u_6\}$ with probabilities

u	$P_U(u)$
u_1	0.27
u_2	0.23
u_3	0.20
u_4	0.15
u_5	0.10
u_6	0.05

5. Find a Huffman code for the random variable U that takes on the six values in the set of outputs $\{u_1, u_2, u_3, u_4, u_5, u_6\}$ with probabilities

u	$P_U(u)$
u_1	0.20
u_2	0.20
u_3	0.20
u_4	0.15
u_5	0.15
u_6	0.10

6. Find a Huffman code for the random variable U that takes on the seven values in the set of outputs $\{u_1, u_2, u_3, u_4, u_5, u_6, u_7\}$ with probabilities

u	$P_U(u)$
u_1	0.30
u_2	0.20
u_3	0.10
u_4	0.10
u_5	0.10
u_6	0.10
u_7	0.10

7. Find the dictionary and codeword lengths when the LZW algorithm is used for the following sentences.

   (a) THE FRIEND IN NEED IS A FRIEND INDEED

   (b) THE CAT IN THE CAR ATE THE RAT

   (c) EARLY TO BED AND EARLY TO RISE MAKES A MAN WISE

   (d) IF WE CANNOT DO AS WE WOULD WE WOULD DO AS WE CAN

   (e) BETTER LATE THAN NEVER BUT BETTER NEVER LATE

   (f) WHO CHATTERS WITH YOU WILL CHATTER ABOUT YOU

8. Consider the following binary sequences

   (a) 100100100110001001111101000010011
       010001111001000010101010101001100011
       00001000010000010000011110010000
       0011100100101000000101010000011000
       00100001000001010001000110000011
       10101000001011010000000010010000
       1110100100000001100101010101011000
       001000010100110000110000000011001
       00001010000000110101001100010000
       1100010011000010111011001011010110110
       0001101110101111100100100000010
       010100110000100100100011010101

   (b) 0010001011110010011111101000011110
       010100000010101001111100000100101
       0001000001010101000000101000010000
       0001100100000101000100111110001101
       0011000110101110000110101011001000
       01100000010010010011010111110001
       100111101101011100100111100000001
       10010100000110000001001101000101
       000000010000100

(c) 001010100001001001010001000011111
0100011000010000100001000110000
0100100100000011100100100000001001
0001101000101011000000010010101000
100001100000101110011000011101001
010100

(d) 1100001010000010001110010011111
0100010011010000111100100010101
0101000010010001101000010100101000101
0110000001100101001100011100011000011
0001100000101000100000001010010101
00111001110010010001000011000000111
11100

generated by the LZW algorithm using the ASCII code described in Figure 3.1. Find the texts that were compressed. Find also the compression ratios, that is, the ratios between the number of binary symbols in the compressed and uncompressed strings.

9. Consider the block code $\mathcal{B} = \{000000, 110110, 011011, 101101\}$.

   (a) $\mathcal{B}$ linear?
   (b) Find the rate $R = K/N$.
   (c) Find, if it exists, a linear encoder.
   (d) Find, if it exists, a nonlinear encoder.
   (e) Determine the minimum distance d_{min}.
   (f) How many errors can we correct with $\mathcal{B}$?

10. Consider the (7,4) Hamming code. It can correct all patterns of single errors and no pattern of more errors. Suppose that this Hamming code is used to communicate over the binary symmetric channel with channel error probability $\varepsilon = 0.1$. What is the *word error probability*, that is, the probability that the decision for the codeword differs from the transmitted one?

    Hint: What is the relation betwen the word error probability and the probability that the decision for the codeword is the transmitted one?

11. Consider the rate $R = 1/2$ convolutional encoder shown in Figure 5.27.

    (a) Find the state-transition diagram.
    (b) Draw the trellis.
    (c) Determine the free distance d_{free}.
    (d) Suppose five information symbols (plus one dummy zero to terminate the trellis) are encoded and transmitted. Use the Viterbi algorithm to decode the received sequence $r = 11\ 11\ 11\ 11\ 01\ 10$.
    (e) How many errors have occurred if the optimal path corresponds to the transmitted codeword?

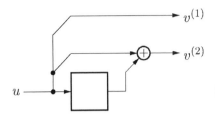

Figure 5.27   Convolutional encoder for Problem 11

12. Consider the rate $R = 1/2$ convolutional encoder shown in Figure 5.17.

   (a) Use the Viterbi algorithm to decode the received sequence $r = 00\ 00\ 01\ 10\ 11\ 00$.

   (b) Suppose that the information sequence is $u = 0000$. How many channel errors are corrected in (a)?

13. Use the rate $R = 1/2$ convolutional encoder shown in Figure 5.24 in a coded QPSK scheme with the mapping shown in Figure 5.28.

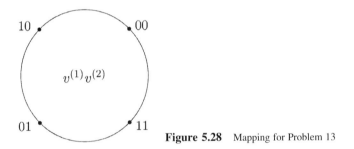

Figure 5.28   Mapping for Problem 13

   (a) Find $d_E^{2(c)}$.

   (b) Determine the asymptotic coding gain for this coded QPSK scheme over an uncoded BPSK scheme.

   (c) Suppose that four information symbols followed by two dummy zeros have been encoded and that the sequence $r = 10\ 10\ 00\ 11\ 01\ 00$ has been received. Which information symbols will the Viterbi algorithm output?

Chapter 6

Cryptology: FUBSWRORJB??

According to the Encyclopaedia Britannica, *cryptology*[1] is the "science concerned with data communication and storage in secure and usually secret form." It is often subdivided into the two disciplines *cryptography* and *cryptanalysis*. Legitimate users obtain security by using a secret key that is known only to them. Cryptography "encompasses the whole area of key-controlled transformations of information into forms that are either impossible or computationally unfeasible for unauthorized persons to duplicate or undo." Cryptanalysis "is the science (and art) of recovering or forging cryptographically secured information without knowledge of the key."

During almost the entire history of cryptology, which dates back some millennia, the sole purpose was to provide secrecy. The information age with, for example, electronic commerce (e-commerce) has led to a huge demand for means to provide evidence that no changes of the data has been made by a third party—*information integrity*—and proofs that a message comes from a certain sender such that neither the sender can deny that he is the actual sender nor can anyone else forge the identity of the sender—*authentication*.

6.1 FUNDAMENTALS OF CRYPTOSYSTEMS

In Figure 6.1 we show the information flow in a model of a cryptosystem for secrecy. The secret *key K* is distributed securely in advance, for example, by a courier or by a more sophisticated key distribution system. The *plaintext* is transformed by the *encrypter* $e_K(\cdot)$ and we obtain the *ciphertext* $C = e_K(P)$, which is transmitted over a *public channel* susceptible of eavesdropping. The enemy cryptanalyst's task is to obtain a reliable decision for the plaintext $\hat{P}$.

The security of the *cipher* should reside entirely in the secret key. The designer of a cryptosystem should always assume that the enemy "by hook or by crook" can

---

[1] The article "Cryptology," written by Gustavus J. Simmons, is highly recommended.

Understanding Information Transmission. By John B. Anderson and Rolf Johannesson
ISBN 0-471-67910-0 © 2005 the Institute of Electrical and Electronics Engineers, Inc.

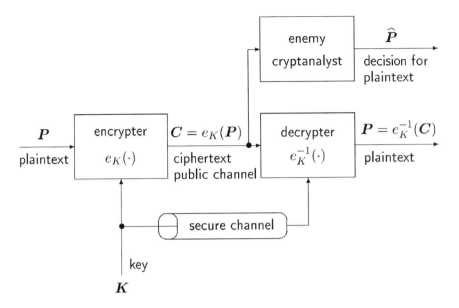

Figure 6.1   Model of a cryptosystem for secrecy

get hold of a detailed description of the cryptosystem; the only thing that is hidden from the cryptanalyst is the actual value of the key. Although this is an old principle formulated by Auguste Kerckhoffs already in 1883, it is still valid [1].

Consider the following simple example.

EXAMPLE 6.1   *Secrecy*

A day-trader would like to send one of the two messages *Buy IBM* and *Sell IBM* to his broker. The communication takes places over the Internet and they have every reason in the world to believe that an eavesdropper has access to their communication. Clearly it is vital to both the day-trader and the broker as well as to the stock market in general that nobody picks up the information being communicated. In order to thwart the eavesdropper both the day-trader and the broker agree in advance as to whether the message should be the genuine one or simply its opposite. They flip a fair coin and if, for example, *Heads* comes up the message is the genuine one and if *Tails* comes up they communicate the opposite of the intended instruction. The encrypter/decrypter function is illustrated by the following scheme:

<table>
<tr><td></td><td></td><td colspan="2" align="center">plaintext</td><td></td></tr>
<tr><td></td><td></td><td>*Buy IBM*</td><td>*Sell IBM*</td><td></td></tr>
<tr><td rowspan="2">key</td><td>*Heads*</td><td>*Buy IBM*</td><td>*Sell IBM*</td><td rowspan="2">ciphertext</td></tr>
<tr><td>*Tails*</td><td>*Sell IBM*</td><td>*Buy IBM*</td></tr>
</table>

Suppose the outcome of coin flipping is *Tails* and the day-trader would like to sell all his IBM stocks, then he sends the message *Buy IBM* to the broker who, knowing that the key this day is *Tails*, decrypts it as *Sell IBM* and acts accordingly.   ∎

If the day-trader and the broker use the scheme described in the example given above the eavesdropper does not get the slightest clue about the plaintext by observing the ciphertext—we say that such a cryptosystem is *perfect from a secrecy point-of-view*.

Can the broker trust that the message he received actually came from the day-trader? In order to address such questions Simmons developed a theory of authentication [2]. While the history of systems for secrecy dates back millennia, authenticity systems date back only a few decades. The concept of authentication is much more subtle than that of secrecy. We must, for example, give the intruder more freedom; now he is not only a simple eavesdropper. He can choose an *impersonation attack* where he simply pretends that he is the legitimate sender—he impersonates the sender—and creates a message that he hopes the legitimate receiver will accept. Alternatively, he can break into the public communication channel and intercept the message from the sender, then he replaces it by another message and again hopes that the legitimate receiver will accept his message. This is called a *substitution attack*. In Figure 6.2 we show the information flow in a model of a cryptosystem for authentication.

The impersonation attack is successful if the receiver accepts the ciphertext C^* that is chosen by the intruder *without knowledge about the genuine ciphertext C*. In the substitution attack the intruder first intercepts the genuine ciphertext C, then he chooses a ciphertext C^* different from C that he hopes will be accepted by the receiver.

In the following examples we return to the day-trader and his broker.

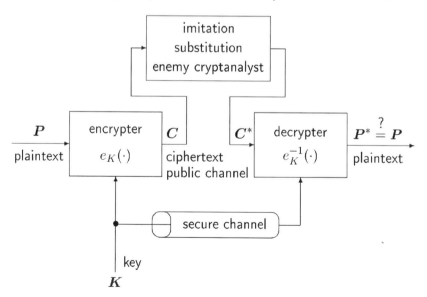

Figure 6.2   Model of a cryptosystem for authentication

EXAMPLE 6.2 *Authenticity without secrecy*

To set up their scheme for authentication the day-trader and the broker flip a fair coin twice in order to choose one of four equally likely keys; for notational convenience we call them *HH*, *HT*, *TH*, and *TT*. Then they use the following scheme.

plaintext

		Buy IBM	Sell IBM	
	HH	Buy IBM-0	Sell IBM-0	
key	HT	Buy IBM-1	Sell IBM-1	ciphertext
	TH	Buy IBM-0	Sell IBM-1	
	TT	Buy IBM-1	Sell IBM-0	

The ciphertext is formed by appending an authentication bit, 0 or 1, to the plaintext.

Suppose that the outcome of the coinflipping is *TH* and that the day-trader's intention is to buy some IBM stocks. Then he sends the ciphertext *Buy IBM*-0 corresponding to the key *TH* and the plaintext *Buy IBM*. The broker checks the row corresponding to the agreed upon key *TH* and finds indeed the ciphertext *Buy IBM*-0, which he, of course, decrypts to *Buy IBM* and acts accordingly. ∎

Can the broker trust that the ciphertext actually came from the day-trader?

First we consider an impersonation attack. The intruder selects without knowing the key the ciphertext that maximizes the probability that he will deceive the broker. Since the keys are equiprobable and the appended authentication bits appear in a symmetric manner, he simply chooses a ciphertext at random. We notice that the two ciphertexts *Buy IBM*-0 and *Sell IBM*-1 appear in the row of the chosen key *TH*. Hence, if the intruder chooses either one of these two ciphertexts it will be accepted by the broker who then will be deceived. If the intruder, however, chooses *Buy IBM*-1 or *Sell IBM*-0 the broker immediately finds out that something fishy is going on since neither of them corresponds to the chosen key *TH*. So what is the probability that the impersonation attack is successful? It is simply the probability that the intruder chooses one of the two ciphertexts in row *TH* among all four ciphertexts; that is, the probability of a successful impersonation attack is $Pr(I) = \frac{1}{2}$.

In the substitution attack the intruder picks up the sent ciphertext *Buy IBM*-0 and from the scheme he concludes that the key is either *HH* or *TH* since the ciphertext *Buy IBM*-0 appears in the corresponding two rows. He selects one of these rows. If he chooses the row corresponding to the key *HH*, then he sends the ciphertext *Sell IBM*-0. This immediately alerts the broker since this ciphertext does not correspond to the selected key *TH*! If the intruder, on the other hand, chooses the key *TH*, then he sends the ciphertext *Sell IBM*-1, which the broker will accept. He consequently sells the day-trader's IBM stocks—a successful substitution attack. Clearly, the intruder will succeed if he selects the correct row and he has two alternatives; hence, if the plaintexts are equiprobable, the probability of a successful substitution attack is $Pr(S) = \frac{1}{2}$.

Does this scheme provide any secrecy? No, since from the ciphertext we can without knowing the key immediately deduce the corresponding plaintext.

If the day-trader and his broker are not satisfied with a 50–50 chance of detecting fraud, they have to choose a more advanced scheme with more ciphertexts. However, regardless of how sophisticated a scheme they use, they can never achieve complete protection against these types of fraud!

Simmons showed a combinatorial lower bound on the probability of a successful impersonation attack, namely,

$$Pr(I) \geq \frac{|\mathcal{P}|}{|\mathcal{C}|} \tag{6.1}$$

where $|\mathcal{P}|$ and $|\mathcal{C}|$ are the numbers of plaintexts and ciphertexts, respectively. The scheme in Example (6.2) has two plaintexts and four ciphertexts; hence, inequality (6.1) yields

$$Pr(I) \geq 2/4 = 1/2 \tag{6.2}$$

and we conclude that this scheme for protection against an impersonation attack is as good as it gets with a scheme of the given size.

We conclude this section by an example showing that we can obtain both secrecy and authenticity.

EXAMPLE 6.3 *Secrecy and authenticity*

The scheme in this example is a slight modification of the scheme in Example (6.2):

		plaintext		
		Buy IBM	*Sell IBM*	
	HH	*Buy IBM-0*	*Sell IBM-0*	
key	*HT*	*Buy IBM-1*	*Buy IBM-0*	ciphertext
	TH	*Sell IBM-1*	*Buy IBM-1*	
	TT	*Sell IBM-0*	*Sell IBM-1*	

Regardless which ciphertext we consider, if we do not have any knowledge about the key, both plaintexts are equally likely; hence, our scheme gives perfect protection from a secrecy point-of-view. Each ciphertext appears in two rows; hence, the probability of a successful impersonation attack is $Pr(I) = \frac{1}{2}$.

Regardless of which ciphertext an intruder picks up, he must choose between two ciphertexts when he makes his substitution attack; hence, assuming that the plaintexts are equiprobable the probability of success is $Pr(S) = \frac{1}{2}$.

6.2 CAESAR AND VIGENÈRE CIPHERS

When Julius Caesar wrote to Cicero and other friends in Rome more than 2000 years ago he used a very simple *substitution cipher* in which the cipher alphabet is a cyclic shift of the plaintext alphabet. In a general substitution cipher each plaintext letter is replaced by a ciphertext letter according to a specified mapping; the ciphertext alphabet is a permutation of the plaintext alphabet. Caesar shifted the cipher alphabet three steps such that A is encrypted as D, B as E, C as F, and so on. As an example we have

```
plaintext     CAESAR
ciphertext    FDHVDU
```

Caesar always shifted three steps, but nowadays a cipher obtained by any shift is called a *Caesar cipher*. The number of steps in the shift is the key; that is, the classical Caesar cipher has key $K = 3$ [1].

There is no evidence that Brutus or anybody else during Caesar's time broke his simple cipher. Breaking is, however, readily done since we have, assuming for simplicity the English alphabet, only 26 different keys corresponding to the 26 possible cyclic shifts determined by the 26 letters in the alphabet. Consider as an example the ciphertext

```
DIAJMHVODJI
```

```
DIAJMHVODJI
EJBKNIWPEKJ
FKCLOJXQFLK
GLDMPKYRGML
HMENQLZSHNM
INFORMATION
JOGPSNBUJPO
KPHQTOCVKQP
LQIRUPDWLRQ
MRJSVQEXMSR
NSKTWRFYNTS
OTLUXSGZOUT
PUMVYTHAPVU
QVNWZUIBQWV
RWOXAVJCRXW
SXPYBWKDSYX
TYQZCXLETZY
UZRADYMFUAZ
VASBEZNGVBA
WBTCFAOHWCB
XCUDGBPIXDC
YDVEHCQJYED
ZEWFIDRKZFE
AFXGJESLAGF
BGYHKFTMBHG
CHZILGUNCIH
```

Figure 6.3   Breaking a Caesar cipher

To find the plaintext we try all 26 different keys in a systematic way by writing the complete alphabet below each letter in the ciphertext; see Figure 6.3. Then we look for a row with "meaningful" text and find INFORMATION.

The Caesar cipher is a special case of a *monoalphabetic substitution cipher*, where "mono" indicates that only one alphabet is used in the substitution. An arbitrary permutation of the English alphabet is used as the key for a substitution done letter by letter. For example, the mapping

```
plaintext alphabet    ABCDEFGHIJKLMNOPQRSTUVWXYZ
cipher alphabet       XGUACDTBFHRSLMQVYZWIEJOKNP
```

is a key that enciphers the plaintext WOODSTOCK as the ciphertext OQQAWIQUR.

There are many keys as there are permutations of the 26 different letters in the alphabet; that is, for a monoalphabetic substitution cipher we have 26! keys. Since 26! is greater than 4×10^{26} it is not tempting to try all keys. The cryptanalysis can, however, be carried out rather easily by a statistical analysis that exploits the fact that we have the same relative frequencies for the ciphertext letters as for the plaintext letters; they are only reordered by the permutation. Since E is the letter that is most frequently used in English, it is likely that the most frequent letter in the ciphertext corresponds to E, and so on.

To make a cipher less vulnerable to statistical attacks we can try to conceal the varying relative frequencies for the plaintext letters by using more than one substitution alphabet. A popular example of a so-called *polyalphabetic substitution cipher* is the *Vigenère cipher* named after the French cryptographer Blaise de Vigenère (1523–1596). For a couple of centuries his cipher was known as *le chiffre indéchiffrable*, the "unbreakable cipher" [1].

Consider the Vigenère table in Figure 6.4. The horizontal alphabet at the top is the plaintext alphabet. Below this alphabet we have 26 "Caesar alphabets," of which the first one is a copy of the plaintext alphabet. The remaining 25 are copies cyclically shifted one step at a time. These 26 Caesar alphabets are indexed by the key letters. To encrypt, the cipher letter is found at the intersection between the column headed by the plaintext letter and the row indexed by the key letter. To decrypt, the plaintext letter is found at the head of the column determined by the intersection of the diagonal containing the ciphertext letter and the row indexed by the key letter. The key consists of a word that is repeated periodically. For example, if the key is THOMPSON and the plaintext is FOR WOODSTOCK MY FRIEND OF FRIENDS, then we obtain the ciphertext as follows:

```
plaintext    FORWOODSTOCKMYFRIENDOFFRIENDS
key          THOMPSONTHOMPSONTHOMPSONTHOMP
ciphertext   YVFIDGRFMVQWBQTEBLBPDXTEBLBPH
```

In 1863 the retired army officer and amateur cryptanalyst Friedrich W. Kasiski (1805–1881) published his epochal book *Die Geheimschriften und die Dechiffrirkunst* (Secret Writing and the Art of Deciphering). Kasiski's cryptanalysis of the Vigenère cipher opened up the doors to the cryptology of today. Kasiski had noticed that if the first letter of two repeated plaintext strings are a multiple of the

```
    A B C D E F G H I J K L M N O P Q R S T U V W X Y Z

A   A B C D E F G H I J K L M N O P Q R S T U V W X Y Z
B   B C D E F G H I J K L M N O P Q R S T U V W X Y Z A
C   C D E F G H I J K L M N O P Q R S T U V W X Y Z A B
D   D E F G H I J K L M N O P Q R S T U V W X Y Z A B C
E   E F G H I J K L M N O P Q R S T U V W X Y Z A B C D
F   F G H I J K L M N O P Q R S T U V W X Y Z A B C D E
G   G H I J K L M N O P Q R S T U V W X Y Z A B C D E F
H   H I J K L M N O P Q R S T U V W X Y Z A B C D E F G
I   I J K L M N O P Q R S T U V W X Y Z A B C D E F G H
J   J K L M N O P Q R S T U V W X Y Z A B C D E F G H I
K   K L M N O P Q R S T U V W X Y Z A B C D E F G H I J
L   L M N O P Q R S T U V W X Y Z A B C D E F G H I J K
M   M N O P Q R S T U V W X Y Z A B C D E F G H I J K L
N   N O P Q R S T U V W X Y Z A B C D E F G H I J K L M
O   O P Q R S T U V W X Y Z A B C D E F G H I J K L M N
P   P Q R S T U V W X Y Z A B C D E F G H I J K L M N O
Q   Q R S T U V W X Y Z A B C D E F G H I J K L M N O P
R   R S T U V W X Y Z A B C D E F G H I J K L M N O P Q
S   S T U V W X Y Z A B C D E F G H I J K L M N O P Q R
T   T U V W X Y Z A B C D E F G H I J K L M N O P Q R S
U   U V W X Y Z A B C D E F G H I J K L M N O P Q R S T
V   V W X Y Z A B C D E F G H I J K L M N O P Q R S T U
W   W X Y Z A B C D E F G H I J K L M N O P Q R S T U V
X   X Y Z A B C D E F G H I J K L M N O P Q R S T U V W
Y   Y Z A B C D E F G H I J K L M N O P Q R S T U V W X
Z   Z A B C D E F G H I J K L M N O P Q R S T U V W X Y
```

Figure 6.4   The Vigenère table

length of the key apart, then these strings will be encrypted as identical ciphertext strings. The cryptanalyst looks for such repetitions in the ciphertext. In our example we find the repeated string TEBLBP:

```
plaintext    FORWOODSTOCKMYFRIENDOFFRIENDS
key          THOMPSONTHOMPSONTHOMPSONTHOMP
ciphertext   ..............TEBLBP..TEBLBP.
```

If we find a few such repetitions we can guess the length of key and separate the ciphertext letters into, in our example, eight Caesar ciphers (only seven are different since O occurs twice in THOMPSON) that can easily be solved by statistical methods. Notice that all repetitions are not the result of the described phenomenon; some repetitions are simply coincidences.

6.3 THE VERNAM CIPHER AND PERFECT SECRECY

In 1917 the American engineer Gilbert S. Vernam suggested an important variant of the Vigenère cipher [1, 3]. He considered a random sequence of equiprobable binary digits that he added positionwise modulo 2 to a plaintext consisting of binary digits; see Figure 6.5. If the key digit is 0, then the plaintext digit passes unaltered through the system, while if the key digit is 1, the plaintext digit is complemented twice, both by the encrypter and by the decrypter. The drawback with the *Vernam cipher* is that it requires a key of the same length as the plaintext.

By adding the coinflipping sequence modulo 2 in the Vernam cipher, we introduce randomness to at least the same degree as it is reduced by the structure between the plaintext symbols, thereby eliminating the correlation between the ciphertext symbols. The statistics on which the successful methods for cryptanalysis of the Vigenère cipher is based are simply destroyed. Almost 30 years after Vernam's invention Claude Shannon proved that Vernam's intuition about the unbreakability of his cipher was correct.

Shannon defined a cryptosystem to provide *perfect secrecy* if the plaintext and the ciphertext are independent random variables [4]. For such systems we obtain no information at all about the plaintext by observing only the ciphertext. We could do just as well by guessing the plaintext without observing the ciphertext and trusting to luck!

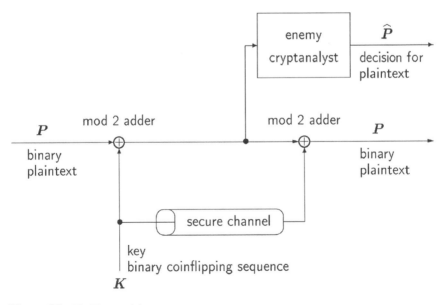

Figure 6.5 The Vernam cipher

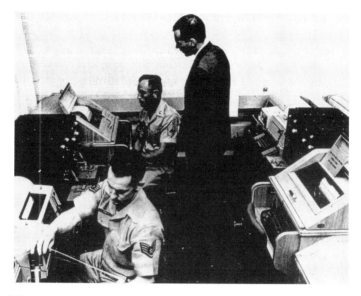

Figure 6.6 One end of the "hot line" (U.S. Army photo)

We can regard the Vernam cipher as a binary symmetric channel with the key as the error pattern. Since the key is a coinflipping sequence we have crossover probability $\varepsilon = \frac{1}{2}$, which corresponds to channel capacity 0. In other words, the conditional uncertainty of the plaintext (channel input) given the ciphertext is the same as the uncertainty of plaintext; that is, the plaintext and ciphertext are independent random variables (see Theorem 5.3) and, hence we have perfect secrecy.

For the first time in history a truly secure cryptosystem had been constructed. It is secure not because the enemy cryptanalyst has not been clever enough, but because he faces an impossible task. Another provably secure cryptosystem besides the Vernam cipher is based on quantum cryptography, which is a subject within the rapidly evolving field of quantum computing and quantum information theory.

The Vernam cipher is sometimes called a *one-time key* system, since the key is used only once. It is commonly called *one-time pad*, which refers to the times when the random one-time key was written on a pad. It was (is?) often used by spies. The Russian master-spy Rudolf Abel had a Vernam cipher when he was arrested in New York in 1957. Moreover, it was used on the "hot line" between Washington and Moscow during much of the cold war [1] (Fig. 6.6).

6.4 STREAM CIPHERS

Since the Vernam cipher requires prior distribution of the key of the same size as the message, it is usually impractical. A variant that is suitable for fast hardware

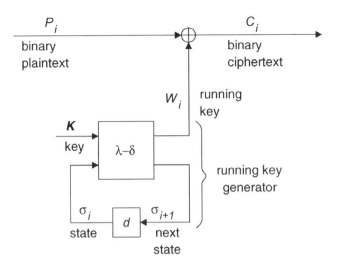

Figure 6.7   General model of a stream cipher

implementation is the important class of *stream ciphers*. In Figure 6.7 we give a general model of a (binary additive) stream cipher. The encryption process is simply a positionwise modulo 2 addition of the plaintext symbol P_i and the *running key* symbol W_i. The stream cipher differs from the Vernam cipher in an important way. The running key W_i is not a coinflipping sequence. It is generated from a finite key K by a *running key generator* that consists of a *memory d*, a combinatorial circuit realizing the binary *Boolean function*[2]

$$W_i = \lambda(K, \sigma_i)$$

and a bank of Boolean functions, where contents of the memory d, σ_i, are called the *state*. Its initial value σ_0 may be determined from the key; if not, it must be known by the decrypter as well as the encrypter. The input of the memory is called the *next state* σ_{i+1} and is determined by the bank of Boolean functions

$$\sigma_{i+1} = \delta(K, \sigma_i)$$

A well-designed running key generator is often built around so-called *linear feedback shift registers*. These are easy to implement in hardware and generate binary sequences that have good statistical properties and long periods. In a linear feedback shift register (Fig. 6.8), the memory contents are shifted left one position at each step. The bit stream at the memory element at the extreme left is regarded as the

---

[2] A binary Boolean function $u = f(x_1, x_2, \ldots, x_n)$ is a mapping

$$f: \quad \{0, 1\}^n \rightarrow \{0, 1\}$$
$$(x_1, x_2, \ldots, x_n) \longmapsto u$$

that can be realized by, for example, NOT, AND, and OR gates.

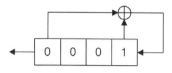

Figure 6.8   A linear feedback shift register of length $L = 4$ with initial register contents 0001

In 1943, a young school teacher, Miss Gene Grabeel, was assigned by the U.S. Army's Signal Intelligence Service, a forerunner of the National Security Agency (NSA), to start a top secret program that later became known as VENONA. The task was to collect, study, and, if possible, read encrypted Soviet, KGB, and GRU messages. The VENONA success story is quite remarkable since the cryptosystems used by the Soviets should have been impossible to crack! First the plaintext was encrypted using a so-called code book in which letters, words, and phrases were replaced by numbers. Then the sequence of digits was encrypted using a one-time pad. How could ciphertexts obtained by theoretically secure ciphers be read? Through sweat-of-the-brow analysis it was discovered that occasionally the key for the one-time pad had been used more than once. This is a fatal mistake since then the cryptanalysts can subtract one ciphertext from the other and obtain the difference of the two plaintexts – the effects of the identical keys are cancelled. The task of obtaining the two plaintexts from their difference is relatively simple. When a fragment of the plaintext had been obtained it was subtracted from the ciphertext and the corresponding fragment of the key was recovered. Then the cryptanalysts went back to other cryptotexts and checked whether the newly found key fragment was of any help there. When it was no longer expected that agents mentioned in the 1942–1945 messages were active, the cryptanalytic efforts were terminated and in 1995 the silence surrounding the VENONA project was ended and more than 3000 messages were declassified. Among these were messages related to atomic bomb espionage that disclosed some of the clandestine activities of infamous spies such as Julius and Ethel Rosenberg, Harry Gold, and Klaus Fuchs.

During World War II, Sweden collected many encrypted Soviet radio transmissions. This material was almost forgotten until the end of the 1950s when Sweden secretly became a partner in VENONA. Then some of these messages could be read. Here is an example [5]:

"From: STOCKHOLM
To: MOSCOW
No: 1523
June 25 1945
To VIKTOR. For FEDEROV.
On June 22 1945 the following Latvians who are agents of ours, left for their country: "OEOLZILE" Peter ROSENFELD, born 1902, and "ZEPPELIN" Karlis VILTSME-JERS, born 1898 (FELLOWCOUNTRYMAN) (17 groups unrecovered), maintaining radio communication (65 groups unrecoverable)."

output and the new right-hand bit is obtained as the modulo 2 sum (a linear combination) of the bits at some prescribed positions. Suppose that the initial register contents are 0001. Then we obtain the output sequence

$$\underbrace{000111101011001}_{\text{one period}}\,0001\ldots$$

After one period the sequence repeats. We notice that if the output sequence is read 4 bits at a time by successively shifting this 4-bit window one position to the right, we obtain all possible nonzero binary 4-tuples. If the initial contents are 0000 then the output will be a sequence of zeros. We can conclude that 15 is the longest possible period obtainable with a length $L = 4$ linear feedback shift register. The corresponding sequence is called a *maximum-length sequence*. In general, with appropriately chosen positions for the feedback, a length L linear feedback shift register can generate maximum-length sequences of length $2^L - 1$ corresponding to the $2^L - 1$ different nonzero L-tuples.

Show as an exercise that a length $L = 4$ linear feedback shift register in which all four positions are added and fed back to the memory element at the extreme right yields three essentially different nonzero sequences of period 5 (depending on the nonzero initial contents).

Linear feedback shift registers can be used to generate sequences with long periods that can be used as running keys in stream ciphers. Such devices have, however, a serious drawback: they are also easily predictable from their output sequences. We can overcome this weakness by taking nonlinear combinations of several linear shift register sequences. The nonlinearity makes it much harder for the cryptanalyst to obtain the plaintext. Many ciphers used both commercially and by the military are of this general type.

6.5   BLOCK CIPHERS

A block cipher breaks the plaintext into blocks of the same size. Then each block is mapped into a ciphertext block of the same size using a common key. The mapping (encryption) is memoryless outside the current block. While the block size for a classical cipher such as Playfair is as short as two, it is much longer for modern electronic block ciphers, typically 64 or 128 or even as long as 256 bits.

In 2000 the *National Institute of Standards and Technology* (NIST) announced that a block cipher called *Rijndael* had been chosen to become the *Advanced Encryption Standard* (AES), which is a new U.S. Government standard. Its block length is 128 bits and the key length can be chosen to be 128, 192, or 256 bits. Rijndael was designed to meet both the needs of smart cards and other equipment that have a limited computational capability, as well as the needs of the Internet and e-commerce. These needs were formulated as the following design criteria:

- resistance against all known attacks;

- speed and code compactness on a wide range of platforms;
- design simplicity.

Rijndael consists of 10 to 14 so-called rounds depending on the key size. The structure of a single round is as follows. We have block size 128 bits, that is, 16 bytes. Then the input to a round is represented by a four by four array of bytes. First we perform a nonlinear substitution operation on each byte of the input. The rows of the resulting array are permuted and then we operate on the columns with a linear transformation. Finally, the round key is added modulo 2 to the array. The resulting array is used as input to the next round.

Before the first round there is an initial key addition to the plaintext block since otherwise the layer before the first key addition could simply be "peeled off" in a so-called known plaintext attack. The resulting array from the last round is taken as the ciphertext block.

Rijndael is also well-suited for applications such as automated teller machines (ATM), high-definition television (HDTV), broadband integrated services digital network (B-ISDN), voice, and satellite.

6.6   CRYPTOMACHINES DURING WORLD WAR II

During World War II there were several cryptanalytic triumphs that contributed to ending the war. The cryptomachines were either mechanical or electromechanical. A well-known example of a mechanical masterpiece is the Hagelin M-209 Converter constructed by the Swedish Engineer Boris Hagelin. On April 9, 1940, when the Germans invaded Denmark and Norway, he decided to bring his cryptomachine to the United States, and after some modifications it was accepted by the U.S. Army. In 1942, L. C. Smith & Corona Typewriters, Inc., produced 400 Hagelin M-209 Converters per day. After the war Boris Hagelin moved his company from Sweden to Switzerland where it prospered as Crypto AG.

Next we will briefly describe two German electromechanical cryptomachines. They played an important role for Nazi Germany but cryptanalyzing them played an even bigger role for the Allies.

6.6.1   Enigma

The original version of the famous Enigma cryptomachine (Fig. 6.9) was invented in the Netherlands but it was further developed in Germany in the 1920s and became a commercial machine that anybody could buy. Among the customers were the German military as well as the Schutzstaffel (SS).

In Figure 6.10 we show a diagram of the Enigma. It is a so-called rotor machine consisting of three rotating rotors with 26 spring-loaded contacts on each side corresponding to the 26 letters on the keyboard. Each time the operator presses a key, the right-hand rotor rotates one notch. After rotating 26 notches it causes the middle rotor to rotate one notch and so on. The rotors rotate like an odometer. When the

Figure 6.9   Enigma, as used by Germany in World War II.
Source: National Communications Security Authority, Government of Sweden

operator presses key A, say, a current goes from the battery through the keyboard letter A, via the plugboard that introduces a permutation, then through the three rotors, reaching a reflector, which is a fixed rotor with spring-loaded contacts on only one side. These contacts are pairwise connected so the current enters via one contact and leaves the reflector via another contact. Then the current passes the rotating rotors in reversed order and via the plugboard it reaches a bulb that lights, and the current then returns to the battery completing the circuit. The letter at the bulb is the cipher letter corresponding to the pressed key A. Suppose that plaintext letter A yields the ciphertext letter Q, then, because of the reflector, the plaintext letter Q yields the ciphertext letter A. This phenomenon can be regarded as a weakness of this cipher, but it is very convenient since it explains why the Enigma works both as encrypter and decrypter. The secret key determines both the wiring between the spring-loaded input and output contacts on each rotor as well as the plugboard connections.

Every day the operator had to choose the plugboard connections and choose three rotors out of a set of five, which could be done in $5 \times 4 \times 3 = 60$ different three-rotor orders. Then he chose the starting positions for the rotors. When the operator should send an encrypted message he chose himself three letters to be used as the message key. This 3-tuple was encrypted twice. Then the rotors were reset according to the 3-tuple and the message encrypted. When the legitimate operator

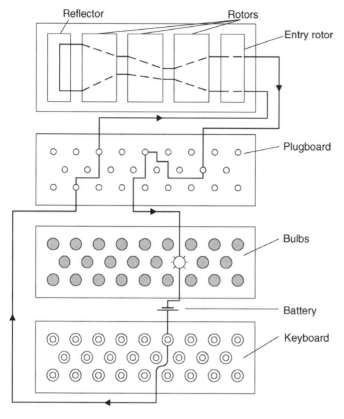

Figure 6.10   Schematic diagram of the Enigma

at the receiving side, using the daily settings, decrypted the first six letters, he expected to obtain a 3-tuple repeated twice. If the 3-tuple was not repeated, he knew that an error had occurred. This yielded a certain robustness. The rotors of the Enigma on the receiving side were reset according to the obtained 3-tuple, the message key, and the rest of the ciphertext was decrypted.

At a first glance it seems to be a good idea to encrypt the message keys twice, but somewhat surprisingly, it turned out that it would have been much better if the message keys had not been encrypted at all! This double encryption was a weakness that was successfully exploited by Marian Rejewski, a Polish mathematician, who together with his colleagues Jerzy Różycki and Henryk Zygalski struggled to read the Enigma messages in the early 1930s. In 1939, when the German invasion of Poland was imminent, they turned over their material to the British cryptanalysts at the legendary Bletchley Park. Alan Turing is one of many geniuses at Bletchley Park who kept solving a steady flow of modifications of the Enigma. The Polish and British solution of the German Enigma was a great moment in the history of cryptanalysis. These cryptanalysts were war heros who worked in utmost secrecy and made important contributions to shortening World War II.

6.6.2 Geheimschreiber

In the morning of April 9, 1940, the Swedish government was taken by surprise when the Nazi German Wehrmacht occupied its neighbours, Denmark and Norway. The following day, the German Minister in Stockholm presented a list of demands to the Swedish government, one of them was permission to use the Swedish west coast cable in order to facilitate the communication between Berlin and Oslo. The Swedish govenment complied – but reluctantly in order hide their intention to tap the cable.

The Germans used tone telegraphy for five-channel teleprinter traffic that by the end of April was encrypted by their *Geheimschreiber*. The teleprinter alphabet consists of 32 binary 5-tuples. These are encrypted by the electromechanical Geheimschreiber as follows: first the 5-bit running key is added positionwise modulo 2 to the 5-bit plaintext symbol (substitution) and then a permutation of the bits in the sum is performed. The resulting 5-tuple is the ciphertext symbol. See Figure 6.11, where we illustrate the principles of the Geheimschreiber. It consists of ten wheels of lengths 47, 53, 59, 61, 64, 65, 67, 69, 71, 73. These lengths represent the total number of 0s and 1s along the wheels; this is part of the key. The ten wheels output a 10-digit binary number whose period is the product of the wheel lengths (893,622,318,929,520,960) since these lengths are relatively prime, that is, they have no factor in common. The 10 bits are permuted by a wired connection that yields $10! = 3,628,800$ combinations. The Germans usually changed these wired connections, as part of the key, every third to ninth day. The resulting left 5-tuple determines the running key for the substitution and the right 5-tuple determines the permutation, which is realized with five controlled switches. If the control bit to a switch is 0, then its two inputs are swapped, otherwise not.

It was Sweden's most eminent cryptanalyst, Arne Beurling, who took a stab at the enormously difficult problem of solving the Geheimschreiber cipher using only intercepted material. Born in 1905, he became a Professor of Mathematics at Uppsala in 1937. In 1952 he joined the Advanced Study Institute, Princeton, where he stayed until his death in 1986. He was a legendary teacher and was generally considered to be a genius. Trying to solve the Geheimschreiber was indeed a task worthy a genius.

Quite remarkably, after only a few weeks Beurling could present fragments of plaintext! He had realized that the Germans often made the mistake of sending several messages with the same key (cf. VENONA) and by combining this with the characteristics of the teleprinter alphabet he could figure out a mathematical model for the Geheimschreiber.

The information obtained from the Geheimschreiber messages were invaluable for not only the Swedish government but also for the Swedish counter-intelligence.

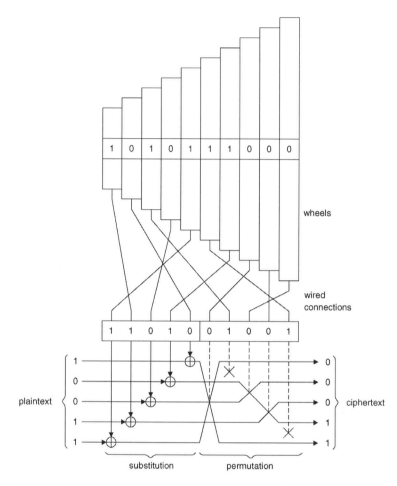

Figure 6.11 Schematic diagram of the *Geheimschreiber*

In 1976 when Beurling was asked what had led him to the solution he answered: "A magician does not reveal his tricks!"

6.7 TWO-KEY CRYPTOGRAPHY

All schemes we studied so far are characterized by the need for a secure method of distributing the key. In 1976, Whitfield Diffie and Martin Hellman suggested that it is possible to exchange secret keys without using a secure channel [6]. This remarkable idea has dramatically changed cryptological research.

Diffie and Hellman introduced the concepts of *one-way functions* and *trapdoor one-way functions*. A one-way function is a function $f(x)$ that is "easy" to compute for all x, but for essentially all y it is computationally infeasible to find x such that

$y = f(x)$. A trapdoor one-way function is a family of invertible functions f_K such that when K is known, we easily can find algorithms E_K and D_K that compute $f_K(x)$ and its inverse $f_K^{-1}(y)$, for all x and y, but when K is not known, for almost all K and y it is infeasibly hard to compute $f_K^{-1}(y)$, even if we know E_K. The algorithm E_K depends on a secret *trapdoor parameter* T such that D_K and hence $f_K^{-1}(y)$ are easy to find when we know T but hard when we do not know T. It is far from obvious that such functions exist, but if they do, they are quite useful in cryptography.

An application of one-way functions is the personal identity number (PIN) (PIN), a password that must be entered into, for example, an automated teller machine (ATM) together with a bankcard in order to verify that the user is authorized to access the bank account. The PIN is transformed by a one-way function and the result is compared to the contents of the bank's computer files. An intruder who obtains the encrypted PIN from the bank's files cannot compute the PIN since the transformation is one-way.

Using a trapdoor one-way function we can design a so-called *two-key* or *public-key cryptosystem*. Such a system can be arranged by the intended *receiver* of encrypted information as follows. The receiver selects his trapdoor one-way algorithm E_K, keeps the trapdoor parameter T secret, but publishes openly the encryption algorithm E_K. Anyone who would like to send an encrypted message to the receiver looks up the public algorithm E_K and uses it to encrypt his plaintext. Since only the receiver knows the secret trapdoor parameter T, only he can find the corresponding secret decryption algorithm D_K, which he uses to decrypt the ciphertext. In Figure 6.12 we show a model for a two-way cryptosystem for secrecy. Notice that there is no need for a secure channel for communicating the key.

A trapdoor one-way function can be used to identify a sender—to obtain a *digital signature*—but at the expense of giving up secrecy. If the domain and range of f_K and f_K^{-1} coincide for all K, then the *sender* who would like to create an unforgeable digital signature uses his *secret* algorithm D_K and creates a ciphertext by using, for example, his name as plaintext. Anybody can use the senders' *public* algorithm E_K to decrypt the ciphertext, and, hence, recover the sender's plaintext. Since this plaintext was obtained using the sender's public algorithm E_K, the corresponding ciphertext must have been created by the sender's secret algorithm D_K. Since this algorithm is known only to the sender he should not be trusted if he denies that he created the digital signature. In Figure 6.13 we show a model for a two-key cryptosystem for authentication or digital signatures.

6.7.1 A Practical Two-Key System

In ref. [7], Diffie writes that "the single most spectacular contribution to public key cryptography..." was made by the three Massachussets Institute of Technology researchers Ron Rivest, Adi Shamir, and Len Adleman (RSA) when they in 1978 proposed a trapdoor one-way function that is based on the difficulty of factoring large integers into primes [8]. Before we can describe their remarkable two-key cryptoscheme we need some results from number theory.

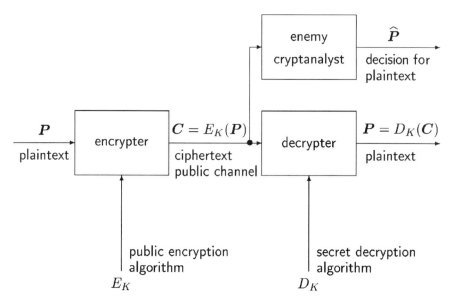

Figure 6.12   Model of a two-key cryptosystem for secrecy

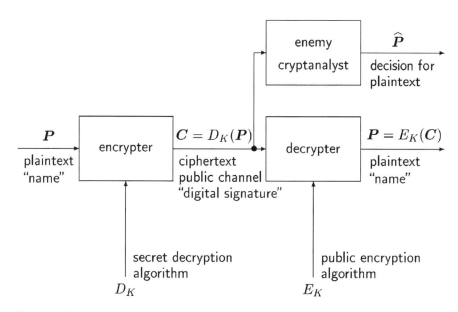

Figure 6.13   Model of a two-key cryptosystem for digital signatures. The cipertext C serves as a digital signature

The solution to the problem of finding the *greatest common divisor* of two natural numbers[3] was given by Euclid (300 B.C.).

Euclid's Algorithm   Given two natural numbers n_1 and n_2, where $n_1 > n_2$. Divide continually the larger by the smaller as follows (q_i is the quotient and r_i the remainder):

$$n_1 = q_0 n_2 + r_0 \quad \text{(dividing } n_2 \text{ into } n_1)$$
$$n_2 = q_1 r_0 + r_1 \quad \text{(dividing } r_0 \text{ into } n_2)$$
$$r_0 = q_2 r_1 + r_2 \quad \text{(dividing } r_1 \text{ into } r_0)$$
$$r_1 = q_3 r_2 + r_3 \quad \text{(etc.)}$$
$$\vdots$$
$$r_{i-2} = q_i r_{i-1} + r_i$$
$$r_{i-1} = q_{i+1} r_i$$

Then r_i is the greatest common divisor of n_1 and n_2, denoted $r_i = \gcd(n_1, n_2)$.

Euclid's algorithm has the following important and useful consequence.

Theorem 6.1   (Bezout's Identity)   *Given integers n_1 and n_2 not both zero, there exist integers s and t such that*

$$\gcd(n_1, n_2) = sn_1 + tn_2 \tag{6.3}$$

EXAMPLE 6.4

Let us use Euclid's algorithm to find $\gcd(858, 84)$. We begin with $n_1 = 858$, $n_2 = 84$, and proceed as follows:

$$858 = 10 \cdot 84 + 18 \tag{6.4}$$
$$84 = 4 \cdot 18 + 12 \tag{6.5}$$
$$18 = 1 \cdot 12 + 6 \tag{6.6}$$
$$12 = 2 \cdot 6 + 0$$

Since the last nonzero remainder is the greatest common divisor, we conclude that

$$\gcd(858, 84) = 6$$

---

[3] The set of *natural numbers* or *counting numbers* is $N = \{1, 2, 3, 4, \ldots\}$.

Now we shall find s and t such that (cf. Eq. (6.3))

$$6 = s \cdot 858 + t \cdot 84$$

Let us first solve for the remainders in Eqs. (6.4)–(6.6) and write them in reverse order. Then we obtain

$$6 = 18 - 1 \cdot 12 \tag{6.7}$$

$$12 = 84 - 4 \cdot 18 \tag{6.8}$$

$$18 = 858 - 10 \cdot 84 \tag{6.9}$$

Next we substitute the expression for the remainder 12, that is, Eq. (6.8), into Eq. (6.7) and obtain

$$\begin{aligned} 6 &= 18 - 1 \cdot (84 - 4 \cdot 18) \\ &= -1 \cdot 84 + 5 \cdot 18 \end{aligned} \tag{6.10}$$

Then we substitute the expression for the remainder 18, that is, Eq. (6.9), into Eq. (6.10), which yields

$$\begin{aligned} 6 &= -1 \cdot 84 + 5 \cdot (858 - 10 \cdot 84) \\ &= 5 \cdot 858 - 51 \cdot 84 \end{aligned}$$

Hence, $s = 5$ and $t = -51$.

Notice that the pair s and t is not unique. For example, $s = -9$ and $t = 92$ also satisfy

$$6 = s \cdot 858 + t \cdot 84 \qquad\blacksquare$$

The number of integers between 1 and n that are *relatively prime* with n, that is, they have no common factors with n, is of particular interest. It is expressed by the Euler's totient function and denoted $\phi(n)$. Suppose that n is the product of two primes, that is,

$$n = pq \tag{6.11}$$

where p and q are prime. Then Euler's totient function can be obtained as follows. Assume that $p < q$ and consider the integers

$$1, 2, \ldots, p, \ldots, q, \ldots, 2p, \ldots, 2q, \ldots, pq$$

Delete all multiples of p and all multiples of q. Then we obtain

$$\phi(n) = pq - q - p + 1 = (p-1)(q-1) \tag{6.12}$$

where we add 1 because p and q were both "deleted" in pq.

EXAMPLE 6.5

(a)

$$\phi(6) = 2 \tag{6.13}$$

The two integers are 1 and 5.

(b)

$$\phi(8) = 4$$

The four integers are 1, 3, 5, and 7.

(c)

$$\phi(16) = 8$$

The eight integers are 1, 3, 5, 7, 9, 11, 13, and 15.

(d) Since 6 is the product of two primes, namely, $6 = 2 \cdot 3$, we conclude from Eq. (6.12) that

$$\phi(6) = (2 - 1)(3 - 1) = 2$$

in agreement with Eq. (6.13). ■

Our trapdoor one-way function rests on the following pillar.

Theorem 6.2 (Euler) *Let a and n be two integers that are relatively prime. Then*

$$a^{\phi(n)} \equiv 1 \qquad (\text{mod } n) \tag{6.14}$$

or, equivalently,

$$R_n(a^{\phi(n)}) = 1 \tag{6.15}$$

where $R_d(i)$ denotes the remainder r when the integer i is divided by the divisor d, that is, $i = qd + r$, $0 \leq r < |d|$.

EXAMPLE 6.6

Let $a = 2$ and $n = 55$. Clearly, a and n are relatively prime. Furthermore, since 55 is the product of the two primes, 5 and 11, we obtain

$$\phi(55) = (5 - 1)(11 - 1) = 40$$

and, hence,

$$
\begin{aligned}
a^{\phi(n)} = 2^{40} &= (2^{10})^4 = 1024^4 \\
&= (18 \cdot 55 + 34)^4 \equiv 34^4 = (34^2)^2 \\
&= 1156^2 = (21 \cdot 55 + 1)^2 \equiv 1^2 \\
&= 1 \qquad (\text{mod } 55)
\end{aligned}
$$

in agreement with Euler's theorem.   ■

We are now well prepared to set up the two-key cryptosystem suggested by Rivest, Shamir, and Adleman.

Two large primes, p and q, are chosen. What do we mean by "large"? The U.S. government security standards call for p and q to be about 155 decimal digits each. Then n is roughly a 310-digit decimal number and it is believed that it will not be feasible to factor such a number within several decades. Let $n = pq$ and compute $\phi(n) = (p - 1)(q - 1)$. Choose an arbitrary integer e, $1 < e < \phi(n)$, such that e and $\phi(n)$ are relatively prime.

Next we shall find the inverse of e (mod $\phi(n)$), that is, find d such that

$$d \equiv e^{-1} \qquad (\text{mod } \phi(n))$$

or, equivalently, such that

$$ed \equiv 1 \qquad (\text{mod } \phi(n))$$

or, again equivalently, such that

$$1 = ed + t\phi(n) \tag{6.16}$$

where t is an integer. Remember that we know e and $\phi(n)$, and would like to solve Eq. (6.16) for d when we do not know t. Let us compare Eq. (6.16) with Bezout's identity (6.3). Since e and $\phi(n)$ are relatively prime, $\gcd(e, \phi(n)) = 1$ and, hence, the unknown d is simply s in Bezout's identity and we can calculate d (and t if we would like to) by following the procedure outlined in Example 6.4.

EXAMPLE 6.7

Let $p = 41$, $q = 167$, and $e = 23$. Then we have $n = pq = 6847$ and $\phi(n) = (p-1)(q-1)$ $= 40 \cdot 166 = 6640$. In order to obtain s (and t) in Bezout's identity we start with Euclid's algorithm and find the greatest common divisor of $e = 23$ and $\phi(n) = 6847$ (although we know that it is 1, since e and $\phi(n)$ were chosen to be relatively prime).

Euclid's algorithm yields

$$
\begin{aligned}
6640 &= 288 \cdot 23 + 16 \\
23 &= 1 \cdot 16 + 7 \\
16 &= 2 \cdot 7 + 2 \\
7 &= 3 \cdot 2 + 1 \\
2 &= 2 \cdot 1 + 0
\end{aligned}
$$

Next we solve for the remainders and write them in reversed order:

$$
\begin{aligned}
1 &= 7 - 3 \cdot 2 \\
2 &= 16 - 2 \cdot 7 \\
7 &= 23 - 1 \cdot 16 \\
16 &= 6640 - 288 \cdot 23
\end{aligned}
$$

(6.17)
(6.18)

Then we substitute the expression for remainder 2, that is, Eq. (6.18) into Eq. (6.17) and obtain

$$
\begin{aligned}
1 &= 7 - 3 \cdot (16 - 2 \cdot 7) \\
&= -3 \cdot 16 + 7 \cdot 7
\end{aligned}
$$

(6.19)

Substituting successively the expressions for the remainders 7 and 16 we get

$$
\begin{aligned}
1 &= -3 \cdot 16 + 7 \cdot (23 - 1 \cdot 16) \\
&= 7 \cdot 23 - 10 \cdot 16 \\
&= 7 \cdot 23 - 10 \cdot (6640 - 288 \cdot 23) \\
&= -10 \cdot 6640 + 2887 \cdot 23
\end{aligned}
$$

(6.20)

Let us rewrite Eq. (6.20) as

$$
23 \cdot 2887 = 1 + 10 \cdot 6640
$$

then we have immediately

$$
23 \cdot 2887 \equiv 1 \qquad (\text{mod } 6640)
$$

Hence, the inverse of $e = 23$ (mod 6640) is simply $d = 2887$. ∎

We shall now describe the *RSA two-key cryptosystem*.

The pair (n, e) is published by the receiver while the trapdoor parameter

$$T = (p, q, d) \tag{6.22}$$

is kept secret. The plaintext that should be encrypted is represented by a sequence of digits that are grouped into blocks; let the integer P, where $0 \leq P < n$, denote such a block.

RSA Encryption

The *encryption* is performed by the sender who looks up the public parameters n and e; then he takes his plaintext P and raises it to the power of e (mod n) and obtain the ciphertext

$$C = E_K(P) \equiv P^e \qquad (\text{mod } n) \tag{6.23}$$

which is transmitted.

EXAMPLE 6.8

Let the public parameters be $n = 6847$ and $e = 23$. Then the plaintext $P = 17$ is encrypted by the RSA two-key cryptosystem as

$$C \equiv P^e \qquad (\text{mod } n)$$
$$= 17^{23} \qquad (\text{mod } 6847)$$

It is often convenient to compute such exponentiations by the method of successive squarings as we illustrate below. The exponent $e = 23 = 16 + 4 + 2 + 1$. Hence, we evaluate first

$$17^2 = 289 \qquad (\text{mod } 6847)$$
$$17^4 = 289^2 = 83521 \equiv 1357 \qquad (\text{mod } 6847)$$
$$17^8 \equiv 1357^2 = 1841449 \equiv 6453 \qquad (\text{mod } 6847)$$
$$17^{16} \equiv 6453^2 = 41641209 \equiv 4602 \qquad (\text{mod } 6847)$$

Then we have

$$17^{23} = 17^{16+4+2+1}$$
$$= 17^{16} \cdot 17^4 \cdot 17^2 \cdot 17$$
$$\equiv 4602 \cdot 1357 \cdot 289 \cdot 17$$

By multiplying the first two and last two numbers we obtain

$$17^{23} \equiv 6244914 \cdot 4913$$
$$\equiv 450 \cdot 4913 = 2210850$$
$$\equiv 6116 \quad (\text{mod } 6847)$$

Hence, we have the ciphertext $C = 6116$ which we transmit. ■

The receiver who knows the trapdoor parameter T proceeds as follows.

RSA Decryption

The receiver uses his secret inverse of e, namely d, and computes the exponentiation

$$D_K(C) \equiv C^d \quad (\text{mod } n) \tag{6.24}$$

It remains only to show that the exponentiation (6.24) recovers the plaintext P. We insert our expressions for the ciphertext, that is, Eq. (6.23) into Eq. (6.24) and obtain

$$C^d \equiv (P^e)^d \equiv P^{ed} \quad (\text{mod } n) \tag{6.25}$$

Next we exploit Eq. (6.16), rewrite ed as $1 - t\phi(n)$, and insert this into Eq. (6.25); then we conclude that

$$C^d \equiv P^{ed} = P^{1-t\phi(n)}$$
$$= P^1 \cdot P^{-t\phi(n)} = P(P^{\phi(n)})^{-t} \tag{6.26}$$
$$\equiv P \quad (\text{mod } n)$$

where the last congruence follows from Euler's theorem (6.14)!

EXAMPLE 6.8   *(continued)*

In Example 6.7 we showed that the inverse $d = 2887$ solves $ed \equiv 1 \ (\text{mod } \phi(n))$ for $e = 23$ and $n = 6847$.

The ciphertext $C = 6116$ is decrypted by the RSA two-key cryptosystem in the following way.

$$P \equiv C^d \quad (\text{mod } n)$$
$$= 6116^{2887} \quad (\text{mod } 6847)$$

At a first glance it seems to be a tough task to carry out the exponentiation. As before we use the method with successive squaring and write the exponent d as

$$d = 2887 = 2048 + 512 + 256 + 64 + 4 + 2 + 1$$

Then we compute

$$6116^2 \equiv 295 \qquad\qquad (\text{mod } 6847)$$
$$6116^4 \equiv 295^2 \equiv 4861 \qquad (\text{mod } 6847)$$
$$6116^8 \equiv 4861^2 \equiv 324 \qquad (\text{mod } 6847)$$
$$6116^{16} \equiv 324^2 \equiv 2271 \qquad (\text{mod } 6847)$$
$$6116^{32} \equiv 2271^2 \equiv 1650 \qquad (\text{mod } 6847)$$
$$6116^{64} \equiv 1650^2 \equiv 4241 \qquad (\text{mod } 6847)$$
$$6116^{128} \equiv 4241^2 \equiv 5859 \qquad (\text{mod } 6847)$$
$$6116^{256} \equiv 5859^2 \equiv 3870 \qquad (\text{mod } 6847)$$
$$6116^{512} \equiv 3870^2 \equiv 2511 \qquad (\text{mod } 6847)$$
$$6116^{1024} \equiv 2511^2 \equiv 5881 \qquad (\text{mod } 6847)$$
$$6116^{2048} \equiv 5881^2 \equiv 1964 \qquad (\text{mod } 6847)$$

Thus, we have

$$6116^{2887} = 6116^{2048+512+256+64+4+2+1}$$
$$\equiv (1964 \cdot 2511)(3870 \cdot 4241)(4861 \cdot 295)6116$$
$$\equiv (1764 \cdot 411)(2972 \cdot 6116)$$
$$\equiv 6069 \cdot 4814$$
$$\equiv 17 \qquad (\text{mod } 6847)$$

The receiver obtained the plaintext $P = 17$, which indeed is the number that was encrypted by the sender. ∎

Everybody can look up the public parameters n and e, but only those who know at least one of the secret parameters p, q, and d that are included in the trapdoor parameter T can decrypt. If the enemy cryptanalyst, however, can factor n, then he can easily compute $\phi(n)$ and obtain the secret decryption exponent d, and, hence, obtain the plaintext.

Since an essentially larger amount of computation is involved in a two-key cryptosystem than in a comparably secure single-key cryptosystem, two-key cryptosystems are mainly used in hybrid systems. The two-key cryptosystem is used for authentication and digital signatures or for an exchange of a key to be used as a session key in a high-speed single-key cryptosystem that provides secrecy for the main communication. When the information transfer is completed, the session key is discarded.

6.8 CONCLUSIONS

While the need for cryptography in connection with affairs of state and the military has generally been accepted for centuries, it was not until we entered the information age that society experienced similar needs in the private sector.

- *Secrecy:* When we store or transmit data we want to protect it from unauthorized access. Properly designed single-key cryptosystems provide the required degree of secrecy. Two-key cryptosystems can also provide secrecy, but are mainly used for key distribution or for authentication.

- *Authentication:* In both commercial and private transactions it is of vital concern to all involved that the information is authentic, that is, that the received message comes from a purported sender. Two-key cryptography solves this problem; it gives us the possibility to create digital signatures. In June 2000 the U.S. Congress gave digital signatures the same legal status as handwritten signatures.

REFERENCES

1. KAHN, D. 1967. *The codebreakers: The story of secret writing.* Macmillan: New York.
2. SIMMONS, G. J. 1984. Authentication theory/coding theory. In G. R. BLAKLEY and D. CHAUM, eds. *Advances in cryptology, Proceedings of CRYPTO'84.* Lecture Notes in Computer Sciences, No. 196, Springer-Verlag: Berlin.
3. VERNAM, G. S. 1926. Cipher printing telegraph systems for secret wire and radio telegraphic communications. *J. Am. Inst. Electr. Engin.*, XLV, 109–115.
4. SHANNON, C. E. 1949. Communication theory of secrecy systems. *Bell System Tech. J.*, 28, 656–715.
5. AGRELL, W. 2003. *Venona – Spåren från ett underrättelsekrig* (in Swedish). Historiska Media: Lund, Sweden.
6. DIFFIE, W. and HELLMAN, M. E. 1976. New directions in cryptography. *IEEE Trans Information Theory*, IT-22, 644–654.
7. DIFFIE, W. 1992. The first ten years in public key cryptology. In G. J. SIMMONS, ed. *Contemporary cryptology: The science of information integrity.* IEEE Press: Piscataway, N.J.
8. RIVEST, R., SHAMIR, A. and ADLEMAN, L. 1978. A method for obtaining digital signatures and public-key cryptosystems. *Comm. ACM*, 21, 120–126.

PROBLEMS

1. Consider the following scheme.

		plaintext		
		Buy IBM	*Sell IBM*	
key	*HH*	*Buy IBM*-0	*Sell IBM*-1	
	HT	*Buy IBM*-1	*Sell IBM*-0	ciphertext
	TH	*Sell IBM*-0	*Buy IBM*-1	
	TT	*Sell IBM*-1	*Buy IBM*-0	

Does this scheme provide any secrecy?

What is the probability of a successful impersonation attack?

What is the probability of a successful substitution attack?

2. Consider the scheme in Example 6.3 and assume that $Pr(\textit{Buy IBM}) = p < 1/2$.

    (a) What is the probability of a successful impersonation attack?

    (b) What is the probability of a successful substitution attack?

3. Find a scheme for authentication of a situation with two plaintexts, Buy IBM and Sell IBM, such that the probability for a successful impersonation attack is $Pr(I) = 1/4$. There is no requirement that your scheme should provide any secrecy, nor does it have to provide any protection against substitution. However, you must state whether your scheme provides secrecy and find the probability $Pr(S)$ for a successful substitution attack.

4. Recover the plaintext from the following ciphertext.

    YREEZSRCZJTFDZEXREUYVYRJVCVGYREKJ

5. Design an RSA two-key cryptosystem with the trapdoor parameter $T = (p, q, d) = (17, 43, 29)$.

6. An RSA two-key cryptosystem is set up with the public parameters $n = 7849$ and $e = 25$. The plaintext is $P = 2728$ (it is converted text to an integer by a method we in this example do not care about). Find the ciphertext.

7. Consider an RSA two-key cryptosystem with the public parameters $n = 143$ and $e = 23$. Factor n and find the plaintext P corresponding to the ciphertext $C = 9$.

8. Find the plaintext P that corresponds to the ciphertext $C = 2401$ obtained with the RSA two-key cryptosystem defined in Problem 6.6.

    Hint: One of the factors is $p = 167$.

Chapter 7

Communication Networks: Let's Get Connected

A network is a means of transporting things. The "things" can be grain, electricity, garbage, people, postal letters, or in our case, information. Organizing networks is a fundamental human activity that helps distinguish us from less intelligent species. Without networks that collect, store and distribute food, we would live precariously from hunting and gathering. Networks direct how we move around or communicate in any organized way. They allow us to cause actions at a distance or at a future time. Networks function according to rules and procedures, sometimes very complicated ones. Almost all networks are accessed through a *terminal*, which serves as a gateway to the network. This can be a computer or a telephone instrument, or an electrical outlet or a garbage container. The user is not allowed any other access.

In this chapter we will take a look at information networks. These are based on the technologies and the natural and mathematical laws of the earlier chapters. We will begin with some major examples of such networks and then look at the building blocks that they have in common. Some networks are straightforward and others are very complex. Later sections focus on two complex networks that we use every day, the telephone network and the Internet.

7.1 AN OVERVIEW OF INFORMATION NETWORKS

The way that a network is arranged, both physically and in terms of rules, is called its architecture. Many functions need to be organized, but at the highest level there is an *overall scheme*, and it is worth spelling out four of them before getting into details.

A relatively simple overall scheme is the *broadcast* or the opposite, the *collection* network. These transfer information in only one direction, out to the user, or into

Understanding Information Transmission. By John B. Anderson and Rolf Johannesson
ISBN 0-471-67910-0 © 2005 the Institute of Electrical and Electronics Engineers, Inc.

a collection point, along a set path dedicated to that user. Everyday examples outside information technology are distribution systems for water and electricity on the one hand and garbage collection on the other. Information network examples are radio and TV broadcasting. In these there is a dedicated pathway, even if it is electromagnetic waves through cables or space, and users consume what they want, without the possibility of answering back.

Another overall network scheme is *circuit switching*. In this kind of network, users submit an address and request a pathway for their goods; one is set up, it serves as long as needed, and then it is shut down. The classic example is the telephone network. We saw in Chapter 1 that circuit switching was devised by Bell and his coworkers almost immediately after the telephone was first marketed.

An older scheme of networking, exemplified by the post office and the telegraph, is called *message switching*. In these networks, a message arrives at the post or telegraph office and an operator or algorithm decides on a routing to the next office. This repeats until the message arrives at its destination. It is possible for operators to store messages for a while and forward them in bulk. There are many examples of message switching, large and small. Another one is a request for information to a bureaucracy, such as the tax office; the request is passed from mailroom to clerk to clerk until (hopefully) one is found who answers the request.

A much newer networking scheme is *packet switching*. Now the message is broken into small standard pieces called packets, each with the address attached. These make their way through the network, more or less as wanderers, taking possibly different paths, until they are reassembled at the destination. This kind of network appeared with the development of the Internet.

7.1.1   Some Well-Known Information Networks

These four schemes of network organization show themselves in various ways in the electrical information networks that we use. Some of the more important of these are as follows. The list here is organized by the service provided. Afterward, we will look at the component functions that all these have in common.

- *Radio and television broadcasting.*   Here the user is passive and simply accepts service whenever he or she desires. Considerable transmission delay is tolerable, but the quality of the information must be high. In all the rest of the networks that follow, communication is two-way.

- *Telephone.*   This is actually two networks, the one that sets up the circuit (the "signaling" network) and the voice network itself. The voice part needs good security and reliability, and moderate quality; it needs to be real time and an assigned circuit must be maintained as long as needed. The signaling network needs very high security and quality (i.e., low error probability), but need not be strictly real time.[1]

---

[1] Before the 1980s, both signaling (in the form of audio tones) and voice traveled over the same network. The security of the voice network was not enough to prevent fraud in the form of stolen long-distance calls.

- *Mobile telephony.* Cellular telephony presents yet a third telephone network type, and here a lower level of security, reliability, and quality are acceptable, compared to a fixed telephone system. The network is still circuit switched, but the physical reality of the circuit changes from time to time as the user moves.

- *Email.* Electronic mail can tolerate long delays, but it needs an almost perfect error rate, high security, and a high reliability that the message eventually will be delivered. In this and the next two examples, much more complicated interactions between terminal and network are allowed, compared to the previous examples.

- *Audio/video streaming.* This refers to downloading of audio or visual material that should "play back," without interruption. The transmission need only be moderately real time, since the terminal can have a storage that evens out small irregularities in delivery. Widely varying demands for quality need to be served, from the MPEG levels in Chapter 3 down to slow-scan video conferencing. Streaming delivery is an example of an *asymmetric* network, one where the down direction to the user carries much more information than the up direction back to the network. A network that carries text, audio, and visual information with radically differing bit rates is called a *multimedia* network.

- *Client–server interactions.* These embrace a variety of networks that handle requests for information from a "client" to a database or a computer program called the "server." Everyday examples include the worldwide web (hereafter called the WWW), airline reservation systems, and all sorts of online and telephone ordering systems. Computer-terminal examples of these networks are often asymmetric and multimedia. Neither end needs to be human. Relatively moderate security and response time are often acceptable. Client–server sessions tend to be packet switched and the network pathway is formed and open only during an actual information exchange.

7.1.2 Functions and Structures Within Networks

In order to set up a network, many decisions about its design need to be made. A number of functions such as address handling and the physical transmission need to be carried out, and such things as the arrangement of nodes and paths needs to be designed. We will look at the major decisions now, one at a time. The examples will be information networks old and new. The way that different functions are carried out is summarized in Table 7.1 for three of them, the postal system, the telephone, and the Internet. We will carry along as a comparison a network that transports something more physical than information, a network that everyone knows well: Collecting the garbage.

Table 7.1   Implementation of network functions in the postal, telephone, and Internet networks

Function	Postal net	Telephone net	Internet
Overall scheme	Msg. switching	Ckt. switching	Packet switching
Addressing	Geographical address	Hierarchical	Hierarchical
Routing	Manual selection by rules	Circuit setup by rules	Packet passing
Store & forward?	Much	None	Some
Transmission method	Paper	Analog & digital	All digital
Original use	Letters	Voice	Email
Present major use	Printed material, packages	$\frac{1}{2}$ voice, $\frac{1}{2}$ data	WWW; streaming downloads
Terminal	Mailbox	Phone instrument	PC
Topology	Rings with hierarchy	Stars with hierarchy	Random arrangement
Security	Strong	Moderately strong	Moderately weak

Network Topology

A good place to start a network design is its topology; that is, the arrangement of its interconnections. We think of networks as consisting of paths and nodes. A node can be a switching point, a broadcasting point, or just a user terminal; paths connect the nodes. Figure 7.1 shows some different network topologies. The choice of topology is a fundamental decision to make about a network. Which arrangement works best depends on who needs to be connected and what is being carried.

We can look now in more detail at some topologies and examples. Figures 7.1*a* to *c* show three simple examples in pure form, the ring, star, and tree topologies. The ring consists of a server and a number of terminals connected in a ring, around which flows all the information in the network. Each terminal takes what it needs from the total flow. A ring that does not come back to the server is called a backbone. Rings are more reliable, however, since a single break does not isolate a group of users. An information example is the Ethernet, a system that finds use in departments and work groups where a number of small computers are together in a few rooms. The transmission medium is a coaxial cable, a medium that easily carries all the information with high reliability, provided that it is only a few hundred meters long.

If the users were widely separated, say, many kilometers apart, a ring with a cable would be a poor design. Perhaps Figure 7.1*b*, the star topology, would work better. Now the server has a direct line running out to each user terminal. A classic example of a star network is a communication satellite, consisting of a central satellite and many separate users, which can be potentially anywhere visible on Earth from the satellite. The links are now electromagnetic radio channels. Terminals are much more expensive and the radio links are less reliable than cable, but if service is needed over a wide area, the satellite system is cheaper. A third basic topology is the tree in Figure 7.1*c*. A tree has no loops, and its nodes are now of two

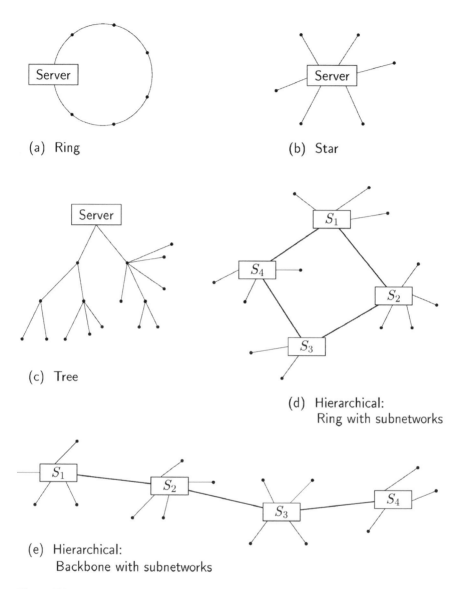

(a) Ring

(b) Star

(c) Tree

(d) Hierarchical:
    Ring with subnetworks

(e) Hierarchical:
    Backbone with subnetworks

Figure 7.1   Ring, star, and tree basic network topologies, plus two hierarchical topologies

types, those where there is a split, with a pass onto another node, and those that are final nodes.

Most networks are not pure in their topology and consist of regions with whatever topology is convenient. An important topological concept in more complex networks is hierarchy. Now there is a large-scale network of major nodes, each of which connects in turn to its own set of minor nodes. The major nodes have a higher capacity and perhaps carry out more functions. We can call them the servers. The networks in Figures 7.1*d* and *e* illustrate hierarchy in two ways. The first is a ring of servers, each with its own subnetwork of users, and the second is a backbone network of servers and their subnetworks along in a line. National telephone networks usually have a multilevel hierarchy. The highest nodes are a network of servers for the different areas of the country; these nodes connect down to a second level in the hierarchy, which consists of towns and districts in large cities; each second-level node connects to a set of local subscribers that are assigned to it. At the highest level in the hierarchy, a telephone topology is typically a collection of rings within rings. At the local lowest level, individual subscribers tend to connect to the next level up through star topologies.

And what about garbage collection? Local garbage collectors probably follow ring-like routes more than anything else. In this way they are like mail carriers, but not like local telephony. When the garbage truck fills up, the load is taken to a single permanent dumping site, although it may reach there through a hierarchy of collection sites. Before the garbage reaches the garbage can, it is collected from the house. What collection topology is used in your living space?

Addressing

Garbage goes to a single place and thus needs no address. Broadcast radio and television pass in reverse from one to many, and need no address either. However, most telephone calls and email must pass through a complex network and end up at precisely one chosen terminal. A method of addressing the information is needed. Simply assigning a one-piece address to every user is called flat addressing. Examples of this are telephone calls inside a company or a university, which lack any sort of prefix, and emails sent to users within the same server. Addressing on a wider scale requires a hierarchical addressing scheme. The international telephone numbering scheme is an example of such addressing. The first digits of the number indicate the country, the second a region within the country, the third the local exchange, and the fourth the user within the exchange. In processing the number, the equipment views the digits one after the other, and declares the country to be the first legal country group that it sees; it repeats the procedure with the digits that follow, declaring the region again to be the first acceptable group that appears; the rest of the digits are the local number.[2] For example, the international number 4646143356 has to mean the local number 143356 in Lund, Sweden, because the first legal country code encountered is 46 (meaning Sweden), and the first regional code after that is also 46 (which as a regional code means Lund).

Another hierarchical address scheme is used with email. Here the parts of the address are denoted by the "@" and "." marks. The part of the address before the "@" is the user name within the mail server's domain, and the part that comes after, called the domain name, identifies the server itself. The domain name consists

---

[2] We have not counted the international long-distance access code, which is typically "00". In information theory, an encoding scheme like this is called an instantaneous code.

of several hierarchical parts, separated by "." symbols. These may indicate companies, schools, or regions; the last part is always a network within the Internet structure, with a name like edu, com, jp, or se, the last two denoting countries. Part of this scheme is found in the URL (Universal Resource Locator) addressing method that is used for WWW sites.

Protocols

A protocol is a set of rules. For example, the HTTP (HyperText Transfer Protocol) is the set of rules by which we obtain documents, pictures, and sound from the world-wide web; our computer terminal sets up a client–server relationship with the desired web server and then requests, receives, and confirms material according to the HTTP rules. A link to the web server must first be set up, and this is done according to another set of rules. Protocols are essential in an information network, and they are found at every physical place in a network and at every level in its organizational structure. Some are so commonplace that they are easily overlooked. For example, every interaction requires "handshaking" in some way. This is the method by which the receiver acknowledges that it has received information or taken an action. When we make a telephone call, the answering end signifies that the connection is set up by saying hello. The receiver formally gives a name in some countries, or may just say "Yes" in others, but the call cannot begin until a handshaking has taken place. The response from the receiving end also fulfills another function, authentication. If we do not recognize who says "Yes", we branch to another protocol, the one that handles unknown responders.

Terminals

Users access the network through terminals. For our garbage collectors, the terminal is a garbage can. In an information network, the choice of features is much more complicated. Perhaps the hardest design decision is intelligence: What should the terminal be able to do on the one hand, and how smart should a human user be on the other. The postal and telegraph systems (like the garbage system) require only that the message with proper address be dropped in the right place. The telephone system, in the present day, has a user interface consisting of a 10 position digit selector. With the Internet came the need for a very intelligent terminal, in fact, a full computer. The human user must be able to operate rather complex programs and needs to be able to compose readable text in the case of email. As we saw in Chapter 1, the Internet had to await the development of cheap computers.

Transmission Links

Garbage collectors use trucks for transmission, but just as with terminals, many link types await the information network designer. These can be wire, cable, or fiber links, all of which are highly reliable and cheap if short. Radio links are much less reliable, but are essential if the terminals are moving. The unreliable radio links require a different set of protocols that handle the retransmissions, lost links, and delays that happen. All these links were discussed in Chapter 4.

Switching

We have seen that networks can transfer two-way information by switching the whole message through a path in an organized way (message switching), by setting up a dedicated pathway and handing it over to the users (circuit switching), or by more or less blindly passing the message in small unit pieces (e.g., packet switching). These all have advantages in different situations. Postal and telegraph-type messages—and garbage—are carried by message switching. The user does not have to understand much about the network, and the network operators can save money by storing many messages and carrying and delivering them all at once. Users, however, have to be trained, as we all have been, to say what they have to say all at once and then wait until a future delivery time for the answer. The telephone system uses circuit switching. This is real time, but setting up and maintaining custom pathways is expensive.[3]

The overhead of setting up circuits can be avoided with packet switching. The message is broken into fixed-size packets and these are simply passed from node to node. A protocol sets rules for where a node should pass a packet, what to do if the node cannot accept a packet, and how to reassemble packets. In effect, the packets find their own way, blown along by the protocol rules. This kind of switching works well with emails and website interactions, which are not real time and which break easily into packets. It works less well when the Internet is used for an ongoing vocal or written conversation, or for listening or watching downloaded audio and video ("streaming" applications); now the packets must march across the net more or less in real time, and a stricter set of rules is called for.

Storing/Forwarding/Concentrating/Routing

Nodes in a network can have storage. That opens many avenues for a more efficient design. A garbage can is a node with storage, and a garbage network is otherwise rather useless. Once storage is available, there need to be rules for how to take in and empty out material. This is forwarding. With the garbage, there is simply an agreed-upon day, but the rules in an information network can be very complex. With a packet switched network, the protocol for storing and forwarding packets is a central issue in the switching design.

An efficient network often must concentrate traffic so that a large number of messages are carried in bulk through an expensive pathway. Postal mail is sorted into bulk quantities and sent by airplane to different high-level stations in the network. Email meant for a destination a continent away is concentrated and sent in a single high-speed transmission. The wandering packet model of the Internet

---

[3]Roughly speaking, half the cost of a telephone network is in its switching, with most of the rest in the local links out to customers.

breaks down here: packets are instead collected, stored, concentrated into one large message, and sent by message switching perhaps through a dedicated channel.

The decision to carry messages to certain destinations in a certain way is called a routing decision. Routing is also done in the telephone network when there are several pathways between switching stations. Routing is often dynamic, meaning that it adapts to the quantity of traffic at different times and places. Our garbage collectors may have to change their truck route to adapt to road repairs and traffic jams. Similar problems arise in an information network: The object is to maintain the most efficient flow possible and avoid overfilling any of the storage locations along the way.

How to coordinate topology, storing, forwarding, and routing is not an easy problem to solve, and its study, called queueing theory, is a major area of networking research. Just how to combine all of these functions into an efficient design is a problem without any precise solution.

Security

Customers expect some level of message security, although they may not be consciously aware of it. In the long run, they will not pay for service that is insecure. There are many facets to security, beyond the fact that users do not like someone else reading their mail. Authentication, as we have mentioned, is the process of confirming that the correct party is reached. The network components themselves need to be able to resist attacks, of both the software and hardware kind.[4] A secure system of billing needs to be devised. Historically, the telephone network was held to a high degree of security, which it often enjoys even today. It is legal in many countries, for example, to record images of people without their permission (as in banks), but not their audio conversations. Mobile telephones, especially the analog kind, are much less secure, but this is accepted by the public. The Internet has a low level of security, both with respect to eavesdropping and to attacks on its structure. In a sense, this was intentional, because its designers gave higher priority to other network functions in order to promote a rapid development. Now we are trying to make the Internet more secure.

Network Management

Last and not least, a network must be managed. Our garbage collectors need to be hired and fired and paid, and if they go on strike, management needs to respond. In an information network, nodes and links need to be repaired and added or taken away. Many networks monitor congestion, and take special action if normal routing and store/forward procedures are insufficient.

---

[4]To describe the security business more fairly, we should say that to a security analyst, there are no Good Guys or Bad Guys. It is as important to look at breaking the security of a system as protecting it. There have been examples of governments that insisted that the security of information networks be designed to be vulnerable.

7.1.3   Layered Architectures: The ISO Reference Model

Another way to think about network architecture is to think of it in levels or *layers*. For example, there is the transmission layer where bits are actually carried. Bit modulation and error correction are of interest here. Then there are the points where packets or other basic messages are fed in or taken out of the network. Here, issues of storing, forwarding, and routing are of interest. An equipment manufacturer might have an interest in these, but not in modulation or error correction, and this manufacturer sees the network only as a packet system. A customer sees the network at an even higher layer, for example, as a means to access the WWW or to send email. This user thinks only about how easy the network is to use, how fast it is, and how much it costs.

These different parties see different layers in the network. If the architecture can be organized throughout into consistent layers, it will be much easier for them all to relate in their own way. It will be easier to develop and modify a network, and to interface it to a different applications. Providers of services over the web, for example, would like to have a fixed set of rules for how these interact with the network, and they would like to be unconcerned with whether bits are carried by fiber or radio, or how they are formed into packets. Early networks tended to be proprietary, meaning that they were not designed to be compatible with other companies' systems, or were even designed in secret. As a business practice, this was often done to isolate smaller competitors, and it still goes on.

The opposite of a proprietary system is an *open system architecture*, with entry points at several layers, each subject to a known set of rules and open without license fee to any provider of equipment or services. After an initial period where large companies tried to dominate networking, the International Organization for Standardization (the ISO) in the late 1970s adopted a standard model for information networks called the Open Systems Interconnection (OSI) model. It consists of seven layers. Even though it is not followed exactly in many networks, it has had a major influence and it tends to be the way people discuss networking. The full framework is shown in Figure 7.2.

We will take the OSI layers now, one at a time. The first layer in the figure is the application layer. By this is meant the layer that provides services directly needed by applications. These include WWW browsing, email, and file transfers, to name a few. The browser, for example, must implement the HTTP protocol, a set of procedures for obtaining documents, and the URL protocol to handle addresses.

The presentation layer is less important to us here. It is supposed to convert the output of the application layer above into machine-independent form.

The session layer supports the dialog-type information flow that needs to exist between the application layer and the actual transport in the network. Applications tend to create sporadic flows, which need to be evened out and stored in buffers. These flows can go in the up and down directions, even though a given line into the network proper can flow in only one direction at once.[5] The session layer

---

[5] Almost all lines accept data in one direction at a time. A line that accepts data in either direction, but not both at once, is called half-duplex. A double line that maintains two-direction flow is called full duplex.

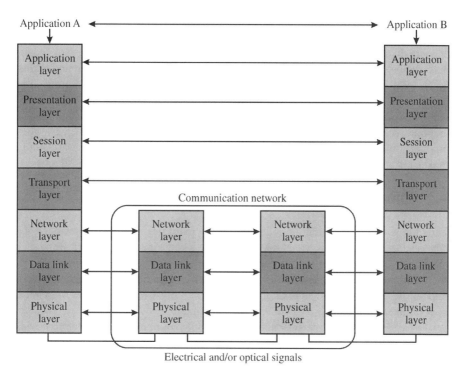

Figure 7.2   The standard OSI reference model, with its seven layers.
Source: Communication Networks [1], copyright 2000, McGraw-Hill, used with permission

takes care of resetting the line to accept data in one direction or the other, and buffering incoming data from the application or the line while this is done. A download of a long audio or video stream needs session layer support as well, since transmission errors and dropouts may need processing and buffering.

The transport layer begins the network proper. In the true OSI model, the transport layer does not know for what purpose the customer is using the network, although it may know that a certain grade of service (e.g., error probability or delay) is required. The layer breaks the data into proper-sized segments containing data and information for use by protocols. It provides error correction and assures that address information is attached to the segments.

The network layer accepts and receives frames of bits. It sees that each frame ends up at the proper geographical address in the network. In a packet switched network, bit frames in the form of packets are passed to another node, perhaps according to a routing algorithm that specifies all or part of the path. If there is congestion, it is dealt with in this layer. It can happen that the network contains certain dedicated paths between node pairs, and if so, these form a lower layer, the data link layer. A stream of bit frames is sent directly down this path, as soon as it is free. Framing information, which tells how to break the stream up into frames, may need to be added. A large network may have fixed-link parts, so it is natural to view these as a lower architectural layer.

Finally comes the physical layer. It includes the actual fiber, wire, or radio channels, the modulation method and its speed, and equipment for setting up and taking down the links. The last three layers are lumped together as the "communication network" in Figure 7.2, since the three often work closely together and can be hard to separate. They blur especially in the Internet, because the Internet is a collection of networks that makes only limited assumptions in one net about what goes on in the others. In some cases, everything below the transport layer (layer 4) simply makes up an "Internet layer," which works to accept and pass on addressed packets.

7.2   CIRCUIT SWITCHING: THE TELEPHONE NET

The classic example of circuit switching is the fixed telephone network. Now we take a closer look at this venerable institution. Much of its layout and principles have changed little since the first systems of the 1880s, but the implementation of such subsystems as switches, transmission lines, and path setup has changed very much. The greatest change is digital conversion—most transmission systems are now digital and the majority of messages are data.

Why has the telephone system survived so long? Not many major technologies from the 1880s are still universal today. Can you think of any? A reason for telephone survival is that it provides a basic function, connecting us together, in a cheap way, and it does it by an overall scheme, circuit switching, that has proved to be effective. A naysayer can always respond that telephones only *look* the same, and that almost all their internal workings have changed. We will look at these workings in detail, and you can be the judge.

7.2.1   An Overview

What follows is a summary of the telephone technology as it most often appears. There are many exceptions in, for example, hotels and networked work places (see the Ethernet discussion in Section 4.1). Cellular telephone operation is quite different, and will be taken up in Section 7.3.

The telephone system consists of local groups of lines to subscribers, switches, and trunk transmission links between the groups. A typical arrangement in a city might be as shown in Figure 7.3*a*. Since Bell's time, a local switch has been called a *central office*. Interconnecting these to each other and to an upper hierarchy of long-distance switches are *trunk lines*. A simple set of procedures regulates how these parts work together. They are the network protocols, although we tend to reserve that word for more complicated sets of rules. A telephone call, whether it carries voice or data, has three phases.

- *Call setup.*   Picking up the phone (taking it "off hook") sets in motion the sequence of events in Figure 7.4, a sequence that has hardly changed since the 1880s. An off hook telephone closes a switch that lowers the resistance

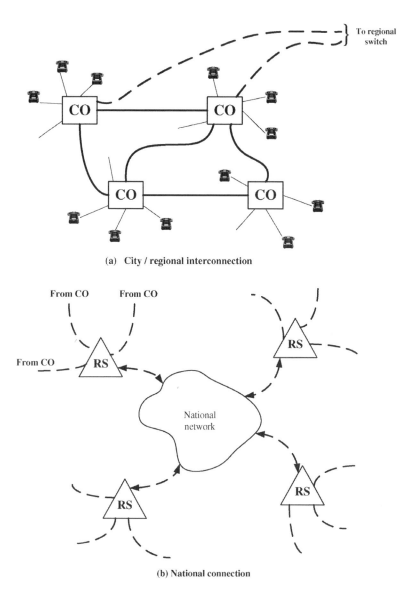

(a) **City / regional interconnection**

(b) **National connection**

Figure 7.3   A national telephone network, in two pictures. (a) Interconnection of central office switches (COs) within a city or region. Heavy solid paths are connections between COs; dashed paths lead out of the region. (b) Regional switches (RSs) gather traffic from a region of COs and connect to other RSs by a national network

of the local telephone line (see Box 7-1). This line is ordinarily a wire pair that forms a simple circuit called the *local loop*. When not in use (when "on hook"), the local loop path still forms a completed circuit, but it has relatively high resistance. The entire set of local loops is energized at 48 V DC.

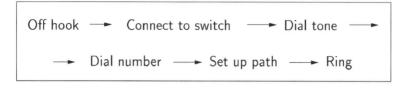

Figure 7.4   The event sequence in setting up a telephone circuit

BOX 7-1

A century ago, circuit technology consisted of coils, transformers and relays. The off hook current energized a relay, which closed a path directly to the switch. A dial was a mechanism that alternately closed a pair of contacts, which drove the telephone switch step by step to the desired position (see the switch discussion). Today, signaling is by a pair of audio tones that represent the twelve symbols $0, \ldots, 9, \#, *$. Dial tone seems to appear almost instantly, but gaining access to the switch is still a separate, distinct step.

An off hook phone increases the line current, which signals the local switch that service is needed. An entry path to the switch is connected to the local loop, an event that is signaled by the appearance of a dial tone. Only then can a user signal the desired number, by tones or dial pulses. For a local call these drive the switch to close a path to the desired party; on completion of the circuit, the switch notifies both parties of this by ringing. The ringing signal is a large (130 V) AC voltage that overcomes the high on hook line resistance and rings the called party. Picking up that phone lowers its circuit resistance and signals the switch to stop ringing.

- *Message.*   Now the parties—or computers—talk (see Box 7-2). The local loop connection to the switch is usually a single wire pair (a "2-wire connection") that carries signals in both directions in an analog fashion.[6] Inside the switch, and between switches along a trunk path, there are separate digital paths in each direction (in a holdover from analog times, the pair is called a "4-wire connection"). Local lines reach the switch through a line card, a circuit that converts signals to a common digital form. The interface between the 4-wire and 2-wire circuits is tricky and requires a device called a hybrid transformer; reflections of signal can occur here, which create annoying echos, and these need to be removed by special echo cancelation circuitry. A true digital connection along the entire user path can be set up as a special service; one such service is an ISDN (Integrated Services Digital Network) connection. Paths among central office switches and regional switching centers are now almost entirely digital, and can be fixed

---

[6]Even when the transmission is data, the signal is still treated as an analog signal until it reaches the switch.

in place or set up in response to demand. A system that sets up high-capacity links between switches in response to demand is called a digital cross connect system.

● *Call release.*   Parties signal the end of the call by placing their phones on hook. The change in DC line current signals the central office switches to disconnect the local lines from them, release pathways through them, and release trunk paths if any.

BOX 7-2

Communication between switches was once by human operators. It is reported that the earliest calls across North America took more than 20 minutes to set up! By mid-century, network signaling was automatic, but signaling and calls were carried over the same network, the signals being carried by standard audio dial tones. This scheme was slow, since the tones were slow and had to be registered and passed from switch to switch, and unscrupulous callers could fool the system by creating their own tone sequences. Today, network signaling can take place in less time than pushing a tone button, so that call setup appears to be instant.

As mentioned in Section 7.1, telephone central offices are connected together in a hierarchical pattern to form a long distance network. Some idea of this was shown in Figure 7.3. The top part shows an interconnection of central offices in a city or region. These offices can connect with each other directly or indirectly, and all have a link, possibly indirect, out of the region. They form a unit, which can be thought of as a telephone area or city code, but practices vary over the world, and such units are not necessarily synonymous with such codes. In order to provide long distance service, these units communicate with each other over a network of interties. Two units with a lot of traffic between them might have their own link, or a number of units can be tied to a higher order national switching node. This is shown in the bottom part of the figure. By extending the hierarchy one level higher, international calls are handled.

As an example, we can take the network in North America, with its 3+7 digit numbering system. Central offices are identified by the first three digits of a standard 7-digit local number, although sometimes several such offices are physically combined. City and regional collections of central offices are called local access and transport areas (LATAs), and they can be operated by different companies. A telephone area code, designated by the first three of the 10 digits, may embrace several LATAs. Links and switching among LATAs are provided by long distance companies called interexchange carriers. Other companies may provide international links.

Network signaling in a telephone network refers to the message passing that is required to set up a call circuit. The initial stage of it consists of the off hook current shift, followed by dial tones, which instruct the local office switch. The content of the dial tones is held in a register; the switch is controlled by software (so-called stored program control), which acts on the register contents. Such a switch can carry out a great many extra services directed by the tones, such as access to stored messages, call waiting, and so on, and it can also store detailed billing information. If the call is to be connected outside the local region, the local office switch must signal a regional switch, and possibly switches at higher levels. This is done by a separate, fast packet-switched system called the signaling network. Software higher in the system makes decisions about how to route the call and passes instructions back down the hierarchy.

7.2.2   Telephone Switching

The simplest kind of telephone switch is shown in Figure 7.5, and is called a *crossbar* switch. All lines come in from the bottom and all come in from the left, and there is a matrix of possible connection points. By making a connection at point (n, m) in the matrix, a path between line m and line n is established. Mechanical crossbar switches were popular during the middle period of telephone history. They are not subject to *blocking*; this means that connection is always available to any user pair, no matter how many calls are handled by the switch.

The first central office switching technology, in common use as late as the 1960s, was the Strowger mechanism, whose history is in Section 1.3. This switch consisted of a cylinder of contact points and a wiper arm that moved up and down inside. The arm was directly driven by dial pulses. The first two digits dialed, say 2 and 8, drove the wiper arm up 2 and around 8; a second pair of digits drove a second mechanism, and so on, until a complete path was established. The Strowger mechanism was direct, fast, and relatively simple, but it would block when the bank of mechanisms was fully taken up with calls.

Modern switching is electronic and depends on the sampling and digitizing of all signals. A typical method is called time-slot interchange. The principle of it is to place sets of bits for all active customers in a big frame; if there are N active lines and b bits per customer, the frame encompasses a total bN bits. The information in the frame is said to be time-division multiplexed, and each active line occupies a "slot" in the frame. N slots of incoming information are written into the frame

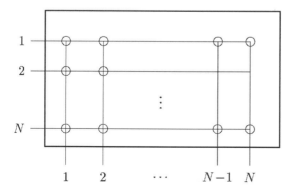

Figure 7.5   A crossbar switch

during each cycle. Information is read out in a pattern that reflects the desired connections. If lines m and n are "connected," for example, slot n will be read out by user m and slot m by user n, and they will thus exchange b bits. Hundreds of calls can be connected in this way by one frame. In order to handle more calls, more complex switches can be designed using these principles.

7.2.3 Multiplexing and Fiber Optic Transmission

Digital transmission by light passing through a fiber entered our book in Section 4.1. A major application of this technology is the interconnecting of telephone central offices across cities and across the world. A single fiber, no bigger than a hair, can carry many billions of bits per second by interrupting and detecting a light beam, and it can do so over 100 km or more without amplification. By sending many distinct wavelengths of light through the same fiber, a method called wavelength-division multiplexing, a great many such transmissions can be carried in the same fiber. The result is a carrying of many *hundreds* of gigabits per second, at a cost not much different from that of a single copper wire pair. As we discovered in Section 4.1, a wire pair without repeater amplifiers can carry only a few hundred megabits per second over a few hundred meters.

However, this powerful method of transmission, with its vanishingly small cost per message and per kilometer, is not inherently cheaper if it carries only a single local telephone call. The key to its use is combining many calls and messages into one transmission, a process called *multiplexing*, which is only really cheap if the calls are in digital form. Optical fibers were thus a major driver in the digital revolution. They dominate the network that interconnects telephone local offices. They offer much less advantage in running lines to local subscribers, and they have been very slow to appear there.

Before entering the subject of optical networking, we need to explore the multiplexing concept a little. The concept is to combine many signals into one, which, hopefully, is not much harder to carry than one of the component signals. In wavelength-division multiplex, a number of light wavelengths, each carrying independent data, combine to form a single light signal. By building detectors that are sensitive to each wavelength, we can separate out each component signal. Ordinary radio broadcasting demonstrates the same idea with radio frequencies instead – many signals are carried by the FM band, and by tuning the radio we select out the one we wish to hear. In the switching discussion a few pages back, switching by time slot interchange worked by placing pieces of each message in slots in a long frame of bits. This is an example of time-division multiplexing. There, it was done for switching purposes, but by transmitting the frame as a unit, we could send all the messages at once.

A very common time-division multiplex application is the *T-1 carrier*. The idea of it is to combine 24 digital single-direction telephone channels into one transmission. We saw in Section 3.2 that standard telephone speech consists of 8000 samples per second and 8 bits per sample. Twenty-four such channels makes a total bit rate $24 \times 8 \times 8000 = 1.536$ Mbits/s. In a T-1 carrier system, the bits for one sample each of the 24 channels are combined into a single frame of 192 bits. To these is added one "housekeeping" bit, to allow the network to send its own control messages. The frame contains 193 bits in total, and 8000 frames appear per second, the same rate as the speech samples. The overall bit rate in these frames is thus $193 \times 8000 = 1.544$ Mbit/s. Although the T-1 carrier system was envisioned (in the 1960s) for speech, it can be used to carry any digital data at 1.536 Mbit/s.

The "*T*" in T-1 originally meant "transmission". The "1" refers to the fact that T-1 is only the first level in a whole hierarchy of time-division multiplex schemes. In North America and Japan, four T-1 type signals may be further multiplexed to form a level 2 signal; housekeeping bits at the rate 136 kbits/s (an overhead of 2.2%) are added, for a total level-2 bit rate of $0.136 + 4 \times 1.544 = 6.312$ Mbit/s. This hierarchy, called "DS", continues up several further levels, as illustrated in Table 7.2 (top).[7] The bit rates were chosen to match the needs of various sources (e.g., TV) and the capabilities of different media (e.g., wires, coaxial cables).

Time-division multiplexing was devised originally for wire and radio channels. With the advent of fibers, some modification was needed. First, *electrical* signals arrive at the fiber, but it transmits *lightwave* signals. Thus every signal for transmission exists in two forms, electrical and lightwave. All sorts of techniques—such as precise time-division multiplexing—are available for electrical signals, but light technology is still rather crude. Today, light signals carry bits by being modulated on and off, and they are not easily switched through complex pathways. Second, wire and radio multiplexing are based on precise and complex timing that is impossible with light technology. In the level 1-to-2 DS multiplex, for example, the second line at the top of Table 7.2, the four incoming 1.544 Mbit/s streams can arrive at slightly different speeds, and they are brought up to precisely the same speed by adding a few fake bits before combining; furthermore, individual bits from different streams are interleaved and the final stream is a complicated jigsaw puzzle.[8] It is not only this complicated technology that we would like to be free of in a fiber. Multiplexing and framing systems in the world differ, and it would be convenient if all could be easily carried by the same fiber optic backbone.

The fiber backbone that has evolved is much simpler than this. After some early standards that were controlled by single companies, two relatively open standards evolved, SONET in North America and SDH as the CCITT international standard.[9] SONET and SDH work more like a conveyor belt, on which optical transmissions can be placed by various users. The timing of these objects need not be extremely precise, and a system of pointers helps mark the boundaries of objects. Data streams can be added as desired to the flow without taking apart the whole

---

[7]DS is a generic term meaning "digital signal"; hierarchies with names T and DR exist and refer to wireline, cable, and radio implementations of the same hierarchy. A parallel hierarchy called E (or CEPT) exists in Europe; its level 1, 2, 3 rates are 2.048, 8.448, 34.37 Mbit/s.

[8]A relatively simple description of this complex process appears in Section 4.9 of ref. [2].

[9]SONET means Synchronous Optical NETwork, SDH is Synchronous Digital Hierarchy, and CCITT is Comité Consultatif International de Téléphonie et Télégraphie, the international standard setting body in telecommunications.

Table 7.2   Some important time-multiplex binary transmission hierarchies. (i) North America–Japan (Japan does not use DS-3, DS-4). (ii) The SONET and SDH hierarchies for optical fibers (partial)

The DS radio/cable/wireless hierarchy

Name	Composition	Bit rate (Mbit/s)	Comments
DS-1 (or T-1)	—	1.544	1 km wireline; carries 24 tel 1-way calls
DS-2	$4 \times$ DS-1 + HKG	6.312	Carries compressed TV or 96 calls
DS-3	$7 \times$ DS-2 + HKG	44.74	Carries std. TV or 672-call "Mastergroup"
DS-4	$6 \times$ DS-3 + HKG	274	1 km coax cable, one microwave radio channel

The SONET/SDH optical hierarchy

Electrical signal std.		Optical signal std.	Bit rate (Mbit/s)	Comments
SONET	SDH			
STS-1	—	OC-1	51.84	Matches DS-3
STS-3	STM-1	OC-3	155.5	Matches CEPT-4
STS-9	STM-3	OC-9	466.6	
STS-18	STM-6	OC-18	933.1	
STS-24	STM-8	OC-24	1244	
STS-48	STM-16	OC-48	2488	Widely deployed backbone std.

HKG = housekeeping bits; STS = synchronous transport signal; OC = optical channel.

transmission. SONET and SDH also have better monitoring and handling of transmission failures. They can use the extra bandwidth of the fibers to carry the same data by two paths in case one fails, or they can instantly substitute a new path for a failed one. The method depends to some degree on whether the network topology is a ring or not.[10]

The lower parts of the SONET and SDH network hierarchies are shown in Table 7.2 (the diagram continues upward past 10 Gbit/s). Except for the lowest level, they are similar, and each level has corresponding electrical and optical signals. Changing one of these optical signals generally means demodulating to the electrical form, changing that, and then modulating a laser to regain the optical form. It can be seen that the lowest level is still rather fast compared to the wire/radio hierarchy at the top of the table. The intention is that a DS-3 or a similar high-level signal in another system, or perhaps a digitized television signal, can be mapped conveniently into the optical backbone without much loss. The backbone itself is intended to run at a very high rate.

[10]Details about how these functions work can be found, for example, in ref. [1], Chapter 4.

BOX 7-3

Around 1990, in the early days of the cellular revolution, apocryphal studies in the United States showed that significant numbers of cellular users never paid their bills or were men trying to impress women in some way; these two groups could be as much as 20% of the market. Whatever we may think of these groups, a successful business plan had to take them into account. Otherwise, the largest cellular users in the United States at that time were doctors, lawyers, and so on returning calls to patients, salespersons phoning in sales and inventory information, and realtors. The insecurity of analog phones played havoc with some of these users. Today, almost everyone has used a mobile phone, and in a few countries, their use even exceeds fixed telephony.

7.3 MOBILE TELEPHONY

Like fixed telephony, mobile telephony depends on a cheap, high-capacity backbone network. Otherwise, it is very different. Instead of fixed lines to geographical *places*, it maintains virtual connections to a set of *terminals*. These are free *to change location*, even to a new country, and within limits they can even be in motion. The telephone number is associated with the user, not with the place. Mobility is the hallmark of this more modern telephone system. We use the word terminal instead of the old word handset because handsets are not free to move.

Allowing customers to move means a lot more tracking and record keeping. This is done with software, data bases, and complex protocols. Universal mobile telephony had to await the invention of these, and they appear now for the first time in our networking story. By contrast, the simple connecting of two moving terminals is a century old, and as we saw in Chapter 1, was the original application of radio. Radio is of course still the only medium available for the "last mile" of a mobile network. Through the 20th century radio grew more easy to use, but mobile links still functioned basically as set down by Marconi. The chief customers were police, the military, transport, and those perhaps with money to spend.

Early cellular system capacity was small, with only a few dozen channels available in a major city. A revolutionary change occurred around 1983 with the introduction of AMPS (Advanced Mobile Phone System) in the United States, the first *cellular* system. This AMPS was one of the last major contributions of the old Bell Laboratories. As we will see, the cellular idea greatly increases the capacity of a mobile system. A second major innovation was *digital* cellular telephony, together with some further innovations, the most important of which was caller roaming. These appeared with the European GSM system, introduced commercially after the mid 1990s. By contrast, GSM was developed by an organization of 19 telecommunication authorities in Europe.[11] It is the dominant standard in the world today.

---

[11] The Conference of European Post and Telecommunications administrations (CEPT). Development and supervision of GSM continues today and is the responsibility of the Special Mobile Group of the European Telecommunication Standards Institute (ETSI). Standard setting in the United States is primarily through industry trade associations.

The AMPS cellular system and similar systems in the rest of the world are called First Generation systems, meaning that they are cellular, analog, and used almost exclusively for telephone calls. A Second Generation system like GSM is digital, allows international roaming, offers low-speed data service such as email, and is only a few times more expensive per minute than fixed telephone. By 2000, Europe was predominantly Second Generation, with other regions soon to follow. A country can jump direct to Second Generation, and many with poor fixed service have done just that, as a way to get a reliable, if somewhat more expensive, basic service. The ease of doing so, together with the overwhelming popularity of mobile phones, has made mobile telephony a boom business. A Third Generation has been standardized and the equipment is ready to enter production. This generation is marked by high data rate services in some parts of the network, such as downloaded music and video, and by Internet access, in addition to ordinary telephone service. The unanswered question at this writing (2002) is whether enough people want these wideband mobile services at the higher price that must be charged.

Now we will look at the engineering of a mobile cellular system in more detail. We will focus mostly on the GSM system.

7.3.1 Cellular Technology

The heart of a mobile telephone system is its partitioning of the radio "last mile" into cells. An idealized picture of the cells is shown in Figure 7.6. The structure is based on repeating seven radio frequencies, and each cell has a *base station* at its center. The station operates at a frequency that differs from any of the immediate neighbors. In fact, its frequency does not reappear until the third tier of neighbors. The frequencies are endlessly reused, and this is the key to supporting many more callers than a single, tall, powerful base station would support.

In a real network, the cells are anything but perfectly repeating hexagons. "Cell design," as it is called, is more an art than a science. Cells in the countryside are 20 km or more in size, with powerful base stations and taller antennas. City cells are 1 km or less, with stations carefully placed to illuminate canyons between buildings and reduce interference among same-frequency cells. It is important to keep transmitter powers as low as possible, both at the base station and the individual mobile terminals; this reduces interference to outer cells and lengthens battery life at the terminals. The base station constantly issues these "power control" orders as the terminals move around. Powers in GSM vary over 0.8–8 W per call channel. Also, GSM does not transmit during the short silences between speech sounds; this reduces interference and battery drain another 50%. The hardest part of siting cells is getting permission to place the base station. Property owners, local government, and people who do not like to look at cell towers all need to be satisfied. Often several cells will have to be serviced from the same tower by directional antennas, even though the cells are separate.

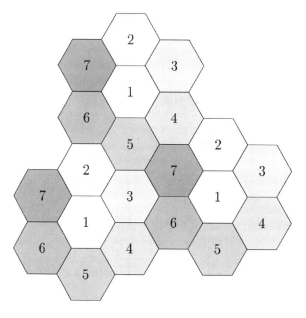

Figure 7.6 A hexagonal cell structure based on seven radio frequency sets

We have acted as if each cell operates on a single frequency, but in reality each cell has a separate *set* of frequencies. Altogether, the system has 124 pairs of radio channels. The uplinks (mobile terminal to base) of each pair are spaced every 200 kHz from 890 to 915 MHz, and the downlinks (base to mobile) from 935 to 960 MHz.[12] Each of these radio carriers transmits bits at the rate 271 kbit/s. The modulation method is a sophistication of those in Section 4.3. The plan here amounts to frequency-division multiplexing; but GSM actually combines time- and frequency-division, because each 271 kbit/s radio channel carries eight digital one-way calls in time-division. This is organized in a rather complicated way but can be summarized as follows. A bit frame lasts 4.6 ms (about 1250 bits). It is divided into eight slots, one for each one-way call, to which are added a number of bits that control the radio system and keep it in precise synchro- nization. The speech digitizing algorithm in GSM converts speech waveforms to 13 kbit/s (see Chapter 3). To this are added almost as many bits for error correction (see Chapter 5), encryption (see Chapter 6), and identification of the call. Then there are the synchronization bits and bits that keep house. In all, more than 30 kbit/s in the cell are needed per one-way call. And every part of this book plays a role some- where in the design!

---

[12]We leave out many small details in what follows. The frequency assignment here applies to Europe. Somewhat different frequencies may be used in other regions, and a second band of frequencies around 1800 MHz is available in Europe. GSM also has provision for transmitting data and email, and for a more advanced 6.5 kbit/s voice coder that allows carriage of twice as many calls. Advanced references [3–5] give details about GSM and the other cellular systems.

We can now look at how a simple GSM call is set up. All the individual base stations connect to the fixed network through a Mobile Switching Center (MSC). To start, assume that one telephone is a mobile terminal and the other is in the ordinary, fixed network. In brief, the base station monitors a special uplink setup channel over which the mobile terminals can signal a demand for service, and the terminals, if they are turned on, monitor a downlink setup channel over which incoming calls to them are announced; once a call is set up, it takes place over an assigned pair of the one-way channels that are associated with the cell. When a terminal is first turned on, before any calls can begin, the terminal decides which cell it is "in." Generally, this is the strongest of the base stations available to the mobile terminal. This outcome is announced to the MSC and throughout the cellular system. Now consider a call originating at a mobile terminal. The setup proceeds as:

Turn on terminal →

Find strongest base station →

Request service over uplink setup channel →

Send validation code →

Base station contacts fixed net via MSC →

Ring fixed party →

Call channel pair is set up →

Call takes place. . . .

For a call that originates from the fixed network, the procedure would be as follows. Here we assume that the mobile terminal is on, with its location registered at the MSC; otherwise, the fixed caller receives a busy signal.

Fixed phone dials central office →

Central office contacts MSC →

MSC looks up terminal location →

MSC signals base station →

Base signals terminal over downlink setup channel →

Call channel pair set up →

Ring terminal →

Call takes place. . . .

A call between two mobile terminals begins like the first procedure and ends like the second. After the call setup reaches an MSC it goes direct to the same or another base station; if it is destined to another cellular system, it goes via fixed lines to an MSC for that system.

A crucial function in a cellular system is the maintenance of a Home Location Register (HLR). Information about every subscriber is kept there, including all their *present locations*. When a mobile terminal is switched on, the base station that it finds is checked against the HLR value, and the HLR is updated if necessary. All calls are routed by means of information in this Register. Other information kept in the HLR includes restrictions on service, extra services subscribed to, terminal characteristics, billing data, and security codes. There is usually one HLR per cellular provider.

In some cellular standards, the uplink and downlink setup channels are two of the radio channels, but in GSM all radio channels carry frames composed of eight call channel slots and smaller slots that carry system control and synchronization bits. Setup communications are carried in the system control slots. They are thus in time division with ongoing calls.

7.3.2 Handoff and Roaming

Cellular communication is a step more complicated when the telephones move during the call. Assuming that they stay within their own cellular systems, they will eventually undergo *handoff* to a new base station. A general description of this procedure is as follows. The base station observes the signal strength of all calls. When a strength falls below a certain level, the base station asks neighboring bases if they have a better signal. If one does, the mobile terminal is ordered to switch frequencies, the two bases adjust accordingly, and the HLR registers a new base location for the terminal. The bargaining among bases here can take several seconds, but the actual handoff takes place almost instantly.

The term *roaming* refers to mobile terminals that have left their home provider or even their home country. Second Generation systems, notably GSM, were designed for easy, economical roaming, and this has been the case for some years over all of Europe. As other regions have adopted GSM, roaming has slowly extended over much of the world. Roaming is both a problem of protocols and physical system design and of cellular standards in different regions. Systems in different parts of the world, for example, operate over different radio bands or may even use wholly different cellular standards. This can be accommodated by building several cellular systems into the same telephone, so-called "dual mode" telephones.

In order to look at roaming within a single cellular standard in more detail, we will once again turn to GSM. When a mobile terminal leaves its home provider or country, it needs to re-register with a new provider. This takes place as usual between terminal and base station, but now the base station, through its Mobile Switching Center, must contact an MSC of the terminal's home provider. By this exchange, the new MSC learns about the new customer and the services it subscribes to, finds out where to send billing, and validates the customer's identity and equipment. Finally, the new customer is placed in the Visiting Location Register (VLR), a temporary version of the HLR. Security and validation are particularly important in a cellular standard that supports roaming.

An interesting example of roaming occurs when subscribers in two cars drive together to a new country and then have a telephone conversation between cars. They may be only 10 m from each other, but the mobile phones must both still register in the new-country VLR. It is possible that the parties may only patch together at the home Mobile Switching Center. If so, each caller connects to a new-country base station, then via fixed lines back to the home country MSC, and back again, a path of perhaps thousands of kilometers in order to call 10 m. As odd as this routing may sound, its cost is almost entirely in the new-country base station system, not in the long backbone links. With digital transmission, there will be no reduction in quality.

7.3.3 Conclusion

Making a cellular system work requires some very sophisticated hardware and software. Affordable mobile communication had to await many new technologies. Obviously, software and cheap computing had to be available. We have skipped over all the network protocols and algorithms in order to simplify the story, but we should emphasize that it takes fast real-time control and large control information flows to keep a cellular system operating. A number of hardware innovations also had to appear. The necessary radio bandwidth is available only at UHF and microwave frequencies, and this technology appeared only in recent decades. The chip revolution had to take place to make digital circuitry small enough. All analog functions, including radio circuitry, had to be miniaturized as well, and this itself is a distinct technology. Finally, handoff, roaming, and control depend on a cheap, high-speed backbone fixed network—ironically, mobile networks are largely fixed—and the heart of this is fiber optic technology.

7.4 THE INTERNET

The Internet, whose roots we traced in Chapter 1, began to take its modern form in the early 1990s. What exactly is the Internet? It is hard to answer this question with a fixed system or an international standard, but by the end of this section we will see that it has at least the following characteristics.

- Even though the Internet was the killer application for the new technique of packet switching, it often employs other networking schemes. It is more accurate to call it un-circuit-switched – "connectionless" is the technical term—meaning that messages can be passed without first setting up a network circuit.

- The Internet can easily grow—in technical jargon it is "scalable"—and no-one directs or limits its growth. New parts can be added at any time.

- The Internet is open to all. Users need not understand the physical network parts and these parts do not have to meet a set of bit rates, error rates and other physical specifications, as do telephone network parts. Rather, users and network must obey *rules*, the central ones being the TCP/IP and HTTP protocol sets.

Ideally, a message is simply presented to the Internet, in a legal form and with a legal address, and it appears at the destination sometime later. Each Internet node passes on the packet, by applying its routing scheme to the address information. If the message is long, it is broken into packets; these will have to be reassembled in order at the receive end. An "end" here is a point where the Internet becomes available to the user. We will use the more technical term *host*, meaning the processor that interfaces to the Internet, that enforces legal packets. It is the first name to the right of the @ in an address, for example, the "it" in it.lth.se. Alternate terms are server, mailserver, or less precisely, domain name.

The standard OSI model in Figure 7.2 is helpful in understanding all this. Users of the Internet see at most down to level 4, the local transport layer; what a human user most likely sees is the top layer, the application layer, which contains a mail program or WWW browser. In any case, the host is responsible for seeing that layers 1–4 are carried out properly and that legal packets are presented to level 5, the network layer. That layer signals the transport layer when new packets come in. Layers 6 and 7, the data link and physical layers, should be invisible to the local group of users, and are of interest only if they fail to work or have excessive delay. For an email going between two hosts in the same company, layers 5–7 may simply be an Ethernet wire. In this case the network path is a formal connection, fixed, error-free, and nearly instant. The opposite extreme is a path that is complex and delay-prone and spans the Earth. The packets pass from node to node, and nodes provide what is called "best effort service", meaning that they pass on packets as best they can but offer no guarantee of success. With only a little fantasy, we could imagine a network layer that puts a typed-out packet in a box and carries it by camel across a desert!

Whatever the nature of the network layer, the transport layer, not the network, is responsible for getting the message through correctly or notifying the user that the transmission has failed. This means error detection, deciding when that the message is lost, breaking the message into packets, and assigning routing instructions.

7.4.1   Physical Arrangement of the Internet

No-one can conceive of the whole arrangement of the Internet—it is believed to have tens of millions of hosts—but a certain general arrangement has grown up and we can describe that. Figure 7.7 shows a simplified view of some physical parts.

The smallest subsystem is a *domain*, a collection of hosts that works as an autonomous unit. Technically, a domain is a collection of servers that work under common control and route outgoing packets according to the same protocol. The term domain should not be confused with domain name, which means the full name of a server (for example, it.lth.se or aol.com). The domain is generally the second-last part of an Internet address ("lth" or "aol" in the example). At first, domains were universities ("lth" is Lund Technical University) or research labs (an early Arpanet domain was "ames", an arm of the National Aeronautics and Space Administration in the United States). Today, the largest domains are Internet

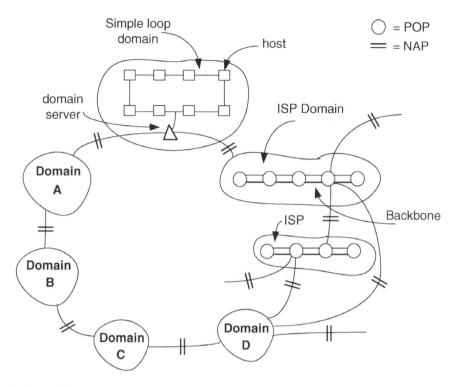

Figure 7.7   The physical Internet, showing some domains. Two ISP providers with POPs and backbones are shown, and a smaller domain with a wire loop of hosts. Domains A–D form a chain and can only communicate through it. NAPs connect domains. The two ISPs have special links to Domain D

service providers (ISPs) and large companies. Email to the General Electric Company goes to an address of the form

```
[user address]@[company subdivision].ge.com
```

Email to an ISP such as AOL or Yahoo goes to addresses of the form

```
[user name]@aol.com or [user name]@yahoo.com
```

Here the domains are ge, aol, and yahoo.

Some domains are huge and consist of a great many hosts connected together in some way peculiar to the provider. A large commercial provider has points of presence (POPs) in the different cities it serves, which are interconnected by some kind of high-speed backbone. A user can access mail or the web from any one of them, most often reaching one over the telephone network. Other domains pass messages to a local host server, which acts as a division of the domain. One or more further subdivisions of the address may carry this host information; for example, "it" in it.lth.se means the Information Technology Department within Lund Technical University, a separate host within the domain lth.

The internal topology of a domain or a host subunit can be a loop, star, hierarchical backbone, or just an ad hoc collection of links. A small local network together with a host is often a local area network (LAN). This special term refers to a nearly error-free high-speed line (e.g., an Ethernet wire) that runs from user to user. Users share peripherals such as printers and backup disks, as well as Internet access through the host. Each user computer has a network interface card that watches for data directed to that computer and passes the rest on to the next computer.

BOX 7-4

Packetizing helps relieve data error problems that arise when messages are very long or are passed through many domains. Consider a message of 10^7 bits and let the link be a good one, with an error rate of 10^{-7}. If sent as a single message, probability theory shows that the message arrives correctly only with probability $P_c = (1 - 10^{-7})^{10000000} \approx 1/e \approx 0.368$. If the message arrives incorrectly (indicated by an error-detecting code), it is sent again. Another calculation shows that the average number of transmissions is

$$1 \cdot P_c + 2 \cdot (1 - P_c)P_c + 3 \cdot (1 - P_c)^2 P_c + \cdots = 1/P_c \qquad (7.2)$$

which is about 2.72. Thus an average of 27 Mbits are required to send the 10 Mbit message. If the message is passed through five similar links in order to reach its destination, the probabilities are the same at each link, and the expected number of bits carried over any link is five times as large, or 136 Mbits. Now assume that the message is broken into 10,000 1000-bit packets. A packet arrives correctly over one link with probability $P_c = (1 - 10^{-7})^{1000} \approx 0.9999$. Another application of Eq. (7.2) shows that an average 1.0001 uses of the link are required to send a packet, so that the 10,000 packets require average transmission 10.001 Mbits, far less than before. To progress five links requires 50.005 Mbits. The savings here are even more dramatic with poorer links. We see that packet transmission can pay large dividends. Probability theory and a subdiscipline called queueing theory are important tools in the study of networks.

Domains are connected to each other by network access points (NAPs). It is here that domains can exchange messages and every NAP includes a routing server that decides the next destination for packets. Often a NAP includes a store-and-forward system that collects all the message packets before passing them on to the next domain. In principle, the Internet can expand indefinitely by adding domains and connecting new ones to existing ones through a NAP. In reality, a router in a size-N Internet must know how to handle $N(N - 1)/2$ domain pairs, a number that grows uncomfortably fast. Also, domains strung out like sausage links will pass messages slowly. A better solution has been to set up private NAP links between large providers and transmit packets directly.[13] We will return to routing presently.

---

[13] These links and links inside ISPs can take many forms, from telephone-like lines to new technologies such as ATM (asynchronous transfer mode) transmission (see ref. [1]).

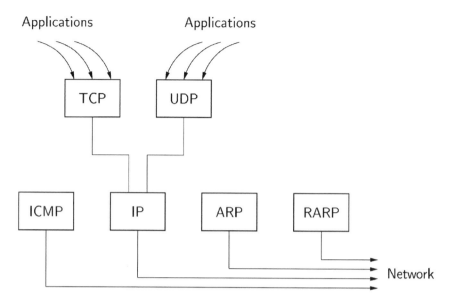

Figure 7.8   The blocks of the TCP/IP protocol suite, showing the two main levels. Standard packets go out to a partly unknown network

7.4.2   The TCP/IP Protocols

Now we have some idea of what might be physically present in the Internet. How can these diverse parts work together? Some Internet links are fixed, but others are not and we need to assume the worst case, that the outside network is not circuit switched (it is "connectionless") and that it can only make a "best effort" to deliver our message. The different parts of the unknown network must cooperate to move messages to their destination. All quality control is the responsibility of the Internet terminals and the applications lying above them, not the outside network. This includes such matters as error detection, retransmission of missing packets, and limiting the delay of transmission. The way that all this happens is a set of rules called *TCP/IP*. Such an agreed-upon large set is called a protocol suite. It is summarized in Figure 7.8.

There are six major parts to TCP/IP, only two of which form the name of the suite. These form the transport layer 4 in the OSI model of the information system.[14] Applications such as email or WWW enter the TCP and UDP parts of the structure at the top, and the four blocks at the bottom interface to the connectionless, best-effort network. Here are their functions, and the key to all the acronyms.

---

[14] Several important Internet utilities are considered to be part of TCP/IP, even though they are applications, not transport-layer protocols. These include HTTP (for WWW access), TELNET (romote login) and FTP (file transfer).

- The User Datagram Protocol (UDP) is a simple, one-shot, unreliable service. It accepts segments from applications (we will use segment to denote a piece of data presented to one of the six suite blocks and reserve the word packet for an output to the network); it can only attach destination and return addresses, check for errors, and break down and reassemble segments. If a UDP segment is lost, nothing is done about it, and action if any must be taken at a higher level. Some applications that use UDP are TFTP (Trivial File Transfer Protocol), SNMP (Simple Network Management Protocol), and DNS (Domain Name Server). The last submits requests for the correct numerical Internet address that corresponds to an easier-to-read alphabetic email address.

- The Transmission Control Protocol (TCP) carries the lion's share of the information load. It provides reliable service, which appears to come from a real connection. It tries to provide full duplex service; that is, it allows a back and forth exchange of the sort that one would use with an interactive website. It also attempts to provide stream service; this means data such as a sound or image download that needs to arrive continuously and in sequence. We need to understand that parts of the Internet are still connectionless and unreliable while TCP operates, that reliability is a relative, not an absolute term. What TCP tries to do is announce higher priorities for streaming/duplex packets, raise the odds of their arriving together, and start the transmission only when conditions are good enough. Some of its methods are sounding the net, request–repeat (a method of repeating packets until they get through), and controlling buildups of congestion. Most applications that we use over the Internet work through TCP. Perhaps the most common example is HTTP (HyperText Transfer Protocol), which manages WWW sessions.

- The heart of the next suite level is IP, the Internet Protocol. It multiplexes TCP and UDP segments to form network packets, exchanges these with other IP blocks over the network, and converts received packets back into TCP and UDP segments. With the IP block, the best-effort question comes up again: IP promises no error rate and no limit on delay, and the upper suite or the application level must provide these if they are desired. Internet Protocol also implements address interpretation and the parts of the routing that are done at the Internet host. If the packets are just being passed through the host to another host, IP does this as well.

- Of the remaining lower suite blocks, ICMP (Internet Control Message Protocol) handles transmission problems. Typically, ICMP becomes aware that a packet has failed to forward properly, or to forward in time. It then reports and handles the problem.

- ARP (Address Resolution Protocol) and RARP (Reverse ARP) request address information that appears to be missing. This can happen, for example, because a part of the Internet has broken down or changed, or because the packets are known to be heading for a special subnet, such as an Ethernet.

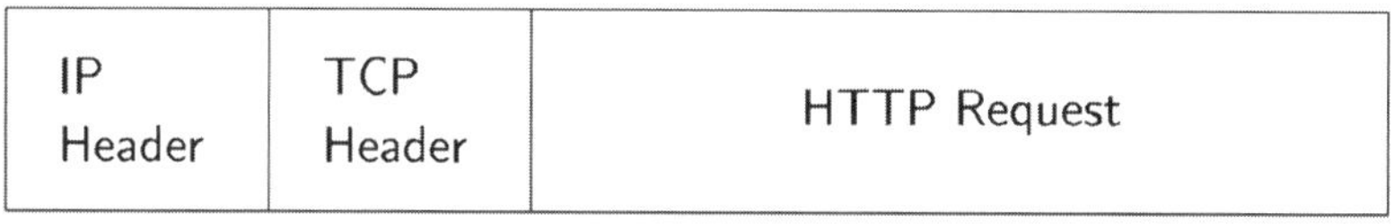

IP Header	TCP Header	HTTP Request

Figure 7.9 How an HTTP Request packet appears in an IP packet ready to go out on the net

An everyday transaction between a user and the Internet is an HTTP request, that is, a request for a website component. This is handled by the TCP. Figure 7.9 shows how the HTTP code is encapsulated into a larger TCP segment that contains a TCP header. The TCP segment is in turn part of one or more IP packets (here only one), each with their own IP header. These packets go out over the Internet.

All TCP/IP segments and packets have a strictly defined structure. The header part of the most basic one, the IP packet, is discussed in the box.

TCP/IP principles are probably not as hard to learn as, say, Fourier transforms, but TCP/IP does comprise a mass of detail that needs to be learned by those who create applications, program hosts, and maintain Internet parts. The suite is also in a constant state of evolution. For those wanting to learn more, Leon-Garcia and Widjaja [1] give a one-chapter summary. Full book treatments may be found in Comer [6] and in the old standby [7].

BOX 7-5

By looking at the form of the basic IP packet header, we can learn a lot about how the Internet works. A standard header consists of 48 bytes (192 bits), which can be arranged for convenience in 6 rows of 8 bytes as in Figure 7.10. Rows 4 and 5, respectively, are the source and destination addresses, which must appear on all packets. (The 32 bits in these addresses have proven insufficient, and a technique with submasks has had to be devised.) The smaller fields are as follows.

Row 1: Version refers to the current IP software version, Length is that of the packet to follow, Service Type is the packet priority, Total Length is the whole packet length ($\leq 65,535$ bytes).

Row 2: The Identification and Fragmentation fields control reassembly of the message from packets.

Row 3: Time to Live shows the time the packet has left to live in the net (successive routers decrement it by 1); in case a packet is resent, the field prevents more than one copy in the net at once. The Protocol field indicates that the packet is UDP, TCT, or some other type.

Row 6: Options can specify a number of routing, security, and other advanced options; Padding fills out the 8 bytes.

It is not easy to design the headers and other parts of a protocol suite. One must leave space for options not yet imagined!

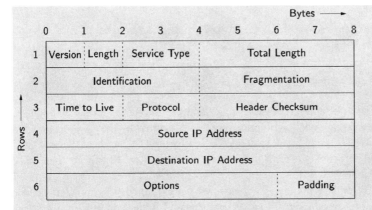

Figure 7.10   A TCP/IP version 4 IP packet header. Header consists of 48 bytes, arranged here in 6 rows of 8. The packet then follows

7.4.3   Routing

One of the fascinating parts of the Internet is how it directs packets to their destination. This is called *routing*. Routing algorithms are complex, but we can take time to look at the principles.

Figure 7.11 is a small Internet that we will use as an example. The nodes are of two types: outer nodes reached by a single path, which are hosts that send and accept packets, and six inner nodes that are hosts but also pass through packets that are on their way somewhere else. The numbers on the branches are costs of some kind. The cost in the figure could be money costs or delays; we might also want to minimize hops (then each branch would have a cost of 1) or try to find the pathway with the widest bandwidth (this "cost" we would want to maximize).

The job of a routing algorithm is to find a good path connecting every pair of nodes in the net. To do this well it needs to know the whole net. It creates a

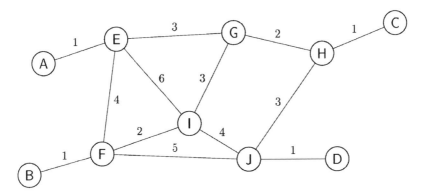

Figure 7.11   A 10-node network example, showing the costs of using each link

routing table from these decisions and distributes it to every node. Routing information travels around the Internet in packets, just like other kinds of information. New tables can be shipped around from time to time, or more often, small revisions and warnings about conditions. A node can copy the whole table, or use the known algorithm and new routing information to create it.

By noting a packet destination and performing a table lookup, a pass-through node learns where the packet goes next. Some routing decisions are trivial, for example a tie line between two major service providers, but those that direct progress through connectionless parts of the net can be challenging indeed. A major problem is that the Internet keeps rearranging itself! A second problem is that the net—and the table—keep growing. Engineers are dealing with this by devising algorithms that distribute only partial tables to each locality, or arrange the addresses in a hierarchical way. Here are some hallmarks of a good routing algorithm.

1. Packets cannot take unreasonably long; few should get lost; above all, they should not travel in circles. Note that "unreasonably" depends on the packet content: Email can take much longer than streaming video.

2. The algorithm must know what is going on in the network; it must sense failures and congestion points.

3. It must adapt rapidly to link failures and send around new instructions.

4. It must devise new pathways on the fly to direct traffic around congestions.

Finding good paths through a known network is part of a branch of mathematics called optimization theory. One of the best-known methods is the Bellman–Ford algorithm.[15] An easy way to understand this algorithm and routing in general is to make an analogy to finding the shortest path between two cities. Suppose that we wish to drive from Denver to New York, and we happen to know that the shortest road leads through Chicago. Then we can solve the Denver–New York problem by solving two shorter problems, the Denver–Chicago and the Chicago–New York problems. Similarly, we can try to break Denver–Chicago into shorter problems, and so on, until the whole problem is solved. If we do not know whether Chicago is on the optimal path, we can solve the problem with that assumption, then with another half-way assumption (St Louis perhaps), and compare outcomes. This is the idea of Bellman–Ford.

Now we apply the idea to sending a packet between B and C in Figure 7.11. Paths BF and HC must be used no matter what, so the problem reduces to finding the cheapest path between F and H. A packet entering/leaving H has two choices, it must pass through G or J. Assume it is node J. The FIJ subnet is small and it is clear that minimum J to F path is J–F, with cost 5. Similarly, it is clear that the best way through the FEIG subnet is G–I–F, with cost 5. Summarizing, we have:

---

[15] Also called the Ford–Fulkerson algorithm, or dynamic programming. A sharp reader will note that the Viterbi decoding algorithm in Chapter 5 is an application of Bellman–Ford.

Initial path	Cost	Remaining min cost	Total
HG	2	5	7
HJ	3	5	8

Thus the minimum cost path is H–J–F, with cost 8. Adding in outer branches C–H and F–B, which do not affect the minimization, we get the complete solution C–H–J–F–B, with cost 10. We have used some standard tricks here. Network parts were removed that do not affect the path outcome. A more subtle trick was to cut the network first on the right, where only two alternatives are generated, rather than in the middle (across E–G, E–I, F–I, F–J) where there would be four. By successive reductions, a large problem can be reduced to smaller ones.

Another procedure is the Dijkstra algorithm. Starting from the source node, it finds the least-cost node, then the second-cost, then the third, and so on, in an organized way. Algorithms like these are an important part of network engineering.

All of this has assumed that the least-cost path is the desirable one for a packet. In special situations, there may be other priorities. Flooding means that each node sends packets to all immediate nodes except the one on which the packet arrived. This may be necessary at network startup, when enough routing information has not reached the nodes. Multicast routing is used when the same message is broadcast to a set of nodes, with the aim that nodes along the way do not carry the same packets many times. Other routing methods are designed for particular network topologies.

Routing in TCP/IPs

As stated before, routing information travels around the Internet by packets. This proceeds according to several protocols. The Routing Information Protocol is a simple method of sending updates from a node to its neighbors; in this way, nodes can keep track of each other every minute or so. A more sophisticated scheme is the Border Gateway Protocol, which allows whole domains to exchange information on, for example, what parts of the network each domain can easily reach at the moment.

7.4.4   Conclusions

The Internet is thus the ultimate virtual object. As a physical object, the best we can say is that it consists of a number of computing engines. These are programmed to carry out a set of rules called TCP/IP, which are what really defines this virtual monster. Other software carries out our Internet applications. The Internet is the apotheosis of the 20th century software revolution. About the network itself we can say little; we do not even know how big it is.

Where will the Internet go? The integrated circuit and optical fiber revolutions have made it almost free on a per-bit basis, but the Internet presents us with some intriguing challenges. Like many new technologies in this book, the Internet was undisciplined at the start and free of commercial exploitation. It often happens that communication media bog down in middle age, and many governments and large corporations are not sure they like uncontrolled information flow. The Internet was in fact set up to have no one in charge. What can we expect from such a system?

REFERENCES[16]

1. LEON-GARCIA, A. and Widjaja, I. 2000. *Communication networks: Fundamental concepts and key architectures.* McGraw-Hill: New York.
2. ANDERSON, J. B. 1999. *Digital transmission engineering.* IEEE Press: New York.
3. STEELE, R., ed. 1995. *Mobile radio communications.* Pentech Press: London; reprinted by IEEE Press: New York.
4. RAPPAPORT, T. S. 1996. *Wireless communications.* Prentice-Hall PTR: Upper Saddle River, N.J.
5. PANDYA, R. 2003. *Introduction to wireless local loop systems and their deployment.* IEEE Press: New York.
6. COMER, D. E. 1995. *Internetworking with TCP/IP,* various volumes and editions. Prentice-Hall: Englewood Cliffs, N.J.
7. LEIDEN, C., WILENSKY, M. and LAUDRY, J. 2000. *TCP/IP for dummies.* 4th ed. Wiley: New York.

---

[15] References marked with an asterisk are recommended as supplementary reading.

Appendix A

Complex Numbers

$\mathbf{A}$s we see in Chapter 2, *complex numbers* play an important role in the study of linear systems. All complex numbers can be written in their *Cartesian form* $x + jy$, where x and y are real numbers, and j denotes $\sqrt{-1}$. (Mathematicians use the notation $i = \sqrt{-1}$, but electrical engineers use i for electrical current and hence they have adopted the notation $j = \sqrt{-1}$, which we use throughout this book.) We refer to the set of all complex numbers by the symbol $\mathbb{C}$. We also let $\mathbb{C}$ denote the complex plane calling the x-axis by the name *real axis*, and the y-axis the *imaginary axis*. In Figure A.1 we show a few examples of complex numbers plotted in the complex plane. For simplicity we write 0 instead of $0 + j0$, 2 instead of $2 + j0$, $-j$ instead of $0 - j$, and so on.

To add or subtract two complex numbers, we simply add or subtract the corresponding real and imaginary parts. For example, the sum of $5 + j2$ and $-2 - j3$ is $3 - j$. These three complex numbers form together with 0 a parallelogram (Fig. A.1) which is a geometrical illustration of addition.

The *absolute value* $|z|$ of a complex number $z = x + jy$ is the distance from the origin 0 to the point z in the complex plane $\mathbb{C}$. The distance $|z|$ is found by using the Pythagorean theorem. Consider the right-angled triangle shown in Figure A.2. The horizontal side of the triangle has length $|x|$, the vertical side has length $|y|$, and, using the Pythagorean theorem, the hypotenuse has length

$$|z| = \sqrt{|x|^2 + |y|^2} \tag{A.1}$$

For example, if $z = 3 + j4$, then $|z| = 5$. The *unit circle* is the circle of radius 1 centered at the origin 0. All complex numbers on the unit circle have absolute value 1, that is, the unit circle can be written $|z| = 1$.

As an alternative to the Cartesian form $z = x + jy$, we can write a complex number in *polar form* $r(\cos\theta + j\sin\theta)$, where r specifies the distance from the origin 0 to the point z, that is, r is the absolute value $|z|$, and θ is the angle between the positive x-axis and the line from the origin 0 to z (Fig. A.3). Sometimes

Understanding Information Transmission. By John B. Anderson and Rolf Johannesson
ISBN 0-471-67910-0 © 2005 the Institute of Electrical and Electronics Engineers, Inc.

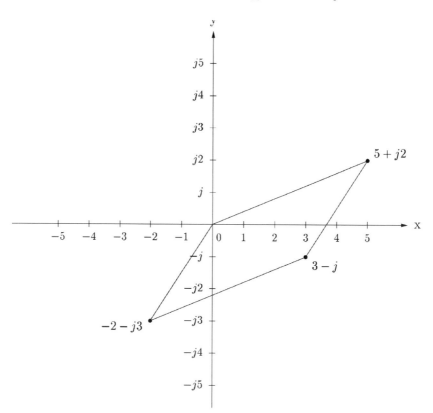

Figure A.1   Complex numbers plotted in the complex plane

we use the notation arg(z) instead of θ. We conclude that the conversion from Cartesian to polar form is performed according to the rules

$$\begin{cases} r = \sqrt{x^2 + y^2} \\ \theta = \arctan(y/x) \end{cases} \tag{A.2}$$

and the conversion from polar to Cartesian form according to the rules

$$\begin{cases} x = r\cos\theta \\ y = r\sin\theta \end{cases} \tag{A.3}$$

For example, the complex number $z = -1 + j\sqrt{3}$ has absolute value $|z| = \sqrt{(-1)^2 + (\sqrt{3})^2} = 2$ and angle $\theta = \arctan(\sqrt{3}/(-1)) = 2\pi/3$. Its polar form is $z = 2(\cos\frac{2\pi}{3} + j\sin\frac{2\pi}{3})$.

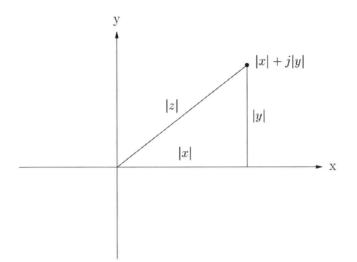

Figure A.2   Absolute value of a complex number

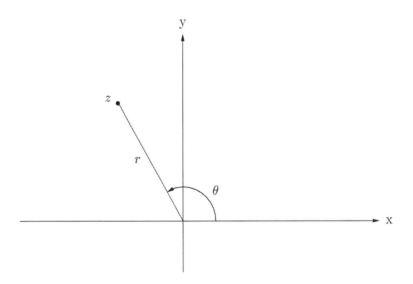

Figure A.3   Polar form of a complex number

Often we use Euler's formula for the complex exponential

$$e^{j\theta} = \cos\theta + j\sin\theta \tag{A.4}$$

and write the polar form as $re^{j\theta}$. In engineering literature the notation $r\angle\theta$ is common.

It is more difficult to multiply two complex numbers than to add or subtract them. Consider for example $z_1 = -3 + j2$ and $z_2 = 2 - j5$; then we obtain the product algebraically as

$$
\begin{aligned}
z_1 z_2 &= (-3 + j2)(2 - j5) \\
&= -6 + j15 + j4 - j^2 10 \\
&= 4 + j19
\end{aligned}
$$

where we have used the fact that $j^2 = -1$. In general we have

$$(x + jy)(u + jv) = (xu - yv) + j(xv + yu) \tag{A.5}$$

where $(xu - yv)$ is the real part and $(xv + yv)$ is the imaginary part. If we write our complex numbers in polar form it follows that the absolute value of the product is the product of the absolute values of the factors and that the angle of the product is simply the sum of the angles of the factors; that is, if $z_1 = |z_1| e^{j\theta_1}$ and $z_2 = |z_2| e^{j\theta_2}$, then

$$
\begin{cases}
|z_1 z_2| &= |z_1| |z_2| \\
\arg(z_1 z_2) &= \arg(z_1) + \arg(z_2) = \theta_1 + \theta_2
\end{cases} \tag{A.6}
$$

Multiplication of a complex number by j corresponds to a rotation of the number in the complex plane by $90°$ or $\pi/2$, which is exploited when we study electronic circuits. For example, the voltage across an inductor is $90°$ ahead of the current through it; hence, the inductor has only a reactance (imaginary part) and no resistance (real part) (cf. Appendix B).

We regard division as multiplication by the reciprocal, that is, we seek $1/z$ for a given complex number z. In other words, for a given complex number $z = x + jy$, find another complex number $w = u + jv$ such that $zw = 1$. Let us rewrite $1/z$ as

$$
\begin{aligned}
\frac{1}{z} = \frac{1}{x + jy} &= \frac{x - jy}{(x + jy)(x - jy)} \\
&= \frac{x - jy}{x^2 - jxy + jxy - j^2 y^2} \\
&= \frac{x - jy}{x^2 + y^2}
\end{aligned}
$$

that is,

$$u = \frac{x}{x^2 + y^2}$$

$$v = \frac{-y}{x^2 + y^2}$$

If $z = x + jy$, then the complex number $z^* = x - jy$ is called the *complex conjugate* of z, and it is easily verified that

$$zz^* = |z|^2 \tag{A.7}$$

where the superscript * denotes the complex conjugate. Thus we can formulate division of two complex numbers as

$$\frac{w}{z} = \frac{wz^*}{|z|^2} \tag{A.8}$$

For example,

$$\frac{2 - j3}{4 + j5} = \frac{2 - j3}{4 + j5} \cdot \frac{4 - j5}{4 - j5} = \frac{(2 - j3)(4 - j5)}{4^2 + 5^2} = \frac{8 - j10 - j12 - 15}{4^2 + 5^2} = -\frac{7}{41} - j\frac{22}{41}$$

Finally, if we write the complex numbers in polar form we obtain the polar form of the quotient z_1/z_2 as

$$\begin{cases} |z_1/z_2| & = |z_1|/|z_2| \\ \arg(z_1/z_2) & = \arg(z_1) - \arg(z_2) = \theta_1 - \theta_2 \end{cases} \tag{A.9}$$

Appendix B

Sinusoids and Circuit Theory

In Chapter 2 we show the importance of the frequency function $H(f)$. The goal of this appendix is to show how we can determine the frequency function for a given linear, time-invariant system built from resistors, inductors, and capacitors. We introduce these three circuit components in Figure B.1.

According to *Ohm's law*, the voltage $v(t)$ volts [V] across a resistor with resistance R ohms [Ω] is proportional to the current $i(t)$ amperes [A] through the resistance; that is,

$$v(t) = Ri(t) \tag{B.1}$$

(MKS units are shown in brackets [ ] here.) In particular, for $i(t) = e^{j\omega_0 t}$, $\omega_0 = 2\pi f_0$, we have

$$v(t) = Re^{j\omega_0 t} \tag{B.2}$$

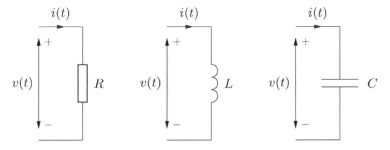

Figure B.1   A resistor R, an inductor L, and a capacitor C

Understanding Information Transmission. By John B. Anderson and Rolf Johannesson
ISBN 0-471-67910-0 © 2005 the Institute of Electrical and Electronics Engineers, Inc.

The voltage across an inductor with inductance L henries [H] is proportional to the derivative of the current $i(t)$ through the inductor; that is,

$$v(t) = L \frac{di(t)}{dt} \tag{B.3}$$

In particular, for $i(t) = e^{j\omega_0 t}$ we have

$$v(t) = j\omega_0 L e^{j\omega_0 t} \tag{B.4}$$

Since the current in Eq. (B.4) is multiplied by j we conclude that the voltage across the inductor is 90° (or $\pi/2$ radians) *ahead* of the current through the inductor. Alternatively, let the current be $i(t) = \sin \omega_0 t$, then it follows from Eq. (B.3) that

$$v(t) = \omega_0 L \cos \omega_0 t \tag{B.5}$$

and the voltage is again 90° ahead of the current. Try drawing both $\sin \omega_0 t$ and $\cos \omega_0 t$; convince yourself that $\cos \omega_0 t$ is 90° ahead of $\sin \omega_0 t$.

The charge $q(t)$ coulombs [C] of a capacitor with capacitance C farads [F] is proportional to the voltage across the capacitor; that is,

$$q(t) = Cv(t) \tag{B.5}$$

Since $q(t) = \int_{-\infty}^{t} i(\tau) \, d\tau$, we have

$$v(t) = \frac{1}{C} \int_{-\infty}^{t} i(\tau) \, d\tau \tag{B.6}$$

In particular, $i(t) = e^{j\omega_0 t}$ yields

$$v(t) = \frac{1}{C} \int_{-\infty}^{t} e^{j\omega_0 \tau} \, d\tau = \frac{1}{j\omega_0 C} e^{j\omega_0 t} \tag{B.7}$$

where we have used that $\lim_{t \to -\infty} e^{j\omega_0 t} = 0$ in the *distributional* sense.

For the capacitor, the current is divided by j, which we can interpret as the voltage being 90° (or $\pi/2$ radians) *behind* the current. Alternatively, let the current be $i(t) = \sin \omega_0 t$, then we deduce from Eq. (B.6) that

$$v(t) = -\frac{1}{\omega_0 C} \cos \omega_0 t \tag{B.8}$$

so that again the voltage is 90° behind the current.

Now define the *one-port* shown in Figure B.2. It is a network consisting of resistors, inductors, capacitors, voltage sources, and current sources. Assume that

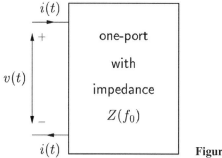

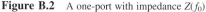

Figure B.2 A one-port with impedance $Z(f_0)$

the voltage across the one-port is the complex exponential signal $v(t) = e^{j\omega_0 t}$, $\omega_0 = 2\pi f_0$. Then the current $i(t)$ will also be a complex exponential signal, but with different amplitude and phase. We have

$$v(t) = Z(f_0)i(t) \tag{B.9}$$

where the proportionality constant $Z(f_0)$ is called the *impedance*. Equation (B.9) is sometimes called *Ohm's law for alternating current*. Ohm's law (B.9) holds *only for stationary sinusoidal voltages and currents*, including of course the special case when the frequency $f_0 = 0$.

The impedance is in general a complex number that depends on the frequency, but if the one-port consists only of resistors, then its impedance will always be real and independent of f_0; that is, it is a resistance, and Eq. (B.9) will be identical to Eq. (B.1). In general, both the real and imaginary parts are frequency dependent. The imaginary part is often called *reactance* and denoted by $X(f_0)$. Hence, we can write the impedance as

$$Z(f_0) = R(f_0) + jX(f_0) \tag{B.10}$$

When we analyze an electric circuit that consists of resistors, inductors, and capacitors, as well as voltage and current sources, we often use *Kirchhoff's laws*. They state general restrictions on the voltages and currents in a circuit.

Kirchhoff's current law (KCL) states that the algebraic sum of the currents entering any node is identically zero at all instants of time.

By *node* we mean any connection point. *Algebraic sum* means that we take the sign (direction) of the current into account; that is, we can alternatively express KCL as: Sum of currents flowing into a node = sum of currents leaving the node.

Kirchhoff's voltage law (KVL) states that the algebraic sum of the voltages around any closed path, or loop, in a circuit is identically zero at all instants of time.

Let us for simplicity first study a circuit with a battery, that is, a *direct current* (DC or frequency $f_0 = 0$) source. The circuit has three resistors.

EXAMPLE B.1

Consider the circuit given in Figure B.3.

The KCL applied to node a yields:

$$i_1 - i_2 - i_3 = 0 \tag{B.11}$$

The KVL applied to loop 1 ($V \to R_1 \to R_2 \to V$) yields:

$$v - v_1 - v_2 = 0 \tag{B.12}$$

The KVL applied to loop 2 ($R_2 \to R_3 \to R_2$) yields:

$$v_2 - v_3 = 0 \tag{B.13}$$

Notice that if we apply KVL to the outer loop ($V \to R_1 \to R_3 \to V$) we obtain

$$v - v_1 - v_3 = 0 \tag{B.14}$$

which is simply the sum of Eqs. (B.12) and (B.13). The three linear equations (B.12), (B.13), and (B.14) are linearly dependent and one of them should be deleted from our system of equations. We have so far obtained three independent linear equations; for example, (B.11), (B.12), and (B.13) for our six unknowns i_1, i_2, i_3, v_1, v_2, and v_3. We need three more before we can solve our system, and we must exploit that the resistors obey Ohm's law. Thus we have

$$v_1 = R_1 i_1$$
$$v_2 = R_2 i_2$$
$$v_3 = R_3 i_3$$

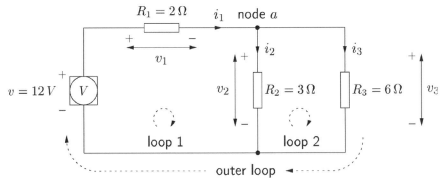

Figure B.3   Circuit analyzed in Example B.1

Inserting the given values $v = 12$ V, $R_1 = 2\,\Omega$, $R_2 = 3\,\Omega$, and $R_3 = 6\,\Omega$ yields the six equations

$$i_1 - i_2 - i_3 = 0 \tag{B.15}$$
$$12 - v_1 - v_2 = 0 \tag{B.16}$$
$$v_2 - v_3 = 0 \tag{B.17}$$
$$v_1 = 2i_1 \tag{B.18}$$
$$v_2 = 3i_2 \tag{B.19}$$
$$v_3 = 6i_3 \tag{B.20}$$

We see immediately from Eq. (B.17) that $v_2 = v_3$. Hence, from Eqs. (B.19) and (B.20) it follows that $i_2 = 2i_3$. Then Eq. (B.15) can be rewritten as

$$i_1 - 3i_3 = 0 \tag{B.21}$$

Combining Eqs. (B.18) and (B.19) with Eq. (B.16) and using $i_2 = 2i_3$ yield

$$12 - 2i_1 - 6i_3 = 0 \tag{B.22}$$

Subtracting two times Eq. (B.21) from Eq. (B.22) yields

$$12 - 4i_1 = 0$$

and we have $i_1 = 3$. From Eq. (B.21) follows $i_3 = 1$ and, hence, that $i_2 = 2$. In summary, we have $i_1 = 3$ A, $i_2 = 2$ A, $i_3 = 1$ A, $v_1 = v_2 = v_3 = 6$ V. ∎

In Figure B.4 we show a circuit consisting of three impedances connected in a serial manner. Assuming that the current $i(t)$ is sinusoidal with frequency f_0, let $Z_s(f_0)$ denote the impedance of this serial circuit. Clearly, $Z_s(f_0)$ satisfies

$$v(t) = Z_s(f_0)i(t) \tag{B.23}$$

From Kirchhoff's voltage law it follows that

$$v(t) = v_1(t) + v_2(t) + v_3(t)$$

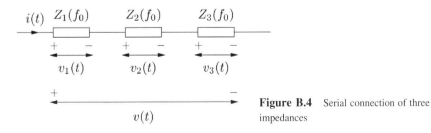

Figure B.4   Serial connection of three impedances

If we use Ohm's law for alternating current to express the voltages across the three impedances we obtain

$$
\begin{aligned}
v(t) &= Z_1(f_0)i(t) + Z_2(f_0)i(t) + Z_3(f_0)i(t) \\
&= (Z_1(f_0) + Z_2(f_0) + Z_3(f_0))i(t)
\end{aligned}
\tag{B.24}
$$

Finally, by comparing Eqs. (B.23) and (B.24) we obtain that the impedance for the serial circuit is simply the sum of the individual impedances:

$$
Z(f_0) = Z_1(f_0) + Z_2(f_0) + Z_3(f_0)
\tag{B.25}
$$

The generalization to more than three impedances is obvious.

EXAMPLE B.2

Consider the circuit shown in Figure B.5. The current $i(t)$ is a sinusoid of frequency f_0 Hz. The impedance of this circuit is

$$
\begin{aligned}
Z(f_0) &= R + j\omega_0 L + \frac{1}{j\omega_0 C} \\
&= R + j\left(\omega_0 L - \frac{1}{\omega_0 C}\right) \\
&= \sqrt{R^2 + \left(\omega_0 L - \frac{1}{\omega_0 C}\right)^2}\, e^{j \arctan \frac{\left(\omega_0 L - \frac{1}{\omega_0 C}\right)}{R}}
\end{aligned}
\tag{B.26}
$$

For $i(t) = e^{j\omega_0 t}$, $\omega_0 = 2\pi f_0$, we obtain

$$
v(t) = Z(f_0)i(t) = \sqrt{R^2 + \left(\omega_0 L - \frac{1}{\omega_0 C}\right)^2}\, e^{j(\omega_0 t + \phi(f_0))}
$$

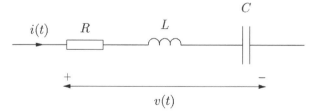

Figure B.5   A resistor R, an inductor L, and a capacitor C in series

where

$$A(f_0) = \sqrt{R^2 + \left(\omega_0 L - \frac{1}{\omega_0 C}\right)^2}$$

is the amplitude and

$$\phi(f_0) = \arctan \frac{\left(\omega_0 L - \frac{1}{\omega_0 C}\right)}{R}$$

is the phase of the voltage $v(t)$. We notice that the reactance

$$X(f_0) = \omega_0 L - \frac{1}{\omega_0 C}$$

can assume both positive (when $\omega_0^2 > \frac{1}{LC}$) and negative (when $\omega_0^2 < \frac{1}{LC}$) values. Furthermore, when $\omega_0^2 = \frac{1}{LC}$ the reactance is identically zero. The frequency

$$f_0 = \frac{1}{2\pi\sqrt{LC}} \tag{B.27}$$

is called the *resonance frequency* of the circuit. At the resonance frequency the phase is zero and the circuit behaves simply as a single resistor with resistance R.   ∎

Next we consider three impedances connected in parallel (Fig. B.6). Assuming that the voltage $v(t)$ is sinusoidal with frequency f_0, we shall determine the impedance $Z_p(f_0)$ of this parallel circuit. It satisfies

$$v(t) = Z_p(f_0)i(t) \tag{B.28}$$

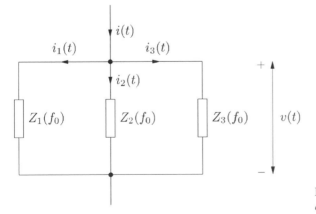

Figure B.6   Parallel connection of three impedances

or, equivalently,

$$v(t) \frac{1}{Z_p(f_0)} = i(t) \tag{B.29}$$

From Kirchhoff's current law it follows that

$$i(t) = i_1(t) + i_2(t) + i_3(t)$$

Using Ohm's law for alternating current we can write

$$\begin{aligned}
i(t) &= \frac{v(t)}{Z_1(f_0)} + \frac{v(t)}{Z_2(f_0)} + \frac{v(t)}{Z_3(f_0)} \\
&= v(t) \left(\frac{1}{Z_1(f_0)} + \frac{1}{Z_2(f_0)} + \frac{1}{Z_3(f_0)} \right)
\end{aligned} \tag{B.30}$$

Combining Eqs. (B.29) and (B.30) yields the following formula for the impedance for the parallel circuit:

$$\frac{1}{Z_p(f_0)} = \frac{1}{Z_1(f_0)} + \frac{1}{Z_2(f_0)} + \frac{1}{Z_3(f_0)} \tag{B.31}$$

with the obvious generalization to an arbitrary number of impedances.

EXAMPLE B.3

Consider the circuit shown in Figure B.7. The voltage $v(t)$ is a sinusoid of frequency f_0 Hz. The impedance $Z(f_0)$ of this parallel circuit is obtained as follows (cf. Eq. (B.31)):

$$\frac{1}{Z(f_0)} = \frac{1}{R} + \frac{1}{j\omega_0 L} + j\omega_0 C$$

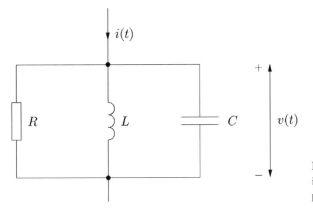

Figure B.7   A resistor R, an inductor L, and a capacitor C in parallel

or, equivalently,

$$Z(f_0) = \cfrac{1}{\cfrac{1}{R} + \cfrac{1}{j\omega_0 L} + j\omega_0 C}$$

$$= \cfrac{1}{\cfrac{1}{R} + j\left(\omega_0 C - \cfrac{1}{\omega_0 L}\right)}$$

$$= \cfrac{1}{\sqrt{\cfrac{1}{R^2} + \left(\omega_0 C - \cfrac{1}{\omega_0 L}\right)^2}} \, e^{-j \arctan \frac{\omega_0 C - \frac{1}{\omega_0 L}}{1/R}}$$

For $i(t) = e^{j\omega_0 t}$, $\omega_0 = 2\pi f_0$, we obtain

$$v(t) = Z(f_0)i(t) = \cfrac{1}{\sqrt{\cfrac{1}{R^2} + \left(\omega_0 C - \cfrac{1}{\omega_0 L}\right)^2}} \, e^{j(\omega_0 t + \phi(f_0))}$$

where

$$A(f_0) = \left(\sqrt{\cfrac{1}{R^2} + \left(\omega_0 C - \cfrac{1}{\omega_0 L}\right)^2}\right)^{-1}$$

is the amplitude and

$$\phi(f_0) = -\arctan \frac{\omega_0 C - \dfrac{1}{\omega_0 L}}{1/R}$$

is the phase of the voltage $v(t)$.

In order to determine the reactance we have to rewrite $Z(f_0)$ in a real part and an imaginary part:

$$Z(f_0) = \frac{1}{\dfrac{1}{R} + j\left(\omega_0 C - \dfrac{1}{\omega_0 L}\right)}$$

$$= \frac{1}{\dfrac{1}{R} + j\left(\omega_0 C - \dfrac{1}{\omega_0 L}\right)} \frac{\dfrac{1}{R} - j\left(\omega_0 C - \dfrac{1}{\omega_0 L}\right)}{\dfrac{1}{R} - j\left(\omega_0 C - \dfrac{1}{\omega_0 L}\right)}$$

$$= \frac{\dfrac{1}{R}}{\dfrac{1}{R^2} + \left(\omega_0 C - \dfrac{1}{\omega_0 L}\right)^2} - j\frac{\omega_0 C - \dfrac{1}{\omega_0 L}}{\dfrac{1}{R^2} + \left(\omega_0 C - \dfrac{1}{\omega_0 L}\right)^2}$$

and hence the reactance is

$$X(f_0) = -\frac{\omega_0 C - \dfrac{1}{\omega_0 L}}{\dfrac{1}{R^2} + \left(\omega_0 C - \dfrac{1}{\omega_0 L}\right)^2}$$

If we choose f_0 to be the resonance frequency, that is, f_0 is chosen according to Eq. (B.27), then the reactance becomes identically zero and this so-called *parallel resonance circuit* behaves as a single resistor with resistance R. ∎

Often we have only two impedances in parallel. Then we can simply write

$$\frac{1}{Z_p(f_0)} = \frac{1}{Z_1(f_0)} + \frac{1}{Z_2(f_0)}$$

as

$$Z_p(f_0) = \frac{Z_1(f_0)Z_2(f_0)}{Z_1(f_0) + Z_2(f_0)} \tag{B.32}$$

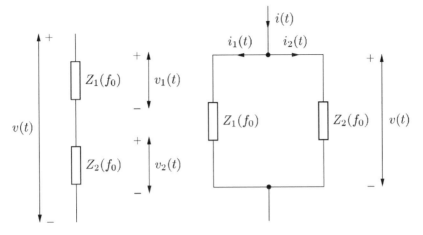

Figure B.8 Voltage and current division

A basic fact about circuits is that with a sinusoidal current of frequency f_0, *impedances in series divide the voltage in the ratio of the impedances* (see Fig. B.8):

$$v_1(t) = \frac{Z_1(f_0)}{Z_1(f_0) + Z_2(f_0)} v(t) \tag{B.33}$$

This follows immediately from Ohm's law for alternating current and the fact that the same current flows through both impedances.

Similarly, *impedances in parallel divide the total current in the ratio of the inverted impedances* (see Fig. B.8):

$$i_1(t) = \frac{\dfrac{1}{Z_1(f_0)}}{\dfrac{1}{Z_1(f_0)} + \dfrac{1}{Z_2(f_0)}} i(t) \tag{B.34}$$

$$= \frac{Z_2(f_0)}{Z_1(f_0) + Z_2(f_0)} i(t)$$

To show Eq. (B.34), we write the voltage across the impedances in two different ways:

$$v(t) = Z_1(f_0) i_1(t) = \frac{Z_1(f_0) Z_2(f_0)}{Z_1(f_0) + Z_2(f_0)} i(t) \tag{B.35}$$

where we have used the Eq. (B.32) to express the total impedance. Then Eq. (B.34) follows immediately.

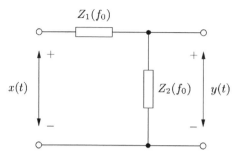

Figure B.9   A simple linear, time-invariant system

Now we have aquired enough knowledge about circuits in order to determine the frequency function $H(f)$. Consider the linear, time-invariant system shown in Figure B.9.

Assume that the input is

$$x(t) = e^{j\omega_0 t}$$

Then we obtain the output (cf. Eq. (B.33) and Fig. B.8)

$$y(t) = \frac{Z_2(f_0)}{Z_1(f_0) + Z_2(f_0)} e^{j\omega_0 t} \tag{B.36}$$

Comparing Eq. (B.36) with Eq. (2.53) from Chapter 2, that is, $y(t) = H(f_0)e^{j\omega_0 t}$, yields

$$H(f_0) = \frac{Z_2(f_0)}{Z_1(f_0) + Z_2(f_0)}$$

Since the frequency f_0 of the sinusoidal input $e^{j\omega_0 t}$ was chosen arbitrarily we have the following important expression for the frequency function

$$H(f) = \frac{Z_2(f)}{Z_1(f) + Z_2(f)} \tag{B.37}$$

EXAMPLE B.4

Consider the linear time-invariant system shown in Figure B.10.

We identify the impedance $Z_1(f)$ as the capacitor, that is,

$$Z_1(f) = \frac{1}{j\omega C} = \frac{2}{j\omega}$$

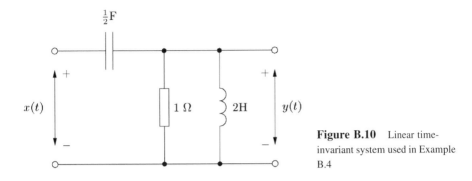

Figure B.10   Linear time-invariant system used in Example B.4

and the parallel combination of the resistor and inductor as $Z_2(f)$, that is,

$$Z_2(f) = \frac{R \cdot j\omega L}{R + j\omega L} = \frac{1 \cdot j\omega 2}{1 + j\omega 2}$$

Then we have

$$H(f) = \frac{Z_2(f)}{Z_1(f) + Z_2(f)} = \frac{\dfrac{1 \cdot j\omega 2}{1 + j\omega 2}}{\dfrac{1}{j\omega \frac{1}{2}} + \dfrac{1 \cdot j\omega 2}{1 + j\omega 2}} = \frac{\dfrac{j\omega}{1 + j\omega 2}}{\dfrac{1 + j\omega 2}{j\omega} + j\omega}$$

$$= \frac{(j\omega)^2}{1 + 2j\omega + (j\omega)^2}$$

$$= \frac{1 + 2j\omega + (j\omega)^2 - 1 - 2j\omega}{1 + 2j\omega + (j\omega)^2}$$

$$= 1 - \frac{1}{(1 + j\omega)^2} - 2j\omega \cdot \frac{1}{(1 + j\omega)^2}$$

■

Below we give some problems that have been selected to illustrate the methods described in this appendix. Only one of them Eq. (B.7), addresses the frequency function. In Chapter 2 there are, however, many problems that involve determining the frequency function.

PROBLEMS

B.1. The circuit shown in Figure B.11 can be replaced by a resistor with resistance R. Find R.

B.2. Consider the circuit shown in Figure B.12.
   Find R such that the total resistance of the circuit is

   (a) 6 Ω

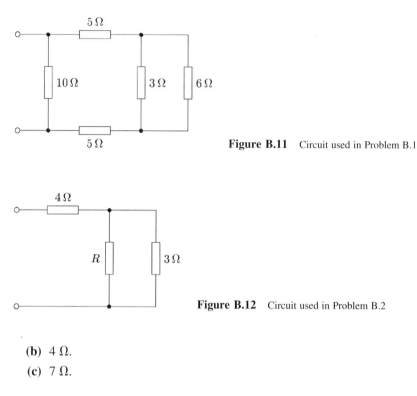

Figure B.11   Circuit used in Problem B.1

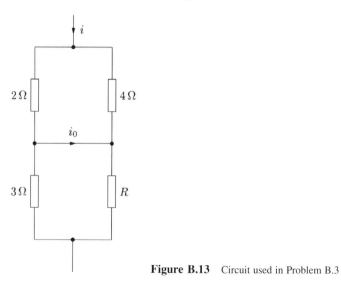

Figure B.12   Circuit used in Problem B.2

(b) 4 Ω.

(c) 7 Ω.

B.3. Consider the circuit shown in Figure B.13.

Figure B.13   Circuit used in Problem B.3

Find R such that $i_0 = 0$.

B.4. The circuit shown in Figure B.14 can be replaced by a single capacitor with capacitance C. Find C.

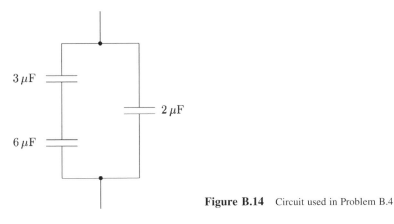

Figure B.14   Circuit used in Problem B.4

B.5. A parallel LC (inductor and capacitor) circuit is often used as a frequency selective device. In practice, we regard the capacitor as a "pure" capacitance, but the inductor is often regarded as a "pure" inductance in series with a resistance.

   (a) Use a capacitor C, an inductor L, and a resistor R to model the "practical" LC circuit described above and draw the circuit.

   (b) Find the resonance frequency; that is, the frequency at which the impedance of the circuit is a real number.

   (c) Let $R = 0$ and find the resonance frequency.

B.6. Consider the circuit shown in Figure B.15.
Find R such that $i_0 = 0$.

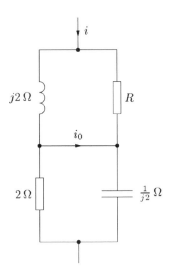

Figure B.15   Circuit used in Problem B.6

B.7. Consider the circuit shown in Figure B.16.

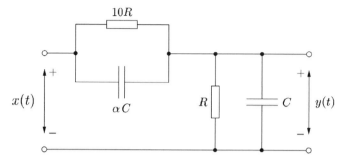

Figure B.16   Circuit used in Problem B.7

Find, if it exists, the value of α such that the frequency function is independent of the frequency.

B.8. Find the source current I for the circuit shown in Figure B.17.

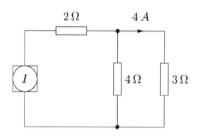

Figure B.17   Circuit used in Problem B.8

Appendix C

Probability Theory: A Primer

$\mathbf{P}$robability theory has its roots in the analysis of games of chance in 16th-century Italy and 17th-century France. Names such as Cardano, Pascal, and Fermat are connected with the early developments of this subject. Nowadays probability theory is considered to be an indispensable tool when engineers design and analyze systems in general and information technological systems in particular. Probability theory is readily used when we model information sources or the ever-present noise in communication systems. Here we give a brief review of the minimum amount of probability theory needed in this book.

Let us start with three definitions:

Outcome: The result of a random experiment is called an *outcome*.

Sample space: The set of all possible outcomes of a random experiment is called the *sample space*, Ω.

Event: Any collection of outcomes, that is, any subset of Ω, is called an *event*.

We also have the *impossible event*, $\emptyset$ (the empty subset of Ω), and the *certain event*, Ω.

EXAMPLE C.1

Let us cast a dice. Then we have six different outcomes which we denote 1, 2, 3, 4, 5, and 6 and, hence, we have the sample space $\Omega = \{1, 2, 3, 4, 5, 6\}$. The events "even number of dots" and "odd number of dots" can be written as $Even = \{2, 4, 6\}$ and $Odd = \{1, 3, 5\}$, respectively. ∎

When we study various combinations of events we often use a convenient tool from *set theory* called *Venn diagrams*. In Figure C.1 we use these diagrams to illustrate some important events.

Next we assign to each event A a real number $Pr(A)$ between 0 and 1 inclusive, which we call the *probability* of that event, that is, $0 \leq Pr(A) \leq 1$. If the event A is

Understanding Information Transmission. By John B. Anderson and Rolf Johannesson
ISBN 0-471-67910-0 © 2005 the Institute of Electrical and Electronics Engineers, Inc.

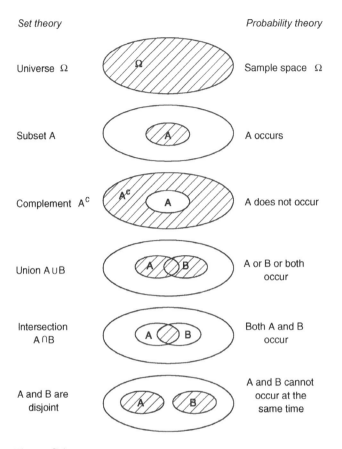

Figure C.1   Important events illustrated in set theoretic form

equal to the sample space Ω, that is, if $A = \Omega$, then the event A will certainly occur when we perform our random experiment and we conclude that we should have $Pr(\Omega) = 1$.

If the events A and B cannot occur at the same time, then the probability that the event $A \cup B$ occurs should be the sum of the probabilities that A and B occur, that is, we should have $Pr(A \cup B) = Pr(A) + Pr(B)$. As an example, flip a fair coin and assume that it cannot stay on its edge. Then we have two possible outcomes, *Head* and *Tail*, both with probability $1/2$. Since we cannot have both *Head* and *Tail* at the same time, the probability that we will get either *Head* or *Tail* is $Pr(Head \cup Tail) = Pr(Head) + Pr(Tail) = 1/2 + 1/2 = 1$, corresponding to the certain event *Head* $\cup$ *Tail*.

In the early 1930s the Russian mathematician A. Kolmogorov formulated three axioms that describe the general structure of random models. The probability $Pr(A)$ of an event A is chosen to satisfy the following conditions:

Axiom 1: $Pr(A) \geq 0$

Axiom 2: $Pr(\Omega) = 1$

Axiom 3: If $A \cap B = \emptyset$, then $Pr(A \cup B) = Pr(A) + Pr(B)$

From these axioms we can easily show (do as exercise!):

$$Pr(A) + Pr(A^c) = 1$$
$$Pr(\emptyset) = 0$$

If the events A and B are not mutually exclusive, then in general

$$Pr(A \cup B) \neq Pr(A) + Pr(B)$$

In this case we have

Theorem C.1 (Adding Two Events)

$$Pr(A \cup B) = Pr(A) + Pr(B) - Pr(A \cap B) \tag{C.1}$$

Proof. We write the events $A \cup B$ and B as sums of two mutually exclusive events (use as an exercise Venn diagrams to illustrate these equalities)

$$A \cup B = A \cup (A^c \cap B)$$
$$B = (A \cap B) \cup (A^c \cap B)$$

Then we have

$$Pr(A \cup B) = Pr(A) + Pr(A^c \cap B) \tag{C.2}$$
$$Pr(B) = Pr(A \cap B) + Pr(A^c \cap B) \tag{C.3}$$

Eliminating $Pr(A^c \cap B)$ by subtracting expression (C.3) from (C.2) yields (C.1). $\square$

Consider casting a fair dice. Since the sample space $\Omega = \{1, 2, 3, 4, 5, 6\}$ and we treat the six outcomes as "equally likely" we have $Pr(\{k\}) = 1/6$, $k = 1, 2, 3, 4, 5, 6$. Suppose that we know that the outcome is even, that is, either 2, 4, or 6. Then what is the probability that we get a 2? We denote this probability $Pr(\{2\} \mid Even)$ and call it "the conditional probability for the event $\{2\}$ given that the event $Even$ has occurred." It seems reasonable to let $Pr(\{2\} \mid Even) = 1/3$, which can be written

$$Pr(\{2\} \mid Even) = \frac{1/6}{1/2} = \frac{Pr(\{2\} \cap Even)}{Pr(Even)}$$

since $Pr(\{2\} \cap Even) = Pr(\{2\}) = 1/6$ and $Pr(Even) = 1/2$. We normalize the joint probability $Pr(\{2\} \cap Even)$ by $Pr(Even)$. From this example we conclude that it is natural to choose the following.

Definition C.1 Given an event B with nonzero probability, that is, $Pr(B) > 0$, we define the *conditional probability of the event A given that the event B has occurred* by

$$Pr(A \mid B) = \frac{Pr(A \cap B)}{Pr(B)} \tag{C.4}$$

Alternatively we can write

$$Pr(A \cap B) = Pr(A \mid B)Pr(B) \tag{C.5}$$

that is, *the probability that two events occur is equal to the probability that the first occurs given that the second has occurred, multiplied by the probability that the second occurs.*

EXAMPLE C.2

Suppose that we cast a fair dice and know that the event $A = \{1, 2, 3\}$ occurred. The probability that the outcome is odd given that the outcome is either 1, 2, or 3 is then

$$Pr(Odd \mid A) = \frac{Pr(Odd \cap A)}{Pr(A)}$$

Clearly $Pr(A) = 1/2$ and since there are two odd outcomes among the three outcomes in the set A we have $Pr(Odd \cap A) = 2/6$. Hence, it follows that

$$Pr(Odd \mid A) = \frac{2/6}{1/2} = 2/3$$

The following theorem is often useful. ■

Theorem of Total Probability If the events $B_1, B_2, \ldots, B_n$ are mutually exclusive and have positive probabilities such that $\sum_{i=1}^{n} Pr(B_i) = 1$, then for any event A we have

$$Pr(A) = \sum_{i=1}^{n} Pr(A \mid B_i)Pr(B_i) \tag{C.6}$$

Proof.

$$Pr(A) = Pr(A \cap \Omega) = Pr\left(A \cap \bigcup_{i=1}^{n} B_i\right)$$

$$= Pr\left(\bigcup_{i=1}^{n} (A \cap B_i)\right) = \sum_{i=1}^{n} Pr(A \cap B_i)$$

$$= \sum_{i=1}^{n} Pr(A \mid B_i) Pr(B_i)$$

where the second equality follows from the fact that our assumption $\sum_{i=1}^{n} Pr(B_i) = 1$ is equivalent to $\bigcup_{i=1}^{n} B_i = \Omega$. Since the events $A \cap B_i$, $i = 1, 2, \ldots, n$, are mutually exclusive the fourth equality follows from a straightforward generalization of Axiom 3 to n events. The last equality follows from expression (C.5). □

For an exercise, illustrate the theorem on total probability using a Venn diagram.

If every point in the set A belongs to the set B, then we say that A is *included* or *contained* in B and that A is a *subset* of B which is written $A \subset B$. Let the event A be contained in the event B, that is, if A occurs then B occurs. Then the conditional probability that B occurs given that A occurred equals 1, $Pr(B \mid A) = 1$.

Consider two events A and B such that $Pr(A \mid B) = Pr(A)$, that is, the probability that A occurs is the same regardless if B has occurred or we do not know anything about it, then it is reasonable to say that A and B are independent. Since expression (C.5) always holds, we have motivated the following definitions as important.

Definition C.2   Given two events A and B, if

$$Pr(A \cap B) = Pr(A)P(B) \tag{C.7}$$

then the events A and B are *(stochastically) independent*.

EXAMPLE C.3

Let us both flip a fair coin and cast a fair dice. Then we have $2 \cdot 6 = 12$ possible joint outcomes which we may regard as equally likely:

$$
\begin{array}{ll}
\{Head, (1)\} & \{Tail, (1)\} \\
\{Head, (2)\} & \{Tail, (2)\} \\
\{Head, (3)\} & \{Tail, (3)\} \\
\{Head, (4)\} & \{Tail, (4)\} \\
\{Head, (5)\} & \{Tail, (5)\} \\
\{Head, (6)\} & \{Tail, (6)\}
\end{array}
$$

Let A be the event that the coin flip yields *Head* and B be the event that the dice cast yields an even number of dots. Then the event A contains six joint outcomes, namely those in the left column given above. The event B contains also six joint outcomes, namely those in the even rows. Consider now the joint event $A \cap B$. It contains the joint outcomes given in the even rows of the left column. Hence, we have six joint outcomes in both A and B (although not the same six!) and three in $A \cap B$. Using mathematical notation, we have

$$| A |=| B |= 6$$
$$| A \cap B |= 3$$

where $| \ldots |$ denotes the *cardinality* or *size* (number of elements) of the set. Since all 12 joint outcomes are equally likely we have

$$Pr(A) = Pr(B) = \frac{6}{12} = \frac{1}{2}$$

and

$$Pr(A \cap B) = \frac{3}{12} = \frac{1}{4}$$

It is easily verified that $Pr(A \cap B) = Pr(A)Pr(B)$ holds, so we can conclude that the events A and B are independent.   ∎

We shall now introduce two more important concepts in probability theory.

Definition C.3   A *discrete random variable* X is a mapping from the sample space Ω into a specified finite or countably infinite set.

$$X : \Omega \to X(\Omega)$$

Definition C.4   The *probability distribution* of a random variable X, denoted P_X, is a mapping from $X(\Omega)$ onto the interval $[0,1]$ such that

$$P_X(x) = Pr(X = x) \tag{C.8}$$

where $Pr(X = x)$ denotes the probability of the event that X takes on the value x, that is, the event $\{X = x\}$.

From expression (C.8) and Kolmogorov's axioms it follows immediately that

$$P_X(x) \geq 0, \qquad \text{all } x \in X(\Omega)$$
$$\sum_{x \in X(\Omega)} P_X(x) = 1$$

We can extend these definitions to vector-valued random variables, for example, $X = (X_1, X_2)$, where X_1 and X_2 are random variables on Ω. Then we have the *joint probability distribution*

$$P_{X_1X_2}(x_1, x_2) = Pr(\{X_1 = x_1\} \cap \{X_2 = x_2\}) \tag{C.9}$$

Clearly, we have

$$P_{X_1X_2}(x_1, x_2) \geq 0, \qquad \text{all } (x_1, x_2) \in X_1(\Omega) \times X_2(\Omega)$$

and

$$\sum_{x_1 \in X_1(\Omega)} \sum_{x_2 \in X_2(\Omega)} P_{X_1X_2}(x_1, x_2) = 1$$

For the values of x_2 such that $P_{X_2}(x_2) > 0$, we have the *conditional probability distribution*

$$P_{X_1|X_2}(x_1 \mid x_2) = \frac{P_{X_1X_2}(x_1, x_2)}{P_{X_2}(x_2)} \tag{C.10}$$

Moreover, if X_1 and X_2 are independent, then

$$P_{X_1,X_2}(x_1, x_2) = P_{X_1}(x_1)P_{X_2}(x_2) \tag{C.11}$$

If $F(X)$ is a real-valued function whose domain contains $X(\Omega)$, then its *(mathematical) expectation* or *average* is the real number $E(F(X))$ given by

$$E(F(X)) = \sum_{x \in X(\Omega)} P_X(x)F(x) \tag{C.12}$$

EXAMPLE C.4

Let X be a random variable with values in the set $\{0, 1, 2\}$ and with the following probability distribution:

x	$P_X(x)$
0	1/4
1	1/2
2	1/4

To obtain the expectation of X, denoted $E(X)$ or $\overline{X}$, we simply insert $F(X) = X$ into expression (C.12):

$$E(X) = \sum_x P_X(x)x$$

$$= \frac{1}{4} \cdot 0 + \frac{1}{2} \cdot 1 + \frac{1}{4} \cdot 2 = 1$$

For $F(X) = X^2$ we obtain

$$E(X^2) = \sum_x P_X(x)x^2$$

$$= \frac{1}{4} \cdot 0 + \frac{1}{2} \cdot 1 + \frac{1}{4} \cdot 4 = \frac{3}{2}$$

Let $F(X) = -\log_2 P_X(x)$, then we have

$$E(-\log_2 P_X(x)) = \sum_x P_X(x)(-\log_2 P_X(x))$$

$$= -\sum_x P_X(x) \log_2 P_X(x)$$

which we call the *uncertainty* of the random variable X in Chapter 5. ∎

So far we have only discussed discrete random variables taking on a countable set of values. When we discuss, for example, noise in a modulation system we often use a sample space that is not countable. In general, continuous random variables need more advanced mathematics for a careful explanation. In the case of random variables with "densities" $f_X(x)$ instead of probability distributions, the sums are replaced by integrals. The *density function* $f_X(x)$ defined on $(-\infty, +\infty)$ satisfies

$$f_X(x) \geq 0$$

$$\int_{-\infty}^{\infty} f_X(x)\, dx = 1$$

$$E(F(x)) = \int_{-\infty}^{\infty} f_X(x)F(x)\, dx$$

Consider the event that the random variable X takes on values in the interval $[a, b]$. Then we have

$$Pr(a \leq X \leq b) = \int_a^b f_X(x)\, dx$$

When we study telecommunication systems we often use the *Gaussian* density function

$$f_X(x) = \frac{1}{\sigma\sqrt{2\pi}} e^{-(x-m)^2/2\sigma^2}$$

where m denotes the expectation of x, that is, $m = E(X)$, and σ^2 denotes the *variance* of X, that is,

$$\sigma^2 = E((X - m)^2)$$

The variance is a measure of the "spreading" of the data. When the variance is small, the data are concentrated around their expected value.

For various applications the Gaussian density function is in good agreement with the collected data. Furthermore, it has several nice mathematical properties that make it very useful. Its famous bell shape is shown in Figure C.2.

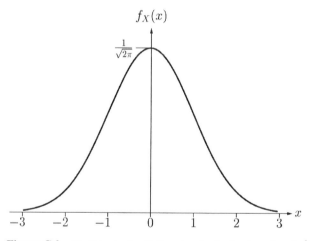

Figure C.2   The "standardized" Gaussian distribution ($m = 0$ and $\sigma^2 = 1$)

Index

Understanding Information Transmission. By John B. Anderson and Rolf Johannesson
ISBN 0-471-67910-0 © 2005 the Institute of Electrical and Electronics Engineers, Inc.

About the Authors

John B. Anderson received the Bachelor of Arts, Master of Science, and Ph.D. degrees in electrical engineering from Cornell University in 1967, 1969, and 1972. From 1972 to1980, he was a faculty member of the Electrical and Computer Engineering Department at McMaster University, Hamilton, Canada, and from 1981 to 1998, he was a professor in the Electrical, Computer and Systems Engineering Department at Rensselaer Polytechnic Institute, Troy, New York. Since 1998, he has held the Ericsson Chair in Digital Communication at Lund University, Sweden. His research work includes coding and communication algorithms, bandwidth-client coding, and the application of these to data transmission; he has served widely as a consultant in these fields. Dr. Anderson served on the Publications Board of the IEEE during 1989–1991 and 1994–1996, and was editor-in-chief of the IEEE Press from 1994–1996. He has served as associate editor of the *IEEE Transactions on Information Theory* (1980–1984) and as guest editor of the *IEEE Communications Transactions*. He currently serves as series editor for the IEEE Press Series on Digital and Mobile Communication. He is a Fellow of the IEEE since 1987 and received the Humboldt Research Prize (Germany) in 1991. In 1996, he was elected Swedish National Visiting Chair in Information Technology. He received the IEEE Third Millennium Medal in 2000.

Rolf Johannesson received the Master of Science and Ph.D. degrees in 1970 and 1975 from Lund University, Lund, Sweden, where he has been a professor of Information Theory since 1976. He became a Fellow of the IEEE in 1998 and in 2000, was awarded the degree of Professor, honoris causa, from the Institute for Information Transmission Problems, Russian Academy of Sciences, Moscow. Dr. Johannesson's scientific interests include information theory, error correcting codes, and cryptography. In addition to papers and book chapters in the area of convolutional codes and cryptography, he has authored two textbooks on switching theory and digital design and one on information theory. He coauthored *Fundamentals of Convolutional Coding*, IEEE Press, 1999. During the 1980s, Professor Johannesson co-chaired seven Russian–Swedish Workshops, which were the chief interactions between Russian and Western scientists in information theory and coding during the Cold War.

Understanding Information Transmission. By John B. Anderson and Rolf Johannesson
ISBN 0-471-67910-0 © 2005 the Institute of Electrical and Electronics Engineers, Inc.